seasonal samplings from the junior league of chicago

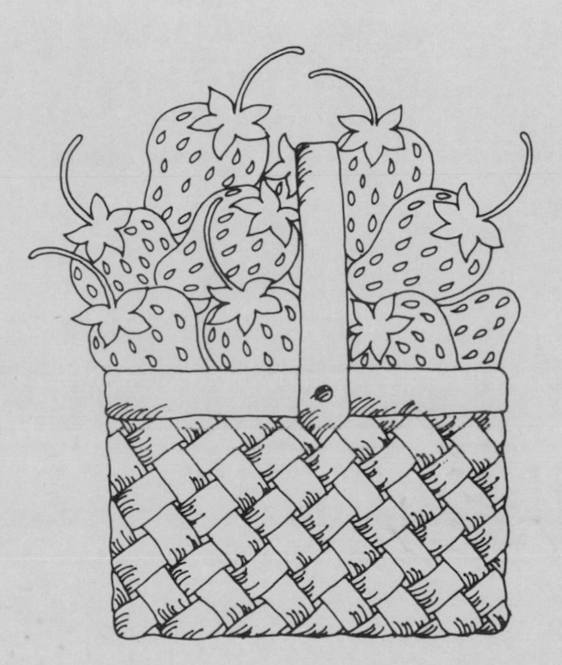

COVER DESIGN AND ILLUSTRATIONS BY NANCY PEIL

THE JUNIOR LEAGUE OF CHICAGO, INC.
CHICAGO, ILLINOIS
1974

The purpose of The Junior League is exclusively educational and charitable and is: to promote voluntarism; to develop the potential of its members for voluntary participation in community affairs; and to demonstrate the effectiveness of trained volunteers.

The proceeds from the sale of SOUPÇON I and SOUPÇON II assist the community projects of the Junior League of Chicago, Inc.

THE JUNIOR LEAGUE OF CHICAGO, INC.
CHICAGO, ILLINOIS

FIRST EDITION

FIRST PRINTING	OCTOBER 1974	10,000 COPIES
SECOND PRINTNG	JULY 1975	10,000 COPIES
THIRD PRINTING	MARCH 1976	20,000 COPIES
FOURTH PRINTING	DECEMBER 1976	40,000 COPIES
FIFTH PRINTING	OCTOBER 1979	15,000 COPIES
SIXTH PRINTING	OCTOBER 1980	20,000 COPIES
SEVENTH PRINTING	NOVEMBER 1981	10,000 COPIES
EIGHTH PRINTING	JULY 1983	20,000 COPIES

For additional copies, use order blanks in the back of the book or write directly to:

SOUPÇON
The Junior League of Chicago
1447 North Astor Street
Chicago, Illinois 60610

SOUPÇON may be obtained by organizations for fund raising projects or by retail outlets at special rates. Write above address for further information.

Published in the United States of America by
THE JUNIOR LEAGUE OF CHICAGO, INC.
CHICAGO, ILLINOIS

Printed by R.R. Donnelley & Sons Co., Crawfordsville, Indiana
ISBN: 0-9611622-0-1

ORIGINAL COOKBOOK COMMITTEE

Co-Chairmen	Marcia M. Patterson Melinda M. Vance
Cover and Illustrations	Nancy R. Peil
Text	Virginia C. Gerst
Professional Home Economists	Marcia W. Smith Annette Ashlock Stover
Testing Chairman	Mary M. Southworth
Seasonal Chairmen	Irene M. BonDurant Marcia M. Hines Marcia M. Patterson Marcia W. Smith Mary M. Southworth Melinda M. Vance Barbara T. Whitney Diane P. Zwilling
Chicago Restaurants	Susan B. DePree
Production	Melinda M. Vance
Wine Chairman	Sally S. Eklund
Wine Consultant	Mr. Joseph B. Glunz House of Glunz Wine Merchants Chicago, Illinois
Marketing Chairman	Karla S. Gillette
Treasurer	Ann M. Buckley

TABLE OF CONTENTS

INTRODUCTION

ith pride we present SOUPÇON: SEASONAL SAMPLINGS FROM THE JUNIOR LEAGUE OF CHICAGO.

The recipes included in this book were chosen from over 1,100 submitted by Chicago Junior League members. Each selection has been tested and professionally edited to insure accuracy of ingredients and that the most efficient method of preparation has been prescribed. Our aim has been to present unusual recipes, ones not found in basic cookbooks, with the emphasis on dishes most appropriate for special meals—parties, holiday celebrations, or elegant repasts for two, although a few unique but more simple everyday type selections have also been included.

The book is a soupcon of gastronomic information. In addition to favorite recipes, we have included some facts about foods, menus and suggested wines for a variety of occasions. Finally, we have selected 15 of Chicago's finest restaurants to be represented with favorite recipes from their chefs' repertoires.

With the exception of the restaurant section, the book is arranged according to the seasons, This approach was chosen because the best culinary results are achieved by using ingredients when they are most fresh. This is seasonal cooking. It is the oldest rule of good eating and one that still produces the best results despite the modern refrigeration and transportation methods which bring out-of-season foods to us throughout the year. The best cook is the seasonal cook. She determines her menu based on the fresh produce available in the market. In so doing, she not only gets better flavor, she saves money, for vine ripened ingredients are almost invariably less expensive than their bland, hot house relatives.

The recipes in SOUPÇON are as varied as the geographic origins of the women who contributed them. Because of Chicago's central location and historic importance as a center of trade and commerce, the city has long been a magnet for people from throughout the nation and the world. All who have come have brought with them their favorite recipes, producing for the city not a regional cuisine, but one which is a combination of the best dishes of all areas. The foods enjoyed by our members reflect the city's diversity.

This diversity is also mirrored in Chicago's many ethnic and specialized restaurants, for which the city is known and justly proud. It has not been easy to select 15 of our favorites from among the many which thrive throughout the city, but we have done so, always with an eye toward variety, popularity, and, above all, excellence. Each of the restaurants selected has generously contributed some of its best liked recipes to SOUPÇON.

Chicago's seasons are a further aspect of the city's diversity, as they range from its famous cold and windy winters to its less well known but much enjoyed summers. Chicagoans look forward to each season for its own particular pleasures, from boating on Lake Michigan in the summer to ice skating at one of the city's many parks in the winter. It is hoped that this book will help its users create a cuisine which will add yet another dimension to their enjoyment of each of the four seasons.

CHATEAU MARGAUX
GRAND VIN
1966
PEIL

INTRODUCTION TO THE SELECTION AND SERVING OF WINES

he Connoisseur and the Gourmet are facets in the designs of God's creation. We are born with an intrinsic drive for food—a craving which sustains life. Added to this basic urge, God also gave man a palate—a sense of taste—one of the five senses. Our palates help us discern the likes and dislikes within us. If one considers his palate, or sense of taste, as legitimate a sense as sight and hearing, then the palate has a need for an art form as do our eyes and ears. We have then, to form rules for the art of dining, develop an aesthetic format with guide lines to follow. At rare times, however, it is good to deliberately contradict rules. This offers a relief, a chance to "do your own thing," to experiment or innovate.

The basic rules we are concerned with here, are those that apply to the joining of wine and food. This is a marriage requiring both balance and harmony. You are the matchmaker, as it were. As most meals consist of a menu which builds to an entree as the highlight, wine selections must also be building blocks which step by step have a design alongside the food. The most basic of all considerations is to complement the wine and food. Seldom should one ever overpower the other.

This balance necessitates the rule: "White wines with white meats; red wines with red meats." As most white wines are more delicate than red wines and white meats more delicate than red meats, we have a basic harmony. Time, experience, indulgence and advice help to sophisticate the application of this blend.

Certain white wines are more delicate and subtle than others. Likewise, some reds are more robust than others. Sophistication, degree and nature of taste, plus personal preference are some of the many factors which contribute to the perfect wine-mate for a particular food course.

The finest starting point is to seek advice of your local wine merchant. He is familiar with all the wines he sells and has in his mind a taste picture of each wine. Describing your menu, he will be able to offer suggestions. Eventually, you will have favorite wines with your favorite foods at which point you will feel comfortable beginning to experiment.

To select wines for an entire meal, plan for the aperitif, which like Kir (white wine and cassis) may be very slightly sweet but generally should be light and dry. With each course, the wines may ascend to fuller, more flavorful wines, avoiding any really sweet ones until dessert. Contrary to popular opinion, there are no "all purpose" wines unless one is dining so casually as a picnic. The most deceptive traps to avoid are underestimating a sauce, marinade, or seasoning, as frequently they take a light, delicate food and greatly change its character. In selecting wines with graduated ascent there are some exceptions which you may make, such as a very dry delicate sherry accompanying a soup course, or break the ascent with a champagne for dessert. There are difficult compromises which arise when the choice of courses themselves do not follow a graduated ascent. Your high point of flavor may be reached before the main entree. In this case, you have no choice but to serve the proper wine for the particular course.

Cheese courses also seem to present a difficulty as one should not have his best wine with cheese, even though the cheese follows the entree. Since cheese so drastically alters the taste of wines, making them full and sweet on the palate, one should not distort a great bottle but possibly help out a lesser wine.

The proper service of wines is almost as important as their selection. White wines should be chilled according to their sweetness—dryer ones, only iced, sweeter wines served quite cold. As your taste buds are like pores of the skin, they open and close with temperature. If a delicate wine is served too cold, the only taste which penetrates the closed taste buds will be acid. Likewise, a Sauterne will appear far too sweet if not chilled enough (the acidity will not have its proper balance.) Red wines, unless extremely fruity, should never be served chilled. Even these fruity wines should only receive a very light chill. Other reds should be served just below room temperature, thus making them more palatably refreshing. Remember, chilling amplifies acidity in the wines. It is most important to open a red prior to serving by at least one hour for wines under ten years of age and less time for older ones. Reds which have eight to ten years of age should probably be decanted. Anything older definitely should be decanted.

Decanting is both easy and fun. Basically, you are pouring the clear wine off, leaving the sediment behind. At the same time, you are aerating the wine. Bring up the bottle from your cellar in the same position it was in while on the rack. Set the bottle in a wine basket or a cradle made from a towel. Remove the lead with a knife but cutting just below the lip on the neck. Clean the head of the cork and the lip. Then insert the corkscrew and lift the neck of the bottle enough so that the wine does not run out after the cork is extracted. Pour off the clear wine withholding the last ounce or so, depending on your professionalism. Ideally, a short candle lit under the neck of the bottle while pouring, makes it easier to see the sediment moving, thus enabling you to use as much clear wine as possible.

Sparkling wines should be chilled according to their sweetness—dryer, less cold than sweeter ones. Sparkling wines are never decanted.

Fortified wines should be served at room temperature and decanted if they have a deposit.

Your wine and food expertise will only go as far as your enthusiasm. Try to make it fun and do it right, so that your enthusiasm is not stunted. Have no fear of making an occasional mistake in the learning and experimentation stages of wine-and-food matchmaking.

I toast your health and dining pleasure.

Sincerely,

Joseph B. Glunz

PEIL

SPRING KITCHEN

urdon Hubbard, a fur trader during the frontier days of Illinois, and one of the state's first citizens, left an early written testament to seasonal cooking when, in 1818, he described the food he and his fellow traders enjoyed during his first expedition to Illinois: "Our fare . . . varied as spring approached with swan, geese, and crane, besides almost every variety of duck. Prairie chickens and quail were also abundant, but these we did not consider edible. Our game was cooked in the French style, and, to our mind, could not be excelled in any kitchen . . . The woods abounded in wild honey, and we kept a large wooden bowl full at all times, of which we partook whenever we desired."

Just as Illinois' early inhabitants looked forward to the varied foods of spring, so do today's residents. The months of March through May are times of anticipation, and the foods of the season are delicate and young. These should be cooked simply, with mild sauces and spices to enhance their natural flavors.

At the top of spring's vegetables is, of course, asparagus. Thin, green, and delightful, it can be served in the European manner as a separate course, heaped on a plate, or as a vegetable accompaniment to a meal. The thinner the stalk, the milder the sauce that should go with it. Try a light lemon and butter sauce for the thinnest, and a hollandaise or one of its varieties on the thicker stalks.

Also to be enjoyed in the spring are artichokes, baby carrots, peas, young new spinach, the first fresh herbs of the year, and berries: strawberries, blackberries, blueberries, logenberries, and raspberries.

Salads, which should be served with the lightest of dressings to highlight the tender flavor of the greens, might include white celery, chicory, cucumbers, Belgian endive, escarole, bibb, limestone and romaine lettuce, radishes, watercress, and the first sproutings of chives.

In fruits, look for apricots, cantaloupes, coconuts, grapes, grapefruit, lemons, limes, nectarines, oranges, papayas, pineapples, rhubarb, and ugli fruit.

Spring lamb, a delicacy that is difficult to find, is worth the search, and spring pork in March and April is delicious. Long Island duckling is at its best in April, maple trees are tapped for their syrup in March and April, and salmon becomes available beginning in May.

Also in fish, seek out the freshwater varieties from the Great Lakes: mullet, yellow perch, carp, pickerel, blue and yellow pike, trout, and whitefish. Saltwater fish particularly abundant at this time of year are sea bass, bluefish, cod, flounder, pompano, mackerel, and shad. Crab, clams, lobster, and mussels are also excellent during this season.

When selecting foods and planning meals for spring, remember that meals should be light and simple, with the accent on the delicate flavors nature has provided.

SPRING MENUS

LADIES TEE-OFF LUNCHEON

SEAFOOD CURRY WITH CONDIMENTS

Tavel Rose

WHITE RICE SPINACH SALAD

* *

RHUBARB MERINGUE PIE

DERBY DAY BUFFET

MINT JULEPS

* *

CHILLED WATERCRESS SOUP IN MUGS

* *

CREOLE JAMBALAYA

Hermitage Blanc

TOSSED GREEN SALAD WITH ARTICHOKE HEARTS

OIL AND VINEGAR DRESSING

CRESCENT ROLLS

* *

LEMON ICE BOX CAKE

FORMAL DINNER

OLIVE CHEESE BALLS

* *

SHRIMP REMOULADE

Muscadet

* *

LEG OF LAMB MANCHU

Cote du Rhone

* *

ASPARAGUS SOUFFLE

PARSLEY BUTTERED NEW POTATOES

* *

MIXED GREEN SALAD

* *

STRAWBERRY CREPES

Sparkling Anjou Rose

SPRING MENUS

BRIDAL LUNCHEON

GOLDEN PUNCH

* *

CHICKEN GOURMET

Piesporter Goldtropfchen Riesling

* *

ASPARAGUS VINAIGRETTE   LEMON BREAD

* *

CORNFLAKE RING WITH FRESH STRAWBERRIES

California Champagne Extra Dry

SPRING BRUNCH FOR A CROWD

MAY WINE TOPPED WITH CHAMPAGNE

* *

LOBSTER CASSEROLE   EGGS IN A BASKET

Muscadet

TOMATO ASPIC

FRUIT SALAD WITH POPPY SEED DRESSING

RHUBARB NUT BREAD

* *

MAPLE RING WITH STRAWBERRIES

EASTER DINNER

ARTICHOKE CLAM PUFFS

* *

HERBED BAKED HAM

Oakville Sauvignon Blanc

BUTTERED BROCCOLI SPEARS

POTATOES DEL MONICO

MANDARIN ORANGE SOUFFLE SALAD

* *

STRAWBERRY SUNSHINE PIE

Vin Mousseux

SPRING TABLE OF CONTENTS

BEVERAGES

TEQUILA-CHAMPAGNE PUNCH — About 2 Gallons

Perfect for brunch parties or luncheons

2 quarts white wine, chilled
2 cans (6 oz. each) frozen concentrated pineapple juice, reconstituted with water
1 bottle (fifth) tequila
2 bottles (fifths) champagne, chilled
2 quarts soda water, chilled
Strawberry halves or orange slices

In punch bowl, combine wine, pineapple juice, and tequila (or mix in the proportions your punch bowl will hold). Just before serving, add champagne and soda water. Float fruits in punch. Or freeze strawberries or other fruits with water in ring mold; unmold and float in punch.

Mrs. Phillip J. Stover
(Annette Ashlock)

STRAWBERRY DAIQUIRI — 6 Servings

1 can (6 oz.) frozen daiquiri mix
1¼ cups light rum
2 pkg. (10 oz. each) frozen strawberries (or raspberries)
Finely crushed ice (about 30 cubes)
6 whole strawberries (or mint sprigs if using raspberries)

Place first 3 ingredients in blender. Cover and blend until smooth. Place crushed ice in ice bucket; stir in daiquiri mixture. When ready to serve ladle into large stemmed goblets. Garnish each with whole strawberry. May be prepared in advance and kept in freezer until 20 minutes before serving.

Mrs. Dennis F. Muckermann
(Betty Graham)

COFFEE PUNCH

2½ Quarts

1 qt. milk
1 qt. strong brewed coffee
½ cup sugar
3 whole cloves
Pinch cinnamon
½ qt. ice cream (vanilla or coffee)
Several drops almond extract

Scald milk; add coffee, sugar, and spices. Chill thoroughly. Put ice cream in a punch bowl; break up into small pieces. Add coffee, milk mixture and almond extract; stir.

Mrs. Bart Mosser
(Carol Clements)

COLORADO PUNCH

5 Cups; 8-10 Servings

1 can (6 oz.) frozen orange juice concentrate
1 can (6 oz.) frozen concentrated lemon juice (not lemonade)
3 cans water
1 cup bourbon
3 T. grenadine
⅓ cup maple syrup

Mix all ingredients. Serve chilled

Mrs. Peter Theis
(Jill Pendexter)

SLOE GIN COOLER WITH PINEAPPLE

25-30 Servings

1 fifth Sloe Gin
1 fifth regular gin
1 cup sugar
2½ cans (6 oz. each) frozen lemon juice concentrate
2 cans (46 oz. each) pineapple juice
MOLD:
1 can (20 oz.) pineapple chunks
1 jar (8 oz.) maraschino cherries, drained
Water

Combine 2 kinds of gin, sugar, lemon juice (undiluted), and pineapple juice; mix well and chill. In 1½-qt. ring mold, put pineapple chunks with juice and cherries; fill rest of mold with water. Freeze solid. When ready to serve, place liquid mixture in punch bowl. Unmold frozen pineapple and float in punch bowl.

Mrs. Nelson Shaw
(Judith Ann Kochs)

MAPLE BARBECUE RIBS

15-20 Servings

- **3 lbs. St. Louis cut ribs, cut individually**
- **1½ cups maple syrup**
- **2 T. chili sauce**
- **2 T. cider vinegar**
- **2 T. finely-chopped onion**
- **1 T. worcestershire sauce**
- **1 tsp. salt**
- **½ tsp. dry mustard**
- **Pepper**

Place ribs on baking sheet in single layer. Combine remaining ingredients. Brush sauce over ribs. Bake at 350° for 1½ hours or until tender, basting frequently with remaining sauce to obtain an even glaze.

Mrs. William D. Roddy, Jr.
(Joanne McDonald)

STUFFED BREAD

6-8 Servings

- **1 large loaf crusty French bread**
- **2 pkgs. (8 oz. each) cream cheese, softened**
- **¼ cup beer**
- **¼ cup chopped watercress**
- **¼ cup chopped onion**
- **¼ cup chopped radishes**
- **1 T. dry mustard**
- **½ lb. liverwurst, cut into small cubes**

Cut loaf of bread vertically into 3 pieces. Slice off ends; discard. Pull out as much of the bread's insides as possible, leaving about ¼-inch crusty shell. Crumble bread; toast on cookie sheet in 350° oven for about 15 minutes. Stir cream cheese until smooth and soft; stir in beer, watercress, onion, radishes and mustard. Gently fold in liverwurst cubes and toasted bread. Pack into bread shells. Wrap in foil; refrigerate at least 4 hours, or overnight. To serve, unwrap; slice as thinly as possible. Serve as an appetizer.

Mrs. James F. Peil
(Nancy Rodgers)

SPINACH BALLS

60-70 Balls

2 pkg. (10 oz. each) frozen spinach, cooked, drained very well
2 cups packaged stuffing mix
1 cup grated parmesan cheese
6 eggs, beaten
¾ cup butter, softened
Salt
Pepper

Combine all ingredients, mixing well. Roll into balls the size of walnuts. Freeze. Before serving, place on cookie sheet still frozen. Bake 10 minutes at 350°

Mrs. William D. Roddy, Jr.
(Joanne McDonald)

CLAMS CASINO

About 5 Cups

¼ cup chopped green peppers
¼ cup minced onions
35 Ritz crackers, crushed
1 lb. bacon, well cooked, crumbled
3 cans (7 ozs. each) minced clams
Dash garlic salt

Mix together ingredients, using the clam juice of 2 cans and draining third can. Put in shallow casserole. Bake 350° for 50 minutes, or until well browned. Serve on crackers.

Mrs. Robert L. Shirley
(Pamela Materne)

ARTICHOKE CLAM PUFFS

24-48 Puffs

2 pkgs. (10 oz. each) frozen artichokes; or 2 cans (16 oz. each) artichoke hearts
1 pkg. (8 oz.) cream cheese
2½ T. sherry
¼ tsp. hot pepper sauce
1 can (7 oz.) minced clams, drained
Paprika

Halve or quarter artichokes. Cook frozen artichokes according to directions (do not overcook). Drain; put on broiler-proof plate. Combine cream cheese, sherry and pepper sauce. Mix well. Stir in clams. Spoon mixture onto cut sides of artichokes. Sprinkle with paprika. Broil until browned.

Mrs. J. Stephen Laing
(Suzanne Reyburn)

BAKED MEAT BALLS IN SWEET SOUR SAUCE

50 Small Meat Balls

1½ lbs. ground chuck
1 can (4½ to 5 ozs.) water chestnuts, drained, chopped
½ cup rolled oats
½ cup milk
2 eggs
1 tsp. salt
½ tsp. onion salt
½ tsp. garlic salt
1 cup catsup
1 jar (12 oz.) currant jelly

Combine meat, water chestnuts, oats, milk, eggs, and seasonings. Form into small balls. Place in shallow baking pan. Combine catsup and jelly; pour over meat balls. Bake, uncovered, at 325° for 1 hour. Turn meat balls every 15 minutes.

Mrs. David Holman
(Alicia Bresee)

OLIVE CHEESE BALLS

20-30 Balls

¼ lb. sharp cheddar cheese, grated
¼ cup soft butter
½ cup flour, sifted
Pinch of salt
Pinch of paprika
1 T. sherry
20 to 30 large stuffed green olives (drained dry)

Blend cheese and butter. Mix together flour, salt and paprika. Combine cheese and flour mixtures. Add sherry. Add more flour, if necessary, to form soft dough. Using 1 to 2 tsp. dough per olive, make a ball, then flatten. Wrap around olives and place on ungreased cookie sheet. Bake at 400° for 12 to 15 minutes. (Can be made ahead and refrigerated until ready to bake.)

Mrs. Kenneth J. James
(Constance Lind)

SALMON TIDBITS

4-6 Servings

1 can (1 lb.) salmon
1 egg, lightly beaten
Flour (approx. ½ cup)
1 tsp. baking powder
Fat for frying

Drain salmon, reserving juice. Add egg to salmon; add enough flour to make mixture thick. Add baking powder to ¼ cup juice from salmon; quickly add to salmon. Drop from teaspoon into hot fat. They cook and brown quickly and are textured like snow flakes.

Mrs. E. J. Mooney
(Mary Martha May)

DEVILED CRAB

12 Servings

- **¼ cup butter**
- **5 T. flour**
- **2 cups whipping cream**
- **1 cup milk**
- **4 tsp. salt**
- **4 tsp. dry mustard**
- **Dash each: red and black pepper**
- **2 T. worcestershire sauce**
- **6 egg yolks, hard-cooked and chopped**
- **⅓ cup minced parsley**
- **⅓ cup lemon juice**
- **2½ lbs. crab meat, inspected for shells**
- **1 cup buttered bread crumbs**

Melt butter; stir in flour. Cook slowly for several minutes. Gradually stir in cream, milk and seasonings. Cook, stirring constantly, until thickened. Add yolks (and chopped whites if you desire a larger amount), parsley and lemon juice. Taste; add more worcestershire sauce or lemon juice, if needed. Add crab meat; mix thoroughly. Place in 12 individual serving shells. Sprinkle with buttered bread crumbs. Bake at 450° for 15 to 20 minutes, or until brown.

Mrs. William A. Patterson, Jr.
(Marcia Motley)

MOULES MARINIERE

6-8 Servings

- **4 qts. mussels**
- **½ cup white wine**
- **⅓ cup olive oil**
- **2 cloves garlic, pressed**
- **3 T. chopped parsley**
- **1½ tsp. minced onion**
- **1¼ tsp. oregano**
- **Salt to taste**
- **Pinch cayenne pepper**

Scrub mussels thoroughly. Mix all ingredients in large covered kettle; stir until mussels are well coated. Steam, covered, 10 to 15 minutes. Discard any mussels that do not open. Adjust seasonings. Serve in soup plates, shells and all.

Mrs. Denis R. Chaudruc
(Jeannene Nixon)

ANCHOVY-FILLED MUSHROOMS — 6-8 Servings

24 medium to
40 small mushrooms
¼ cup olive oil
1 can (2 oz.) flat
anchovy fillets
1 garlic clove,
finely-minced
1 tsp. fresh lemon juice
¾ cup (or less) fresh
soft bread crumbs
¼ cup minced parsley
Freshly-ground black
pepper to taste

Remove stems from washed mushrooms; chop. Saute in 3 T. oil for 3 minutes. Chop anchovies; mix with garlic. Add lemon juice, bread crumbs, parsley, anchovies, sauteed stems and pepper. Fill caps with mixture. Place in shallow baking dish. Drizzle remaining oil over mushrooms. Bake at 350° for 15 minutes or until hot.

Mrs. J. D. MacDonald
(Charie Roberson)

SOLE en ESCABECHE — 6 Servings

A delightful cold fish appetizer

¾ cup olive oil
2 T. butter
6 small fillets of sole
Flour
Salt and pepper
1 onion, thinly-sliced,
separated into rings
1 green pepper,
cut in thin rings
1 clove garlic, minced
½ cup orange juice
Juice of 2 limes
¼ tsp. hot pepper sauce
Orange slices
Lime slices
1 T. grated orange rind
Minced parsley

Heat ¼ cup olive oil and 2 T. butter. Dredge fish fillets lightly in flour; saute until delicately brown on both sides or until just tender. Seaon to taste with salt and pepper. Arrange the fillets in a flat serving dish; top with onion rings, pepper rings, and garlic. Combine remaining ½ cup oil, orange juice, lime juice, hot pepper sauce, and salt and pepper to taste; pour over fish while still warm. Let stand in refrigerator 12 to 24 hours. Serve cold. Garnish with orange and lime slices, orange rind, and parsley.

Mrs. Doyle G'Sell
(Ella Doyle)

SHRIMP REMOULADE

8-10 Servings

- **¼ cup fresh lemon juice**
- **¼ cup cider vinegar**
- **¼ cup prepared mustard**
- **¼ cup prepared horseradish**
- **2 T. catsup**
- **2 tsp. paprika**
- **½ tsp. freshly-ground pepper**
- **1 tsp. salt**
- **1 cup salad oil**
- **½ cup finely-chopped celery**
- **½ cup finely-chopped green onions**
- **¼ cup finely-chopped fresh parsley**
- **2 to 2½ lbs. shrimp**

Blend first 8 ingredients in blender; slowly add oil until thick. Add last 3 ingredients except shrimp. Place 8 cooked shrimp on individual shells or ramekins. Pour sauce over top. Serve as first course.

Mrs. Bruce G. Southworth
(Mary Monek)

ASPARAGUS WITH LEMON CREAM SAUCE

4 Servings

- **1 lb. fresh asparagus**
- **¾ cup butter**
- **3 egg yolks**
- **2 tsp. water**
- **1½ T. lemon juice**
- **2 T. cold butter**
- **Salt and pepper**
- **½ cup whipping cream, lightly whipped**

Steam asparagus over boiling water for 12 to 18 minutes until tender. Drain. Melt ¾ cup butter; cool. In heavy saucepan, over very low heat, beat egg yolks until thick. Beat in water and lemon juice. Add 1 T. cold butter; beat until thick. Remove from heat; add 1 T. cold butter to stop cooking. Slowly beat in cooled butter several drops at a time. Add salt and pepper to taste and more lemon if needed. Just before serving, fold in whipped cream. Serve warm, not hot, over asparagus.

Miss Virginia C. Franche

SALMON MUSHROOM QUICHE

4-6 Servings

A perfect way to use leftover salmon

2 T. minced green onions
⅓ lb. mushrooms, finely-chopped
3 T. butter
1 cup cooked, flaked salmon
1 tsp. lemon juice
2 tsp. finely-minced dill
1 partially-baked 9-inch pastry crust
1 cup whipping cream
3 eggs
Salt and pepper
Nutmeg, freshly-grated
3 T. grated gruyere cheese

Saute green onions and mushrooms in butter until moisture has evaporated. Add salmon, lemon juice and dill; heat through. Spread onto crust. Mix cream, eggs, salt, pepper and nutmeg; pour over salmon. Top with cheese. Bake at 375° for 35 to 40 minutes. Test with toothpick which should come out clean. Serve either as an appetizer or luncheon dish.

Mrs. Thomas D. Hodgkins
(Mary Ann BonDurant)

CHICKEN LIVERS IN ASPIC

6 Servings

1 env. plain gelatin
2½ cups clear consomme madrilene
6 large whole chicken livers
2 T. butter
1 T. cooking oil
2 T. finely-chopped green onions or shallots
Salt, pepper, allspice
½ cup Madeira
Lettuce
Mayonnaise

Soften gelatin in ½ cup consomme. Add to remaining consomme; heat and stir until dissolved. Pour about ⅛-inch of liquid in each of 6 individual molds; chill until set. Saute chicken livers in butter and oil until lightly browned. Add onions; cook 1 minute longer. Drain off fat; sprinkle livers with seasonings. Add Madeira; cover and cook very slowly for 6 to 8 minutes. Remove livers. Reduce liquid by boiling to a syrupy consistency. Roll livers in syrup. Chill. Add livers to pre-lined molds; fill molds with remaining consomme. Chill until set. To serve, unmold onto bibb lettuce leaves. Top with a teaspoon mayonnaise and grind fresh black pepper over top.

Mrs. William Sutter
(Helen Stebbins)

SPRING VEGETABLE SOUP

4-6 Servings

May be served hot or cold

- **3 T. butter, melted**
- **½ cup finely-minced green onions**
- **3 T. flour**
- **6 cups chicken broth**
- **4 cups fresh peas**
- **2 cups fresh spinach**
- **1 head Boston lettuce, shredded**
- **1 T. sugar**
- **Salt**
- **1 cup whipping cream**
- **3 egg yolks**
- **Freshly-ground pepper**
- **1 T. minced fresh mint**

Cook green onions in butter 5 minutes; add flour and cook another few minutes. Stir in broth. Add 3 cups peas, spinach, lettuce and sugar. Bring to a boil. Reduce heat, cover and cook 50 minutes. Cook remaining peas; reserve. Puree soup in blender. Return to heat. Mix cream and egg yolks; add to soup but do not let boil. Garnish with whole peas and mint.

Mrs. Benson T. Caswell
(Margaret Graham)

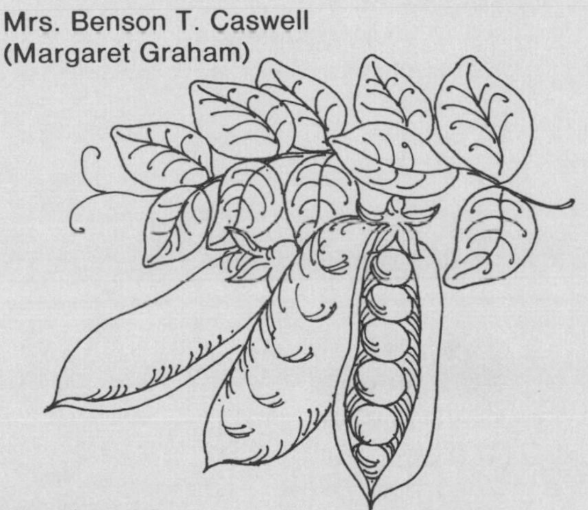

CREAM OF ASPARAGUS SOUP

4 Servings

Don't throw away those tough stem ends

- **3 cups tough stem ends of fresh asparagus (from about 2½ lbs. stalks)**
- **2 cups water**
- **1 tsp. salt**
- **½ tsp. garlic salt**
- **¼ tsp. white pepper**
- **1½ cups medium white sauce (unseasoned)**

Place asparagus and water in saucepan; cover and simmer for 40 minutes. Puree in blender; blend in salt, garlic salt, and pepper. Force through sieve; discard dry tough pulp. (Makes about 2 cups liquid.) Mix with white sauce. Adjust seasonings, if necessary. Serve hot or cold. Garnish with minced chives.

Mrs. Phillip J. Stover
(Annette Ashlock)

SCOTCH BROTH

8 Servings

Bone from 6 lb. lamb
1 large onion, quartered
2 large carrots, peeled and quartered
2 sprigs parsley
1 lemon slice
1 tsp. salt
2 whole allspice
¼ cup uncooked barley
½ cup finely-diced celery
½ cup finely-diced carrots
½ cup finely-diced turnip
½ cup cooked chopped lamb
2 T. finely-chopped parsley

Simmer lamb bone, onion, carrots, parsley sprigs, lemon slice, salt, and allspice in 2 quarts water for 2 hours. Discard bone; strain broth. Chill. Skim fat from surface of broth; combine broth with barley. Cook for 30 minutes. Add vegetables and lamb; cook 30 minutes longer. Garnish with chopped parsley.

Mrs. David Smith
(Marcia Williamson)

CHILLED WATERCRESS SOUP

6 Servings

2 T. butter
1 onion, sliced
1 stalk celery, cut up
1½ cups water
1 pkg. chicken noodle soup mix
½ bunch watercress, bottom stalks discarded
2 cups milk
Grated lemon peel

In hot butter, saute onion and celery 3 minutes. Stir in water and soup. Bring to boil; reduce heat, cover, and simmer 7 minutes. Pour enough hot soup in blender to cover blades. Cover; start blender. Uncover and slowly add rest of soup. Blend until smooth. Add watercress; blend 1 minute. Pour into bowl. Stir in milk. Refrigerate. Serve well chilled, topped with grated lemon peel.

Mrs. Bart Mosser
(Carol Clements)

CHILLED CREAM OF ARTICHOKE SOUP

4 Servings

- **2 artichokes (1½ to 2 lbs. each)**
- **1 can (10½ oz.) chicken broth, undiluted**
- **1 cup water**
- **¼ cup chopped onion**
- **2 T. lemon juice**
- **¼ tsp. dried thyme leaves**
- **⅛ tsp. pepper**
- **1 cup light cream**

Trim stalks from base of artichokes; discard tough outer leaves. Wash; drain. Cut artichokes lengthwise into quarters. Remove inner purple leaves and chokes. In 3½-qt. saucepan, combine artichokes, chicken broth, water, onion, lemon juice, thyme, and pepper. Bring to boiling; reduce heat, cover, and simmer 30 minutes, or until artichokes are tender. Remove artichokes from liquid, reserving liquid. Remove leaves; cut up hearts. With back of knife or spoon, scoop flesh from artichoke leaves. In blender, combine strained cooking liquid, artichoke flesh and hearts, and cream. Blend, at high speed, 2 minutes, or until smooth. Add cream. Refrigerate, covered, several hours or overnight, until well chilled.

Mrs. H. Alex Vance, Jr.
(Melinda Martin)

COLD RASPBERRY SOUP

12 Servings

Courtesy of "The Twin Chefs" at John Gardiner's Tennis Ranch, Arizona

1½ T. unflavored gelatin
⅓ cup cold water
¾ cup hot water
4 cups pureed fresh raspberries
3½ cups sour cream
1⅓ cups pineapple juice
1⅓ cups half and half
1⅓ cups good sherry
⅓ cup grenadine
Juice from 1 lemon
Sugar to taste

Soak gelatin in cold water 5 minutes; stir in hot water. Dissolve over low heat. Combine remaining ingredients; place them in a stainless steel container. Cover; refrigerate overnight. Garnish with a few whole raspberries and a mint leaf.

Mrs. H. Alex Vance, Jr.
(Melinda Martin)

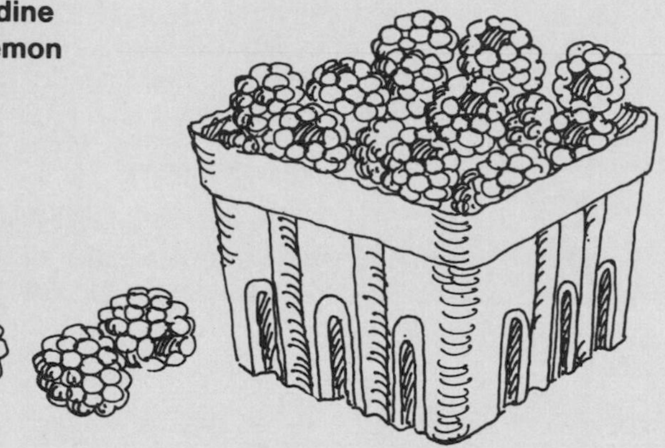

CREAM OF SPINACH SOUP WITH CHEESE

6 Servings

¼ cup boiling water
2 pkg. (10 oz. each) frozen spinach
¼ cup finely-chopped onion
¼ cup butter
¼ cup flour
4 cups milk
1 tsp. salt
Dash MSG
Provolone cheese, coarsely-grated

Add boiling water to the spinach; let stand until spinach is heated through. Put into blender; blend thoroughly. Brown onion in butter; stir in flour. Cook until bubbly; slowly add milk. Cook, stirring constantly, until thickened. Add spinach, salt and MSG. Let stand at least 15 minutes. When serving, put a teaspoonful of provolone cheese on top.

Mrs. Dennis F. Muckermann
(Betty Graham)

RHUBARB-NUT BREAD

1 Large Loaf

- 2½ cups flour
- 1 tsp. baking soda
- ¾ tsp. salt
- ¾ cup butter
- 1½ cups brown sugar
- 1 egg
- 1 tsp. lemon extract
- 1 tsp. grated lemon rind
- 1 cup buttermilk
- 1½ cups finely-diced fresh rhubarb
- ¾ cup finely-chopped pecans
- 1 T. melted butter
- ½ cup sugar

Sift flour with soda and salt. Cream butter until soft; gradually add brown sugar, beating until light and fluffy. Add egg; beat well. Stir in lemon extract and rind. Stir in dry ingredients alternately with buttermilk, mixing until smooth after each addition. Stir in rhubarb and nuts. Pour batter into a 11 x 7 x 3-inch loaf pan or one 10-inch tube pan. Combine 1 T. melted butter and ½ cup sugar; sprinkle over top of batter. Bake at 350° for 1 hour and 10 minutes or until bread tests done.

Mrs. Thomas D. Hodgkins
(Mary Ann BonDurant)

ORANGE RAISIN LOAF

1 Loaf

- ⅔ cup shortening
- ¾ cup sugar
- 2 tsp. grated orange rind
- 1 egg
- 3 cups sifted all-purpose flour
- 3½ tsp. baking powder
- 1½ tsp. salt
- 1 cup milk
- ⅔ cup orange juice
- 1 cup chopped walnuts
- ½ cup raisins

ORANGE GLAZE:

- ¾ cup sifted confectioners' sugar
- 1 T. orange juice
- ½ tsp. grated orange rind

Cream shortening and sugar until light and fluffy. Add rind and egg; beat well. Sift flour with baking powder and salt. Blend into creamed mixture alternately with milk and orange juice. Stir in walnuts and raisins. Turn into 9 x 5 x 3-inch greased loaf pan. Let stand 20 minutes. Bake at 350° about 1 hour and 10 minutes. Cool 10 minutes; remove from pan onto cake racks. To make glaze, combine sugar, orange juice, and orange rind; stir until smooth. Spoon over loaf while still slightly warm.

Mrs. Robert T. DePree
(Susan Barker)

MONKEY BREAD

1 Large Ring

2 pkgs. dry yeast
1 tsp. sugar
¼ cup warm water (110-115°)
½ cup butter
⅓ cup sugar
1 tsp. salt
¾ cup scalded milk
5 cups flour
3 large eggs
½ lb. or more melted butter for dipping

Dissolve yeast and 1 tsp. sugar in warm water. Combine butter, ⅓ cup sugar and salt; add scalded milk. Stir to melt butter. Cool; add yeast, half the flour and eggs. Beat thoroughly. Stir in rest of flour to make a soft, but not sticky dough. Turn out onto a floured bread-board; knead until smooth and satiny, 8 to 10 minutes. Place in a buttered bowl; cover and let rise in warm place free from drafts until doubled in bulk. Punch down; turn out onto a floured board. Roll out ¼-inch thick. Cut dough into diamonds, or any shape preferred. Dip each piece into melted butter; arrange in a buttered 10-inch tube pan. Cover and let rise again until almost doubled in bulk. Bake at 375° 45 minutes or until browned and done. Serve warm. Guests just pull off the buttery delicious diamonds.

Mrs. Jules N. Stiffel
(Lisbeth Cherniack)

LEMON BREAD

1 Loaf

½ cup butter
1¼ cups sugar
2 eggs
1½ cups flour
½ tsp. salt
1 tsp. baking powder
½ cup milk
Grated rind and juice of 1 lemon

Cream shortening and 1 cup sugar until light and fluffy. Add eggs; beat well. Sift flour with salt and baking powder. Add in thirds to creamed mixture alternately with milk. Add grated rind. Pour into a greased 8½ x 4½-inch loaf pan. Bake at 325° for 1 hour, or until done. Combine lemon juice and remaining ¼ cup sugar; spoon evenly over bread while still warm. Remove from pan.

Mrs. Georga Cross III
(Gwendolyn Rendall)

BOCK BEER BREAD

1 Loaf

1 cup bock beer
1 pkg. active dry yeast
3 cups all-purpose flour (or more if needed)
3 T. brown sugar
1 tsp. salt
1 egg, beaten
3 T. soft butter
½ cup wheat germ

Warm beer to 110 to 115°; pour into large mixing bowl. Sprinkle yeast on top; let stand 3 to 5 minutes. Add 1½ cups flour along with the sugar, salt and egg. Beat until smooth. Mix butter with remaining flour and wheat germ; gradually stir into beer mixture until well blended. Add additional flour until dough cleans the bowl. Turn out onto floured board; knead 5 to 10 minutes until smooth and elastic. Cover and let rise in warm place until double in bulk, about 1 hour. Punch down, shape into loaf and place in buttered 9 x 5 x 3-inch loaf pan. Cover and let rise until double in bulk. Bake at 375° for 35 to 40 minutes. Remove from pan; cool on rack.

Mrs. David B. Smith
(Marcia Williamson)

ORANGE CANDY DATE BREAD

1 Loaf

1 cup chopped dates
1 cup water
1 tsp. baking soda
1 cup sugar
¼ cup butter or margarine
2 eggs
1 cup orange slice candy, cut into pieces
1 cup chopped nuts
2¼ cups sifted flour
¼ tsp. salt

Cook dates in water for 5 minutes. Cool completely; stir in baking soda. Cream butter and sugar until light. Add unbeaten eggs and mix well. Stir in cooled date mixture. Add flour and salt, mixing well. Stir in candy and nuts. Pour batter into well-greased 9 x 5 x 3-inch loaf pan. Bake at 350° for 1 hour 10 minutes. Cool in pan 5 minutes; remove and cool on cake rack.

Mrs. William Patterson Jr.
(Marcia Motley)

LIMPA BREAD

2 Loaves

1 pkg. active dry yeast
¼ cup warm water (110-115°F.)
½ cup firmly-packed brown sugar
⅓ cup molasses
2 T. orange marmalade
1 T. butter
1 T. salt
2 tsp. caraway seeds
½ tsp anise
1½ cups hot water
4 to 4½ cups flour
2 cups rye flour

Soften yeast in warm water. Let stand 5 to 10 minutes. Put sugar, molasses, marmalade, butter, salt, caraway seeds and anise in large mixing bowl; add hot water. Blend well. When lukewarm, beat in 1 cup flour. Blend in softened yeast. Add rye flour; beat until very smooth. Beat in enough remaining flour to make a soft dough. Turn onto a lightly-floured surface. Allow to rest 5 to 10 minutes. Knead until smooth and elastic, 7 to 10 minutes. Form dough into a large ball. Put in a deep, buttered bowl. Turn to butter top. Cover with waxed paper and a towel and let stand in warm place (80°) until doubled in bulk, about 1½ hours. Punch down with fist; turn out on a lightly-floured surface. Grease a baking sheet. Divide dough into 2 portions; shape into balls. Cover; allow to rest 5 to 10 minutes. Transfer to greased baking sheet. Cover, let rise until doubled in bulk. Bake at 375° 25 to 30 minutes or until lightly browned. Cool on racks.

Mrs. Karl Rohlen, Jr.
(Carolyn Walker)

MAPLE BRAN MUFFINS

18 Muffins

1 cup sour cream
1 cup maple syrup
2 eggs
1 cup flour
1 tsp. soda
1 cup bran flakes
⅓ cup raisins
⅓ cup chopped nuts

Combine sour cream, maple syrup and eggs. Sift flour and soda; add bran flakes, raisins and nuts. Stir in liquid ingredients. Spoon into greased muffin tins. Bake at 400° for 20 minutes.

Mrs. Arthur S. Bowes
(Patricia Kelly)

IRISH SODA BREAD

1 Loaf

- 3½ cups sifted flour
- ⅔ cup sugar
- 1 T. baking powder
- 1 tsp. baking soda
- 1 tsp. salt
- 1 cup raisins
- 1 T. caraway seeds
- 2 eggs, beaten
- 1½ cups buttermilk
- 2 T. melted butter

Sift together into mixing bowl the flour, sugar, baking powder, soda and salt. Stir in raisins and caraway seeds. Combine beaten eggs, buttermilk and melted butter; add to dry ingredients and mix lightly. Pour into greased loaf pan, 9 x 5 x 3-inches. Bake at 375° for 1 hour or until done.

Mrs. Thomas C. O'Neil
(Jane Stephens)

SOUR CREAM COFFEE CAKE

8-10 Servings

- ½ lb. butter, softened
- 1¼ cups sugar
- 2 eggs
- 1 cup sour cream
- 1 tsp. vanilla
- 2 cups flour
- 1 tsp. baking powder
- 1 tsp. salt

TOPPING MIXTURE:

- 4 T. sugar
- 1 tsp. cinnamon
- 1 cup chopped nuts

Cream butter and sugar; add eggs and sour cream. Add vanilla. Sift flour, baking powder and salt together; stir into first mixture. Pour half this batter into a greased bundt or tube pan. Combine topping mixture ingredients; sprinkle half this on batter. Pour remaining batter on and then remaining topping (or if you are going to invert coffee cake, put topping in pan first). Bake at 350° for 1 hour.

Mrs. Edward H. Hatton, Jr.
(Rana Voss)

FRENCH TOAST

4 Servings

Subtle flavoring makes this special

- 1 loaf unsliced white bread
- 4 eggs
- 1 cup milk
- 2 T. Grand Marnier
- 1 T. granulated sugar
- ½ tsp. vanilla
- ¼ tsp. salt
- ¼ cup bacon grease (or oil)
- Butter
- Confectioners' sugar

Slice bread into eight ¾-inch slices. Beat eggs with milk, Grand Marnier, sugar, vanilla, and salt until well blended. Dip each piece of bread into liquid mixture until well saturated; place in a flat baking dish. Pour the remaining liquid over bread; refrigerate, covered, overnight. In very hot bacon grease, saute bread until golden on both sides. Brush with butter and sprinkle with confectioners' sugar. Serve with maple syrup.

Mrs. H. Alex Vance, Jr.
(Melinda Martin)

LUNCHEON DISHES

ARTICHOKE AND SHRIMP CASSEROLE

4 Servings

- 1 can (20 oz.) artichoke hearts
- 4 or 5 green onions, chopped
- 2 T. chopped parsley
- 2 T. chopped fresh chives
- ½ tsp. each: basil, marjoram, dill weed
- 2 T. French dressing
- ¾ cup grated mild cheddar cheese
- 1 pkg. (14 oz.) shrimp, defrosted
- ¾ cup tomato juice
- 2 T. lemon juice
- 1 tsp. salt
- Dash pepper
- ¼ cup butter
- 2 T. sherry
- Paprika
- Parmesan cheese (optional)

Drain artichokes; arrange in shallow, buttered 2-qt. baking dish. Combine onions, parsley, chives, herbs, dressing, and ¼ cup cheese; sprinkle over artichokes. Heat shrimp in tomato and lemon juices; season with salt and pepper. Pour shrimp and juices over artichokes in baking dish. Sprinkle remaining ½ cup cheese over top. Add dabs of butter to top. Sprinkle with sherry, paprika, and a little parmesan cheese, if desired. Bake at 350° for 25 minutes.

Mrs. William Sutter
(Helen Stebbins)

EGGS IN A BASKET

18 Servings

- 3 pkgs. frozen patty shells (18 shells)
- 18 eggs
- 18 slices Canadian bacon, fried
- Hollandaise sauce

Bake patty shells according to directions (can make a day ahead). Undercook just slightly so they are not very brown. Cool. Cut off tops; scoop middle dough out, being careful not to make holes in side of basket. Line baskets up on a large cookie sheet; crack a raw egg into each. Bake at 300° until egg is set, about ½ hour. Eggs can be put into shells one hour before baking. Serve each egg on a slice of Canadian bacon; top with Hollandaise sauce.

Mrs. Bruce Southworth
(Mary Monek)

CHICKEN CHAUFROID

8 Servings

- 4 chicken breasts, halved
- 2 cans (10½ oz. each) chicken broth
- 1 pkg. (3 oz.) cream cheese
- ¼ cup mayonnaise
- 2 T. snipped fresh dill (or 1 T. dill weed)
- 2 T. lemon juice
- ½ tsp. grated lemon rind
- ¼ tsp. salt
- Romaine lettuce
- 8 tomato slices
- Italian dressing
- Avocado slices
- Toasted almonds

Place chicken breasts and broth in saucepan. Simmer, covered, 30 minutes or until tender. Refrigerate in broth until cool. Remove all skin and bones. Make a paste of cream cheese, mayonnaise, dill, lemon juice, rind and salt. Coat rounded side of each breast with paste. Chill. To assemble; arrange bed of lettuce on each plate, add tomato slice and chicken breast. Garnish long edges of breasts with avocado, sprinkle with almonds and serve with dressing.

Mrs. John S. Jenkins
(Mary Lou Cudlip)

CHICKEN GOURMET

6 Servings

- 5 T. butter
- ½ cup chopped onions
- 3 T. flour
- ½ tsp. salt
- Few grains pepper
- 1 can (4 oz.) mushrooms
- ½ cup sherry
- Milk
- 4 cups (or more) diced, cooked chicken
- 1 can (5 oz.) water chestnuts, drained, sliced
- ¼ cup diced pimiento
- ¾ cup shredded swiss cheese
- 1½ cups soft bread crumbs

Melt 2 T. butter in skillet. Add onion; cook until softened. Stir in flour, salt and pepper. Drain mushrooms, reserving liquid. Combine mushroom liquid with sherry; add enough milk to make 1½ cups. Stir into flour mixture. Cook until smooth, stirring constantly. Fold in mushrooms, chicken, water chestnuts and pimiento. Do not stir. Turn into a greased 2-qt. casserole. Sprinkle with cheese and buttered bread crumbs. Bake at 350° for 30 to 45 minutes (longer if dish has been refrigerated).

Mrs. John W. Bradbury
(Mary Nolen)

CHICKEN SALAD MOLD

10-12 Servings

- **1¼ T. gelatin**
- **¼ cup cold water**
- **½ cup cream**
- **½ cup chicken stock**
- **1 cup mayonnaise**
- **2 T. minced parsley**
- **2½ cups cubed cooked cold chicken**
- **1 cup white grapes**
- **1 cup chopped celery**
- **½ cup sliced blanched almonds**
- **1 tsp. salt**

Soak gelatin in cold water for 5 minutes; dissolve over boiling water. Add gelatin to cream, chicken stock and mayonnaise; stir until it begins to thicken. Fold in remaining ingredients. Place in a mold greased with mayonnaise. Chill.

Mrs. Ronald Schroder
(Margot Trauten)

CHICKEN SALAD DELUXE

8 Servings

- **4 cups cubed, cooked chicken**
- **1½ cups chopped celery**
- **3 green onions, sliced**
- **1 can (5 oz.) water chestnuts, drained, sliced**
- **2 medium pieces candied ginger, finely cut up**
- **1 tsp. salt**
- **1 cup mayonnaise**
- **½ cup whipping cream, whipped**
- **½ cup toasted almonds, slivered**

Mix chicken, celery, onion, water chestnuts, ginger, and salt. Fold mayonnaise into whipped cream; mix with chicken. Chill for 1 hour before serving. Garnish with slivered almonds.

Note: Cook chicken in stock of water, a little white wine, celery, carrot, onion and pieces of ginger. Let chicken cool in liquid overnight before cubing.

Mrs. H. Alex Vance Jr.
(Melinda Martin)

HOT HAM SALAD

4 Servings

1½ lbs. coarsely-ground ham
1¼ cups finely-chopped celery, (can be ground with ham)
6 hard-cooked eggs, finely-diced
¾ cup diced sharp cheese
2 T. grated onion
½ tsp. seasoned salt
¼ cup sliced, stuffed olives

DRESSING:
¼ cup mayonnaise
¼ cup vinegar
⅔ cup catsup
2 T. sugar

Mix ham, celery, eggs, cheese, onion, salt and olives. Moisten with dressing ingredients that have been combined and stirred until smooth. Place on heavy duty foil; seal. Bake at 300° for 20 to 25 minutes.

Mrs. John S. Jenkins
(Mary Lou Cudlip)

HAM SALAD DELUXE

6 Servings

1½ cups diced, cooked ham
1 cup pineapple chunks, well drained
1 cup sliced celery
½ cup cooked rice
½ cup mayonnaise
1 T. lemon juice
1 tsp. grated onion
1 tsp. prepared mustard
½ tsp. salt
Few drops hot pepper sauce

Combine ham, pineapple, celery and rice. Combine mayonnaise and remaining ingredients; add to ham mixture. Chill. Serve in crisp lettuce cups. Garnish with parsley and wedge of tomato.

Mrs. Thomas C. O'Neil
(Jane Stephens)

PINEAPPLE-SHRIMP SALAD WITH ROQUEFORT CHEESE

6-8 Servings

1 large fresh pineapple
¾ lb. cooked, shelled, shrimp (medium size)
Romaine lettuce
⅓ cup crumbled Roquefort cheese
1 cup sour cream
¼ cup mayonnaise
3 T. cream
Salt
Paprika

Cube pineapple into bite-size pieces; toss with shrimp. Arrange romaine on individual plates; top with pineapple mixture. Mash cheese until soft; blend in sour cream until smooth. Add mayonnaise, cream and salt to taste. Spoon dressing over each salad; dust with paprika.

Miss Virginia C. Franche

ASPARAGUS CREPES WITH CHEESE

8 Servings

Lovely for spring luncheon

2 lbs. fresh asparagus spears, cooked, drained
16 crepes
½ cup butter
½ cup flour
¾ tsp. salt
⅛ tsp. pepper
1 qt. milk
3 cups grated cheddar cheese

Place asparagus on crepes; roll up. To make sauce; melt butter, add flour, salt and pepper. Slowly stir in milk. Cook, stirring constantly, until thickened. Cover bottom of 2 baking dishes with a little sauce. Lay crepes on top. Add remaining sauce; cover with cheese. (This can be kept in refrigerator several hours.) Bake at 400° for 25 to 30 minutes, until heated through.

Mrs. Gordon B. MacDonald
(Virginia Fagan)

LOBSTER CASSEROLE

8 Servings

2 cans (10½ ozs. each) condensed cream of mushroom soup
1 cup mayonnaise
¼ cup sherry
½ cup milk
1½ lbs. boneless lobster or crab
3 cups packaged seasoned croutons
2 cans (5 oz. each) water chestnuts, drained, sliced
½ cup minced green onions
1 cup grated cheddar cheese

Mix soup, mayonnaise, and sherry. Stir in milk. Combine with remaining ingredients except cheese. Turn into 3-qt. baking dish; top with cheese. Bake at 350° for 1 hour if it has been refrigerated ahead, 40 minutes if not.

Mrs. Earl J. Niemoth
(Jill Lawrence)

SEAFOOD-CHEESE BAKE

6-8 Servings

½ cup butter
⅓ cup flour
1 tsp. salt
⅛ tsp. dry mustard
Dash of cayenne
1½ cups light cream
2 green onions, sliced
½ lb. fresh mushrooms, sliced
½ cup sherry or dry white wine
1 T. minced parsley
3 egg yolks, slightly beaten
1 cup grated sharp cheddar cheese
2 cans (7½ oz. each) crabmeat
Parmesan cheese
Bread crumbs

Melt ¼ cup butter; stir in flour. Cook over medium heat until well blended. Slowly stir in salt, dry mustard, cayenne and cream. Cook until thick, stirring constantly. Meanwhile, saute onions and mushrooms in ¼ cup butter until light in color. Stir in sherry and parsley. Combine with cream sauce. Stir a small amount of cream sauce into egg yolks; gently stir into remaining cream sauce. Cook an additional 5 minutes, stirring constantly. Cool slightly; add cheddar cheese and crabmeat. Place in buttered casserole or individual shells. Sprinkle top with parmesan cheese and bread crumbs. Bake at 350° for 15 to 20 minutes.

Mrs. Jules N. Stiffel
(Lisbeth Cherniack)

TUNA-VEGETABLE SALAD

6 Servings

- 1 can (6½ to 7 oz.) tuna, drained
- 1 can (16 oz.) peas, drained
- 1 small bottle stuffed olives, halved
- 2 stalks celery, sliced
- 1 hard-cooked egg, sliced
- 1 pimiento, chopped
- 2 crackers, crumbled
- ⅓ cup chopped pecans
- 1 apple, diced
- 2 T. chopped sweet pickles
- Mayonnaise
- Lettuce leaves

Toss all ingredients with enough mayonnaise to moisten. Chill. Serve on lettuce leaves. If desired, garnish with pineapple slice and crackers.

Mrs. Charles H. Lueck, Jr.
(Annabelle Perry)

AVOCADO AND SHRIMP BAKE

8 Servings

- 4 large avocados, halved
- ¾ cup red French dressing
- 1½ lbs. shelled shrimp, cooked
- ¼ cup melted butter
- 1½ cups cornflakes (blend in blender until fine)
- 4 slices bacon, halved
- Rock salt to cover bottom of baking pan

Coat the cut side of avocados with dressing. Pack with shrimp. Pour 1 T. dressing over each half; then pour butter over avocados. Cover shrimp with cornflake crumbs. Place ½ slice bacon on each. Place on rock salt; bake at 350° for 15 to 20 minutes. Then broil for 2 minutes to brown the bacon.

Mrs. H. Dorn Stewart
(Judith Collins)

BROILED TOURNEDOS WITH SAUCE BERNAISE

8 Servings

1 beef filet, about 3 lbs.
12 bacon slices, sauteed
1 cup fresh sliced mushrooms
½ cup chopped onion
2 T. chopped shallots
2 T. butter
8 toast rounds

SAUCE BERNAISE:
¼ cup tarragon vinegar
¼ cup dry white wine
1 T. shallots, chopped
1 T. fresh tarragon or 1½ tsp. dried tarragon
3 egg yolks
2 T. butter
½ cup butter, melted
2 T. chopped parsley or fresh tarragon
¼ tsp. salt
¼ tsp. pepper

WINE SUGGESTION:
Nuits St. George

Cut beef filet in 8 slices. Saute bacon until half done. Drain; wrap 1½ bacon slices around each tournedo, securing with wooden pick or string. Brush with bacon drippings. Saute mushrooms, onion, and shallots in butter until tender. Keep warm. Broil tournedos 6 inches from heat for 2 to 3 minutes per side for medium rare. Set each tournedo on a toast round. Top with mushrooms and onions. Keep warm. To prepare sauce, combine in saucepan vinegar, wine, shallots and tarragon. Bring to boil; cook until reduced by half, about 3 to 4 tablespoons. Place yolks and butter in top of double boiler over hot water. Beat until thick and lemony. Strain vinegar mixture; add to egg mixture. Add melted butter, beating constantly, until thickened; add seasonings. Serve over tournedos. Makes about 1½ cups.

Mrs. J. Stephen Laing
(Suzanne Reyburn)

BULGOGI

6 Servings

"Fire Beef" or bulgogi is the national dish of Korea

2 lbs. flank steak, trimmed of fat and gristle, thinly sliced on the bias
5 scallions, chopped
4 garlic cloves, mashed
½ cup + 2 T. soy sauce
½ cup sugar
¼ cup sesame oil
¼ cup dry sherry
1 tsp. ginger
½ tsp. freshly-ground pepper

Score each piece of meat with an X. Combine remaining ingredients; add meat, coating thoroughly. Marinate meat for 6 hours or overnight in the refrigerator. Grill over charcoal or broil for 6 minutes, turning once. Baste with marinade as necessary.

Mrs. David B. Smith
(Marcia Williamson)

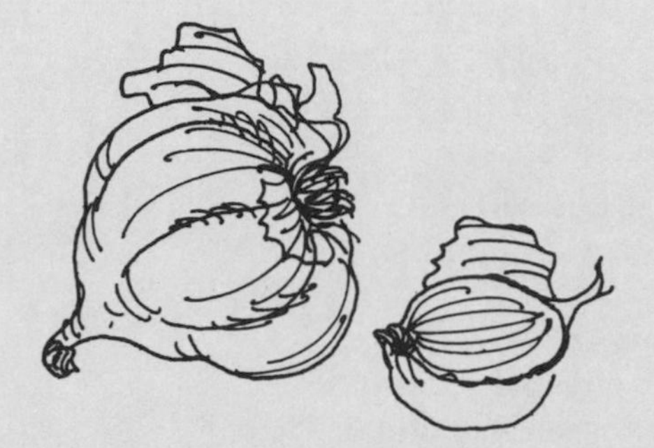

LAMB MANCHU

16 Servings

4 cloves garlic, chopped
⅓ cup honey
½ cup boiling water
1 cup Japanese soy sauce
1 leg of lamb (7 lbs.)
¼ to ½ cup white wine

WINE SUGGESTION:
Cote du Rhone

Mix garlic, honey, and boiling water; stir until honey is dissolved. Add soy sauce. Pour over lamb; marinate 4 to 12 hours, turning lamb several times while marinating. Put in roasting pan and add ½ cup of the marinade. Cook 30 minutes per pound at 325°, adding the wine half way through the cooking. Slice lamb across grain and pour cooking sauce over meat.

Note:
This also makes good post-cocktail party fare, serving hot lamb and sauce on club rolls that have been heated 12 minutes at 400°.

Mrs. Stephan Seftenberg
(Sally Lauder)

SPRING RAGOUT OF LAMB

10-12 Servings

4 lbs. boneless lamb shoulder, cut into 2-inch cubes
¼ cup oil
1½ T. sugar
1½ tsp. salt
½ tsp. pepper
¼ cup flour
3 cups beef bouillon
1 cup fresh tomato pulp or 3 T. tomato paste
3 cloves garlic, mashed
¼ tsp. rosemary
1 bay leaf
12 to 18 small new potatoes, unpeeled
6 carrots, peeled and cut into 1½-inch pieces
6 turnips, peeled and quartered
12 to 18 small white onions, peeled
1½ cups shelled fresh green peas
1½ cups fresh green beans, cut into 1-inch pieces

WINE SUGGESTION:
Beaujolais

Brown lamb a few pieces at a time in hot oil. As they are browned, remove to flame-proof casserole. Sprinkle lamb with sugar and toss over high heat until it carmelizes. Sprinkle meat with salt, pepper and flour. Cook a few minutes until flour browns. Add bouillon to pan; boil to loosen brown bits; pour into casserole; bring to a simmer, stirring to mix liquid and flour. Add tomatoes and seasonings. Cover casserole and simmer slowly 1 hour. Add potatoes, carrots, turnips and onions. Simmer gently, covered, 1 hour longer or until meat and vegetables are tender. Meanwhile, drop peas and beans in rapidly boiling salted water; cook, uncovered, 5 minutes or until almost tender. Drain in colander and run cold water over them to stop cooking. Add to casserole; cover and simmer 5 minutes longer. Taste sauce and correct seasonings.

Mrs. Dennis F. Muckermann
(Betty Graham)

ORANGE MINT LEG OF LAMB

10-14 Servings

A delicious Easter dinner!

1 leg of lamb (5 to 7 lbs.) with sirloin chops removed
3 cloves garlic, slivered (optional)
1 tsp. rosemary
1 tsp. salt
¼ tsp. pepper
½ cup orange juice
¼ cup orange liqueur
½ cup chopped fresh mint or 2 T. dried mint

WINE SUGGESTION:
Margaux

Make a number of incisions in meat; insert garlic slivers. Place lamb, fat side up, on rack in open roasting pan. Rub with mixture of rosemary, salt, and pepper. Roast at 325°. Allow 25 to 35 minutes per pound. About 30 minutes before end of cooking time, combine orange juice and liqueur; pour over lamb. Sprinkle with mint. Continue roasting, basting several times. Pour pan drippings over slices.

Note: Meat therometer should register 170°.

Mrs. Phillip J. Stover
(Annette Ashlock)

LAMB TERRAPIN

6-8 Servings

1 large onion, chopped
3 T. butter
2 to 3 lbs. boneless lamb stew meat
Flour
1 tsp. salt
½ tsp. cinnamon
½ tsp. cloves
½ tsp. nutmeg
Dash pepper
1 cup lamb or chicken broth
½ lb. fresh mushrooms, sliced
1 T. lemon juice
3 hard-cooked eggs, sliced
1 cup half and half
½ cup dry sherry

WINE SUGGESTION:
St. Emilion

Saute onion in butter until tender, but not brown. Dredge stew meat in flour; shake off excess. Add meat to onion; brown. Season with salt, cinnamon, cloves, nutmeg, and pepper. Add broth; cover and simmer about 1½ to 2 hours or until lamb is tender. In separate pan, saute mushrooms lightly; add to meat. Add lemon juice, eggs, half and half, and sherry; heat to serving temperature. Serve with rice. (Meat mixture can be prepared the day before and refrigerated). About ½ hour before serving, saute mushrooms and finish preparation.

Mrs. Robert Shirley III
(Pamela Materne)

HERB BAKED HAM

- 1 cup brown sugar
- ¼ cup fine bread crumbs
- ¼ cup wine vinegar
- 1 T. dry mustard
- 1½ tsp. dried parsley flakes
- ½ tsp. thyme
- ½ tsp. marjoram
- ½ tsp. ground cloves
- 1 bay leaf
- 1 whole ham
- 1½ cups white wine (or vermouth)

WINE SUGGESTION:
Cote Provence Rose

Combine all ingredients except for bay leaf, ham, and wine; mix thoroughly. Place ham on bay leaf in a roasting pan. Spread herb mixture over ham. Pour wine in bottom of pan; cover. Bake at 300°, basting frequently until tender. (Minutes per pound depend on whether the ham is pre-cooked or not, with or without a bone. Follow instructions with ham. Boneless ham gives about 4 servings per pound; bone-in ham gives 2½ to 3.)

Mrs. Walter L. Jones, Jr.
(Jane Frederick)

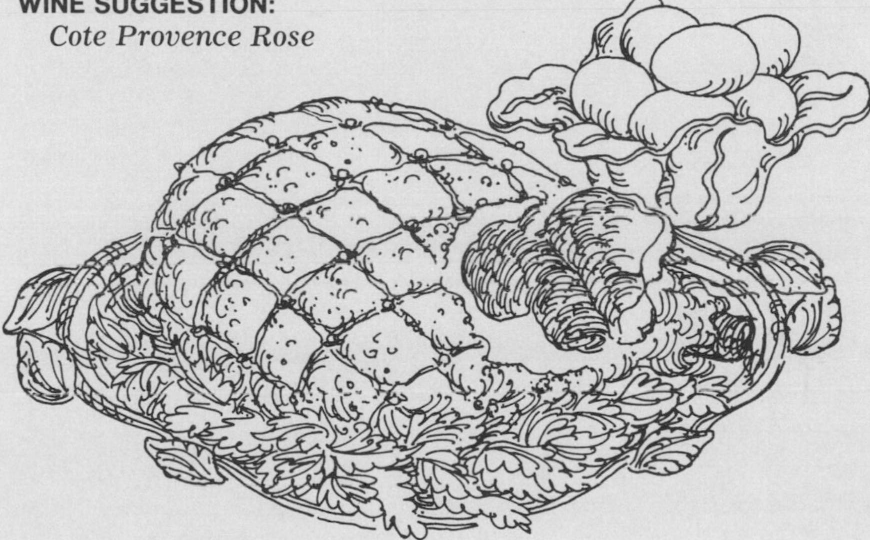

CHILLED APRICOT-GLAZED HAM — 24 Servings

- ¼ cup dark corn syrup
- 1 T. cornstarch
- ¼ tsp. ground cloves
- 1 cup apricot nectar
- 2 T. lemon juice
- 1 canned ham (8 lbs.)

Combine corn syrup, cornstarch and cloves in small saucepan. Stir in apricot nectar and lemon juice. Cook over medium heat, stirring constantly, until mixture comes to a boil; boil one minute. Cool slightly. Spread over ham; chill several hours or overnight. Slice thinly; serve cold.

Mrs. Patrick Callahan
(Patricia Henebry)

SWEET AND SOUR PORK

4 Servings

1½ lbs. boneless lean pork, cubed
1 T. dry sherry
½ tsp. salt
Dash pepper
1 cup flour
½ cup cornstarch
1 tsp. baking powder
1 T. beaten egg
½ cup water
1 tsp. oil

SAUCE:

1½ cups sugar
⅔ cup catsup
2 T. soy sauce
½ tsp. salt
½ tsp. MSG
2 cups water
1 cup vinegar
7 T. cornstarch
1 cup carrots, cut in small chunks, cooked
1 cup green pepper, cut in 1-inch squares
1 cup fresh pineapple chunks

WINE SUGGESTION:
Chenin Blanc

Combine pork, sherry, salt and pepper in a bowl. Mix flour, cornstarch, and baking powder; add egg, water, and oil. Mix until it makes a smooth batter. Dip pork into batter and coat completely. Heat 2-inches oil to 400°. Add pork and deep fry until golden. Drain pork on paper towel. (At this point pork may be refrigerated a day or two. Before serving fry pork a second time at 400°). To make sauce: Combine in a saucepan sugar, catsup, soy sauce, salt, MSG and 1⅓ cups water. Bring to a boil; add 1 cup vinegar. When it boils again add cornstarch mixed with ⅔ cup water. Cook, stirring, until thickened; mix in 2 T. hot oil used to fry pork. Add carrots, green pepper, and pineapple chunks to sauce. At this point both sauce and pork may be kept warm for 15 to 30 minutes. When ready to serve add pork to sweet and sour sauce and toss.

Mrs. H. Alex Vance, Jr.
(Melinda Martin)

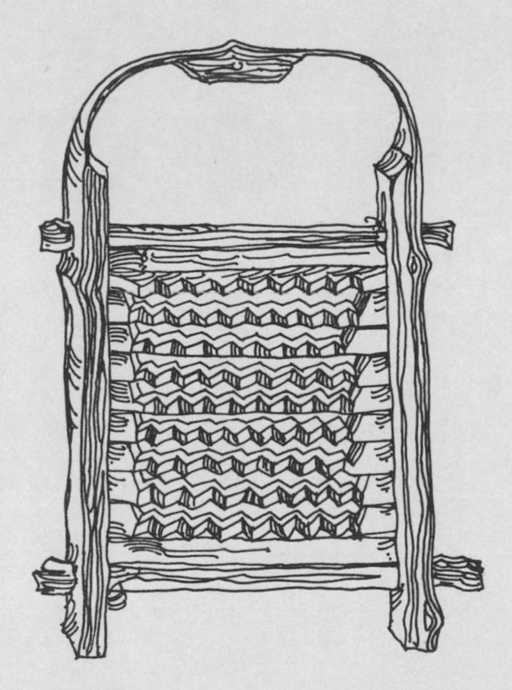

SWEETBREADS POULETTE

6 Servings

- 3 pairs sweetbreads
- Water
- 5 T. lemon juice
- Salt
- 3 T. butter
- 2 T. flour
- 3 cups chicken broth
- 1 cup cream
- 4 egg yolks, beaten
- Pepper to taste
- 1 T. chopped parsley
- ½ lb. fresh mushrooms, sliced and partially sauteed in butter

WINE SUGGESTION:
Beaujolais Blanc

Soak sweetbreads in ice water for 45 minutes. Meanwhile, bring to a boil enough water to cover the sweetbreads; add 2 T. lemon juice, 1 tsp. salt, and sweetbreads. Simmer until white, 15 to 20 minutes. Drain; cool in ice water. Remove all covering and connective tissues. Melt butter; stir in flour. Slowly add chicken broth; cook, stirring constantly, until thickened. Beat cream and egg yolks. Slowly stir half the hot sauce into egg mixture. Slowly stir back into remaining sauce. Season to taste. Add sweetbreads; continue cooking for 4 or 5 minutes over medium heat. Add 3 T. lemon juice, parsley and mushrooms.

Mrs. William A. Patterson, Jr.
(Marcia Motley)

LUXEMBURG STEW

8 Servings

- 2½ lbs. shoulder veal, cubed
- ¼ cup flour
- ⅓ cup butter
- 1 medium onion, sliced
- 1 can (28 oz.) whole tomatoes, drained
- 5 whole cloves
- 1 tsp. salt
- 1 bay leaf
- Pinch each: paprika, thyme, marjoram, rosemary, pepper
- 2½ cups beer
- 6 ginger snaps
- Juice of 1 lemon

WINE SUGGESTION:
Pinot Noir

Roll veal in flour. In heavy pan, melt ¼ cup butter. Brown veal lightly; remove from pan. Add remaining butter; saute onion lightly. Return veal to pan. Add tomatoes, seasonings and beer; cover and cook slowly 2 hours. Moisten ginger snaps with water; crush and add to meat. Cook 30 minutes longer. Just before serving, add lemon juice. Serve with rice or potatoes.

Mrs. William A. Patterson, Jr.
(Marcia Motley)

VEAL CHOPS WITH BELGIAN ENDIVE — 4 Servings

4 loin veal chops
Salt and freshly-ground pepper
¼ cup flour
¼ cup butter
4 firm white heads of Belgian endive
2 T. water
2 T. finely-chopped shallots
3 T. cognac
1½ cups whipping cream
¼ cup grated parmesan cheese

WINE SUGGESTION:
Gewurtztraminer

Sprinkle chops with salt and pepper. Dredge in flour. Melt 3 T. butter and cook chops over moderately low heat 8 to 10 minutes; turn. Cook 15 minutes longer or until done. Place endive in a heavy saucepan; add remaining butter, water, salt and pepper. Cover closely and simmer 25 minutes. If necessary, add a bit more water. Transfer chops to warm platter; cover with foil. Add shallots to skillet; saute for 30 seconds. Add cognac and flame it. Stir to dissolve brown particles in skillet. Add cream; cook, stirring, over high heat for about 5 minutes or until thickened. Strain sauce; add salt and pepper to taste. Arrange chops in one layer in baking dish. Press the endive gently to remove any excess liquid. Arrange around the chops. Spoon sauce over all; sprinkle with cheese. Bake at 400°, uncovered, 15 minutes.

Mrs. James F. Peil
(Nancy Rodgers)

RHUBARB BAKED CHICKEN

8 Servings

- **3 whole chicken breasts, split**
- **2 chicken leg-thighs, not split**
- **¼ cup butter, melted**
- **¼ cup cornstarch**
- **¾ cup sugar**
- **⅛ tsp. salt**
- **3 cups diced fresh rhubarb**
- **2 cups water**
- **2½ tsp. fresh lemon juice**

Arrange chicken in a baking dish, brush with butter; brown under broiler 5 to 10 minutes. Bake at 350° for 30 minutes. Meanwhile, prepare sauce: combine cornstarch, sugar, salt, rhubarb and water in a saucepan. Cook, stirring until mixture boils and thickens. Add lemon juice. Spoon sauce over chicken and bake 20 minutes longer. Serve with hot rice.

Mrs. Benson T. Caswell
(Margaret Graham)

CHICKEN BREASTS IN CREAM

4 Servings

- **¼ lb. uncooked ham, diced**
- **2 whole large chicken breasts, split**
- **1 can (16 oz.) tiny new potatoes**
- **¼ lb. fresh mushrooms, sliced, sauteed**
- **½ lb. seedless green grapes**
- **1 cup white wine**
- **2 cups cream**
- **3 T. butter**
- **2 T. flour**
- **Salt and pepper**

WINE SUGGESTION:
Vouvray

Simmer ham for 15 minutes in a little water. Saute seasoned chicken breasts in butter. Put in deep buttered casserole. Brown new potatoes and put in casserole. Make cream sauce in drippings from chicken by stirring in flour and adding cream and wine; cook, stirring, until thickened. Add drained ham and mushrooms to the casserole. Pour sauce over all. Bake at 350° for 45 to 60 minutes. Add grapes; bake an additional 10 minutes. (Potatoes may be omitted.)

Mrs. Charles A. Ault, III
(Valerie Richards)

HAWAIIAN BAKED CHICKEN — 8-10 Servings

½ cup butter, melted
3 whole chicken breasts, split
4 chicken legs and thighs, not split
Salt and pepper
1 cup fresh orange juice
2 T. fresh lemon juice
½ cup brown sugar
1 T. soy sauce
2 T. cornstarch
1 fresh pineapple, sliced
2 fresh papayas, peeled, seeded and sliced

WINE SUGGESTION:
Portuguese Rose

In ¼ cup melted butter, quickly brown the chicken on both sides. Place in a single layer in a baking dish; add salt and pepper. Brush with remaining butter. Bake at 350° for 40 minutes. Meanwhile combine juices, sugar, soy sauce and cornstarch in a sauce pan; cook stirring constantly, until thick. Stir in fruit. Pour sauce over chicken; bake 15 minutes longer or until chicken is tender.

Mrs. John C. Munson
(Virginia Aldrich)

CHICKEN IN CHAMPAGNE — 8 Servings

2 roasting chickens (4 to 5 lbs. each)
Salt and white pepper
¼ cup butter, melted
1 T. vegetable oil
3 T. butter, melted
¼ cup flour
2 cups milk
2 onions, thinly sliced
2 parsley sprigs, minced
3 T. cream
Dash nutmeg
½ cup finely-chopped mushrooms
2 T. minced shallots
1 split dry champagne

WINE SUGGESTION:
Extra Dry Champagne

Sprinkle chicken inside and out with salt and pepper. Brush with ¼ cup melted butter and oil. Roast at 350° until done, basting frequently. Meanwhile, prepare sauce: Cook 3 T. butter and flour over low heat until blended. Scald milk with onion and parsley. Strain into butter mixture, whisking constantly. Cook and stir until thick and smooth; add cream, nutmeg, and salt and pepper to taste. Add mushrooms and shallots. Simmer 20 minutes, stirring often. Remove chicken from pan; skim off fat. Add champagne to pan liquid. Bring to boil, stirring to dissolve particles in pan. Pour pan juices into sauce and bring to a boil. Strain; adjust seasonings. Place chicken on platter; pour some sauce over it. Serve remaining sauce separately.

Mrs. James F. Peil
(Nancy Rodgers)

BAKED STUFFED CHICKEN BREASTS

4 Servings

4 whole chicken breasts, boned, halved, skinned
2 T. finely-chopped onions
2 T. finely-chopped celery
¼ lb. mushrooms, sliced
2 T. butter
1 tsp. flour
¼ tsp. salt
Dash pepper
1 T. lemon juice
⅓ cup toasted slivered blanched almonds
Melted butter
1¼ cups finely-crushed potato chips
Sauteed whole mushrooms

WINE SUGGESTION:
Piesporter Spatlese

Pound chicken between sheets of waxed paper to flatten to about ⅜ inch thick. Saute onions, celery and sliced mushrooms in 2 T. butter until soft. Blend in flour, salt, and pepper; add lemon juice and almonds. Cook and stir until thickened. Place a spoonful of filling on each piece of chicken; roll, tucking in edges and fasten with skewers or wooden picks. Dip into melted butter; roll into potato chip crumbs. Place in a greased baking dish, skewer sides down. Cover and bake at 350° for 45 minutes; if taken from refrigerator bake 1 hour. Uncover; bake 15 minutes longer or until browned. Garnish with sauteed whole mushrooms.

Mrs. John N. Schmidt
(Joan M. Slauson)

ROCK CORNISH HENS WITH CHERRY SAUCE

2 servings

2 rock cornish hens

CHERRY SAUCE:

1½ T. cornstarch
4 T. sugar
¼ T. salt
¼ T. dry mustard
¼ T. ginger
1 can (1 lb.) water-packed, pitted sour red cherries
1 T. slivered orange rind
½ cup orange juice
¼ cup currant jelly
2 T. dry sherry

WINE SUGGESTION:

Niersteiner Spatlese

Roast hens at 425° for 1 hour or until tender. In saucepan, combine cornstarch, sugar, salt, dry mustard and ginger. Drain the can of cherries. Add liquid to the cornstarch mixture; add orange rind, orange juice and currant jelly. Cook, stirring constantly, until mixture thickens. Add drained cherries and sherry just before serving. Serve with any favorite roasted game bird. (Could make 4 small servings.)

Mrs. Matthew C. Fox
(Amanda Clark)

PLUM DUCKLING

4 Servings

1 fresh or frozen duckling (4 to 5 lbs.)
3 apples, halved

PLUM SAUCE:

1 medium onion, chopped
2 T. butter, melted
1 can (17 oz.) pitted, purple plums
1 can (6 oz.) frozen lemonade
¼ cup soy sauce
2 tsp. prepared mustard
1 tsp. ground ginger
1 tsp. worcestershire sauce
2 drops hot pepper sauce

WINE SUGGESTION:

Cote Rotie

Wash duck, pat dry, stuff with apples. Prick skin with sharp fork several times. Roast on rack, breast side up, at 400° for the first 30 minutes, then at 350° for 2 hours or until tender. To prepare sauce: Saute onion in butter. Puree plums with syrup in blender or food mill; add to onion. Add all other ingredients; simmer uncovered for 15 minutes. (This sauce may be made ahead and refrigerated or frozen.) Baste duck with plum sauce during last 30 minutes of baking.

Mrs. Thomas A. Nickles
(Elizabeth Anne Nelson)

CREOLE JAMBALAYA

18-20 Servings

A savory treat from the bayou-country Cajuns

3 cups dry white wine
1 lemon, sliced
4 cloves garlic, minced
4 bay leaves
Few chopped celery leaves
Dash hot pepper sauce
1 T. salt
1 to 1¼ lbs. shelled shrimp
3 T. butter
1 lb. cooked ham, cubed
5 medium onions, chopped
1 can (28 oz.) tomatoes
1 can (16 oz.) tomatoes
1 lb. chorizo, mild Italian, or Polish sausage, sliced
2 green peppers, coarsely chopped
1 can (6 oz.) tomato paste
¼ cup minced parsley
2 tsp. tarragon
1 tsp. thyme
3 cups raw converted rice
1 lb. scallops, thawed

WINE SUGGESTION:
Rose de Cote de Provence

The day before, combine in sauce pan wine, lemon, 2 cloves garlic, 2 bay leaves, celery leaves, pepper sauce, and 1 tsp. salt. Cover and simmer for 15 minutes. Add shrimp; heat to boiling. Cover and boil gently 4 to 5 minutes, or until done. Cool; marinate in liquid in refrigerator. The next day, melt butter in large pan; add ham, onions, and 2 cloves garlic. Saute 3 to 4 minutes. Add tomatoes with liquid, 1½ cups water, sausage, peppers, tomato paste, parsley, 2 bay leaves, 2 tsp. salt, tarragon, and thyme. Cover and simmer gently 1½ hours. Add strained shrimp marinade, 2 cups water, and rice. Heat to boiling; reduce heat, cover, and simmer for 20 to 25 minutes, or until rice is tender. Add more water, if necessary. Stir in shrimps and scallops during last 5 minutes.

Mrs. Phillip J. Stover
(Annette Ashlock)

SHRIMP AND LOBSTER CURRY — 6 Servings

CURRY SAUCE:

- ¼ cup butter
- ¼ cup chopped onions
- 1 clove garlic, minced
- 1 stalk celery, chopped
- 1 tart apple, diced
- 1 bay leaf
- ⅓ cup flour
- 2 tsp. curry powder
- ½ tsp. salt
- ½ tsp. dry mustard
- 3 cups chicken stock
- ¼ to ½ cup cream or milk (optional)

SEAFOOD:

- ¾ lb. cooked peeled shrimp
- ½ lb. cooked lobster meat

WINE SUGGESTION:
Cote de Provence Blanc

Heat butter. Saute onions, garlic, celery, apple, and bay leaf until cooked but not brown. Sprinkle with flour, curry powder, salt and dry mustard. Gradually add stock. Cook, stirring constantly, until thickened. Add cream, if desired. Simmer 10 to 15 minutes. Add seafood; heat. Serve with rice and desired condiments. (Turkey or chicken may be used instead of seafood.)

Mrs. William A. Patterson, Jr.
(Marcia Motley)

SOFT-SHELL CRAB WITH ALMONDS — 4 Servings

- 12 soft-shell crabs, cleaned
- Flour
- ½ cup oil
- ½ cup butter
- Salt and pepper
- ½ cup chopped almonds
- ¼ cup red wine vinegar
- ½ cup whipping cream

WINE SUGGESTION:
Chablis

Dip crabs in flour; saute in oil and butter about 3 minutes on each side. Sprinkle with salt and pepper. Remove to a serving dish; keep warm. Add more butter to skillet if necessary. Add almonds; toast quickly. Add vinegar; reduce completely. Add cream; cook for 5 minutes. Pour over crabs.

Mrs Thomas C. O'Neil
(Jane Stephens)

SHRIMP KABOBS

4 Servings

Great for a spring cookout

- 2 T. cornstarch
- ⅔ cup pineapple juice
- 2 T. soy sauce
- 2 T. honey
- 1 T. vinegar
- ¼ tsp. powdered ginger
- 24 large shrimp, cleaned, raw
- 1 cup fresh pineapple chunks
- 24 medium whole mushrooms
- 4 green peppers, cut in squares

Blend cornstarch with a little juice; combine with remaining juice, soy sauce, honey, vinegar and ginger. Cook over low heat until thick, stirring constantly. Alternate shrimp, pineapple, mushrooms and green pepper on individual skewers. Broil until lightly browned on all sides, basting with sauce while cooking.

Mrs. H. Dorn Stewart, Jr.
(Judith Collins)

FLOUNDER STUFFED WITH CRAB

6 Servings

- 1 lb. fresh crab meat
- Mayonnaise
- 1 T. lime juice
- 1 T. minced parsley
- 1 onion slice, minced
- 1 tsp. capers
- ½ tsp. salt
- Dash cayenne
- 2 lbs. thin flounder fillets
- ½ cup dry white wine

WINE SUGGESTION:
Pouilly Blanc Fume

Mix crab with sufficient mayonnaise to hold together. Add other ingredients except wine and fish. Place fish in shallow baking dish. Top each fillet with the crab-mayonnaise mixture; fold fish over. Secure with toothpicks. Pour wine over fish. Bake 350° for 18 to 20 minutes or until fish flakes easily. Baste with wine from pan during cooking.

Mrs. Roger O. Brown
(Elizabeth Cluxton)

WHOLE POACHED SALMON IN CHAMPAGNE SAUCE

4-6 Servings

¼ cup butter, melted
2 carrots, finely-diced
1 onion, finely-diced
1 celery stalk, finely-sliced
1 whole salmon (3-4 lbs.), cleaned and head left on
Salt and pepper
1 large bouquet garni, (bay leaf, thyme, parsley)
3 cups dry champagne

SAUCE:
4 egg yolks
1 T. cornstarch
½ cup whipping cream
2 tsp. lemon juice
¼ cup sweet butter
½ lb. button mushrooms, poached

WINE SUGGESTION:
Chinon

In butter, saute vegetables 5 minutes. Spread them on bottom of fish poacher. Season salmon with salt and pepper. Place it on bed of vegetables; add bouquet and champagne. Cover and bake at 350° for 35 minutes or until salmon flakes easily. Remove to serving platter and keep warm. Strain the cooking liquid and over high heat reduce it to 1 cup. Meanwhile, mix egg yolks and cornstarch in double boiler; add cooking liquid; cook, stirring constantly until thickened. If too thick, thin with cream and lemon juice. Add butter and mushrooms. Spoon sauce over salmon and serve.

Mrs. Dennis F. Muckermann
(Betty Graham)

SHAD ROE WITH TOAST POINTS

3 Servings

½ cup butter
2 lbs. fresh shad roe
3 slices fresh bread
Salt and freshly-ground black pepper
Lemon slices
½ cup chopped parsley

WINE SUGGESTION:
Hermitage Blanc

In a skillet, melt butter until warm but not hot. Arrange fresh roe in it. Cover and cook over low heat, turning once, until tender (about 12 minutes). Add more butter if necessary. Toast bread; cut in half, diagonally. Arrange the toast on a warm platter and place roe on top. Season with salt and pepper, garnish with lemon slices and sprinkle generously with parsley.

Mrs. Robert B. Abel
(Mary Beth Turner)

SHAD ROE AUX FINES HERBES

2-4 Servings

¼ cup butter
2 medium shad roe
Salt and pepper
1 T. chopped parsley
2 tsp. lemon juice
2 tsp. chopped chives
1 tsp. chopped fresh tarragon
1 tsp. chopped fresh chervil

WINE SUGGESTION:
Pouilly Fuisse

In a large heavy skillet, heat butter; add shad roe. Sprinkle with salt and pepper. Cook on both sides, turning once carefully, about 12 minutes. When cooked through and lightly browned, transfer to a hot platter. Add remaining ingredients to the skillet. Heat, stirring, and pour over the shad roe.

Mrs. Thomas N. Boyden
(Susan B. Dalton)

ENTREES: SAUCES

SOUR CREAM SAUCE FOR FISH — 1¼ Cups

1 cup sour cream
2 T. prepared mustard
1 T. lemon juice
1 T. minced onion
1 tsp. salt
1 tsp. worcestershire sauce
4 drops hot pepper sauce
Dash pepper

Blend all ingredients. Serve at room temperature.

Miss Gabriele Weissenberger

SAUCE LILI — ¾ Cup

½ cup mayonnaise
1 T. tarragon vinegar
1 tsp. malt vinegar
1 tsp. catsup
1 tsp. chili sauce
¼ tsp. salt
⅛ tsp. paprika
Dash pepper

Combine all ingredients. Mix thoroughly. Serve with cold lamb. This sauce is also good with avocado or seafood cocktail. Can be stored in the refrigerator.

Miss Margo Corrigan Moss

TARTAR SAUCE WITH SHERRY — 1 Cup

1 cup mayonnaise
2 T. minced candied dill pickle strips
1 tsp. chopped chives
1 tsp. chopped parsley
1 tsp. chopped shallots or green onions
1 tsp. chopped green olives
¼ tsp. salt
Freshly-ground pepper to taste
1 to 2 tsp. sherry

Mix all ingredients well; refrigerate until ready to serve.

Mrs. Robert H. BonDurant
(Irene McCausland)

ORANGE SAUCE FOR EASTER HAM

½ can (11 oz. size) mandarin oranges
1 T. cornstarch
⅔ cup orange juice
½ cup orange marmalade
¼ tsp. ginger
2 T. brandy (optional)

Drain oranges, reserving liquid. In saucepan, combine cornstarch with ⅓ cup drained liquid. Add orange juice, marmalade, and ginger. Cook, stirring constantly, until thickened. Add oranges and brandy; heat through. Baste ham with some of sauce during last 15 minutes. Pass remainder. (Brandy may also be warmed, ignited, and poured over sauce for bringing to the table. Sauce is also good with roast fresh pork.)

Mrs. Phillip J. Stover
(Annette Ashlock)

MUSTARD SAUCE — 2 Cups

3 egg yolks
3 T. sugar
2 T. water
¼ cup vinegar
1 tsp. salt
1 T. dry mustard
2 T. butter
2 T. grated horseradish
1 cup whipping cream, whipped

Beat eggs yolks until light. Add sugar, water, vinegar, salt and mustard. Cook in double boiler over boiling water, stirring constantly, until thick. Add butter and horseradish; stir until well blended. Cool. Fold into whipped cream. Serve with baked ham.

Mrs. Walter L. Jones, Jr.
(Jane Frederick)

RAISIN SAUCE FOR HAM — 2 Cups

1 cup sugar
½ cup water
2 T. vinegar
1 T. worcestershire sauce
1 jar (8 oz.) currant jelley
1 cup raisins, chopped
½ tsp. salt
¼ tsp. cinnamon
⅛ tsp. cloves
⅛ tsp. ginger
Dash pepper

Boil sugar and water for 2 minutes. Add remaining ingredients, cook until well blended. Serve hot.

Mrs. David B. Smith
(Marcia Williamson)

VEGETABLES AND ACCOMPANIMENTS

ARTICHOKES ITALIAN

6-8 Servings

2 bacon slices, cut in pieces
1 medium onion, minced
1 can (6 oz.) tomato paste
½ cup white wine
1 tsp. oregano
1½ tsp. salt
¼ tsp. pepper
1 tsp. sugar (optional)
2 pkgs. (9 oz. each) forzen artichoke hearts, thawed
3 to 4 T. butter
Grated parmesan cheese

In small skillet, saute bacon and onion until golden. Add tomato paste, wine, and seasonings. Meanwhile, lightly saute artichoke hearts in butter. Arrange in buttered 8-inch pie plate. Sprinkle with parmesan cheese. Pour sauce over artichokes; brown under broiler. Top with more parmesan cheese.

Mrs. Bart H. Mosser
(Carol Clements)

ASPARAGUS SOUFFLE

6 Servings

1 T. grated parmesan cheese
2 T. minced green onion
3 T. butter
3 T. flour
1 cup milk; or ¼ cup asparagus water and ¾ cup milk
½ tsp. salt
⅛ tsp. pepper
Pinch cayenne and grated nutmeg
½ cup grated swiss cheese
4 egg yolks
¾ cup cooked chopped asparagus
5 egg whites

Butter a 6-cup souffle dish and sprinkle with parmesan cheese. Saute green onion in butter for 2 minutes. Add flour. Cook together 2 minutes; whisk in boiling liquid, add seasonings. Cook, stirring constantly, until thickened. Add cheese; stir until melted. Off heat, whisk in egg yolks one at a time. Add asparagus. Beat egg whites until stiff peaks form. Gently fold whites into the base; turn into prepared dish. Optional: if you have saved the asparagus heads you can gently make a design on top of the souffle mixture. Bake at 375° for 35 minutes. Serve immediately.

Mrs. J.D. MacDonald
(Charie Roberson)

CREAMED ASPARAGUS 8 Servings

2 T. butter
2 T. flour
1 cup cream
1 cup grated cheddar cheese
½ tsp. salt
¼ tsp. pepper
1½ lbs. fresh asparagus pieces
¼ lb. fresh mushrooms, sliced, sauteed in butter
4 hard-cooked eggs, sliced
½ cup toasted, slivered almonds
Bread crumbs, buttered

Melt butter; add flour. Blend until smooth. Slowly add cream. Cook, stirring constantly, until thick. Add cheese and seasonings. Cook until melted. In a greased casserole, alternate layers of asparagus, mushrooms, eggs, almonds, and sauce. Top with bread crumbs. Bake, covered, at 350 for 30 minutes.

Mrs. Bruce G. Southworth
(Mary Monek)

ITALIAN BAKED ASPARAGUS 4 Servings

1 lb. fresh asparagus
¼ cup butter, melted
3 T. minced onion
3 T. finely-chopped celery
2 T. grated parmesan cheese
2 T. freshly-grated bread crumbs
4 canned Italian tomatoes, drained and diced
Pinch of thyme
Pinch of oregano
Salt, freshly-ground pepper

Break off tough ends of asparagus spears. Pour butter in bottom of a rectangular baking dish. Line bottom with asparagus; sprinkle with onion, celery, cheese, bread crumbs, and diced tomatoes, in this order. Season with oregano, thyme, and salt and pepper to taste. Cover and bake at 375° for 45 minutes, or until asparagus is tender. (This looks very attractive if asparagus is arranged in dish with tips pointing alternately to the left and right. Sprinkle topping down the center, leaving tips showing.)

Mrs. James F. Peil
(Nancy Rodgers)

GREEK BULGUR

12 Servings

A marvelous rice substitute!

- ¾ cup butter
- 3 cups coarse bulgur (cracked wheat)
- 2 onions, finely-chopped
- 6 cups chicken or beef broth (or mixed)
- 2 tsp. salt
- 1 tsp. pepper
- 1 tsp. curry powder
- 1 cup pine nuts

Melt ½ cup butter in skillet. Add dry bulgur; saute well. In a separate pan, saute onion in ¼ cup butter until yellow gold. Mix with bulgur; add broth, seasonings and nuts. Stir well. Bake in an uncovered casserole at 375° for 30 minutes. Adjust seasonings; stir. Bake 10 minutes longer. (This freezes well or keeps in refrigerator 2 days.)

Mrs. H. Alex Vance, Jr.
(Melinda Martin)

HERBED CARROTS

4-6 Servings

- 2 bunches carrots, cut in 1-inch pieces
- 1 bunch green onions, chopped
- 2 pinches chopped parsley
- 3 T. sweet vermouth
- ½ cup water
- ¼ cup butter
- 3 T. sour cream
- 1 tsp. Italian seasonings
- Canned French fried onions as desired

Place first five ingredients in pressure cooker; cook 5 to 8 minutes under 15 lbs. pressure. (Can be cooked in foil sealed pot until carrots are just tender.) Drain; place in oven-proof casserole. Blend in butter, sour cream, and seasonings. Sprinkle onions on top. Bake at 350° for 20 minutes.

Mrs. Henry A. Blyth III
(Annis Pechin)

ORANGE-GLAZED CARROTS

6 Servings

Sure to appeal to even the staunchest carrot haters

- 6 to 8 fresh carrots
- ¼ cup butter
- ¼ cup sugar
- 1 T. flour
- Juice of 2 oranges (about ⅔ cup)
- Orange slices for garnish

Peel carrots. Cut into strips lengthwise. Cook, covered, in boiling salted water until tender. Transfer to shallow baking dish. Melt butter; stir in sugar and flour. Gradually add orange juice. Cook, stirring constantly, until mixture bubbles. Pour evenly over carrots. Garnish with twisted halves of orange slices. Bake at 350° for 30 minutes.

Mrs. Donald J. Ross
(Cynthia Stiles)

BAKED CELERY WITH WATER CHESTNUTS

12-14 Servings

8 cups celery, cut in 1-inch pieces
2 cans (5 oz. each) water chestnuts, drained, sliced
½ cup diced green peppers
2 cans (10½ oz. each) cream of chicken soup
½ cup bread crumbs
½ cup toasted slivered almonds
¼ cup butter, melted

Cook celery in salted water 8 to 10 minutes, uncovered. Drain; add soup, water chestnuts, and green pepper. Turn into 2-quart buttered casserole. Toss bread crumbs and almonds with butter; sprinkle on top. Bake at 350° for 35 minutes or until golden brown.

Mrs. M. Jay Tree
(Judith Marks)

SOUTHERN GARLIC GRITS

8 Servings

Not unlike a souffle

4 cups water
½ tsp. salt
1 cup grits
¾ roll garlic cheese
¼ lb. butter
2 eggs, beaten
½ cup milk
1 cup corn flake crumbs

Bring water and salt to a boil; stir in grits; cook 2 to 5 minutes. Add garlic cheese, butter, eggs and milk. Stir until all is well blended. Pour mixture into a 2-qt. buttered casserole; sprinkle top with corn flake crumbs. Bake at 350° for 25 minutes.

Mrs. S. Powell Bridges
(Barbara Best)

MUSHROOMS POLONAISE

6 Servings

1½ lbs. fresh mushrooms, sliced
½ cup butter
1 onion, minced
2 T. flour
1 cup sour cream
¼ cup whipping cream
Salt and pepper to taste
¼ tsp. nutmeg
2 T. minced parsley
¼ cup bread crumbs tossed in ¼ cup melted butter

Saute mushrooms in butter until lightly brown. Add onion; cook until soft. Stir in flour. Cook until thick, stirring constantly. Stir in other ingredients except crumbs. Pour into a buttered casserole. Top with bread crumbs. Bake at 325° for 35 minutes or until brown.

Mrs. Cushman B. Bissell, Jr.
(Judith Roddewig)

POTATOES DELMONICO

6-8 Servings

- ¼ cup butter
- 3 T. flour
- ½ tsp. salt
- ¼ tsp. pepper
- ½ tsp. garlic salt
- 1½ cups hot milk
- ½ cup grated American cheese
- 4 hard-cooked eggs, sliced
- 4 cups sliced (¼-inch slices) cooked potatoes

Melt butter. Add flour and seasonings; stir until well blended. Slowly add milk, stirring constantly. Continue cooking until smooth and thick. Remove from heat; blend in cheese. Pour entire mixture over sliced potatoes and hard-cooked eggs. Mix well, put into a well-greased casserole. Sprinkle top with additional cheese and paprika. Bake 1 hour at 350°.

Mrs. Harold B. Smith, Jr.
(Frederica Harriman)

BAKED PINEAPPLE

10-12 Servings

Excellent accompaniment for roast pork or ham

- 2 cans (20 oz. each) crushed pineapple
- 1 cup brown sugar
- 1 cup white sugar
- 1 T. lemon juice
- 7 slices bread, crusts removed and broken into pieces
- Rice Krispies
- 2 T. butter

Combine pineapple with liquid, sugar, lemon juice, and bread. Place in a casserole; top with Rice Krispies. Dot with butter. Bake at 350° for 45 minutes.

Mrs. Melville C. Hill, Jr.
(Mary Johnson)

MINT MERINGUE PEARS

8-10 Servings

To garnish an Easter leg of lamb

- 8 to 10 canned pear halves
- Green food coloring
- 2 egg whites
- ½ cup mint jelly

Drain pears thoroughly, reserving liquid. Mix liquid with a little water; add food coloring to make liquid a deep green. Add pears. (Pears should be covered with liquid). Let stand until pears take on light green color. Drain pears; partially dry with paper towels. Beat egg whites until stiff; add mint jelly, continuing beating until well mixed. Drop spoonfuls of meringue on cut surface of each pear half. Place in hot oven or broiler just long enough to brown meringue.

Mrs. Phillip J. Stover
(Annette Ashlock)

BRAZILIAN RICE

10-12 Servings

3 cups cooked rice
2 pkgs. (10 oz. each) chopped spinach, cooked and drained
1 lb. brick cheese, grated
1 T. instant minced onion
½ tsp. marjoram
½ tsp. thyme
½ tsp. rosemary
1 T. worcestershire sauce
1 cup milk
4 eggs, lightly beaten

Combine rice, spinach and cheese. Add onion and herbs. Stir in remaining ingredients. Mix well. Pour into a 9 x13-inch baking dish. Bake at 350° for 30 to 40 minutes.

Mrs. Stanley A. Walton, III
(Karen Karser)

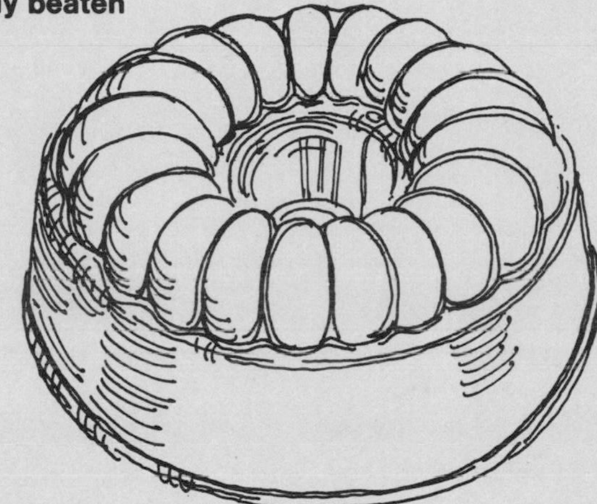

SPINACH RING

10-12 Servings

4 packages (10 ozs. each) frozen chopped spinach, thawed, drained
1 cup medium white sauce
2 T. prepared mustard
2 T. Roquefort or blue cheese, crumbled
1 tsp. grated onion
Salt, pepper
1 cup bread crumbs
3 eggs, separated

Combine spinach, white sauce, mustard, cheese, onion, and salt and pepper to taste. Stir in bread crumbs and beaten egg yolks. Beat egg whites until stiff but not dry; fold into spinach mixture. Turn into greased 2-qt. ring mold. Set in pan of hot water. Bake at 350° for 25 to 30 minutes, or until set. Turn out on round platter. Garnish with parsley.

Mrs. John Wheelan
(Betsy Califf)

SPINACH BALLS GIACOSA

8 Servings

- 2 pkgs. (10 oz. each) frozen spinach
- 1 lb. ricotta cheese
- 1 cup grated parmesan cheese
- 1 cup fine bread crumbs
- 4 eggs, beaten
- ¼ tsp. marjoram
- Garlic salt, Salt and pepper
- Flour
- Prepared Italian spaghetti sauce

Cook spinach according to package directions. Drain thoroughly, pressing to remove as much moisture as possible. Combine with ricotta cheese, parmesan cheese, crumbs, eggs, marjoram, garlic salt, salt and pepper to taste. Form into balls about the size of walnuts. Chill thoroughly. To cook; roll in flour, drop in pan of boiling water. Cook a few at a time until they rise to the top in a single layer, about 5 minutes. Serve covered with spaghetti sauce. If sauce contains meat, this can be a one dish dinner.

Mrs. John N. Schmidt
(Joan Slauson)

TIAN de COURGETTES aux RIZ et EPINARDS

12 Servings

Zucchini, rice and spinach in cheese sauce

- 2½ lbs. zucchini
- ½ cup raw rice
- 1 cup minced onions
- 3 to 4 T. oil
- 1 T. butter
- 2 lbs. fresh spinach; or 2 pkgs. (10 oz. each) frozen spinach
- 2 cloves garlic, minced
- 2 T. flour
- Milk
- ⅔ cup grated parmesan cheese

Grate, salt and drain zucchini, reserving juices. Cook rice according to package directions. Saute onions in oil and butter until almost tender. Add spinach and garlic; cook until tender. Stir in flour. Add enough milk to zucchini juices to measure 1½ cups; stir into spinach mixture. Cook and stir until thickened. Add cooked rice and zucchini, all but 2 T. cheese, and salt and pepper to taste. Turn into baking dish; sprinkle with remaining cheese. Bake at 425° for 25 to 30 minutes, or until bubbly and lightly browned.

Mrs. Franklin McCarty, Jr.
(Ann Fix)

ASPARAGUS VINAIGRETTE

12 Servings

3 lbs. fresh asparagus
Boiling water, salt
¼ cup vegetable oil
2 T. cider vinegar
2 T. olive oil
1 T. fresh lemon juice
1 tsp. salt
1 tsp. paprika
½ tsp. dry mustard
2 sweet gherkins, chopped
½ clove garlic, pressed
¼ tsp. basil
⅛ tsp. freshly-ground pepper
1 hard-cooked egg, chopped

Cut off tough ends of asparagus. Tie stalks into bunch with string; stand upright in deep saucepan. Pour boiling water to depth of 2 inches; add salt. Bring to boil, cover, cook about 15 minutes, or until tender. Drain. Lay stalks in shallow dish. Combine all other ingredients except egg; pour over asparagus. Refrigerate several hours, turning stalks several times. Arrange on platter; sprinkle with egg. This sauce is also good for marinating little beets, artichoke hearts, string beans, etc.

Mrs. Bruce G. Southworth
(Mary Monek)

SPINACH SALAD

6 Servings

1 lb. fresh spinach
3 hard-cooked eggs
6 strips bacon
1 large red onion

DRESSING:

1 egg yolk
2 T. sugar
1½ tsp. paprika
1 T. worcestershire sauce
½ tsp. salt
¼ tsp. dry mustard
¼ tsp. pepper
¾ cup salad oil
¼ cup wine vinegar

Wash and dry spinach; chop eggs finely. Cook bacon until very crisp; crumble. Slice onion thinly. For dressing, mix egg yolk with seasonings and mix until smooth. Slowly add oil (about 1 T. at a time); slowly add vinegar. Toss with salad.

Mrs. Freeman Wood, Jr.
(Roswitha Stephan)

TOMATOES STUFFED WITH SPINACH

6 Servings

6 medium tomatoes
3 pkgs. (10 oz. each) frozen chopped spinach
½ green pepper, chopped
¼ cup chopped onion
2 hard-cooked eggs, chopped
2 stalks celery, chopped
Salt, pepper
Mayonnaise, slightly thinned with lemon juice

Hollow out tomatoes. Turn upside down to drain. Cook spinach quickly in a skillet without adding any additional water. Squeeze out every bit of liquid from spinach. Mix spinach with chopped green pepper, onion, eggs, celery, and salt and pepper to taste. Stir in enough thinned mayonnaise to hold mixture together. Check for seasoning. Fill tomato shells; refrigerate until serving time.

Mrs. Fentress Twerdahl
(Gretchen Fentress)

NO-TOSS SALAD

12 Servings

1 large head lettuce, shredded
¼ cup finely-chopped green onion
¼ cup celery, chopped
1 can (6 oz.) water chestnuts, sliced
1 or 2 pkgs. (10 oz. each) frozen peas (not thawed)
2 cups top-quality mayonnaise
1 T. sugar
¾ lb. bacon, fried and crumbled
3 to 4 hard-cooked eggs, sliced
3 tomatoes, sliced
Parmesan and Romano cheese, grated

Place lettuce in large, shallow serving dish or bowl. Sprinkle next three ingredients on top in layers. Break peas apart and sprinkle on top while frozen. Spread mayonnaise over top like frosting; sprinkle with sugar. Cover and refrigerate overnight. Before serving, add layers of bacon, egg slices and tomato slices. Sprinkle with grated cheeses. Do not toss this salad. Each serving should go to the bottom of the bowl to get the effect of the layers.

Mrs. Donald J. Ross
(Cynthia Stiles)

SPRING RADISH AND CUCUMBER SALAD

6-8 Servings

- 2 cucumbers, halved and seeds removed
- 1 tsp. salt
- 2 bunches radishes, thinly-sliced
- 1 cup sour cream
- 2 T. tarragon vinegar
- 1 tsp. celery seed
- Freshly-ground pepper

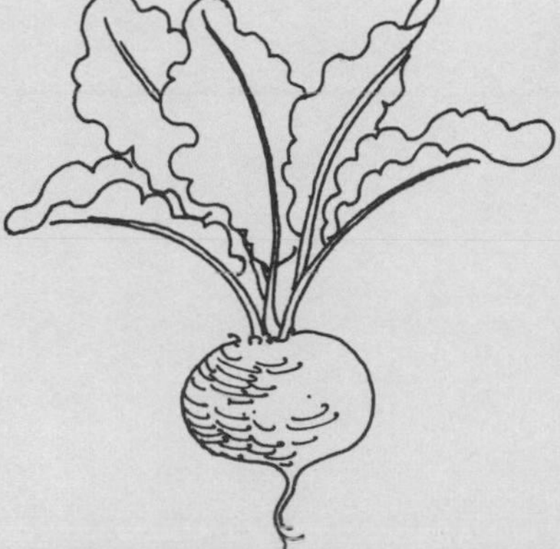

Slice cucumbers very thin. Sprinkle with salt; cover and chill several hours. Drain cucumbers well; combine with radishes. Combine remaining ingredients; blend into cucumbers and radishes. If desired, pile mixture into the center of a tomato aspic ring. Dust with a little ground pepper. May also be served on lettuce leaves.

Mrs. Edwin Holzer
(Josephine Earnest)

MOLDED EGG, CHEESE, AND OLIVE SALAD

6-8 Servings

- 1 pkg. (3 oz.) lemon-flavored gelatin
- 1 cup boiling water
- ½ cup cold water
- ½ cup mayonnaise
- 2 T. lemon juice
- ½ tsp. salt
- Few drops hot pepper sauce
- ½ cup shredded American cheese
- ½ cup diced celery
- ⅓ cup sliced stuffed olives
- 2 T. diced pimiento
- 1 tsp. grated onion
- 4 hard-cooked eggs, sliced

Add hot water to gelatin and stir until dissolved. Add cold water, mayonnaise, lemon juice, salt and hot pepper sauce. Stir until smooth and well blended. Chill until of a syrupy consistency. Beat until light. Fold in cheese, celery, stuffed olives, pimiento and onion. Arrange slices of egg on bottom and sides of a 1-qt. ring mold. Pour in gelatin mixture. Chill until set. Unmold on crisp lettuce. Serve with mayonnaise.

Mrs. Thomas N. Boyden
(Susan B. Dalton)

MANDARIN ORANGE SOUFFLE SALAD

10-12 Servings

2 pkgs. (3 oz. each) orange-flavored gelatin
1 cup boiling water
1 cup orange juice, freshly squeezed
1 cup sour cream
1 pt. orange sherbet
1 cup pineapple tidbits, well drained
2 cups mandarin orange sections, well drained
1 cup flaked coconut
Lettuce leaves

Mix gelatin and boiling water until dissolved. Add orange juice. Chill until mixture begins to thicken. Stir in sour cream and orange sherbet. Beat until thick and foamy. Add drained pineapple tidbits and orange sections. Pour into a 2-qt. ring mold. When set, turn out on lettuce leaves and sprinkle with coconut. If desired, garnish with additional mandarin orange sections.

Mrs. David B. Smith
(Marcia Williamson)

MINTED FRUIT MOLD

4 Servings

½ cup fresh mint leaves
2 cups boiling water
Green food coloring
2 env. plain gelatin
1 cup cold water
½ cup plus 2 T. sugar
½ cup fresh lemon juice
½ tsp. salt

FRESH FRUIT:
Melon balls, berries, grapes, banana slices

DRESSING:
1 pkg. (3 oz.) cream cheese, softened
2 T. honey
Juice of 1 orange
Grated rind of 1 orange

Steep mint in boiling water for 5 minutes. Strain and add a few drops of food coloring. Soak gelatin in cold water for 5 minutes; dissolve over low heat. Add to mint water. Stir in sugar, lemon juice and salt. Chill until almost set; add fruit. Pour into oiled mold; chill. Whip dressing ingredients together. Unmold salad. Serve with dressing.

Mrs. Alexander B. Sharpe
(Marjorie Johnston)

CUT GLASS GELATIN MOLD — 20 Servings

Also makes a pretty dessert

- **6 pkgs. (3 oz. each) flavored gelatin, each different**
- **Water**
- **2 env. plain gelatin**
- **1 cup pineapple juice**
- **1 pt. whipping cream**
- **5 T. powdered sugar**
- **1 tsp. vanilla**

Two days ahead, prepare each flavored gelatin individually by dissolving each pkg. in 1 cup boiling water and ½ cup cold water. Put in separate oiled pans in refrigerator. The next day, place the plain gelatin in ½ cup cold water; let stand 5 minutes. Add pineapple juice; heat slowly and stir until dissolved. Cool. Whip the cream; stir in sugar and vanilla. Cut the 6 pans of flavored gelatin into 1-inch squares. Gently fold in whipped cream and cooled pineapple mixture until well blended. Pour into a 10-inch angel food cake pan. Chill overnight. Unmold onto serving plate.

Mrs. David B. Smith
(Marcia Williamson)

SPRING FRUIT SALAD WITH POPPY SEED DRESSING — 8 Servings

- **¾ cup sugar**
- **⅓ cup vinegar**
- **1 tsp. dry mustard**
- **1 tsp. salt**
- **1½ T. grated onion**
- **1 cup salad oil**
- **1½ T. poppy seeds**
- **4 heads bibb lettuce**
- **2 avocados, sliced**
- **2 grapefruits, sectioned**
- **1 pint fresh strawberries**

Blend sugar, vinegar, mustard, salt and onion; add oil slowly through top of blender; add poppy seeds last. Arrange lettuce on individual plates. Alternate sections of fresh grapefruit and avocado. Top with dressing; garnish with strawberries.

Mrs. E.J. Mooney
(Mary Martha May)

PAPAYA SEED DRESSING

3 cups

The piquant flavor is excellent for fruit

- **1 cup tarragon vinegar**
- **1 cup sugar**
- **1 T. salt**
- **1 tsp. dry mustard**
- **1 cup salad oil**
- **1 small onion, chopped**
- **3 T. fresh papaya seeds**

Place vinegar, sugar, salt, and dry mustard in blender. Turn on blender; gradually add salad oil and onion. Blend thoroughly. Add seeds. Blend only until seeds are the size of coarsely-ground pepper.

Mrs. John C. Munson
(Virginia Aldrich)

CHUTNEY DRESSING

2¼ Cups

May also be used as dip for fresh fruit

- **1 cup salad oil**
- **⅓ cup wine vinegar**
- **1 clove garlic, crushed**
- **1 tsp. salt**
- **¼ tsp. MSG**
- **1 cup chutney, finely-chopped**

Mix all ingredients in a jar; shake well and store in refrigerator until ready to use. Shake well before serving. Excellent with fruit or a mixed green salad.

Mrs. Gilbert P. George
(Ann Sullivan)

GREEN GODDESS SALAD DRESSING

4-6 Servings

- **1 cup mayonnaise**
- **3 T. anchovies or 1½ T. anchovy paste**
- **3 T. chopped chives**
- **1 garlic clove, crushed**
- **1 T. lemon juice**
- **3 T. tarragon vinegar**
- **2 T. chopped parsley**
- **½ cup cream**

Blend first 7 ingredients until smooth. Add cream. Keeps several weeks in refrigerator before cream is added. Serve on various types of lettuce.

Mrs. Stephen H. Goulding
(Ann Thomas)

ANGEL CREAM DELIGHT

12-14 Servings

1 angel food tube cake
1 pkg. (3 oz.) instant vanilla pudding
1 can (8 oz.) crushed pineapple
2 cups whipping cream
½ cup chopped pecans
½ cup sliced strawberries
2 to 4 T. rum
Whole strawberries and pecan halves

Cut off top of cake 1 inch down from top. Make tunnel in bottom part of cake, 1 inch from sides and bottom, scooping carefully. Mix dry pudding mix and pineapple (juice and all); let stand. Whip 1 cup of cream; add nuts, sliced berries and pineapple mixture to whipped cream; fold completely. Sprinkle rum around inside cake tunnel and cake top. Fill tunnel with cream mixture. Put top on cake; press gently to seal. Whip remaining cream; fold in remainder of filling. Frost cake; decorate with whole berries and pecans.

Mrs. Walter L. Jones, Jr.
(Jane Frederick)

BLITZ TORTE

8 Servings

½ cup butter
1¼ cups sugar
⅛ tsp. salt
4 eggs, separated
1 tsp. vanilla
3 T. milk
1 cup sifted flour
1 tsp. baking powder
½ cup slivered almonds
1 T. sugar
½ tsp. cinnamon

FILLING:

⅓ cup sugar
3 T. cornstarch
¼ tsp. salt
2 egg yolks
2 cups scalded milk
2 T. butter
1 tsp. vanilla
1 pt. fresh strawberries

Cream butter and ½ cup sugar. Add salt and slightly-beaten egg yolks. Add mixture of vanilla and milk alternately with mixture of flour and baking powder. Spread mixture into 2 greased 8-inch round cake pans. Beat egg whites until foamy. Gradually beat in ¾ cup sugar, continuing beating until stiff peaks form. Spread evenly over dough. Mix almonds, 1 T. sugar and cinnamon; sprinkle over each pan. Bake at 350° for 25 to 35 minutes. Remove from pans; cool on wire racks. For filling, combine sugar, cornstarch and salt in a double boiler. Stir in egg yolks. Slowly add milk. Cook over hot water, stirring constantly, until very thick. Stir in butter. Remove from heat; stir in vanilla. Cool; chill. Spread custard filling between torte layers. Decorate with whole strawberries.

Mrs. Bruce G. Southworth
(Mary Monek)

GRAND MARNIER SAUCE FOR FRUIT

4 egg yolks
¾ cup sugar
1 tsp. lemon juice
Dash salt
2 T. flour
¾ cup Grand Marnier
(or ¼ cup frozen orange juice concentrate and ½ cup Grand Marnier)
1 pt. whipping cream

In top of double boiler, beat egg yolks. Stir in sugar, lemon juice, and salt. Make paste of flour and small amount of Grand Marnier; add to egg mixture along with remaining Grand Marnier. Cook over hot water, stirring constantly, until thick. Cool. Whip whipping cream; fold into thickened mixture. Chill. Spoon over sliced fresh fruit.

Mrs. John Bradbury
(Mary Nolen)

SNOW HUT

10-12 Servings

2 T. plain gelatin
⅓ cup cold water
1 cup boiling water with ½ tsp. salt
1 cup sugar
1 cup fresh orange juice
3 cups whipping cream
1 large orange chiffon cake, broken in pieces
1 can (3½ oz.) flaked coconut
1 can (11 oz.) mandarin orange sections

Soften gelatin in cold water. Add boiling water and sugar. Stir until dissolved. Add fruit juice; mix well over ice water until chilled. Whip 2 cups of the cream; fold into gelatin mixture with cake pieces. Place in a large bowl; refrigerate overnight, unmold on a serving plate. Whip remaining cream and spread over the snow hut. Sprinkle with coconut; arrange a row of orange sections across top. Encircle bottom with orange sections.

Mrs. Patrick Callahan
(Patricia Henebry)

FRUIT-TOPPED MERINGUE

8-10 Servings

1 cup egg whites (about 7)
2 cups sugar
1 T. vanilla
½ tsp. vinegar
½ tsp. water
2 to 3 cups sliced fruits, fresh or thawed frozen (strawberries, peaches, etc.)
1 cup whipping cream, whipped, sweetened

Beat egg whites until soft peaks form. Gradually beat in sugar, 2 tablespoons at a time, continuing beating until stiff, glossy peaks form. Fold in vanilla, vinegar, and water. Turn into 9-inch springform pan. Bake at 350° for 10 minutes; reduce oven to 250°. Bake 1 hour longer. Turn off oven; let meringue sit inside for 15 minutes. Cool to room temperature (do not refrigerate). Cover top with fruits, sweetened to taste. Top with whipped cream. Decorate with a little of the fruit.

Mrs. Ronald Allen
(Ruth Koch)

HEAVENLY PIE

8 Servings

From aunt who is a "heavenly" cook

- **4 eggs, separated**
- **1½ cups sugar**
- **¼ tsp. cream of tartar**
- **3 T. lemon juice**
- **1 T. grated lemon rind**
- **⅛ tsp. salt**
- **1 pt. whipping cream, whipped**

Beat egg whites until foamy. Slowly beat in 1 cup sugar and cream of tartar. Continue beating until stiff peaks form. Place in two 8-inch pie plates, working up onto the sides with a spatula. Bake at 225° for 1 hour. Beat egg yolks in top of double boiler; add ½ cup sugar, lemon juice, rind and salt. Cook over boiling water, stirring constantly, until thick. Cool. Fold in whipped cream. Pour into prepared crusts. Refrigerate for 24 hours.

Mrs. William F. Zwilling
(Diane Poppen)

CORNFLAKE RING

8 Servings

- **5 cups cornflakes**
- **½ cup pecans, coarsely chopped**
- **¼ lb. butter**
- **1 cup brown sugar**
- **¼ cup dark corn syrup**
- **1 tsp. vanilla**
- **2 cups whipping cream, whipped (or vanilla ice cream)**

Combine the cornflakes and pecans in a large bowl. In a saucepan, melt butter; add sugar and corn syrup. Heat to soft ball (238°) stage. Remove from heat; add vanilla. Pour over cornflakes; toss lightly but thoroughly. Place in a buttered ice-cold 6-cup ring mold. Do not refrigerate. Unmold after 20 minutes. Fill center with whipped cream or ice cream.

Mrs. John R. Siragusa
(Sinclair Smith)

LEMON PIE VOLCANO

8 Servings

- **½ cup butter**
- **⅓ cup lemon juice**
- **2 T. lemon rind**
- **¼ tsp. salt**
- **1½ cups sugar**
- **2 eggs**
- **3 egg yolks**
- **1 quart vanilla ice cream**
- **1 baked 9-inch pie shell**
- **3 egg whites**
- **½ empty egg shell**
- **Brandy, warmed**

Melt butter in top of double boiler. Add juice, rind, salt, and 1 cup sugar. Beat 2 eggs and 3 yolks thoroughly. Gradually stir into butter mixture; cook over hot water, stirring constantly, until thick and smooth. Chill. Press half the ice cream (softened) into pie shell. Freeze. Spread half the lemon filling over this and freeze. Repeat layers. Beat egg whites until foamy; add sugar gradually, continuing beating until stiff. Spread meringue on pie, sealing edges. Insert half an egg shell in center; freeze. Just before serving, place in 475° oven until lightly browned, 1 to 3 minutes. Fill egg shell with brandy and ignite.

Mrs. C. Richard Mason
(Mary Cord)

MILE HIGH STRAWBERRY PIE

8 Servings

- **1 pkg. (10 oz.) frozen strawberries**
- **1 cup sugar**
- **2 egg whites**
- **1 T. lemon juice**
- **Dash salt**
- **½ cup whipping cream, whipped**
- **1 tsp. vanilla**
- **1 prepared 9-inch graham cracker crust**

Thaw strawberries. Combine berries, sugar, egg whites, lemon juice, and salt. Beat for 15 minutes or until very stiff. Fold in whipped cream and vanilla. Pour into pie crust. Freeze until firm.

Mrs. Frank Jacobsen
(Julie Hasselbalch)

STRAWBERRY-SUNSHINE PIE

6 Servings

- **1 pt. lemon sherbet, slightly softened**
- **1 baked 9-inch pastry shell**
- **3 egg whites**
- **½ tsp. cream of tartar**
- **½ tsp. vanilla**
- **½ cup sugar**
- **1 qt. strawberries, halved**

Spread sherbet evenly on bottom of pastry shell. Wrap with clear plastic. Seal tightly; freeze overnight. (Don't let sherbet get too soft or it will form crystals when it refreezes.) Just before serving, beat egg whites with cream of tartar and vanilla until frothy. Add 6 T. sugar gradually and continue beating until stiff. Sweeten strawberries with remaining sugar; place on top of sherbet. Pile meringue all over, sealing edges. Place pie on a wooden board; bake at 500° for 3 minutes, until lightly browned. Serve at once. Sherbet must not melt.

Mrs. Fentress Twerdahl
(Gretchen Fentress)

STRAWBERRY CREPES

4 Servings

- **1 pkg. (3 oz.) cream cheese, softened**
- **½ cup sour cream**
- **8 dessert crepes**
- **1½ T. butter**
- **2 cups sliced strawberries (fresh or frozen, thawed)**
- **2 to 4 T. sugar**
- **2 jiggers (6 T.) kirsch**
- **1 jigger (3 T.) strawberry liqueur**

Combine cream cheese and sour cream. Divide between centers of warm crepes; roll up. Place 2 on each of 4 dessert plates. In blazer pan or chafing dish, melt butter; add strawberries and sugar. (Use greater amount of sugar for fresh strawberries.) Simmer a few minutes. Add kirsch and liqueur; ignite. Pour immediately over crepes and serve.

Mrs. James F. Peil
(Nancy Rodgers)

MERINGUE-TOPPED RHUBARB PIE 6-8 Servings

- 2 T. butter
- 1½ cups sugar
- ½ cup flour
- ¼ tsp. salt
- 4 cups diced rhubarb
- 3 eggs, separated
- 1 unbaked 9-inch pastry shell
- Pinch of cream of tartar
- 6 T. sugar

Cream butter and sugar together thoroughly. Sift flour and salt together; add to creamed mixture. Add rhubarb; toss thoroughly. Beat egg yolks until light; add to rhubarb mixture. Fill pastry shell. Bake at 350° for about 1 hour or until set, covering with inverted pie tin for first 45 minutes to prevent crust from burning. For meringue; beat egg whites with cream of tartar until foamy. Gradually add 6 T. sugar, beating until stiff peaks form. Cover pie with meringue; return to oven to lightly brown meringue. Cool at room temperature.

Mrs. Jeffrey L. Parsons
(Peggy Platt)

RHUBARB-STRAWBERRY RING WITH SOUR CREAM-HONEY SAUCE 8 Servings

- 1 pkg. (3 oz.) strawberry gelatin
- 1 cup boiling water
- 1 T. plain gelatin
- ¼ cup cold water
- 3 cups cooked rhubarb
- 1 tsp. lemon juice
- 1½ to 2 pts. fresh strawberries
- 1 cup sour cream
- ⅓ cup honey

Dissolve strawberry gelatin in boiling water. Soften plain gelatin in cold water. Stir over low heat until dissolved; combine with strawberry gelatin. Chill until partly thickened; add rhubarb and lemon juice. Turn into a 5-cup ring mold. Chill until set. Unmold onto round serving platter. Heap whole strawberries in center. For sauce, combine sour cream and honey; serve separately.

Mrs. John A. Kelly, Jr.
(Joyce Judson)

RHUBARB ICE CREAM — 1 Quart

3 cups fresh rhubarb, thinly-sliced
2 cups sugar
1 tsp. lemon juice
1 cup whipping cream, whipped

Place rhubarb in a flat baking dish in layers with sugar sprinkled between. Cover and bake at 375° for 30 to 40 minutes. Cool slightly. Put rhubarb into blender to make a thick puree. Chill 30 minutes. Add lemon juice. Fold puree into whipped cream. Place in a 1-qt. container; do not cover. Place in freezer. Stir every 15 minutes for the first hour. Then let it set for 2 hours, or until firm. Cover.

Mrs. H. Alex·Vance, Jr.
(Melinda Martin)

FRESH CHERRY CREAM PIE — 8 Servings

2 lbs. dark sweet cherries, stemmed and pitted
1 cup sugar
¾ cups water
1½ T. cornstarch
1 unbaked 9-inch pastry shell
12 oz. cream cheese, softened
2 eggs, lightly beaten
½ tsp. almond extract
1½ cups sour cream

In a saucepan, combine cherries with ½ cup sugar and ½ cup water. Cook over low heat 5 minutes. Mix corn-starch with remaining ¼ cup water; add it to cherries. Cook, stirring constantly, until thickened. Spread half the cherry filling over the bottom. Cover pastry edges with foil to prevent browning too quickly. Bake at 425° for 15 minutes. In a bowl beat cream cheese until soft. Gradually stir in remaining ½ cup sugar, eggs, and almond extract; stir until smooth. Pour it over hot cherry filling. Remove foil from crust and bake at 350° for 25 to 30 minutes. Cool slightly. Spoon sour cream around edge of pie and pour remaining cherry filling into center. Serve warm.

Miss Virginia C. Franche

MAPLE RING WITH STRAWBERRIES

10 Servings

- **4 large eggs, separated**
- **1 cup maple syrup**
- **2 env. plain gelatin**
- **½ cup cold water**
- **1 tsp. vanilla**
- **1 pt. whipping cream, whipped**
- **2 pts. fresh strawberries or raspberries**
- **1 pkg. (10 oz.) frozen strawberries or raspberries**
- **2 to 3 T. sugar**
- **1 T. cornstarch**
- **Currant jelly**

In top of double boiler, beat egg yolks until very light. Add maple syrup; cook over hot water, stirring constantly until thickened. Soak gelatin in cold water; add to syrup. Add vanilla. Stir until gelatin is dissolved. Place syrup mixture in a pan over ice water; stir until creamy and cool. Beat egg whites until stiff; fold into syrup mixture. Then fold in whipped cream. Pour into a 6 to 7-cup ring mold; refrigerate overnight. Slice 1½ pints strawberries. Puree frozen strawberries and juice in blender; combine with mixture of cornstarch and sugar. Cook, stirring constantly, until thickened; cool. Mix this syrup with sliced fresh strawberries for sauce. Dip remaining fresh whole strawberries in melted currant jelly; arrange around unmolded maple ring.

Mrs. H. Alex Vance, Jr.
(Melinda Martin)

FROSTY PINEAPPLE DELIGHT — 4 Servings

2 small fresh pineapples
Sugar
1¼ cups pineapple juice
¾ cup water
Grated rind and juice of 1 lemon
1¼ cups whipping cream, whipped
3 T. kirsch

Cut pineapples in half lengthwise, leaving on green tops. Remove flesh and juice, being careful not to break through shell. Discard hard core. Sprinkle insides of shells with a little sugar; chill. Mash pineapple flesh with a fork. Add pineapple juice, water, 1 cup sugar, and lemon rind. Bring to a boil; boil for 5 minutes. Strain; add lemon juice. Freeze for 4 hours. Beat mixture with a fork. Fold in whipped cream and kirsch. Return to freezer. Just before serving, spoon mixture into chilled pineapple shells.

Mrs. James F. Peil
(Nancy Rodgers)

COLD RASPBERRY SOUFFLE — 8 Servings

4 tsp. plain gelatin
3 T. cold water
Pinch of salt
2 pkgs. (10 oz. each) frozen raspberries, thawed
1 T. lemon juice
½ cup sugar
3 egg whites
1 cup whipping cream, whipped

In saucepan, soften gelatin in cold water with salt; heat slowly and stir to dissolve. Puree berries in blender. Combine puree with gelatin, lemon juice and sugar. Place over ice stirring often until thickened. Beat egg whites until stiff; fold into berry mixture. Then fold into cream. Spoon into individual dessert dishes; chill overnight or several hours. Dot with whipped cream and toasted almonds.

Mrs. Bruce G. Southworth
(Mary Monek)

SHERRY SOUFFLE

10-12 Servings

4 eggs, separated
4 tsp. sugar
1 env. plus 1 tsp. unflavored gelatin
½ cup water
1 cup whipping cream, whipped
¼ cup cream sherry
10 Heath bars, crumbled

Beat egg whites until foamy; slowly beat in sugar, continuing to beat until stiff peaks form. Fold in egg yolks, which have been beaten. Soften gelatin in water; dissolve over hot water. Add warm gelatin to egg mixture. Fold in whipped cream and sherry. Sprinkle ⅓ of Heath bar crumbs on bottom of a 1½-qt. souffle dish, which has foil collar around rim. Cover with half of sherry-cream mixture, ⅓ of crumbs, then remaining cream mixture. Top with remaining crumbs. Chill until firm.

Mrs. William D. Roddy, Jr.
(Joanne McDonald)

MAPLE PARFAIT

6-8 Servings

8 egg yolks, beaten
1 cup maple syrup
Rum to taste
1 pt. whipping cream, whipped
Toasted chopped almonds

Mix yolks with maple syrup. Place over low heat and whip until thickened. Mixture should coat the beaters. Remove from heat; whip until cool and very light. Mix in rum. Fold in whipped cream; freeze in individual parfait glasses. Serve garnished with almonds.

Mrs. H. Alex Vance, Jr.
(Melinda Martin)

CHILLED LIME SOUFFLE

6 Servings

1 env. plain gelatin
¼ cup cold water
4 egg yolks, lightly-beaten
1 cup sugar
½ cup lime juice
½ tsp. salt
1 T. grated lime rind
6 egg whites
1 cup whipping cream, whipped
Toasted coconut flakes

Sprinkle gelatin over cold water to soften. In top of double boiler, mix egg yolks with ½ cup sugar, lime juice, and salt. Cook over barely simmering water, stirring constantly with wisk, until slightly thickened. Remove from heat. Add gelatin and lime rind, stirring until gelatin is completely dissolved. Cool. Beat egg whites until they hold a soft shape; beat in remaining sugar a tablespoon at a time until mixture is stiff. Fold in lime mixture and whipped cream. Pour into 1½-quart oiled souffle dish, which has foil collar around it extending above rim. Chill until set. To serve, remove paper collar and press coconut around the sides of the souffle.

Mrs. James F. Peil
(Nancy Rodgers)

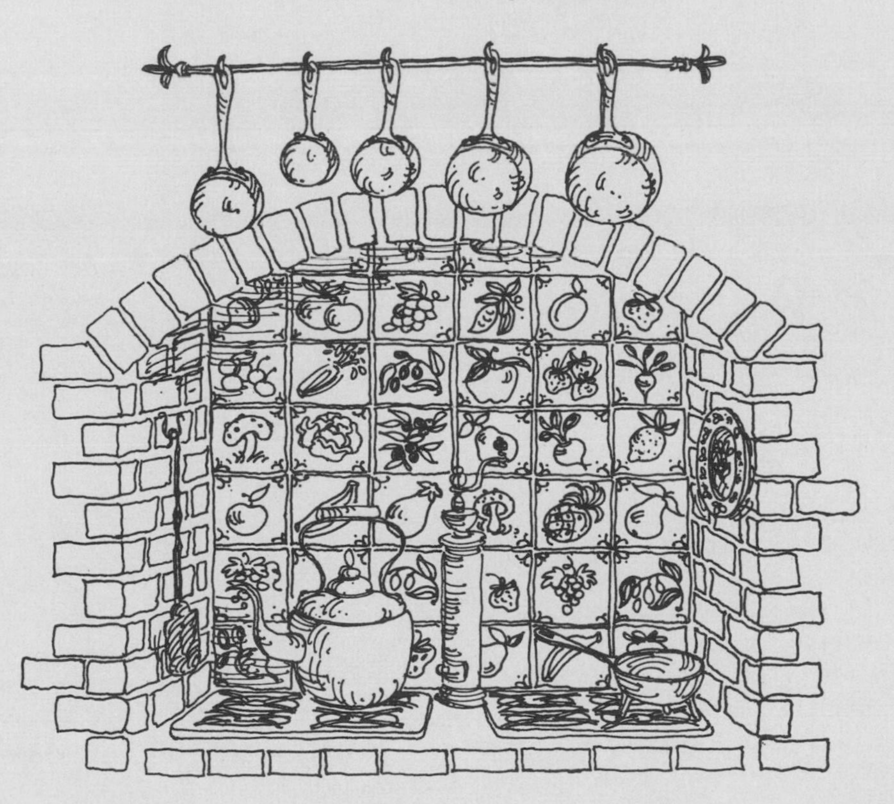

Sugar
Pickle
Pickle
kles

SUMMER KITCHEN

During the summer of 1819, Ferninand Ernst, a wealthy German, visited the southern portion of Illinois to evaluate it as a possible settlement site for a group of his countrymen who desired to migrate to the United States. The observations he sent to them included a description of Illinois' summer produce. "This fertile region is covered with fine farms, where one has the opportunity of admiring the astonishing productiveness of the soil. I found the maize from 12 to 15 feet high on an average. The gardens which have sufficient age for fruit settings are luxuriant with peach trees and other fruit trees . . . Peach brandy and dried peaches are very common here . . . Moreover the gardens produce melons, especially watermelons in great quantity and of unusual size."

Throughout Illinois today summer is still primarily the time of fruits and vegetables. These, like all the foods of this lush season, are best served simply—in a style suited to summer's hot days and their accompanying decline in the desire for formal dining. Many of summer's best liked meals are those that can be prepared in advance, then served beautifully by a cool, collected cook. This is the season of the cold buffet, the magnificent salad, the tall, cool drink, the tray of fruit. Also to be enjoyed during summer are picnics—casual or gourmet, and barbecues, also as elegant or simple as the occasion dictates. Finally, summer is a time to begin preserving fruits and vegetables for enjoyment during the months ahead.

The vegetables which are best enjoyed in summer include green or snap beans, lima beans, red beets, cabbage, collard greens, corn, kohlrabi, okra, sorrel, spinach, summer squash, swiss chard, tomatoes, and white turnips.

Make green salads with chicory, escarole, dandelion greens, bibb, iceberg, or romaine lettuce, chives, red onions, green scallions, green peppers, or watercress.

Use the season's fresh herbs and shallots for seasoning, and look for the first tiny new potatoes to appear in the market.

In fruits, the soft berries—raspberries, strawberries, gooseberries and blueberries, as well as red currants, are available through July, as are apricots, while Bartlett pears, Bing cherries, nectarines, grapes, peaches, and plums are in abundance throughout the season.

Melons—crenshaw, cantaloupe, honeydew, and watermelon—are particularly good at this time, as are Valencia oranges.

Great Lakes fish to look for in summer are carp, coho salmon, herring, mullet, musky, perch, pike, chub, trout, and whitefish. In shellfish, serve shrimp, and clams.

Try serving a variety of meats cold or at room temperature. Lamb, chicken, beef, ham, and veal are particularly good this way, as are many types of summer fish and shellfish. When barbecuing consider lamb and fish as possible offerings as well as chicken, pork, and beef.

Whether preparing a picnic, barbecuing, or cooking in the kitchen oven, remember that summer's meals should be simple, with the spotlight turned to nature and its own spectacular bounty.

SUMMER MENUS

ELEGANT TROUT PATIO DINNER

PATE MOLD WITH SESAME WATER CRACKERS
Pouilly Blanc Fume

* *

COLD CREAM OF CUCUMBER SOUP
California Dry Chenin Blanc

* *

POACHED TROUT WITH BROCCOLI
Puligny Montrachet

TOMATO SLICES MARINATED | HOT BUTTERFLAKE ROLLS

* *

HARLEQUIN PIE
Cream Sherry

A LIGHT SUMMER BRUNCH

STRAWBERRIES IN FRESH ORANGE JUICE

* *

EGGS ELEGANTE
Neuchatel

BAKED TOMATOES STUFFED WITH MUSHROOMS

BUTTERED ENGLISH MUFFINS | LIME-NECTARINE JAM

BEACH PICNIC

THERMOS OF BLENDER GAZPACHO

* *

PICNIC LOBSTER BUNS
Muscadet

BEST EVER SLAW

* *

BLUEBERRY UPSIDE DOWN CAKE

SUMMER MENUS

BRIDAL SHOWER

RALPH'S PUNCH

* *

SALMON MOUSSE WITH DILL SAUCE

Bernkasteler Riesling

BUTTERED BROCCOLI SPEARS

LEMON MUFFINS

* *

CANTALOUPE SUPREME

BARBECUE

KIR

MARINATED SHRIMP

* *

DEVILED STEAK

Italian Barolo

HERBED CORN IN FOIL

SPAGHETTI SALAD

HERB BREAD

* *

WATERMELON SURPRISE

RAVINIA PICNIC

FRESH PEACH DAIQUIRI

* *

FRENCH STUFFED EGGS

BEEF-AVOCADO MARINADE

Beaujolais St. Amour

FRENCH BREAD

* *

BLUEBERRY CAKE

COLD SPICED COFFEE

SUMMER TABLE OF CONTENTS

BEVERAGES

ALEX'S BANANA DAIQUIRI — 1 Serving

Juice of ½ fresh lemon
2 oz. white rum
1 T. sugar
1 fresh banana
4 to 5 ice cubes

Blend first 4 ingredients in blender until smooth. Add the ice cubes and blend until just thickened and ice is crushed.

Mrs. H. Alex Vance, Jr.
(Melinda Martin)

FROZEN PEACH DAIQUIRI — 10 Servings

1 can (6 oz.) frozen daiquiri mix
1½ cups light rum
6 fresh peaches, unpeeled, quartered
1 tsp. almond extract (optional)
1 lime, ends removed, quartered (optional)

Place all ingredients in blender. Cover and blend until smooth. Pour into glasses half filled with crushed ice.

Mrs. John S. Jenkins
(Mary Lou Cudlip)

MARGARITAS — 4 Servings

1 cup plus 2 T. tequila
⅓ cup cointreau
¼ cup superfine sugar
½ cup lemon or lime juice
Coarse salt

Mix the tequila, cointreau and sugar in blender. Dip rim of glass in lemon juice, then into coarse salt. Fill glass with ice and pour in mixture.

Mrs. John S. Jenkins
(Mary Lou Cudlip)

VELVET HAMMER — Makes one and that's enough!

3 to 4 scoops vanilla ice cream
1 oz. brandy
⅛ oz. banana liqueur
⅛ oz. Curacao

Blend in blender. Serve in brandy snifter.

Mrs. William G. McMillian
(Florence Dalrymple)

RALPH'S PUNCH

70 Servings (4 oz. each)

3 bottles (fifths) champagne
3 bottles (fifths) dry sauterne
3 bottles (28 oz. each) club soda
8 oz. orange curacao
8 oz. brandy

Refrigerate champagne, sauterne and soda until well chilled. Combine with Curacao and brandy. Pour over large block of ice in punch bowl.

Mrs. John S. Jenkins
(Mary Lou Cudlip)

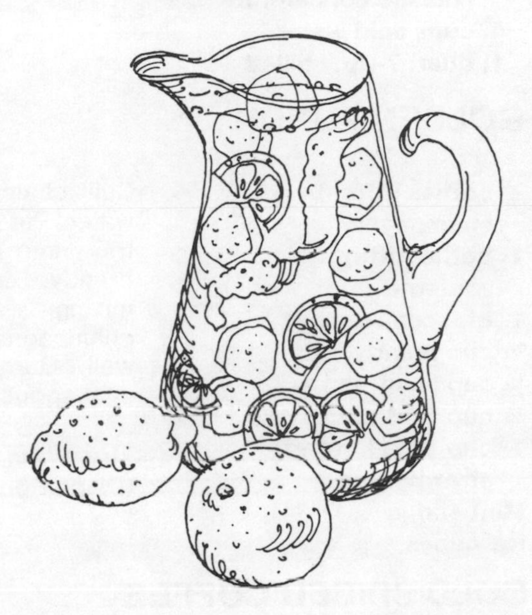

SANGRIA FOR A CROWD

3 Gallons

An authentic drink from Spain

1 gallon water
2 cups sugar
6 oranges, peeled, sliced
4 lemons, sliced
2 gallons red wine
Ice

In large kettle, combine water and sugar; heat until dissolved. Add sliced fruits; let stand at room temperature at least 4 hours. Add wine just before serving. Serve from punch bowl with lots of ice. Note: When mixing in batches, add ingredients in proportions of 2 parts wine to 1 part flavored water.

Mrs. Phillip J. Stover
(Annette Ashlock)

SUNSHINE PUNCH

12-15 Servings

Delicious for children's parties
Perfect for those hot, sultry days on the tennis court

- 1 can (6 oz.) frozen orange juice concentrate
- 1 can (6 oz.) frozen lemonade concentrate
- 1 can (6 oz.) frozen limeade concentrate
- 4 cups cold water
- 1 quart 7-Up, chilled

Combine all ingredients. Mix well. Chill.

Mrs. David B. Smith
(Marcia Williamson)

GOLDEN PUNCH

4½ Quarts

- 2 bottles (fifths) champagne
- 1 bottle (fifth) sauterne
- 1 qt. soda water
- ¼ cup brandy
- ¼ cup cointreau
- ¼ cup light corn syrup
- 1 cup sliced hulled strawberries
- Mint sprigs
- Ice cubes

Chill champagne, sauterne, and soda water. Put ice cubes from two ice cube trays into large punch bowl. Combine brandy, cointreau and corn syrup, mixing well; pour over ice. Add champagne, sauterne and soda; mix well. Garnish with strawberries and mint sprigs.

Mrs. William F. Zwilling
(Diane Poppen)

COLD SPICED COFFEE

4-6 Servings

Fun to take on picnics

- 4 cups strong hot coffee
- ¼ cup sugar
- 10 whole allspice
- 10 whole cloves
- 4 cinnamon sticks
- ½ cup coffee-flavored liqueur
- Ice cubes

Combine hot coffee, sugar and spices in a large mixing bowl. Cover with plastic wrap. Let stand at room temperature for 1 hour, no longer. If serving immediately, strain coffee into a 1-quart pitcher. Add liqueur and 6 ice cubes. If making ahead, strain into pitcher. Discard spices. Add the liqueur (but not ice) and refrigerate, covered. Just before serving, add ice. Serve it plain, over ice, in cups, wine glasses or over ice cream for dessert.

Mrs. R. Barksdale Collins
(Lynn Synder)

PATE MOLD

8 Servings

1 envelope plain gelatin
1 can (10½ oz.) consomme
1 large jigger (1½-2 oz.) sherry
1½ pkgs. (3 oz. size) cream cheese
1 pkg. (4 oz.) liverwurst

Soften gelatin in consomme; heat until dissolved. Add sherry. Rinse mold in cold water and put slightly more than ½ of mixture in it. Set balance aside to cool. Refrigerate mold until set. Bring cream cheese and liverwurst to room temperature. Shape cream cheese into rough size of mold. Spread on firm gelatin. Spread on liverwurst. Add balance of consomme mixture. Chill until jelled. Unmold onto serving plate. Serve with your favorite cracker.

Mrs. John N. Schmidt
(Joan M. Slauson)

CAVIAR A LA SCALORA

16 Servings

1 large cucumber
1 pkg. (8 oz.) cream cheese
1 cup sour cream
1 T. worcestershire sauce
1 tsp. seasoned salt
2 tsp. lemon juice
Chopped chives
2 hard-cooked eggs, seived
1 large jar caviar

Cut cucumber in half. Remove skin and seeds from one half and chop fine. Set other half aside. Combine cream cheese, sour cream, worcestershire sauce, seasoned salt, and 1 tsp. lemon juice. Mix well. Place in serving dish 9 inches wide and at least 1 inch deep. Slice other half of cucumber, unpeeled and scored with fork prongs. Arrange slices around edge standing up. Sprinkle chives generously in an inch strip around edge of plate close to cucumber slices. Place an inch strip of seived eggs next to chives. In the center spread a jar of caviar; sprinkle with 1 tsp. lemon juice. Serve with crackers or cucumber slices.

Mrs. William F. Zwilling
(Diane Poppen)

KOREAN SHORT RIBS

10 Servings

If you don't have a Korean "Genghis Khan" grill which lets the fat drain off without catching fire, use a hibachi or regular barbecue

4 lbs. beef short ribs, well-trimmed and cut through bone at 2½ inch intervals
½ cup soy sauce
½ cup water
⅓ cup sliced green onions and some tops
2 T. sesame seeds
2 T. sugar
2 cloves garlic, mashed
½ tsp. pepper

Score ribs: make cuts halfway to the bone every ½ inch in one direction. At right angles cut every ½ inch, but go only ½ inch deep into the meat. Combine remaining ingredients; pour over ribs. Marinate, covered, in the refrigerator overnight. Cook ribs over charcoal about 15 minutes or until crisply browned on all sides.

Mrs. William B. Miller
(Katherine Hillman)

CRAB SPREAD

8 Servings

1 pkg. (8 oz.) cream cheese
2 to 3 T. mayonnaise
1 T. catsup
1 T. finely-chopped onion
1 T. worcestershire sauce
Dash of Tabasco sauce
Garlic salt to taste
1 can (7½ oz.) crabmeat, drained, flaked

Beat all indredients except crab together until smooth. Stir in crab. Chill. Serve spread on crackers or as a dip.

Mrs. C. Richard Mason
(Mary Cord)

SHRIMP BALLS

50 Balls

1 lb. cooked shrimp, ground
1 T. chili sauce
¼ cup finely-minced celery
2 T. finely-minced water chestnuts
2 T. grated onion
1 hard-cooked egg, sieved
1 pkg. (3 oz.) cream cheese, softened
½ tsp. salt
⅛ tsp. white pepper
Dash cayenne pepper
1 tsp. lemon juice
Minced parsley

Combine all ingredients except parsley; adjust seasonings. Chill. Form into 1 inch balls; roll in minced parsley.

Mrs. David B. Smith
(Marcia Williamson)

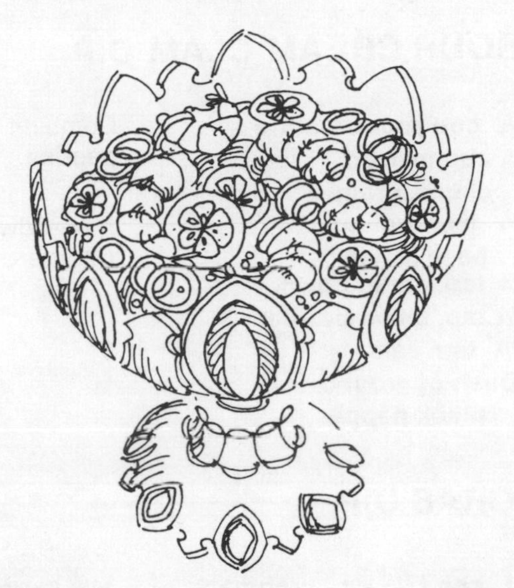

MARINATED SHRIMP

12 Servings

They are delicious

2½ lbs. peeled shrimp, deveined and cooked
2 large onions, sliced into rings
1½ cups salad oil
1 cup white vinegar
2½ tsp. celery seeds
1 T. capers and juice
4 to 5 bay leaves
Several dashes Tabasco sauce

Layer hot shrimp and onions in a crystal bowl. Combine remaining ingredients; and pour over shrimp and onions. Refrigerate at least 24 hours. Drain most of marinade off and serve with toothpicks.

Mrs. Walter L. Jones, Jr.
(Jane Frederick)

FRESH VEGETABLE SPECIALITIES

Carrots
Cauliflower
Cherry Tomatoes
Cucumber slices
Mushrooms
Radishes
Zucchini slices

Prepare fresh vetetables. Serve with one or more of the following dips:

SOUR CREAM CLAM DIP

½ cup sour cream
¼ cup minced clams, drained
¼ tsp. ground basil leaves
¼ tsp. garlic powder
¼ tsp. onion powder
¼ tsp. salt
Dash of ground black pepper

Combine ingredients; garnish with paprika.

Mrs. Edward C. McNally
(Margaret McGann)

CRAB DIP

1 can (7½ oz.) crabmeat
2 pkgs. (8 oz. each) cream cheese
½ tsp. celery salt
½ tsp. garlic salt
½ tsp. onion salt
½ tsp. MSG
2 T. mayonnaise
Juice of ½ lemon

Mix ingredients. Chill.

Mrs. Edward C. McNally
(Margaret McGann)

CURRY DIP

1 can (4½ oz.) tiny shrimp, chopped
1⅓ cups mayonnaise
2 T. honey
2 T. catsup
1 T. grated onion
1 tsp. lemon juice
1 tsp. curry powder
½ tsp. tarragon vinegar
Dash of Tabasco sauce
Salt and pepper to taste

Mix all together; refrigerate overnight.

Mrs. Raymond Olson, Jr.
(Carol Louise Johnson)

WATER CHESTNUT DIP

1 cup mayonnaise (Hellman's preferred)
1 cup sour cream
½ cup finely-chopped green onions
¼ cup finely-chopped parsley
¼ cup minced water chestnuts
1 T. soy sauce
Dash salt

Combine ingredients. Chill.

Mrs. Bruce G. Southworth
(Mary Monek)

WATERCRESS DIP

1 pkg. (8 oz.) cream cheese, at room temperature
3 to 4 green onions, chopped
1 small clove garlic, crushed
1 bunch watercress, washed and dried
3 T. lemon juice
1 T. prepared horseradish
½ tsp. salt
¼ tsp. white pepper

Break up cream cheese; put it in blender with all other ingredients. Blend until smooth.

Mrs. William P. Sutter
(Helen Yvonne Stebbins)

SOUPS

CREAM OF AVOCADO SOUP — 4 Servings

2 avocados
1 cup hot chicken broth
1½ cups sour cream
¼ cup dry white wine
1 T. minced onion
2 T. lemon juice
Salt
Cayenne pepper
Fresh dill

Mash avocados, puree thru a sieve or in a blender. Stir in chicken broth, sour cream, wine, onion, and lemon juice; blend well. Season to taste with salt and cayenne pepper (or chili powder). Garnish with chopped thread-like leaves of fresh dill.

Mrs. J. Stephen Laing
(Suzanne Reyburn)

ICED AVOCADO-CLAM SOUP — 6-8 Servings

2 ripe avocados
1 can (10½ oz.) cream of chicken soup
1⅓ cups milk
1 carton (8 oz.) plain yogurt
1 can (7½ oz.) clams, minced
1 cup half and half
1 T. lemon juice
½ tsp. salt
¼ tsp. pepper
⅛ tsp. nutmeg
1 to 2 drops green food coloring
Parsley sprigs

Mash avocado and put in blender. Add remaining ingredients except coloring and parsley. Blend at high speed for 1 minute until mixture is smooth. Tint with food coloring. Refrigerate 2 to 4 hours until well chilled. Just before serving, add milk or cream to thin soup to desired consistency. Serve in chilled bowls. Garnish with parsley.

Mrs. J. Stephen Laing
(Suzanne Reyburn)

COLD CREAM OF CUCUMBER SOUP — 4-6 Servings

2 large or 3 medium cucumbers
1 medium onion, chopped
1 cup chicken broth
2 T. flour
¼ tsp. white pepper
½ tsp. salt
Dash of garlic powder
1 cup sour cream
Dill weed

Pare, seed, and coarsely chop cucumbers. Place all ingredients except sour cream and dill weed in blender; blend until smooth. Add sour cream; chill. Sprinkle dill weed on top before serving or float a slice of cucumber.

Mrs. G. Dodge Ferreira
(Noni Harrington)

BORSCH

8-10 Servings

6 beets
2 qts. water
1 onion, chopped
1 T. salt
⅓ cup lemon juice
3 T. brown sugar
1 egg, beaten
Sour cream

Grate 3 beets; chop the other 3 beets. Bring water to a boil and add beets, onion and salt. When water returns to a boil, reduce heat, cover and simmer 1 hour. Add lemon juice and sugar. Simmer 30 minutes longer. Add more sugar or lemon juice to taste. Stir small amount of soup into egg. Stirring constantly, add egg mixture to soup pot. Cook, stirring, until thickened. Cool soup. Strain if desired. Chill 3 to 4 hours. Serve with a teaspoon of sour cream on top.

Mrs. Karl V. Rohlen, Jr.
(Carolyn Walker)

CURRIED CRAB SOUP

6 Servings

Hot or cold

2 T. butter
1 small onion, grated
1 tsp. curry powder
4 chicken bouillon cubes
1 qt. milk
1 can (7½ oz.) crabmeat
½ cup white wine
4 egg yolks, beaten

Put butter, onion, and curry powder in top of double boiler; cook over direct heat until onion is tender. Place over hot water. Add bouillon cubes and ½ cup milk, heating until bouillon cubes are blended in. Add remaining milk, crab and juice from can. Cover; keep on low heat until ready to serve. Add wine to yolks; beat in a spoonful of hot soup. Gradually stir eggs into soup. Cook over barely simmering water for a few minutes. Serve hot or chilled. Garnish with chopped parsley.

Mrs. John S. Jenkins
(Mary Lou Cudlip)

BLENDER GAZPACHO

8 Servings

2 cups tomato juice
1 cup peeled and chopped tomatoes
½ cup finely-chopped green pepper
½ cup finely-chopped celery
½ cup finely-chopped cucumbers
¼ cup finely-chopped onions
2 T. fresh parsely
1 clove garlic, minced
2 to 3 T. wine vinegar
2 T. olive oil
1 tsp. salt
½ tsp. worcestershire sauce
¼ tsp. pepper

Blend all ingredients together in blender. Chill until ready to serve.

Mrs. E. J. Mooney
(Mary Martha May)

TEA HOUSE ORANGE SOUP

12 Servings

Courtesy of "The Twin Chefs" at John Gardiner's Tennis Ranch, Arizona

2 qts. fresh orange juice
½ tsp. ground cloves
1/16 tsp. ginger
1/16 tsp. nutmeg
1/16 tsp. mace
1 whole cinnamon stick
2 T. unflavored gelatin
½ cup cold water
2 cups pineapple juice
2 cups good sherry
2 cans (11 oz. each) mandarin orange sections

Bring to a boil 1 pt. orange juice; add spices. Simmer 1 hour. Remove cinnamon stick. Soak gelatin in cold water; add to hot orange juice. Combine the remaining ingredients and put in a glass or stainless steel container. Cover and refrigerate overnight.

Mrs. H. Alex Vance, Jr.
(Melinda Martin)

CASSEROLE DILL BREAD

1 Loaf

- **2 to 2¼ cups unsifted flour**
- **2 T. sugar**
- **1 T. instant minced onion**
- **2 tsp. dill seed**
- **1 tsp. salt**
- **¼ tsp. baking soda**
- **1 pkg. active dry yeast**
- **1 T. margarine softened**
- **¼ cup very hot tap water**
- **1 cup creamed cottage cheese (at room temperature)**
- **1 egg (at room temperature)**

Mix ¼ cup flour, sugar, instant minced onion, dill seed, salt, baking soda and undissolved yeast. Add softened margarine. Gradually add water; beat 2 minutes at medium speed of electric mixer. Add cottage cheese, egg, and ½ cup flour or enough flour to make a thick batter. Beat at high speed 2 minutes. Stir in enough additional flour to make a soft dough. Cover; let rise in a warm place, free 'from draft, until doubled in bulk, about 1 hour and 15 minutes. Stir batter down. Turn into a greased 1½-quart casserole. Cover; let rise in warm place until doubled, about 50 minutes. Bake at 350° about 30 minutes or until done. Remove from casserole and cool on wire rack.

Mrs. Robert G. Walker, Jr.
(Lynn Ingersoll)

LEMON MUFFINS

2 Dozen

These freeze well and are nice when split, toasted and served with salads

- **1 cup butter**
- **1 cup sugar**
- **4 eggs, separated**
- **2 cups flour**
- **2 tsp. baking powder**
- **1 tsp. salt**
- **½ cup lemon juice**
- **2 tsp. grated lemon peel**

Cream butter and sugar until smooth. Add egg yolks; beat until light. Sift flour with baking powder and salt; add alternately with lemon juice, mixing thoroughly after each addition (do not overmix). Fold in stiffly-beaten egg whites and the grated lemon peel. Fill buttered muffin pans ¾ full; bake at 375° about 20 minutes.

Mrs. David B. Smith
(Marcia Williamson)

BOURBON NUT BREAD

3 Loaves

This bread freezes well and is delicious with summer salads

8 eggs, separated
3 cups sugar
1 lb. butter
3 cups sifted flour
½ cup bourbon
2 tsp. vanilla
2 tsp. almond extract
1 cup chopped pecans

Beat egg whites until soft peaks form. Gradually add 1 cup sugar, continue beating until stiff peaks form. Set aside. Cream butter with remaining sugar. Add egg yolks one at a time, beating well after each addition. Add flour in thirds alternately with bourbon, mixing well. Stir in vanilla, almond extract and nuts. Gently fold in egg whites. Pour into 3 well-greased 9 x 5-inch loaf pans. Bake at 350° for 1 hour, or until done.

Mrs. Walter P. Loomis, Jr.
(Carylee Slaughter)

HERB CHEESE BREAD

6-8 Servings

2 cups biscuit mix
1 T. sugar
2 tsp. instant minced onion
½ tsp. dill weed, sweet basil or oregano
1 egg
½ cup milk
¼ cup melted butter
¼ cup sauterne
⅓ cup grated parmesan cheese

Combine biscuit mix, sugar, onion and herbs together in mixing bowl. Beat egg with milk. Add to dry ingredients along with butter and wine. Beat until blended. Turn into a well-greased 8-inch round cake pan. Sprinkle cheese over top. Bake at 400° until crusty and brown, about 25 minutes. Cut into wedges and serve warm.

Mrs. David B. Smith
(Marcia Williamson)

HOT HERB BREAD

2 Loaves

...and variations for your pleasure

½ lb. butter
¾ cup minced fresh chives
¾ cup minced fresh parsley
2 T. minced fresh sweet basil leaves
1 T. minced fresh tarragon leaves

Blend butter and herbs. Split loaves of bread lengthwise. Spread each cut surface with ¼ of the butter mixture. Slice each half in 2-inch wedges almost to the crust. Reassemble the loaves and wrap in foil. To heat, place foil-wrapped loaves in a 350° oven for 30 minutes. Fold the foil back to frame the loaf for serving.

SPREAD VARIATIONS FOR HERB BREAD

2 loaves unsliced french bread

PARMESAN BREAD:

½ cup grated parmesan cheese
½ cup minced parsley
2 tsp. oregano
½ tsp. garlic salt

PATIO HERB BREAD:

2 jars (5 oz. each) processed American cheese
1 tsp. garlic salt
2 tsp. marjoram
1½ T. sesame seeds
¼ cup finely-chopped parsley
¼ cup sherry

BREAD CALEXICO:

2 T. paprika
2 T. chili powder
½ tsp. oregano
½ tsp. sweet basil
2 tsp. grated onion

BARBECUED BREAD:

½ cup prepared mustard
¼ cup poppy seeds
1 onion, grated
1 tsp. worcestershire sauce
Swiss cheese squares (1-inch), inserted into each cut

PERFECT WITH BAKED BEANS BREAD:

⅔ cup brown sugar
2 tsp. cinnamon
1 tsp. nutmeg
¼ tsp. ginger
¼ tsp. cloves
¼ cup dry sherry

Variations: Substitute ingredients listed for the herbs.

Mrs. William F. Zwilling
(Diane Poppen)

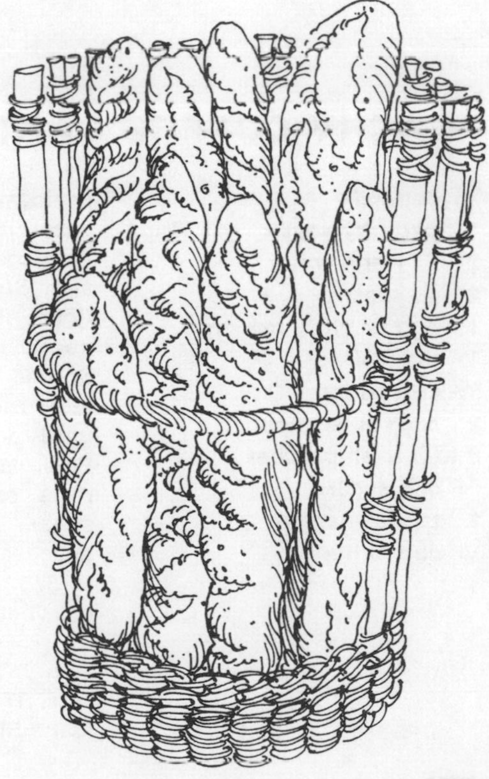

BLUEBERRY BUCKLE BRUNCH BREAD

9 Servings

½ cup butter
1 cup sugar
1 egg
½ tsp. vanilla
1⅓ cups flour
1 tsp. baking powder
¼ tsp. salt
⅓ cup milk
2 cups blueberries
½ tsp. cinnamon
¼ tsp. nutmeg

Cream ¼ cup butter together with ½ cup sugar. Beat in egg and vanilla and stir until smooth. Sift together 1 cup flour, baking powder and salt. Add alternately with the milk to the creamed mixture, starting with the dry ingredients. Pour into a greased 9-inch square baking pan and top with blueberries. Combine the remaining sugar and flour, cinnamon and nutmeg. Using a pastry blender or fork, cut in remaining butter until the texture resembles coarse cornmeal. Sprinkle over blueberries. Bake in preheated oven at 350° for one hour. Cool slightly before serving.

Mrs. Benson T. Caswell
(Margaret Graham)

PEACHY COFFEE CAKE

16 Servings

⅓ cup milk
1 pkg. dry yeast
2 T. warm water
2 T. sugar
1 egg, slightly beaten
½ tsp. salt
½ cup butter
2 cups sifted flour
6 to 8 fresh peaches
¾ cup sugar
1 tsp. cinnamon
¼ cup butter

Scald milk; cool to lukewarm. Dissolve yeast in water. Let stand 5 minutes. Add cooled milk, 2 T. sugar, egg and salt. Stir to blend. Cut butter into flour, as for a pie crust. Add milk and yeast mixture. Beat until smooth. Spread in buttered 15 x 10 x 1-inch jelly roll pan; let rise in warm place until double in bulk (about 1 hour). Peel and slice peaches. Arrange in rows on top of dough. Mix ¾ cup sugar and cinnamon. Sprinkle over peaches. Dot with ¼ cup butter. Bake at 375° for 20 minutes or until lightly browned.

Mrs. Thomas C. O'Neil
(Jane Stephens)

WHOLE WHEAT BREAD

2 Loaves

- **2 cups milk**
- **½ cup light brown sugar, packed**
- **1 T. salt**
- **¼ cup butter**
- **1 cup warm water**
- **2 pkgs. dry yeast**
- **7 cups unsifted whole wheat flour and 1¼ cups unsifted all-purpose flour (or substitute 4 cups whole wheat flour and 4¼ cups white)**
- **3 T. melted butter**

In a saucepan heat milk until bubbles form around the edge; remove from heat and add sugar, salt and butter. Cool until lukewarm. Sprinkle yeast over water in a large bowl. Stir with a fork until dissolved. Stir in milk mixture. Add 4 cups whole wheat flour. Beat until smooth with a wooden spoon. Gradually add remaining flour. Beat thoroughly. Turn out onto a lightly floured board and knead about 10 minutes. Place in a large oiled bowl. Roll dough to cover with oil. Cover with a damp towel. Let rise in a warm place (75 to 85°) until doubled, about 1 hour. Divide in ½ on lightly floured board and let rest 10 minutes. Roll out into 16 x 8 rectangles. (May spread with honey before rolling.) Roll up starting at 1 end. Tuck ends under. Place in greased pans and press dough into corners, slightly flattening top. Brush lightly with melted butter. Let rise until sides come to the top of the pans, about 1 hour in a warm place. Place in middle of a 400° oven. Bake 35 to 40 minutes. If crust seems too brown after 20 minutes, cover with foil. Turn onto wire racks to cool. Brush tops with any remaining butter.

YEAST ROLLS

32 Dinner Rolls

1¼ cups milk
2 pkgs. dry yeast
1 tsp. sugar
8 T. butter, melted
3 eggs, slightly beaten
1 cup milk
½ cup sugar
6 to 7 cups flour, sifted
1½ tsp. salt

In a small saucepan scald ¼ cup of milk and cool to lukewarm. Sprinkle yeast and ½ tsp. sugar over milk. Dissolve and let stand until mixture is foamy. Mix butter, eggs, milk and sugar. Add yeast mixture. Sift flour and salt. Add 6 cups to mixture and mix well. Add additional flour as needed until dough is still soft but not sticky. Place in large bowl; cover with plastic wrap and dish towel. Secure with rubber band. Refrigerate overnight. Divide into quarters. On well-floured board, roll each quarter into 12 inch circle. Brush with melted butter. Cut into eighths. Starting at large end, roll into crescent shaped rolls. Place on ungreased cookie sheet; leave several inches between each to allow for rising. Let rise 3 to 4 hours. Bake at 425° for 5 to 7 minutes. Remove to racks. Serve warm or freeze.

SCOTTISH SHORTBREAD

4 Dozen Bars

A hands-in-the-dough recipe!

1 lb. butter, softened
1 cup sugar
5 cups flour

On clean countertop, pastry sheet or waxed paper, thoroughly combine sugar and butter with hands. Add flour and knead until smooth ball is formed. Press dough into jelly roll pan. With palm of hand make dough as smooth and even as possible. With fork tines, imprint the surface of the dough by pressing into dough about ⅛ inch deep. Make rows of imprints about ¼ inch apart until entire surface is covered. Bake at 325° for 1 hour or until light golden brown. Let cool 15 minutes. Cut into 1-inch x 2½-inch bars.

CALIFORNIA PATIO SALAD — 5-6 Servings

1 pkg. (1 oz.) Italian salad dressing mix
6 T. salad oil
3 oz. wine vinegar
½ cup rose or sauterne wine
Salt to taste
8 oz. fresh or frozen shrimp, cooked and deveined
8 oz. fresh or frozen lobster, or crabmeat, cooked and flaked
1 can (14 oz.) artichoke hearts, halved
1 can (6 oz.) pitted ripe olives, drained
1 jar (2 oz.) sliced pimiento
½ pound fresh mushrooms, or 1 can (4 oz.) drained

Blend salad dressing mix, oil, vinegar, wine and salt. Pour over remaining ingredients. Chill 8 hours or more. Drain off marinade. Spoon on to lettuce cups or other salad greens.

Mrs. Wayne P. Lockwood
(Carol Ann Condon)

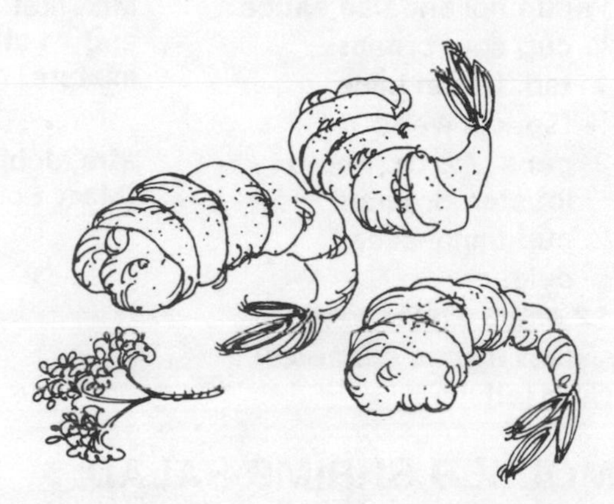

CURRIED CHICKEN SALAD — 6 Servings

3 cups cubed cooked chicken
1 cup celery, diced
1 tart apple, diced
1 can (11 oz.) mandarin oranges
½ cup finely-chopped macadamia nuts
1 cup mayonnaise
2 tsp. curry powder
1 tsp. salt
¼ cup crumbled blue cheese

Combine chicken, celery, apple, mandarin oranges and macadamia nuts. Stir together mayonnaise, curry powder and salt. Toss with chicken mixture. Sprinkle blue cheese over top. Chill and serve.

Mrs. Donald J. Ross
(Cynthia Stiles)

CRABMEAT BROIL
6-8 Servings

1 clove garlic, crushed
6 T. butter
½ lb. processed American cheese
1 tsp. worcestershire sauce
1 tsp. horseradish
2 cans (7½ oz. each) crabmeat, flaked
6 to 8 English muffin halves

Rub the inside of the top of a double boiler with garlic. Add butter and cheese; stir until melted. Stir in worcestershire, horseradish, and crabmeat. Chill. When ready to serve, spread on English muffin halves. Place under broiler until golden.

Mrs. Walter P. Loomis, Jr.
(Carylee Slaughter)

PICNIC LOBSTER BUNS
4-6 Servings

½ cup hollandaise sauce
¼ cup sour cream
1 tsp. lemon juice
⅛ tsp. dill weed
2 cans (7½ oz. each) lobster, drained
⅓ cup thinly-sliced celery
12 small dinner rolls (2½ inches diameter)
Bibb lettuce

Mix first 6 ingredients together. Split and butter rolls; fill with lobster mixture. Add lettuce. Chill.

Mrs. John S. Jenkins
(Mary Lou Cudlip)

MOLDED SHRIMP SALAD
6-8 Servings

This is lovely for a summer luncheon or Sunday night supper

1 can (10½ oz.) tomato soup
1 pkg. (8 oz.) cream cheese
½ cup mayonnaise
1 cup chopped celery
2 T. minced onion
¼ cup shredded green pepper
2 cups cooked shrimp, cut in half
1 pkg. (3 oz.) lemon gelatin
1 cup boiling water
1 cup peas

Heat soup. Add cheese; stir until blended. Add mayonnaise, celery, onion, pepper, shrimp and peas. Stir in lemon gelatin which has been dissolved in hot water. Pour into 2-qt. mold and chill.

Mrs. Harrison I. Steans
(Lois Mae Morrison)

CURRIED SHRIMP SALAD

6-8 Servings

8 oz. medium shell macaroni, cooked and drained
⅔ cup mayonnaise
1 T. red wine vinegar
2 tsp. curry powder
½ cup sliced radishes
½ sweet green pepper, sliced
1½ cups small shrimp, cooked and cleaned
⅓ cup seeded, chopped cucumber
½ cup sliced green onions
⅓ cup chopped celery
½ cup chutney, chopped

Put drained macaroni in a bowl. Combine mayonnaise, vinegar and curry powder; stir into warm macaroni. Add remaining ingredients and toss. Chill. Best made a day ahead.

SPINACH SALAD

6 Servings

½ can (14 oz.) bean sprouts
½ can (7 oz.) water chestnuts, sliced
1 lb. fresh spinach
½ can (16 oz.) chow mein noodles
2 hard-cooked eggs, chopped
6 to 8 slices of bacon, fried crisp and crumbled
1 large red onion, sliced, separated into rings

DRESSING:

¼ cup white vinegar
1 cup corn oil
¾ cup catsup
1 tsp. salt
2 T. Worcestershire sauce

Soak bean sprouts and water chestnuts in cold water; drain and dry. Place all ingredients in glass bowl. Refrigerate. At the last minute, toss together with dressing. For dressing, place all ingredients in processor or blender and mix.

CURRIED TUNA SALAD

4-6 Servings

¼ cup mayonnaise
¼ cup plain yogurt
2 T. chopped onion
1 tsp. lemon juice
1 tsp. curry powder
¼ tsp. salt
2 cans (6½ oz. each) tuna, drained
½ cup raisins
½ cup chopped green pepper
½ cup dry roasted peanuts
¼ cup flaked coconut (optional)
2½ T. chopped chutney
Fresh pineapple slices

Combine mayonnaise, yogurt, onion, lemon juice, curry powder, and salt; chill. Mix tuna, raisins, green pepper, peanuts, coconut, and chutney. Combine with chilled dressing and serve on a bed of lettuce. Pineapple slices are a nice garnish.

CRABMEAT SALAD

6 Servings

2 cans (6½ oz. each) crabmeat or frozen crabmeat
1 pkg. (10 oz.) frozen peas, cooked and drained
1 cup chopped celery
1 small onion, minced
1 can (3 oz.) chow mein noodles
½ cup toasted slivered almonds

DRESSING:

¾ cup mayonnaise
1 T. lemon juice
⅛ tsp. curry powder
1 tsp. soy sauce
⅛ tsp. garlic salt

Drain crabmeat thoroughly; break into large pieces. Mix with peas, celery, and onion. Chill thoroughly. Combine ingredients for dressing; chill thoroughly. Just before serving, mix dressing with crab mixture; stir in chow mein noodles. Top with almonds and serve immediately in lettuce cups.

SALMON MOUSSE 6-8 Servings

Especially delectable in a fish-shaped mold with slices of pimiento, olive, and thin slices of radish set in appropriate places for eyes, scales, etc.

3 T. flour
3 T. powdered sugar
2 tsp. Dijon-style mustard
2 tsp. salt
Few grains cayenne pepper
4 eggs
1½ cups milk
½ cup tarragon vinegar
3 T. melted butter
2 envelopes plain gelatin
¼ cup cold water
3 cups flaked salmon
1 cup whipping cream, whipped

Mix flour, sugar, mustard, salt and cayenne in top of double boiler. Add eggs and whisk until smooth. Add milk. Stir in vinegar, slowly (or will curdle); mix well. Cook over hot water until thickened, stirring constantly. Add butter. Soften gelatin in cold water; add to hot mixture. Stir until gelatin is completely dissolved. Add salmon. Chill, stirring occasionally. When slightly thickened, fold in whipped cream. Turn into a 2 quart mold (rinsed with cold water). Chill until firm. Unmold on lettuce. Serve with cucumber-dill sauce. (This can be made the day before. Cover with plastic wrap.)

Mrs. Halbert S. Gillette
(Karla Spiel)

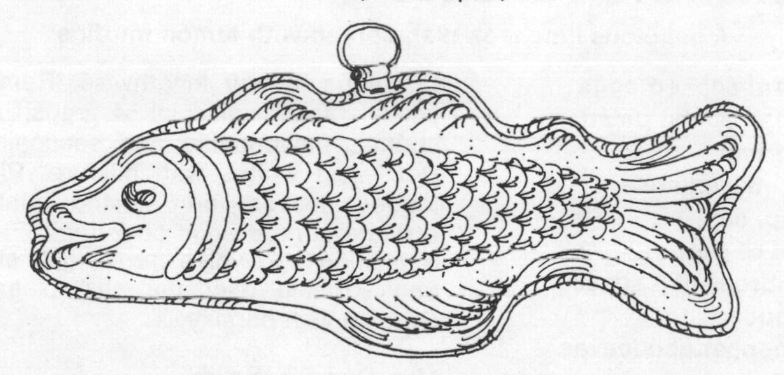

CUCUMBER-DILL SAUCE 1¾ Cups

1 cucumber, peeled and seeded
Salt
1 cup sour cream
1 T. lemon juice or tarragon vinegar
1 tsp. dill weed
1 tsp. chopped chives
¼ tsp. white pepper

Shred cucumber with coarse grater. Sprinkle with salt; let stand at room temperature for 1 hour. Drain thoroughly. Combine with remaining ingredients. Chill.

Mrs. Halbert S. Gillette
(Karla Spiel)

BROCCOLI MOLD 8 Servings

Fill ring mold with chicken salad for a luncheon or marinated mushrooms to serve with a hot meal

- 1 envelope plain gelatin
- ¼ cup cold beef broth (bouillon)
- ¾ cup hot beef broth
- ¾ cup mayonnaise
- ¼ cup plain yogurt or sour cream
- ½ tsp. worcestershire sauce
- Salt
- 2 pkg. (10 oz.) frozen chopped broccoli, cooked, well drained
- 6 hard-cooked eggs, chopped

Dissolve gelatin in ¼ cup cold beef broth. Add to hot broth. Add mayonnaise, yogurt, worcestershire and salt to taste; mix well. Stir in broccoli and eggs. Turn into 5-cup mold. Chill until firm.

Mrs. Robert L. Shirley
(Pamela Materne)

FRENCH STUFFED EGGS 6 Servings

A delicious luncheon dish served with lemon muffins

- 6 hard-cooked eggs
- ½ cup cooked diced shrimp
- 3 T. mayonnaise
- ½ tsp. salt
- Dash of pepper
- Few drops of Tabasco sauce
- 6 crisp lettuce leaves
- Parsley

Cut eggs in half lengthwise. Remove yolks. Mash yolks of 4 eggs; add shrimp, mayonnaise and seasonings. Refill egg whites with mixture. Place lettuce leaves on serving platter; arrange stuffed eggs on lettuce. Force remaining egg yolks thru a fine sieve and sprinkle over the stuffed eggs. Garnish with parsley.

Mrs. David B. Smith
(Marcia Williamson)

LUNCHEON EGGS ELEGANTE 12 Servings

- 2½ cups hot milk
- 1 pkg. (3 oz.) cream cheese
- 12 eggs
- 1 tsp. salt
- Pepper to taste
- ½ cup melted butter
- ½ lb. crabmeat or shrimp

Blend milk and cheese. Beat eggs slightly; add cheese mixture, salt and pepper. Pour butter in bottom of greased 2-qt. casserole. Pour egg mixture on top of butter. Bake at 350° for 1 hour. Stir after 20 minutes. After 40 minutes stir in crabmeat or shrimp. Stir again after 55 minutes. Serve immediately.

Mrs. Donn P. Alspaugh
(Kathleen Duffey)

BEEF AND AVOCADOS DELUXE

6 Servings

Great for a Ravinia Park Picnic

- 2 avocados, peeled and sliced
- 2 lbs. leftover roast beef, rare and sliced
- 1 sweet red onion, sliced very thin
- ½ cup vegetable oil
- ¼ cup olive oil
- ½ cup wine vinegar
- 2 tsp. dijon mustard
- 2 tsp. salt
- ¼ tsp. pepper
- Chopped parsley

WINE SUGGESTION:
Bourgogne Blanc

Arrange in a casserole layers of avocado, beef, onion, avocado, beef, onion. Mix other ingredients; pour over top. Marinate several hours.

Mrs. Gordon B. MacDonald
(Virginia Fagan)

DEVILED STEAK

6 Servings

Serve steak sliced on crisp toast points with a green salad

- 2 lbs. sirloin steak, cut 2 inches thick
- 2 T. prepared mustard
- 2 tsp. lemon juice
- Seasoned salt
- ¼ cup catsup
- ¼ cup water
- ¼ cup olive oil or salad oil
- 2 T. wine vinegar
- 2 T. soy sauce
- 3 T. plum or cherry jam
- 3 T. brown sugar
- ⅛ tsp. coarsely-ground black pepper
- Few drops Tabasco sauce

WINE SUGGESTION:
Hermitage

Combine prepared mustard and lemon juice. Spread mustard mixture onto both sides of steak. Sprinkle generously with seasoned salt. Combine other ingredients; heat to boiling. Pour sauce over steak; allow to stand 2 hours longer, turning occasionally. Grill over charcoal. Baste with sauce as steak is grilled.

Mrs. David B. Smith
(Marcia Williamson)

FILET MIGNON FACON DU CHEF

6 Servings

Extremely elegant

6 filet mignon, 1-inch thick
9 slices bacon
2 cups diced fresh mushrooms
½ cup minced fresh parsley
¼ cup minced onions
¼ cup butter
1 tsp. salt
⅛ tsp. pepper
6 very large mushrooms caps
3 to 6 oz. brandy

WINE SUGGESTION:
Pommard

Wrap each steak with a slice of bacon securing with wooden picks. Dice remaining bacon; cook until crisp. Drain fat. Add mushrooms, parsley, onions, and butter to pan; brown lightly. Add seasonings; keep warm. Broil steaks on grill to desired doneness. Place on large platter; top with mushroom mixture. Place a mushroom cap, cup side up, on each steak; fill with warm brandy. Ignite brandy and serve flaming.

Mrs. Chalres A. Ault III
(Valerie Richards)

TERIYAKI STEAK

12 Servings

4 to 5 lbs. beef round steak
Meat tenderizer
2 cups water
2 cups soy sauce
¾ cup finely-chopped onions
2 garlic cloves, finely chopped
1 small piece ginger root, mashed
2½ T. brown sugar

WINE SUGGESTION:
Cotes du Rhone

Sprinkle meat with tenderizer, following label directions. Cut round steak in 12 medium pieces. Combine remaining ingredients; pour over meat. Marinate in refrigerator 12 to 14 hours. Cook over charcoal. Serve either plain or on potato rolls.

Mrs. Donald J. Ross
(Cynthia Stiles)

STIR-FRIED BEEF WITH VEGETABLES

2-4 Servings

- **½ lb. flank steak**
- **2 tsp. cornstarch**
- **¼ tsp. sugar**
- **1½ T. soy sauce**
- **1 T. water**
- **3 T. vegetable oil**
- **1 medium onion, very thinly sliced**
- **2 cups evenly and very thinly-sliced vegetables (green pepper, cabbage, broccoli, cauliflower, green beans, zucchini, cucumber, mushrooms, bamboo shoots or water chestnuts)**
- **1 tsp. shredded fresh ginger**

WINE SUGGESTION:
Napa Gamay

Slice beef against the grain into 2x1x½-inch pieces. Combine cornstarch, sugar, soy sauce, and water. Add to beef. Set aside. Heat wok until very hot. Reduce heat to moderate. Add 1 T. oil; add onions and vegetables; stir-fry for 2 minutes. Don't let them brown or wilt; remove them and onions; set aside. Heat wok to very hot. Add remaining 2 T. oil, ginger, and beef. Stir-fry until beef pieces separate and just change color. Add cooked vegetables; stir to blend. Cook about 1 minute, being careful not to overcook. Serve hot with plain boiled rice.

Mrs. James F. Peil
(Nancy Rodgers)

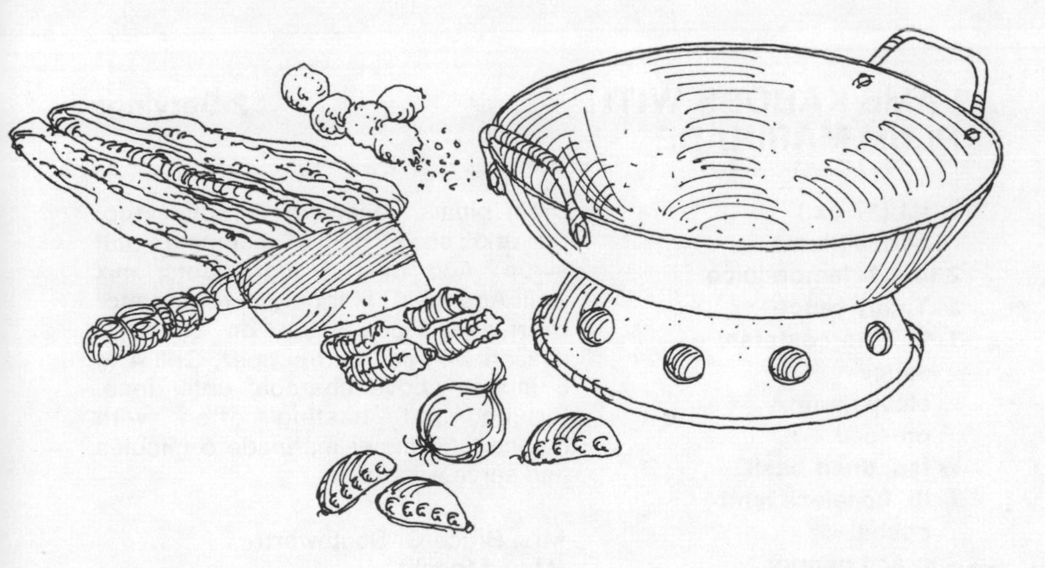

RED WINE HAMBURGERS

8-10 Servings

4 medium onions, chopped
¼ cup butter
1½ lbs. ground chuck
1½ lbs. ground round
1 cup red wine
2 tsp. celery salt
2 tsp. dry mustard
1 tsp. salt
1 tsp. pepper
½ tsp. garlic salt
½ tsp. thyme

WINE SUGGESTION:
Zinfandel

Saute onions in butter until just browned. Mix with remaining ingredients; form into patties. Grill over charcoal until done.

Mrs. William B. Allbright
(Claudia Ruch)

LAMB KABOBS WITH PLUM MARINADE

2 Servings

1 jar (17 oz.) purple plums
2 to 4 T. lemon juice
1 T. soy sauce
1 tsp. worcestershire sauce
½ clove garlic, pressed
½ tsp. dried basil
1 lb. boneless lamb, cubed
Salt and pepper

WINE SUGGESTION:
Chauteauneuf du Pape

Drain plums, reserving ¼ cup syrup. Pit and sieve plums; combine with syrup. Add next 5 ingredients; mix well. Add meat. Marinate in refrigerator overnight. Place meat on skewers; season with salt and pepper. Grill 4 to 6 inches above charcoal until done, turning and basting often with marinade. Simmer marinade 5 minutes and serve with meat.

Mrs. Bruce G. Southworth
(Mary Monek)

BARBEQUED LAMB — 8-10 Servings

Hearty, tangy, barbecue specialty

1¼ cups red wine
⅓ cup olive oil
2 T. red currant jelly
3 bay leaves
5 peppercorns
1 boned and rolled leg of lamb (4 to 5 lbs.)

WINE SUGGESTION:
Rully

In a saucepan warm all but lamb until jelly melts. Pour over lamb. Marinate at least 1 hour. Skewer lamb on revolving rotisserie. Baste with sauce while cooking. Build charcoal fire around edge of grill and have aluminum foil pan to catch fat drippings. This prevents burning of meat. For rare meat cook 1 hour 15 minutes. Cook longer for more well done lamb.

Mrs. John R. Gardner
(Catherine Corrigall)

BUTTERFLIED LEG OF LAMB — 12 Servings

1 large leg of lamb
2 cups dry vermouth
½ cup vegetable oil
2 T. tarragon vinegar
⅓ cup finely-chopped onion
1 T. finely-chopped parsley
1 tsp. dried basil
1 tsp. garlic powder
1 tsp. worcestershire sauce
1 bay leaf, crumbled
½ tsp. pepper
1 lemon, thinly sliced

WINE SUGGESTION:
St. Estephe

Have butcher butterfly the leg of lamb (the bones are removed and the meat is split lengthwise part way through, then spread flat like a thick steak). Remove all possible fat, as it tends to catch fire while barbecuing. Combine remaining ingredients. Pour into a large shallow dish or roasting pan. Add meat to marinade. Marinate in refrigerator a day or two, turning occasionally. Grill out of doors, basting frequently with marinade, 12 to 15 minutes on each side. If broiled indoors, cook approximately the same amount of time. This is especially good with wild rice. Spoon heated marinade over rice and lamb, and serve with fresh sliced tomatoes.

Mrs. Harrison I. Steans
(Lois Morrison)

MARINATED PORK CHOPS — 4 Servings

4 pork chops, cut 1-inch thick
½ cup olive oil
½ cup wine vinegar
1 clove garlic, minced
1 bay leaf, crushed
2 peppercorns
Salt and pepper to taste
Pinch dry mustard

WINE SUGGESTION:
Stein-wein

Place pork chops in a flat container. Combine all remaining ingredients. Pour over chops, cover, and marinate several days in the refrigerator, turning occasionally. When ready to serve grill over charcoal until done.

Mrs. George Yapp
(Charlene Brooks)

PRUNE-STUFFED PORK LOIN — 10 Servings

Acquires a rich smoked flavor and deep brown glaze

1 pork loin roast (6½ to 7 lbs.)
Dried pitted prunes, 3 per pocket
2½ cups orange juice (or sherry or both)
1 jar baby food prunes
Hickory charcoal

WINE SUGGESTION:
Chinon

Have butcher crack loin bones to make carving easier. Make deep pockets through meaty side of loin every 1¼ inches. Soak prunes in mixture of orange juice and jar of strained prunes for at least 2 hours. Stuff prunes into pockets; tie whole loin lengthwise to keep pockets from opening. Cook on a covered grill over an even bed of hickory coals at 300° to 350° about 2 hours or until meat temperature is 170°. Baste meat 2 or 3 times with reserved orange-prune marinade.

Mrs. H. Alex Vance, Jr.
(Melinda Martin)

BARBECUED HAM STEAK — 4-5 Servings

1 thick center-cut ham steak (about 1½ lbs.)
1 T. prepared mustard
1 T. catsup
1 T. honey
2 T. wine vinegar
2 T. dry sherry

WINE SUGGESTION:
Tavel

Slash fat edge of ham at 1-inch intervals, but do not cut into the meat. Combine remaining ingredients. Grill ham about 5 or 6 inches above the coals, brushing often with the barbecue sauce. Cook about 5 minutes on each side before turning, making 3 turns in all.

Mrs. Robert T. DePree
(Susan Barker)

GRILLED GERMAN BRATWURST — 4 Servings

4 bratwurst
Cooking oil
1½ cups chopped onion
1 can (12 oz.) beer
2 T. butter
½ tsp. onion salt
4 frankfurter buns
½ cup grated sharp cheddar cheese
4 slices bacon fried, crumbled

WINE SUGGESTION:
Ingelheimer Rote

Brown bratwurst over medium heat in a little oil. Add onions and beer. Simmer, uncovered, for 20 to 30 minutes. Stir together butter and onion salt; spread on buns. Make a lengthwise cut in each bratwurst to within ½ inch from end. Spoon on drained onion; sprinkle with cheese. Place in a foil "boat", leaving side open. Broil 4 inches from heat for 2 minutes. Top with crumbled bacon. (Can be done ahead except for final heating, which can also be done on an outside grill; put bratwurst on a baking sheet and cover grill a few minutes. Watch so they do not burn on the bottom.) Serve with German potato salad.

Mrs. James F. Peil
(Nancy Rodgers)

SAVORY BARBECUE SAUCE — 2 Cups

½ can beer
½ cup molasses
½ cup chili sauce
¼ cup prepared mustard
1 small onion, chopped
Dash worcestershire sauce
Salt and pepper

Blend all ingredients together in a saucepan; bring to a boil. Simmer for 10 minutes. If sauce gets too thick, add more beer. May be stored for several weeks in the refrigerator.

Mrs. Thomas N. Boyden
(Susan Dalton)

SWEET-SOUR SPARERIBS — 6 Servings

3 lbs. spareribs, cut into 2-inch pieces
2 T. soy sauce
3 T. flour
½ tsp. salt
Cooking oil
1 can (13½ oz.) pineapple chunks
¾ cup cider vinegar
⅔ cup dark brown sugar
½ cup water
1 tsp. grated fresh ginger root

WINE SUGGESTION:
Grenache Rose

Rub spareribs with soy sauce, flour, and salt. Brown in hot oil. Pour off excess fat. Drain pineapple, reserving ½ cup juice. Set chunks aside. Mix reserved juice with remaining ingredients. Pour over spareribs. Cover and simmer until tender. Just before serving, add pineapple chunks. If sauce is not thick enough, add cornstarch paste. Sauce may need more sugar or vinegar, depending on individual preference.

Mrs. Donald J. Ross
(Cynthia Stiles)

CHINESE BARBECUED SPARERIBS — 6 Servings

4 lbs. spareribs
½ cup soy sauce
½ cup dry sherry
½ cup water
¼ cup dark brown sugar
2 cloves garlic, crushed

WINE SUGGESTION:
Rioja Burgundy

Arrange ribs in large roasting pan. Combine remaining ingredients; pour over ribs. Cover pan with foil. Bake 45 minutes at 350°, turning ribs once or twice. Transfer ribs to grill; reserve sauce. Set grill as high above gray coals as possible. Cook for 20 to 30 minutes or until meat is browned and tender, turning and basting frequently with sauce.

Mrs. Gilbert H. Marquardt, Jr.
(Martica Heyworth)

SPARERIBS WITH BOURBON — 4 Servings

1 cup catsup
⅓ cup bourbon
¼ cup molasses
¼ cup vinegar
1 T. lemon juice
1 T. worcestershire
2 tsp. soy sauce
½ tsp. dry mustard
¼ tsp. pepper
1 clove garlic, crushed
3 lbs. lean spareribs

WINE SUGGESTION:
Petite Syrah

Several hours before baking, mix together all ingredients except ribs; let stand. Cut ribs into serving pieces and place on a rack in a shallow roasting pan. Bake at 425° for 30 minutes. Pour off fat. Pour half of sauce over ribs; bake at 325° for 45 minutes. Pour remaining sauce over ribs; bake another 45 minutes.

Mrs. David B. Smith
(Marcia Williamson)

CHICKEN GRAND MARNIER AU PECHE

6-8 Servings

4 large chicken breasts, split
Salt and flour
Peanut oil (no substitute)
6 T. brown sugar
2 T. butter
2 large oranges, sectioned
4 fresh nectarines (or peaches), halved
½ cup Grand Marnier
¾ cup toasted almonds

WINE SUGGESTION:
Vouvray

Lightly salt and flour chicken. Fry chicken over medium heat in peanut oil until nicely browned and almost cooked. Remove chicken and set aside. Pour off all oil in pan; add brown sugar and butter. Simmer, stirring until smooth. Add chicken and orange sections. Place a halved nectarine on each piece of chicken. Add Grand Marnier and simmer while basting for 5 minutes. Arrange chicken and fruit on a platter; sprinkle with toasted almonds.

Mrs. H. Alex Vance, Jr.
(Melinda Martin)

POULET JARDIN

4 Servings

1 frying chicken (2½ to 3 lbs.), cut up
Seasoned salt
Flour
2 T. butter
2 T. shortening
1 cup dry sherry
1 cup chicken broth
½ green pepper, sliced
3 whole tomatoes, peeled and quartered
2 medium onions, sliced
1 pkg.(10 oz.) frozen artichoke hearts
Salt and pepper to taste
Cooked rice

WINE SUGGESTION:
Macon Blanc

Sprinkle chicken with seasoned salt; dredge in flour. Brown in butter and shortening (360° if using electric frying pan). Pour off any excess fat. Add sherry and chicken broth. Cover and simmer 45 minutes (230° if using electric frying pan). Push chicken to one side of pan; add salted vegetables. Cook 15 to 20 minutes, making sure artichoke hearts are heated through. Serve over rice.

Mrs. Michael A. James
(Mary Rife)

BARBECUED STUFFED CHICKEN BREASTS

8 Servings

8 whole cnicken breasts, boned, unsplit, not skinned
Salt and pepper

STUFFING:
1 egg, beaten
1 pkg. (8 oz.) herb-seasoned croutons
½ can condensed cream of mushroom soup
1 can (7 oz.) crabmeat, flaked
¼ cup chopped green pepper
1 T. lemon juice
2 tsp. worcestershire sauce
1 tsp. prepared mustard
¼ tsp. salt

BASTING SAUCE:
½ can condensed cream of mushroom soup
¼ cup salad oil
¼ tsp. onion juice
1 tsp. Kitchen Bouquet
Dash pepper

WINE SUGGESTION:
Bernkasteler Riesling

Sprinkle inside of chicken breasts with salt and pepper. Mix stuffing ingredients. Spread over chicken. Skewer chicken breasts closed. Grill 30 minutes over medium coals. Combine basting sauce ingredients; brush over chicken. Continue grilling 15 minutes more, turning and basting frequently.

Mrs. Donn P. Alspaugh
(Kathleen Duffey)

BARBECUE SAUCE FOR CHICKEN

1 medium onion, quartered
½ cup butter
½ cup vinegar
1 T. prepared mustard
1 T. worcestershire sauce
1 square lemon peel (1-inch)
¼ cup chili sauce
2 T. brown sugar
1 tsp. salt
¼ tsp. pepper

Saute onion in butter. Pour into blender and add remaining ingredients. Blend until onion is finely chopped. If desired add several drops of Tabasco sauce.

Mrs. David B. Smith
(Marcia Williamson)

WINE-POACHED TROUT EN GLACE

4 Servings

For that extra special picnic

1¼ cups chicken stock
1¼ cups white wine
1 tsp. chicken broth concentrate
2 T. lemon juice
1 tsp. salt
1 sprig fresh rosemary
4 medium sized trout
1½ env. plain gelatin
3 T. white wine
4 stuffed green olives

WINE SUGGESTION:
Saumur

Combine first six ingredients in pan in which trout can lay flat. Add trout. Cover and poach gently for 5 to 10 minutes. Remove herb sprig. Let trout cool in liquid. Carefully lift trout from stock. Place on a wire rack or a tray. Cover and chill thoroughly. Meanwhile, prepare glaze: Soften gelatin in 3 T. wine. Strain stock. Add gelatin: heat until dissolved. Chill until syrupy. Arrange slices of stuffed green olives on eye and along back of each fish. Spoon glaze over all. Coat 3 to 4 times, chilling between coats and reusing aspic that drips on tray.

Mrs. Robert W. Buckley Jr.
(Ann Middleton)

POACHED TROUT WITH BROCCOLI

5-6 Servings

1½ lbs. fresh broccoli
5 to 6 small trout, cleaned
Juice of 1 lemon
1 cup dry white wine or chicken stock
½ lb. fresh mushrooms
2 T. butter
2 T. flour
½ cup whipping cream
½ tsp. salt
⅔ cup shredded American cheese

WINE SUGGESTION:
Johannisberger Riesling

Cook broccoli until just tender-crisp. Remove heads and tails from trout, if desired. Sprinkle trout with lemon juice and let stand 15 minutes. Cover and simmer in heated wine or chicken stock until almost tender, about 5 minutes. Remove trout. Arrange with broccoli in a shallow buttered baking dish.

Halve mushrooms; saute in butter until lightly browned. Add flour and mix until well blended. Gradually stir in cream and ½ cup of the poaching liquid. Cook, stirring constantly, until mixture boils and thickens. Remove from heat and stir in salt and cheese. Pour over fish; bake covered, at 375° for 20 to 25 minutes.

Mrs. Thomas C. O'Neil
(Jane Stephens)

COLD MARINATED TROUT — 6-8 Servings

From a friend in Colorado

3 to 4 large mountain trout
Juice of 6 limes
Juice of 6 lemons
6 bay leaves
Peppercorns

WINE SUGGESTIONS:
Puligny Montrachet

Place trout in shallow baking dish. Combine remaining ingredients; pour over trout. Place in oven at 150° for 3 to 4 hours or until the skin peels, the eyes are white or until fish flakes with a fork. Refrigerate and serve with dill mayonnaise and lemon.

Mrs. H. Alex Vance, Jr.
(Melinda Martin)

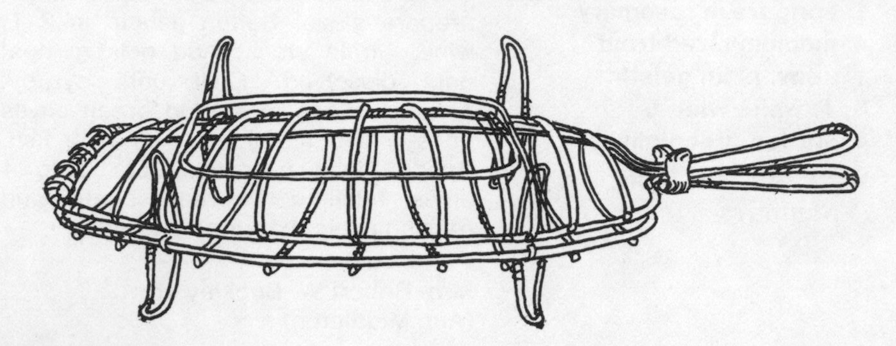

COHO OVER THE COALS — Serves: 6

BEER SAUCE:
1 lb. butter
1 can (12 oz.) beer
Juice of 6 lemons

CUCUMBER SAUCE:
2 cucumbers, finely chopped and seeded (unpeeled)
1 pt. sour cream
1 onion, grated
1 large coho salmon
Lemon or orange slices

WINE SUGGESTION:
Pinot Chardonay

To prepare beer sauce, melt butter; stir in remaining ingredients. Save ½ of sauce to serve warm at table with cooked coho. To prepare cucumber sauce, combine all ingredients; chill. When coho is cleaned, dried and ready to cook, put lemon or orange slices inside. Place on heavy foil; cover with ½ of beer sauce. Seal. Wrap foil-covered fish in chicken wire. Put on charcoal grill over good hot fire with evenly spread coals. Cook for 1 hour or more, depending on type of grill and size of coho. Fish is done when meat flakes with fork at backbone. Pass both sauces.

Use same method and sauces for Atlantic coast or Pacific coast salmon.

Mrs. John S. Jenkins
(Mary Lou Cudlip)

BAKED COHO SALMON WITH SOUR CREAM DRESSING

6 Servings

1 dressed coho salmon (3 to 4 lbs.)
2½ tsp. salt
¾ cup chopped celery
½ cup chopped onion
1 qt. toasted bread crumbs (commercial herb may be used)
½ cup sour cream
¼ cup diced, peeled lemon
¼ cup melted fat or oil
2 tsp. grated lemon rind
1 tsp. paprika
2 T. cooking oil

WINE SUGGESTION:
Sauvignon Blanc

Wash and dry fish. Sprinkle inside with 1½ tsp. salt. To prepare stuffing, cook celery and onion in fat until tender. Combine all ingredients except cooking oil, and mix thoroughly. (Makes 1 quart stuffing.) Place on a well-greased bake-and-serve platter. Stuff fish loosely.

Brush fish with cooking oil. Bake at 350° basting occasionally, 45 to 60 minutes, until fish flakes easily when tested with fork.

Mrs. John S. Jenkins
(Mary Lou Cudlip)

MUSKY DELIGHT

24 Servings

COURT BOUILLON:
4 qts. water
3 carrots, chopped
6 stalks celery with tops, chopped
2 onions, whole
6 scallions, whole
6 sprigs parsley
10 peppercorns
2 cups dry white wine
¼ tsp. basil
¼ tsp. marjoram
2 lemons, sliced
1 pkg. Crab Boil (optional)
1 whole Muskelunge (36 to 46-inches), cleaned
Mayonnaise, lemon juice, lemon slices, olive slice, chopped parsley

WINE SUGGESTION:
Sancerre

For Court Bouillon, combine ingredients; boil for 20 minutes. Wrap whole fish tightly in cheesecloth. Tie ends with string. If too long for poacher, cut off head and tail. Wrap each separately in cheesecloth. Place fish in poacher in 400° oven. Cover fish with boiling Court Boullion. Do not cover; poach for 30 minutes. Test for doneness (140° internal temperature). Unwrap fish. Chill well.

Place fish on platter. Remove skin from top side, sliding knife carefully just under skin. Insert knife carefully along both sides of backbone and ease backbone out of fish. Frost with mixture of mayonnaise and lemon juice. Garnish with lemon slices, an olive slice for an eye, and a parsley "necklace." Replace head and tail; cover gaps.

Mrs. Timothy E. Thompson
(Susan Falk)

CALIFORNIA BEANS
6 Servings

1 can (16 oz.) kidney beans
1 can (16 oz.) pork and beans
6 slices bacon, partially cooked, chopped
½ cup catsup
½ cup brown sugar
½ tsp. chili powder
¼ tsp. cumin
1 onion, chopped
1 cup grated cheddar cheese

Drain kidney beans; combine all ingredients except cheese. Bake at 400° in an uncovered bean pot for 45 minutes. Sprinkle cheese over top; cover pot and continue cooking for 15 minutes.

Mrs. David B. Smith
(Marcia Williamson)

SWEET AND SOUR GREEN BEANS
4-6 Servings

½ lb. bacon
2 eggs
⅓ cup vinegar
½ cup water
¼ tsp. salt
3 T. sugar
1½ lbs. fresh green beans, cooked

Cook ½ lb. bacon until crisp. Drain off all but ¼ cup drippings. Beat together eggs, vinegar, water, salt and sugar. Add to cooled drippings in skillet. Cook over low heat, stirring constantly, until thickened. Pour over beans in dish. Crumble bacon over beans.

Mrs. William F. Zwilling
(Diane Poppen)

HERBED CORN IN FOIL
8 Servings

½ cup butter, softened
2 T. chopped parsley
2 T. chopped chives (fresh or frozen)
½ tsp. salt
Dash of pepper
8 ears of corn

Blend butter with parsley, chives, salt and pepper. Spread 1 T. herbed butter on each of 8 ears of corn. Wrap in heavy-duty foil. Grill over glowing coals for 15 to 20 minutes, turning occasionally, until tender.

Mrs. John N. Schmidt
(Joan M. Slauson)

CARROTS MARINADE

10 Servings

- **2 bunches (2 lbs.) carrots, sliced**
- **1 medium onion, diced**
- **1 green pepper, diced**

MARINADE:

- **1 can (10½ oz.) tomato soup**
- **1 cup sugar**
- **½ cup cooking oil**
- **¾ cup vinegar**
- **1 tsp. dry mustard**
- **1 tsp. worcestershire sauce**
- **1 tsp. salt**
- **1 tsp. pepper**

Cook carrots until just tender crisp. (It is very important that there still be some crispness). Layer the diced onion and green pepper with the carrots. Pour marinade over the vegetables; cover and refrigerate for at least 12 hours. Drain well before serving.

Mrs. Walter L. Jones, Jr.
(Jane Frederick)

MARINATED CAULIFLOWER

8 Servings

Perfect for a Ravinia picnic

- **1 large head cauliflower**
- **Garlic salad dressing mix (Good Seasons preferred)**
- **¼ tsp. cider vinegar**
- **2 T. water**
- **⅔ cup salad oil**
- **½ cup sour cream**
- **¼ tsp. chopped scallions**
- **½ cup crumbled bleu cheese**
- **2 T. slivered almonds**
- **2 T. crumbled bacon**

Steam cauliflower for 20 minutes. Cool. Mix salad dressing mix with vinegar, water and salad oil. Add all other ingredients to dressing. Mix well. Pour over cooled cauliflower. Chill before serving.

Mrs. Lawrence Walter Lauterbach
(Ann Shull)

CORN AND TOMATO CASSEROLE

6-8 Servings

Yummy and party pretty

1 medium onion, chopped medium fine
1 green pepper, chopped medium fine
2 T. butter
6 ears of corn
5 medium tomatoes, sliced thick, unpeeled
¼ cup butter
½ tsp. pepper
2 tsp. salt
1 cup fresh bread crumbs

Saute onion and green pepper in 2 T. butter for 5 minutes. Cut corn off raw ears. Place ½ of corn in 2-qt. well-buttered casserole. Add ½ of tomato slices, then ½ of onion-green pepper mixture. Dot with 2 T. butter, sprinkle with ¼ tsp. pepper and 1 tsp. salt. Repeat. Cover with crumbs. Bake at 375° for 30 minutes.

Mrs. Bowman C. Lingle II
(Jennet Burnell)

KOHLRABI WITH CHEESE

4-6 Servings

8 large kohlrabi, cut into ¼-inch slices
Water, salt
2 T. butter
2 T. flour
½ to 1 cup grated colby or sharp cheddar cheese

Drop kohlrabi slices into boiling, salted water. Cook until tender, reserving cooking liquid. Make a sauce by melting butter and stirring in flour; gradually stir in 1 cup cooking liquid. Cook, stirring constantly, until thick. Stir in cheese; cooking until melted. Add kohlrabi. Pour into a casserole and bake at 300° for about 30 minutes.

Mrs. James T. Wheary
(Victoria Fazen)

FRIED OKRA

4 Servings

1 lb. small tender okra pods
¾ cup cornmeal
Vegetable oil
Salt and pepper to taste

Wash okra and cut off the ends. Cut into ½-inch pieces. Moisten okra slightly; shake in a paper bag containing the cornmeal. Fry in oil until golden, adding more fat when necessary. Season to taste.

Mrs. H. Alex Vance, Jr.
(Melinda Martin)

OKRA GUMBO

4-6 Servings

2 T. butter
½ cup chopped onion
2 cups chopped and peeled tomatoes
1 lb. fresh okra, finely sliced
½ cup chopped green pepper
2 cups water
½ tsp. celery seed
1½ tsp. salt
⅛ tsp. pepper

Heat butter in a saucepan. Add onion and cook until brown. Add rest of the ingredients. Bring to a boil; reduce heat and simmer, covered, about ½ hour until thick.

Mrs. Robert B. Abel
(Mary Beth Turner)

SQUASH CASSEROLE

4 Servings

2 cups sliced and cooked yellow squash
2 T. grated onion
Salt and pepper to taste
2 eggs, beaten
2 T. butter
1 cup bread crumbs (made from toasted white bread)
1 cup milk, scalded
¼ cup grated cheddar cheese

Mash squash; and combine with onion, seasonings and eggs. Add butter and crumbs to scalded milk; cool. Combine mixtures. Put in casserole. Top with cheese. Bake 35 minutes at 350°.

Mrs. Walter L. Jones, Jr.
(Jane Frederick)

SUPER SQUASH

6-8 Servings

1 small butternut squash, peeled cut up
4 to 5 medium zucchini squash, cut up
2 to 3 tomatoes, cut up
¼ cup butter, cut in small pieces
¼ cup chopped onion
2 tsp. sugar
1 tsp. salt
½ tsp. pepper
¼ tsp. oregano
Parmesan cheese, grated

Put all ingredients except cheese in a casserole, mixing well. Cover and bake at 350° for 45 minutes. Sprinkle with parmesan cheese; bake 15 minutes more.

Mrs. Harrison I. Steans
(Lois Mae Morrison)

YELLOW SQUASH SOUFFLE — 8-10 Servings

8 to 10 yellow squash, diced
1 large onion, finely chopped
½ green pepper, finely chopped
¼ cup butter
2 T. flour
1¼ cups milk
3 eggs, separated
½ lb. Roquefort cheese, crumbled
¾ lb. American cheese, grated
1 cup mayonnaise
1 tsp. salt
½ tsp. pepper

Cook squash, onion and pepper in small amount of water, covered, until just tender; drain. Melt butter; stir in flour. Slowly pour in milk. Cook, stirring constantly, until thick. Stir several tablespoons hot sauce into egg yolks. Slowly stir yolks into remaining milk mixture. Cook, stirring constantly, 3 to 4 minutes. Add cheeses; blend until smooth. Cool. Add mayonnaise, squash mixture, and seasonings. Beat egg whites until stiff; gently fold into squash mixture. Turn into casserole; place casserole in pan of water. Bake at 350° for 40 minutes. Serve immediately.

Mrs. Roger O. Brown
(Elizabeth Cluxton)

SUMMER GARDEN CASSEROLE — 10-12 Servings

May be frozen after it is cooked and cooled

3 medium zucchini, unpeeled, sliced
1 small eggplant, peeled, sliced
Salt
1 clove garlic, sliced
Olive oil
1 lb. fresh mushrooms, sliced
2 medium onions, sliced
6 fresh tomatoes, peeled, chopped
½ cup grated cheese (swiss, jarlsberg, cheddar or gruyere)

Sprinkle zucchini and eggplant generously with salt; let stand 5 minutes. Wipe dry, turn slices over and repeat process. Meanwhile, saute garlic in ¼ cup oil. Remove garlic; saute mushrooms, then onions in the same oil. When onions are translucent, add tomatoes; cook over medium-high heat until soft and much of liquid has evaporated. Salt to taste. Set aside. Heat more oil in pan. Lightly flour zucchini and eggplant; quickly saute, uncrowded, until golden brown on both sides. Arrange slices in alternate layers in a baking dish. Pour tomato sauce over all; top with cheese. Bake at 350° for 30 minutes until cheese is melted and golden.

Mrs. J. Stephen Laing
(Suzanne Reyburn)

BROILED TOMATOES WITH STUFFING

8 Servings

Marvelous accompaniment for roast beef

- 2 T. butter
- 1 T. prepared mustard
- ¾ to 1 cup cornbread stuffing mix
- 4 tomatoes, halved
- Salt and pepper
- Parmesan cheese

Melt butter in skillet; add mustard and mix well. Add stuffing mix, mix well. Salt and pepper tomatoes. Put stuffing mix on top; sprinkle generously with cheese. Broil till browned. (Watch as will burn easily.) Stuffing should be moist but not gooey.

Mrs. Walter L. Jones, Jr.
(Jane Frederick)

ARTICHOKE-STUFFED TOMATOES

12 Servings

- 12 large firm tomatoes
- 2 cups chopped onion
- ½ lb. butter
- 3 cans artichoke bottoms (or diced zucchini squash)
- 4 cups seasoned croutons
- Salt and pepper
- Lemon juice

Cut tops off tomatoes. Remove pulp and dry tomatoes with paper towel inside and out. Saute onions in butter. Dice artichoke bottoms. Add to pan. Add croutons; stir for 5 minutes over moderate heat. Season. Fill tomatoes; place in shallow baking dish. Bake at 350° for ½ hour. Sprinkle with lemon juice just before serving.

Mrs. Timothy E. Thompson
(Susan Falk)

BAKED TOMATOES STUFFED WITH MUSHROOMS

4 Servings

Delicious for brunch with eggs or a cheese souffle

- 4 large firm tomatoes
- 2 T. butter
- ½ lb. fresh mushrooms sliced thin
- ½ tsp. flour
- ½ tsp. salt
- Pinch each of dried rosemary and savory
- 3 T. cream

Dip tomaotes in boiling water for 10 seconds, then peel. Scoop out pulp and seeds to form a cup. Melt butter in a skillet and saute mushrooms for 5 minutes. Dust with flour; stir in remaining ingredients. Fill each tomato with mushroom mixture. Bake in a buttered dish for 8 to 10 minutes at 400°. (For a surprise, serve upside down, garnished with a sprig of watercress.)

Mrs. James F. Peil
(Nancy Rodgers)

RATATOUILLE

6-8 Servings

1 small eggplant, unpeeled and diced
2 medium zucchini, unpeeled and diced
2 green peppers, chopped
2 onions, chopped
½ to 1 cup salad oil
4 tomatoes, quartered
Salt and pepper

Salt and drain eggplant on paper towel for 20 minutes. Saute the first 4 vegetables a few at a time in the oil, until lightly browned; transfer to a casserole. Add tomatoes; bake at 325° for 2 hours uncovered. Liquid should evaporate. Can be served hot or cold; freezes well.

Mrs. Lloyd Owens
(Luvian Moore)

ZUCCHINI CUSTARD

4-6 Servings

Plan on people going back for seconds

4 large zucchini, sliced
Salt to taste
1 egg
½ cup sour cream
¾ tsp. seasoned salt
¼ tsp. pepper
1 cup grated parmesan cheese
2 T. butter

Cook zucchini, covered, in salted, boiling water until tender. Drain well. Put in shallow baking dish. Beat together egg, sour cream, salt, pepper and half of cheese. Pour over zucchini. Dot with butter and sprinkle with remaining cheese. Bake at 400° for 15 minutes or until set.

Mrs. Frank W. Gordon II
(Judith Bracken)

ZUCCHINI SOUFFLE

4 Servings

2 lbs. zucchini, sliced
½ lb. cream cheese
White pepper
Buttered bread crumbs
Fines herbs

Cook zucchini covered, in boiling salted water until just tender. Drain thoroughly, about ½ hour in colander. Whip cream cheese; add zucchini and pepper and herbs to taste. Put in quiche pan, cover with buttered crumbs and a sprinkle of fines herbs. Bake at 325° for about 1 hour.

Mrs. Donald J. Ross
(Cynthia Stiles)

GARDEN FRESH TOMATO MARINADE

4 Servings

3 fresh tomatoes, sliced
1 Bermuda onion, sliced
1 cucumber, peeled and sliced
1 green pepper, sliced
½ cup vinegar
2 T. red wine
2 T. sugar
¼ tsp. salt
¼ tsp. basil
Pepper to taste

Place sliced vegetables in a bowl. Combine remaining ingredients. Pour over vegetables; cover and let marinate several hours in the refrigerator.

Mrs. Walter P. Loomis, Jr.
(Carylee Slaughter)

TOMATO ASPIC

6 Servings

3¾ cups tomato juice
1 bay leaf
⅓ cup chopped onion
2 T. vinegar
1 T. worcestershire sauce
1 tsp. seasoned salt
Several dashes Tabasco sauce
2 envelopes plain gelatin
⅔ cup water
Shrimp
Green olives
1 can (16 oz.) artichoke hearts
½ pint sour cream
Black caviar (optional)
Avocado (optional)

Heat tomato juice with bay leaf and onion. Do not boil; simmer 10 to 15 minutes. Add vinegar, worcestershire, salt, lemon juice, and Tabasco. Soften gelatin in water; combine with tomato mixture, stirring until gelatin is dissolved. Cool. Pour in large mold or individual ones; add shrimp and/or olives, and artichoke hearts to degree suitable for mold. Chill until set. Unmold. Serve with bibb lettuce, sour cream topped with caviar, and slices of avocado.

Mrs. Doyle G'Sell
(Ella Doyle)

BEAN SALAD

12 Servings

1 cup sugar
⅞ cup vinegar
½ cup salad oil
½ T. salt
½ T. pepper
3 to 4 cans (16 oz. each) green beans, drained
1 can (5 oz.) water chestnuts, sliced
1 salad onion, sliced (purple is attractive)
1 pkg. (4 oz.) blue cheese, crumbled

Combine sugar, vinegar, salad oil, salt and pepper in a saucepan. Bring to a boil; pour over beans, water chestnuts and onion. Mix in blue cheese. Chill.

Mrs. William B. Allbright
(Claudia Ruch)

SPAGHETTI SALAD

8 Servings

1 lb. spaghetti
½ cucumber, chopped
1 bunch radishes, sliced
1 bunch green onions, sliced
1½ tsp. salt
1 tsp. sugar
¾ tsp. pepper
½ tsp. celery salt
1 large pinch oregano
4 hard-cooked eggs
⅔ qt. salad dressing (see below)

SALAD DRESSING:
4 cups mayonnaise
⅔ cup sour cream
1 cup milk or half and half
¼ cup Durkee sauce
1 tsp. Dijon mustard

Break spaghetti into quarters. Cook in water containing 1 T. cooking oil. Drain. Add remaining ingredients. Mix with the dressing. Cover and refrigerate overnight.

Mrs. Jerome E. Hickey
(Denise Coakley)

BEST EVER SLAW
10 Servings

- 1 large head cabbage, chopped
- 1 green pepper, chopped
- 1 red pepper, chopped
- 1 onion, chopped
- 1½ cups sugar
- 1½ cups vinegar
- 1 T. salt
- 1 T. mustard seed
- 1 T. celery seed

Place all vegetables in a large bowl. Combine remaining ingredients, blending well. Pour over vegetables; mix well. Cover. Refrigerate at least 24 hours.

Mrs. Walter P. Loomis, Jr.
(Carlylee Slaughter)

CHILLED CURRIED RICE
6-8 Servings

- 1 T. olive oil
- 1 tsp. curry powder
- 1 can (13¾ oz.) chicken broth
- 1 cup chopped celery
- 1 cup raw converted rice
- ½ cup water
- ½ cup slivered almonds, toasted
- ⅓ cup mayonnaise

In saucepan, heat oil. Add curry powder. Heat gently about 1 minute. Add broth, celery, rice, and water. Heat to boiling; lower heat, cover and simmer for 20 to 25 minutes or until liquid is absorbed. Chill 6 hours or more. Stir in almonds and mayonnaise. Garnish with tomatoes and parsley.

Mrs. Richard C. Gifford
(Wendy Thorsen)

MACARONI SALAD
6 Servings

At its best several days after it has been made

- 2 cups dry macaroni, cooked
- 1 cup black olives, chopped
- 1 jar (4 oz.) red pimiento, chopped
- ⅓ large green pepper, chopped
- ½ cup salad oil
- 6 T. vinegar
- 1½ tsp. salt
- ½ tsp. garlic salt
- ½ tsp. sweet basil
- ¼ cup chopped parsley

Place macaroni, olives, pimiento, and green pepper in a bowl. Combine remaining ingredients; pour over macaroni mixture. Chill.

Mrs. Robert L. Shirley
(Pamela Materne)

LEMON CREAM MOLD

6-8 Servings

Very refreshing

1 pkg. (3 oz.) lemon flavored gelatin
½ cup sugar
⅛ tsp. salt
1 cup boiling water
1 can (6 oz.) frozen lemonade concentrate
1 cup whipping cream, whipped
Raspberries
Blueberries
Watermelon balls
Cantaloupe balls
Strawberries

Blend gelatin sugar and salt in a bowl. Add boiling water and stir until dissolved. Stir in lemonade concentrate. Chill until mixture has a jelly-like consistency. Fold whipped cream into lemon mixture; pour into a 4-cup ring mold or individual molds. Unmold and fill center with fresh fruit. Garnish with mint leaves.

Mrs. H. Alex Vance, Jr.
(Melinda Martin)

FRUIT SALAD SUPREME

8 Servings

4 pineapples
1 pt. fresh strawberries
1 melon (honeydew or cantaloupe)
White grapes
2 oranges, sectioned
1 grapefruit, sectioned
1 banana, sliced
1 apple, sliced
Fresh blueberries (optional)

Split pineapple lengthwise (keep top leaves intact). Scoop out pineapple, leaving shell intact. Cut ½ the strawberries into bite-size pieces, leaving the small ones whole. Cut some large strawberries into wedges to put into niches. Make melon balls or cut small apple-size wedges. Put fruits into pineapple boats. (Do not allow to stand, as it gets juicy. This needs to be fairly dry, so dressing will show nicely.) Pass following Fruit Salad Dressing in a separate container.

Mrs. Walter L. Jones, Jr.
(Jane Frederick)

FRUIT SALAD DRESSING 1¼ Cups

- ⅓ cup honey
- 2 T. vinegar
- 1 T. frozen orange juice concentrate
- 1 T. prepared mustard
- 1 tsp. salt
- ¾ cup salad oil
- ¼ cup chopped pecans
- 1 tsp. poppy seeds

Combine honey, vinegar, orange juice concentrate, mustard and salt. Add oil slowly, beating thoroughly until well blended. Stir in nuts and poppy seeds. Put into pint jar with lid. Chill well before serving. Shake well before using.

Mrs. Walter L. Jones, Jr.
(Jane Frederick)

TOSSED FRUIT SALAD 6-8 Servings

- 1 medium head boston or bibb lettuce
- ½ head romaine lettuce
- 8 watercress sprigs
- 4 plums
- 4 fresh peaches
- 1 banana
- ⅓ cup lemon juice
- 1 pint fresh strawberries, washed and hulled
- 6 small clusters seedless green grapes

Wash greens; dry well. Store in crisper until ready to use. Refrigerate rest of ingredients. Line shallow salad bowl with crisp outer lettuce leaves. Break rest of lettuce into bite-size pieces to measure 3 cups. Turn into center of bowl. Slice plums into 8 sections. Peel peaches; cut into 8 sections. With tines of fork, flute banana lengthwise; cut into ¾-inch diagonal pieces. Sprinkle plums, peaches and bananas with lemon juice. Reserve 6 strawberries; cut rest in half. Add fruit to greens. Toss with Lime Salad Dressing. Garnish with watercress sprigs, whole strawberries and grape clusters.

Mrs. David Holman
(Alicia Bresee)

LIME SALAD DRESSING 1⅓ Cups

- ¾ cup salad oil
- ¼ cup orange juice
- 3 T. lime juice
- 2 T. sugar
- 2 T. cider vinegar
- ½ tsp. salt
- ⅛ tsp. paprika
- 3 T. chopped fresh mint

Combine all ingredients in pint jar with tight-fitting lid. Shake vigorously to combine well. Refrigerate until ready to use. Shake well just before serving.

Mrs. David Holman
(Alicia Bresee)

HOT BACON DRESSING

4 Servings

This may be served with lettuce, or green or yellow beans

6 slices bacon, cooked and crumbled
2 T. bacon fat
1 medium onion, diced
3 T. water
2 T. vinegar
1 T. brown sugar
1 T. granulated sugar
½ tsp. salt
1 bunch leaf lettuce

Boil all ingredients and pour over lettuce. Serve immediately.

Mrs. James M. Klancnik
(Elizabeth G. Paddock)

"MAINE CHANCE" SALAD DRESSING

2 Cups

Delicious for dieters. Courtesy of Chef Bello

1 bunch parsley
1 bunch watercress
½ cup safflower oil
½ cup olive or vegetable oil
⅓ cup tarragon vinegar
2 egg yolks
8 shallots
2 tsp. dry mustard
1 tsp. horseradish
1 tsp. MSG
1 tsp. worcestershire sauce
Vegetable salt to taste

Put all ingredients in electric blender; blend well. If too thick thin with a few drops of ice water.

Mrs. H. Alex Vance, Jr.
(Melinda Martin)

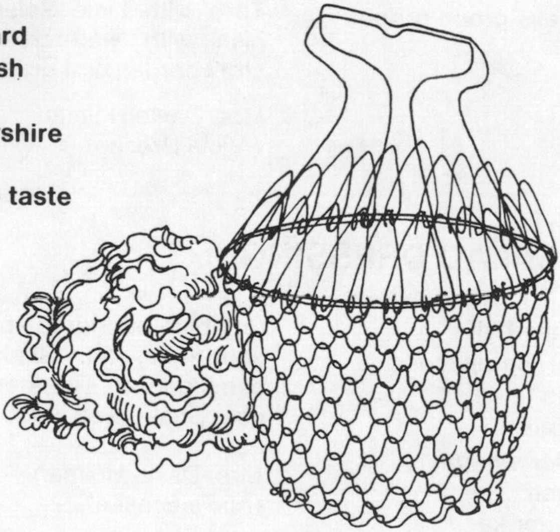

FRESH APRICOT MOUSSE — 6 Servings

1 lb. fresh apricots, peeled and pureed in blender
1 cup sugar
4 eggs, separated
1 cup warm milk
2 tsp. vanilla
3 T. apricot brandy
⅛ tsp. almond extract
1 env. unflavored gelatin
3 T. water
1 cup whipping cream, whipped
6 extra whole apricots, peeled, poached and soaked in additional apricot brandy

Combine the pureed apricots and ½ cup sugar. Reserve. In top of double boiler, beat egg yolks and remaining sugar until light. Pour in warm milk. Cook until thickened, stirring constantly. Add vanilla, apricot brandy and almond extract. Remove from heat. Combine gelatin with water; heat to dissolve. Beat into warm custard. Beat egg whites until stiff; fold into custard. Chill until mixture starts to set. Fold whipped cream and apricot puree into custard. Pour mousse into crystal bowl or individual parfait glasses. Chill. Garnish eash serving with 1 whole poached apricot.

Miss Virginia C. Franche

CANTALOUPE SUPREME — 4 Servings

2 canteloupes
1½ pints strawberries, halved
½ cup sugar
2 egg whites
Kirsch
1 pint vanilla ice cream

Cut bottoms off melons so they sit easily on a cookie sheet. Cut in half and remove seeds. Use a grapefruit knife to loosen fruit from rind. Cut fruit into fairly small pieces; put back in the rind. Add just enough sugar to strawberries to sweeten. Add to melons. Sprinkle with kirsch. Beat egg whites until foamy; add rest of sugar slowly, beating until stiff peaks form. Put one scoop of ice cream on each melon; cover well with meringue. Broil just until lightly browned; serve at once.

Mrs. George Yapp
(Charlene Brooks)

BLUEBERRY UPSIDE-DOWN CAKE

8-10 Servings

1½ cups flour
¼ tsp. salt
½ tsp. soda
½ tsp. cinnamon
½ tsp. allspice
¾ tsp. ginger
½ cup butter, softened
½ cup sugar
1 egg
½ cup molasses
½ cup plus 2 T. buttermilk

TOPPING:
2 T. melted butter
¼ cup sugar
Grated rind of 1 lemon
2 T. corn syrup
1 pt. fresh blueberries

Sift together dry ingredients. Cream butter and sugar. Add egg; beat well. Add molasses; beat vigorously. Stir in flour mixture alternately with buttermilk. For topping, mix butter, sugar, lemon rind and corn syrup in bottom of 9-inch iron skillet or heavy square casserole dish. Add berries. Pour cake batter over berries. Bake at 325° for 1 hour, or until done. Turn upside down immediately over serving plate. Allow to sit for a few minutes so all topping will come out. Serve warm—plain or with whipped cream.

Mrs. Walter L. Jones, Jr.
(Jane Frederick)

SUMMER BLUEBERRY CAKE

9-12 Servings

A nice welcome for new neighbors

2 cups blueberries
2 cups flour
2 tsp. baking powder
½ tsp. salt
¼ cup butter
¾ cup sugar
1 tsp. vanilla
1 egg
½ cup milk
Grated rind of 1 lemon
Dry bread crumbs
½ cup chopped walnuts

TOPPING:
⅓ cup flour
1 tsp. cinnamon
½ cup sugar
¼ cup butter

Wash berries; dry thoroughly. Sift flour, baking powder and salt. Sprinkle berries with 1½ T. of the dry mixture. Toss gently. Set aside.

Cream butter and sugar. Add vanilla and egg; beat until fluffy and light. Stir in remaining dry ingredients alternately with milk. Stir in rind. Spoon stiff batter over berries; fold gently until just mixed. Turn into buttered 9-inch square pan that has been dusted with dry bread crumbs. Spread evenly. Sprinkle with nuts. To make topping, combine flour, cinnamon and sugar. Cut in butter until mixture resembles coarse crumbs. Sprinkle over cake. Bake 50 minutes at 375°. Cool at least 30 minutes.

Mrs. James F. Peil
(Nancy Rodgers)

TROPICAL LEMON CREAM PIE
8 Servings

3 pts. vanilla ice cream
9-inch pastry shell
½ pt. whipping cream, whipped
1 can (1 lb. 6 oz.) lemon pie filling
½ cup orange juice
3 T. rum
Toasted flaked coconut

Scoop ice cream into pastry shell. Pipe a border of whipped cream onto edge of pie. Place in freezer until ready to serve.

Combine pie filling and orange juice in small saucepan; heat, stirring often, until boiling. Stir in rum.

Spoon some of lemon sauce over ice cream; sprinkle coconut onto edge. Cut pie into wedges; spoon more warm lemon sauce over each serving.

JAMAICA CAKE
12-16 Servings

½ cup raisins
6 T. dark rum
1 can (15 oz.) crushed pineapple
2 cups sugar
1½ cups salad oil
3 eggs
2 cups diced bananas (about 3 bananas)
3 cups flour
1 tsp. baking soda
1 tsp. cinnamon
½ tsp. salt
1 cup chopped nuts
1¼ cups confectioners' sugar

Soak raisins in 3 T. rum at least 1 hour. Drain pineapple, reserving juice. Using electric mixer, beat sugar and oil. Add eggs, 1 at a time, beating well after each addition. Beat in bananas. Combine flour, soda, cinnamon, and salt; add to butter. Beat thoroughly. Stir in raisins with rum, drained pineapple, and nuts. Pour into greased 10-inch tube or bundt pan. Bake at 350° for 1 hour and 10 minutes, or until pick inserted into center comes out clean. Cool slightly; remove from pan. For glaze, combine confectioners' sugar, 3 T. rum and 3 T. reserved pineapple juice. Pour over cake while still warm.

AFTER HOURS COFFEE MILK SHAKE
2 Servings

1 pt. good quality coffee ice cream
3 T. milk
4 T. brandy

Put ingredients in blender. Blend until mixture is still slightly lumpy. Pour into tall glasses.

YUMMY FROZEN CHOCOLATE PIE

8 Servings

CRUST:

25 vanilla wafers, crushed
½ cup pecans, finely chopped
¼ cup butter, melted

FILLING:

¾ cup butter
1 cup plus 2 T. sugar
1 tsp. vanilla
2 squares (2 oz.) unsweetened chocolate, melted
3 eggs

For crust, combine wafer crumbs with pecans. Mix with melted butter. Press into a 9-inch pie plate. Bake at 350° for 8 to 10 minutes or until crisp. Cool. For filling, cream butter and sugar. Beat in vanilla and melted chocolate. Add eggs, 1 at a time, beating for 4 minutes after each egg, for a total of 12 minutes. Pour into crust. Freeze for 24 hours before serving. Serve frozen.

LEMON BLUEBERRY MOUSSE

8-10 Servings

Pretty and tart

8 egg yolks
1 cup sugar
½ cup plus 2 T. lemon juice
4 tsp. grated lemon rind
4 egg whites
1 cup whipping cream, whipped
2 cups fresh blueberries

Beat 8 egg yolks until thick and pale. Beat in sugar, lemon juice and lemon rind. Cook in double boiler until thick, stirring constantly. Cool thoroughly. Beat egg whites until stiff. Fold whipped cream and blueberries into cooled sauce. Gently fold in egg whites. Refrigerate in individual sherbet containers or 1 large glass bowl. Serve with tiny butter cookies.

FOURTH OF JULY DESSERT

8-10 Servings

1 pt. blueberries
1 pt. strawberries
1 pt. sour cream or yogurt
½ cup brown sugar

Layer blueberries, strawberries and sour cream in glass souffle dish. Sprinkle brown sugar on top. Chill until ready to serve.

CHOCOLATE-COFFEE ICE CREAM PIE 8-10 Servings

1 ⅓ cups chocolate wafer crumbs
2 T. sugar
¼ tsp. cinnamon
5 T. butter, melted
¾ cup finely chopped blanched almonds
1 qt. coffee ice cream, softened
⅔ cup sugar
⅓ cup water
⅛ tsp. salt
2 egg whites, stiffly beaten
½ cup whipping cream
2 tsp. unsweetened cocoa
Chocolate curls

For crust, mix crumbs, 2 T. sugar, and cinnamon; blend in butter and ½ cup of almonds. Press into a 9-inch pie plate. Chill in freezer. Spoon ice cream over crust; freeze until firm. For topping, combine ⅔ cup sugar with water and salt in 1-qt. saucepan. Bring to boil, cooking until syrup spins a thread, about 7 minutes (soft ball stage, 238°). Beating egg whites at moderately slow speed, pour in the sugar syrup in a thin stream. Continue beating at high speed for at least 5 minutes, until mixture is cool. Chill. In chilled bowl, whip cream with cocoa; fold into topping along with remaining ¼ cup almonds which have been toasted. Mound on pie. Top with chocolate curls or more toasted almonds. Return to freezer.

TOFFEE MERINGUE DESSERT 8-10 Servings

Sinfully rich

4 egg whites
1 cup sugar
1 tsp. vanilla
1 tsp. vinegar
10 large (or 20 small) Heath bars, frozen
1 pt. whipping cream, whipped

Beat egg whites until stiff but not dry. Gradually beat in sugar, then vanilla and vinegar. Pour into 2 greased 8-inch layer cake pans which have been lined with greased brown paper. Bake in 275° oven for 2 hours. Remove and quickly peel off paper. Cool. Put frozen Heath bars into blender, 1 at a time; chop finely and set aside. Whip cream; combine with chopped Heath bars reserving ⅓ cup candy for topping. Spread between and on top of meringues. Sprinkle top with reserved candy. Chill for 24 hours. Serve in small wedge-shaped portions.

CHOCOLATE DROPS

5 Dozen

Very rich chocolate taste

- 1 pkg. (12 oz.) chocolate pieces
- 1 can (14 oz.) sweetened condensed milk
- ¼ cup butter
- 1 tsp. vanilla
- 1 cup flour
- 1 cup coarsely chopped pecans

In top of double boiler, combine and melt the chocolate, milk, and butter. Remove from heat. Stir in vanilla, flour, and nuts. Drop from a teaspoon on an ungreased cookie sheet. Bake at 350° about 7 minutes. Don't overbake; cookies will be soft as they come out of the oven. They harden as they cool. Remove from pan with spatula immediately.

FRESH PEACH VELVET

6 Servings

- 4 medium fresh peaches, peeled, chunked
- 2 egg whites
- 1 cup sugar
- 2 T. fresh lemon juice
- ½ tsp. almond extract
- 1 cup whipping cream, whipped
- 2 cups sliced, fresh peaches sweetened with ½ cup sugar

Put peach chunks into small bowl of electric mixer. Beat to a coarse pulp. Beat egg whites and sugar with peaches until mixture holds stiff peaks. Stir in lemon juice and almond extract. Fold whipped cream into peach mixture. Pour into 2-qt. bowl or ice cube trays. Freeze overnight. Serve frozen, topped with sweetened, sliced fresh peaches.

MOCHA POTS DE CREME

8-10 Small Cups

Easy blender version of a classic French dessert. Coffee liqueur adds a unique touch

- ½ cup sugar
- ½ cup water
- 1 pkg. (6 oz.) semisweet chocolate pieces
- 2 eggs
- Dash salt
- 3 T. coffee liqueur
- 2 T. brandy or Cognac
- 1½ cups whipping cream

Combine sugar and water in saucepan; heat until sugar is dissolved. Place chocolate pieces, eggs, and salt in blender or food processor. Add sugar syrup in slow steady stream, blending until smooth. Cool. Add liqueur and Cognac. Whip cream until slightly thickened but still of pouring consistency. Fold into chocolate mixture. Turn into individual pots de creme or demitasse cups. Chill.

FROSTED GRAPES

4 Servings

- **1 lb. seedless grapes**
- **⅓ cup honey**
- **2 T. good brandy or cognac**
- **2 T. lemon juice**
- **1 pint sour cream**

Wash grapes and remove stems. Place in a serving bowl. Mix honey, brandy and lemon juice; pour over grapes. Mix well; refrigerate overnight. Stir occasionally. When ready to serve, place in dessert dishes and top each portion with ½ cup sour cream.

Mrs. George Yapp
(Charlene Brooks)

CRISP GINGER COOKIES

6 Dozen

- **4 cups sifted flour**
- **½ cup sugar**
- **½ tsp. baking soda**
- **½ tsp. salt**
- **2½ to 3 tsp. ginger**
- **1 tsp. cinnamon**
- **2 cups butter**
- **1¼ cups warm molasses**

Sift together flour, sugar, soda, salt, ginger and cinnamon. Cut in butter, until crumbly. Stir in warm (not hot) molasses, mixing quickly. Cover and chill thoroughly. When quite stiff, divide dough in half and roll into strips about ½-inch in diameter. Wrap in waxed paper or foil; refrigerate or freeze. Slice thin; bake at 350° for 10 minutes. Serve with Cold Lemon Souffle.

Mrs. John S. Jenkins
(Mary Lou Cudlip)

COLD LEMON SOUFFLE

12 Servings

- **2 lemons**
- **6 lumps sugar**
- **6 eggs, separated**
- **1½ cups sugar**
- **1 T. cornstarch**
- **2 cups milk, scalded**
- **2 envelopes plain gelatin**
- **¼ cup lemon juice**
- **1 T. vanilla**
- **1 pt. whipping cream, whipped**
- **Cookie crumbs or pralines**

Wash lemons. To extract extra oil from skins, rub lumps of sugar over them until lumps crumble. Beat egg yolks with these lumps plus sugar and cornstarch until mixture turns light and forms a ribbon. Add scalded milk. Cook over low heat, stirring constantly, until custard thickens. Add gelatin, which has been softening in lemon juice and vanilla; stir to dissolve completely. Cool slightly. Beat egg whites until stiff with a pinch of salt and 1 T. sugar. Fold into custard. Chill, stirring occasionally. When not quite set, fold in whipped cream. Fasten foil collar to extend 3 inches above 2-qt. souffle dish. Pour in mixture. Refrigerate 4 hours. Sift crumbs or pralines generously over the top surface. Remove collar.

Mrs. John S. Jenkins
(Mary Lou Cudlip)

LEMON DESSERT SUPREME
10 Servings

1 envelope plain gelatin
½ cup cold water
4 eggs, at room temperature
1 cup sugar
½ cup fresh lemon juice
1 tsp. grated lemon rind
1 pt. whipping cream, whipped
2 dozen lady fingers
Strawberries

Soften gelatin in cold water. Dissolve over hot water. Separate eggs. Beat yolks; slowly add ½ cup sugar, beating until thick and light. Slowly add lemon juice, rind and gelatin. Beat egg whites until foamy; gradually add ½ cup sugar, beating until stiff peaks form. Gently fold into yolk mixture; then fold in whipped cream. Line a spring form pan with lady fingers. Pour in ½ of custard. Layer broken lady fingers over custard; add remaining custard. Refrigerate 24 hours. Top with more whipped cream and strawberries.

Mrs. James J. Porter
(Jeanne Kegel)

LEMON CRUNCH
9 Servings

FILLING:
½ tsp. salt
2 T. cornstarch
1 cup sugar
1 cup cold water
2 eggs, beaten
¼ cup butter
½ tsp. vanilla
½ cup lemon juice
1 tsp. grated lemon rind

CAKE:
¾ cup soda cracker crumbs
1 cup brown sugar
½ cup melted butter
1 cup sifted flour
½ tsp. soda
1 cup shredded coconut

In top of double boiler, combine salt, cornstarch, and sugar; add cold water. Cook, over direct heat, stirring constantly, until thick. Cook over simmering water 10 minutes, stirring occasionally. Add a little hot mixture to beaten eggs. Return to double boiler. Cook 4 to 5 minutes longer. Remove from heat; add butter, vanilla, lemon juice and rind. Cool. For cake, mix crumbs and brown sugar; add melted butter. Mix flour, soda and coconut; add to cracker crumbs. Sprinkle ¾ of this mixture into buttered 9-inch square cake pan. Pour lemon filling over this. Sprinkle the remaining crumb mixture on top. Bake at 350° 15 to 20 minutes or until lightly browned. Chill. Cut into squares.

Mrs. David B. Smith
(Marcia Williamson)

BAKED PEACHES

6 Servings

6 large whole peaches
1 T. butter, melted
½ tsp. mace
½ cup water
1 cup sugar
1 lemon, juice and rind
¼ cup white wine, brandy or rum

Peel peaches; put in covered glass baking dish. Combine butter, mace, water, sugar, lemon juice and rum; pour over peaches. Grate rind of lemon over top. Bake at 400° until peaches are tender (about 30 minutes). Serve hot or cold.

Mrs. William F. Zwilling
(Diane Poppen)

PEACH LUSCIOUS

8-10 Servings

3 T. butter, softened
Sugar
2 eggs, separated
Grated rind of 1 lemon
½ cup milk
1 cup flour
1 T. baking powder
½ tsp. salt
8 to 10 large peaches, peeled and sliced
1 T. lemon juice

Cream butter and ¼ cup sugar until light. Stir in egg yolks and lemon rind; mix thoroughly. Alternately stir in milk and mixture of flour, baking powder and salt. Blend well. Fill bottom of greased baking dish (13 by 9 inches) with peaches. Sprinkle ⅔ cup sugar and lemon juice over peaches. Pour batter over peaches. Bake at 350° for 45 minutes. Prepare meringue by beating egg whites until foamy. Gradually beat in ¼ cup sugar and continue beating until stiff peaks are formed. Top dessert with meringue. Brown 12 to 15 minutes at 350°. Serve warm.

Mrs. William A. Patterson, Jr.
(Marcia Motley)

PEPPERMINT FRANGOS

24 Servings

1 cup butter
2 cups sifted powdered sugar
4 squares unsweetened chocolate, melted
4 eggs
2 tsp. vanilla
2 tsp. peppermint flavoring
1 cup vanilla wafer crumbs

Cream butter and sugar until light and fluffy. Add melted chocolate gradually. Add eggs, one at a time, beating thoroughly after each addition. Add vanilla and peppermint. Sprinkle half the crumbs in 24 small cupcake liners. Add filling; top with remaining crumbs. Freeze until firm. Serve frozen or cold. This can also be made in a flat pan and cut in squares.

Mrs. Thomas Alexander
(Ann Tomson)

MARGARITA PIE

8 Servings

True to its name and most refreshing

CRUST:
¾ cup pretzel crumbs
⅓ cup butter
3 T. sugar

FILLING:
1 envelope plain gelatin
½ cup lemon juice
4 eggs, separated
1 cup sugar
¼ tsp. salt
1 tsp. grated lemon rind
⅓ cup tequila
3 T. triple sec

Combine all crust ingredients. Press into a 9-inch pie plate. Chill. For filling, sprinkle gelatin over lemon juice; let stand until soft. Beat egg yolks in top of double boiler. Blend in ½ cup sugar, salt and lemon rind. Add gelatin. Cook over boiling water, stirring constantly, until slightly thick. Place in a bowl; blend in tequila and triple sec. Chill. Beat egg whites until foamy; gradually add remaining sugar, continuing to beat until stiff peaks form. Fold into cooked mixture. Pour into crust and chill until set.

Mrs. J. Stephen Laing
(Suzanne Reyburn)

GOOSEBERRY CHIFFON PIE

6-8 Servings

2 cups fresh gooseberries, washed and inspected
1¾ cups water
¼ tsp. salt
1 cup sugar
2 eggs, separated
1 env. plain gelatin
¼ cup cold water
1 9-inch graham cracker crust
1 cup whipping cream
2 T. powdered sugar

Place gooseberries in saucepan with water; cook until just soft but not mushy. Put them through a food mill. Combine strained pulp with salt and sugar; return to heat, bringing to a boil. Beat yolks slightly, stir in a little hot gooseberry pulp, then add yolks to pan, stirring constantly. Cook until mixture thickens slightly. Remove from heat. Soften gelatin in ¼ cup water, then stir into hot gooseberries, stirring until it is all dissolved. Chill mixture until it begins to thicken. Beat egg whites until stiff; fold into gooseberries. Turn filling into crust; chill until firm. Whip cream, add powdered sugar and serve on top of pie.

Mrs. Gilbert P. George
(Ann Sullivan)

FROZEN HARLEQUIN PIE — 8 Servings

1½ cups ground pecans, (medium-fine)
¼ cup sugar
⅛ tsp. salt
1 egg, separated
1 T. instant coffee
½ cup milk
16 marshmallows
1 cup whipping cream, whipped
¼ cup semi-sweet chocolate bits
1 T. milk

Butter a 9-inch pie plate. Line bottom with buttered waxed paper circle. Mix nuts, sugar and salt. Beat egg white until stiff; add to nut mixture. Press firmly on bottom and sides of pie plate (not rim). Bake at 375° for 12 to 15 minutes, until light brown. With spatula carefully loosen crust around sides. Let stand 10 minutes. Lift crust and slip off paper. Cool.

Meanwhile, in saucepan cook coffee, ½ cup milk and marshmallows over low heat, stirring until marshmallows melt. Beat egg yolk lightly. Stir in a little of the hot mixture. Return all to saucepan; cook 1 minute, stirring. Refrigerate, stirring occasionally, until almost set. Fold in whipped cream. Turn into crust.

Melt chocolate over hot water. Stir in 1 T. milk. Cool. Drop by teaspoonfuls onto filled pie. Cut several times with knife to give marked effect. Freeze. Remove about ½ hour before serving.

Mrs. John A. Kelly, Jr.
(Joyce Judson)

PEACH MELBA ICE CREAM PIE — 6 Servings

1 can (3½ oz.) flaked coconut
½ cup finely-chopped walnuts
2 T. melted butter
1 qt. peach ice cream, softened
1 pt. vanilla ice cream, softened
1 pkg. (12 oz.) frozen red raspberries, thawed
½ cup sugar
1 T. cornstarch
2 cups sliced peaches sweetened

Combine coconut, nuts and butter. Press firmly and evenly against bottom and sides of 9-inch pie plate. Bake at 325° for 10 to 15 minutes or until golden brown. Cool. Spoon peach ice cream into crust, spreading to edges. Freeze until firm. Spoon vanilla ice cream over the peach. Freeze. Drain raspberries, reserving syrup. In small saucepan, combine sugar, cornstarch and reserved syrup. Cook over medium heat, stirring constantly, until thickened. Boil 2 minutes longer. Stir in raspberries; cool. Just before serving, arrange peaches on pie. Cut into wedges. Serve with raspberry sauce.

Mrs. Edward C. McNally
(Margaret McGann)

FRESH PLUM PIE

6-8 Servings

5 cups sliced fresh purple prune plums
⅔ cup brown sugar
¼ cup flour
⅛ tsp. salt
1 tsp. grated orange rind
¼ tsp. cinnamon
2 T. butter cut into 12 bits
Pastry for double-crust pie
Milk
Granulated sugar

Combine plums, brown sugar, flour, salt, orange rind and cinnamon. Line 9-inch pie plate with about half of pastry, leaving a good margin around edge. Add plum filling. Dot with butter. Roll out remaining pastry; cut in strips. Weave a lattice top; fold over edges, seal and flute. Brush top with milk; sprinkle with granulated sugar. Bake at 400° for 45 to 50 minutes. Serve topped with sweetened whipped cream, if desired.

Mrs. H. Alex Vance, Jr.
(Melinda Martin)

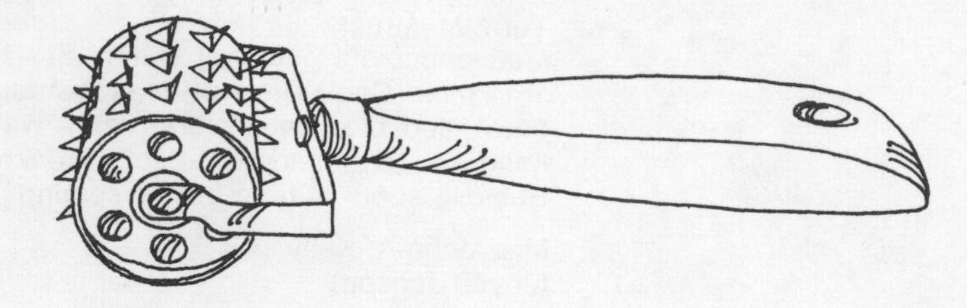

RUM MOUNTAIN

8 Servings

A few minutes work that looks like hours

½ cup dark rum
½ cup water
1 T. sugar
2 pkgs. lady fingers
12 oz. chocolate topping
Vanilla ice cream (good rich brand)
Whipping cream, whipped
Toasted slivered almonds

Line bottom of small charlotte mold with waxed paper. Mix rum, water and sugar. Dip lady fingers into mixture, one at a time; line bottom and sides of mold. Do not soak them. Spoon chocolate topping over fingers. Spoon whipped ice cream on top, then a layer of lady fingers. Continue layering several times, ending with lady fingers. Cover with plastic wrap and freeze. To serve, unmold and garnish with whipped cream and toasted almonds. Can be made several days ahead.

Mrs. Frank W. Gordon III
(Judith Bracken)

RASPBERRY WATERMELON SURPRISE

16-18 Servings

Pretty and delicious, especially good with anything chocolate

Small watermelon
6½ cups water
2 cups sugar
3 pkgs. (16 oz. each) frozen sliced strawberries, thawed
1 box (12 oz.) frozen raspberries, thawed
Chocolate bits or coffee bean candies

Cut watermelon in half lengthwise and scoop out all of the pink fruit; reserve pulp for another use. Cover shell with foil; freeze. Boil water with sugar 5 minutes; chill. Whirl berries in a blender for a few seconds. Put through a fine strainer to remove seeds and coarse pulp. Push down with rubber spatula. Combine with chilled syrup. Freeze in a hand or electric ice cream freezer. Fill watermelon shell. Smooth over the top. Press chocolate bits or coffee bean candies into surface to resemble watermelon seeds. Cover with plastic wrap; freeze.

Mrs. James F. Peil
(Nancy Rodgers)

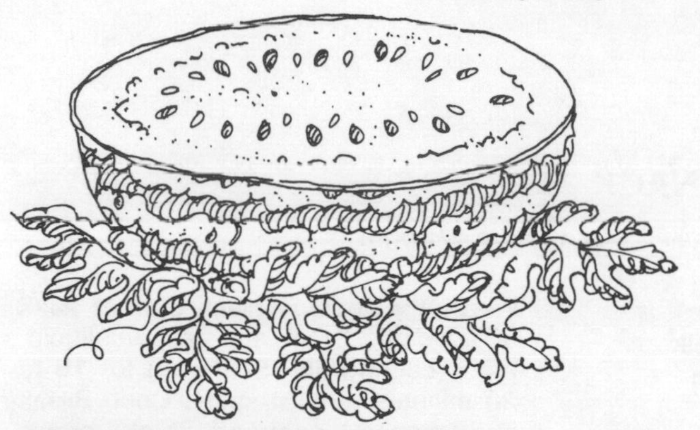

CREME DE MENTHE ICE

2 Quarts

2 cups sugar
4 cups water
¾ cup lemon juice
Dash salt
1 egg white
3 T. green creme de menthe

Combine sugar and water. Boil 5 minutes. Cool to room temperature. Stir in lemon juice and salt. Cover; freeze until firm, several hours or overnight. Beat egg white until foamy; add creme de menthe and the frozen mixture in large spoonfuls, beating well until very smooth. Cover; freeze until firm, at least 8 hours.

Mrs. John N. Schmidt
(Joan M. Slauson)

RED CURRANT AND RASPBERRY PUDDING

6-8 Servings

- 9 slices thin white bread, crusts removed
- 4 cups red currants
- 4 cups fresh raspberries
- 1¼ cups granulated sugar
- ½ tsp. cinnamon
- 1 cup whipping cream
- ¼ cup confectioners' sugar

Line bottom and sides of a 2-qt. bowl or pudding mold with bread slices. Reserve enough bread to cover top of pudding. In a saucepan combine raspberries, currants, water, granulated sugar, and cinnamon. Heat berries and cook 2 minutes; let cool. Pour into mold; cover with reserved bread slices; cover with a plate and put a weight on top. Chill overnight. Unmold onto a serving plate. Whip cream until stiff, gradually adding sugar; serve with pudding.

Mrs. David B. Smith
(Marcia Williamson)

COCONUT SNACK

Can't stop eating it !

- 1 fresh coconut
- ¼ cup coconut milk
- 1 tsp. light brown sugar

Pierce the 3 shiny black dots at peak of coconut. Drain and reserve liquid. Place coconut in 350° oven for 15 to 20 minutes, until it splits. Cool. Break into pieces; peel off thick brown membrane but leave inside brown skin on. With a potato peeler slice coconut into thin slices; combine with ¼ cup coconut milk and the sugar. Spread on a cookie sheet. Bake, stirring occasionally, at 350° until a light golden brown, about 1 hour.

Mrs. Bruce G. Southworth
(Mary Monek)

RUMTOPF

1 stone crock or rumtopf jar
FRUIT: (Well-ripened washed aromatic fruit, each as in season)
Strawberries
Raspberries
Pitted cherries
Diced pineapple
Diced apricots
Diced peaches
Blueberries
Green grapes
Gooseberries
Diced plums
Red currants
Sliced pears
Sugar
Rum (or substitute good brandy)
1 or 2 sticks cinnamon (optional)
Whole cloves (optional)

Begin filling rumtopf jar with first fresh fruit of the season. Add the same weight of sugar as fruit and cover with rum. Then as more fruits become available, add a cup of each at a time along with a cup of sugar for each. More rum is added as needed to keep the mixture covered. Cinnamon sticks and whole cloves may be added if desired. Keep the jar covered and in a cool spot. It takes 6 weeks for one layer to ripen. Stir well before serving. Serve as is or over ice cream.

Mrs. H. Alex Vance, Jr.
(Melinda Martin)

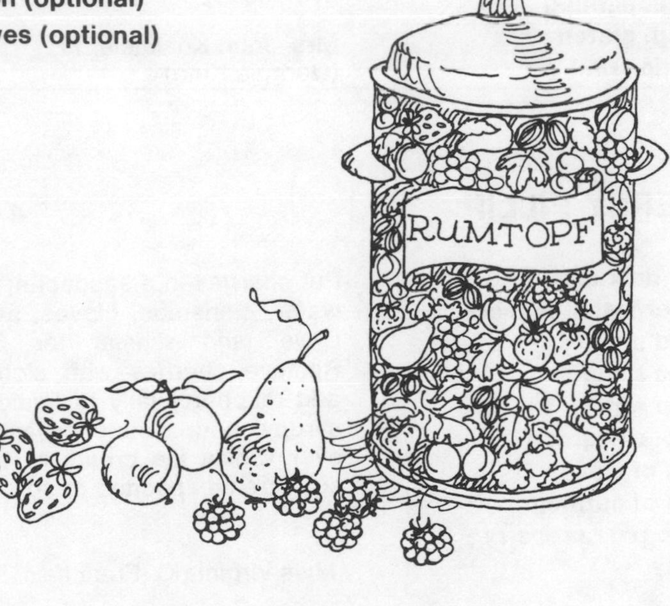

GRAND MARNIER AND ORANGE ICE CREAM

Very easy, but elegant and delicious

Vanilla ice cream
Grand Marnier
Frozen orange juice concentrate

Chill bowl of electric mixer in freezer. Take ice cream directly from freezer, place in bowl. Mix briefly with beaters to break from large lump. Add Grand Marnier and orange juice to taste. Mix as briefly as possible. Pour or spoon into individual serving dishes. Serve either plain or dotted with sweetened whipped cream.

Mrs. John W. Bradbury
(Mary Nolen)

HOT BLUEBERRY SAUCE — 1 Cup

1½ cups fresh blueberries
¼ cup sugar
¾ tsp. cinnamon
¼ tsp. nutmeg
½ tsp. grated lemon rind

Wash and drain berries. Mix with remaining ingredients. Bring to boil; reduce heat and simmer 5 minutes, stirring every few minutes. Serve hot over ice cream or sliced pound cake.

Mrs. John Kohlmeier III
(Georgia King)

CHERRY FILLIP — 4 Servings

1 lb. dark sweet cherries, stemmed and pitted
¾ cup sugar
½ cup water
½ tsp. cinnamon
Pinch of cloves
Pinch of nutmeg
½ cup red raspberry jelly

Put cherries in a saucepan; add sugar, water, cinnamon, cloves, and nutmeg. Cover and simmer for 5 minutes. Remove cherries with slotted spoon; add raspberry jelly to liquid. Boil until syrupy; pour over cherries. Serve hot over vanilla ice cream or chilled with sour cream spooned on top.

Miss Virginia C. Franche

CREME DE CACAO SAUCE ¾ Cup

- 6 sqs. dark sweet chocolate, grated
- 6 T. cold coffee
- 1 T. creme de cacao

Combine chocolate and coffee in a heavy saucepan. Stir over low heat until smooth and velvety. Stir in creme de cacao. Serve hot over coffee ice cream.

Mrs. Robert T. DePree
(Susan Barker)

SUPER FUDGE SAUCE 2 Cups

- ½ cup butter
- 1 cup sugar
- ⅛ tsp. salt
- 1 tsp. instant coffee
- 2 T. rum
- ⅓ cup cocoa
- 1 cup whipping cream
- 2 tsp. vanilla

Melt butter in saucepan; blend in sugar, salt, coffee, rum and cocoa. Add cream; bring to a boil. Lower heat and simmer 5 minutes. Remove from heat; add vanilla. Serve warm or cold.

Mrs. David B. Smith
(Marcia Williamson)

ORIENTAL ICE CREAM SAUCE 1 Quart

- 4 cups sugar
- 2 cups water
- Juice and grated peel of 1 orange
- Juice and grated peel of 1 lemon
- ½ cup candied ginger, cut in small pieces
- 1 cup slivered blanched almonds

Make a syrup of the sugar, water, fruit juices and grated peels. Add ginger and cook until medium thick in consistancy. Add almonds last. Serve hot or cold over vanilla ice cream.

Mrs. Thomas N. Boyden
(Susan Dalton)

RUM SAUCE About 2½ Cups

Keeps indefinitely in refrigerator

- ½ cup butter
- 3 cups brown sugar
- ⅔ cups pineapple juice
- ⅔ cup orange juice
- ⅓ cup rum

Melt butter in skillet; add brown sugar. Cook 3 to 4 minutes. Add pineapple and orange juices; cook until syrup-like. Add rum. Serve with 2 or 3 fresh fruits over vanilla ice cream; top with slivered almonds.

Mrs. Robert A. Paul
(Nancy Williamson Blake)

STRAWBERRY-LIME JAM

Six 8-oz. Glasses

4½ cups very ripe strawberries
2 tsp. grated lime rind
¼ cup lime juice
1 box (1¾ oz.) powdered fruit pectin
7 cups sugar

Stem and crush berries, one layer at a time. Measure 4½ cups into large kettle. Add lime rind and juice. Mix in fruit pectin. Place over high heat and stir until mixture comes to a rolling boil. Immediately stir in sugar. Bring to a rolling boil; boil rapidly for 1 minute, stirring constantly. Remove from heat and skim off foam with metal spoon. Stir and skim for 5 to 10 minutes while cooling to prevent floating fruit. Ladle in sterilized glasses. Cover with ¼-inch parafin.

Mrs. John S. Jenkins
(Mary Lou Cudlip)

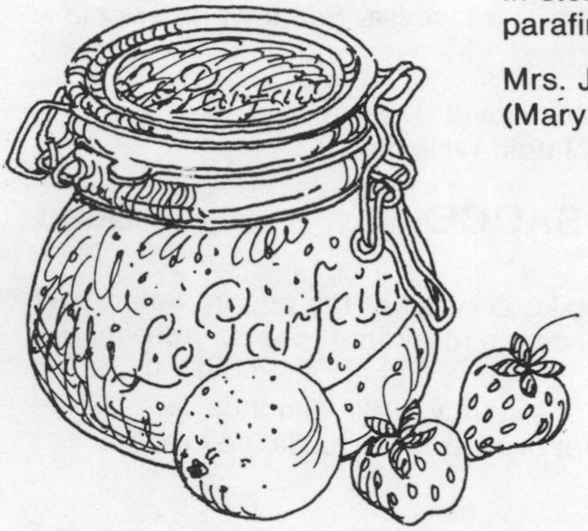

LIME-NECTARINE JAM

10 Glasses

2¼ lbs. nectarines
4 limes
7½ cups sugar
¼ tsp. salt
1 cinnamon stick
½ bottle liquid fruit pectin

Coarsely chop nectarines to measure 4 cups. Grate rind from 1 lime. Halve the other limes and extract 2 T. juice; pare and chop fine (I use blender). Put grated rind, lime juice, chopped pulp, sugar, salt and cinnamon in large kettle. Bring to a full rolling boil. Boil rapidly for 1 minute, stirring constantly. Remove from heat. Stir in pectin. Skim off foam with metal spoon and continue skimming for 5 minutes while jam cools. Ladle into sterile jars and seal.

Mrs. John S. Jenkins
(Mary Lou Cudlip)

JALEPENA JELLY

3 to 4 Half-pint Jars

- **¾ cup green peppers**
- **¼ cup jalepena peppers**
- **1 cup vinegar**
- **5 cups sugar**
- **1 bottle (6 oz.) liquid pectin**
- **Green food coloring, if necessary**

Grind peppers finely; combine with vinegar in blender. Blend 1 minute. Combine pepper mixture with sugar in large saucepan. Bring to boil; cook over low heat, stirring constantly, for 4 minutes. Remove from heat; skim off foam. Cool 1 minute. Stir in pectin and food coloring; pour into hot sterilized jars. Seal. Serve with cream cheese and crackers, cold meats or egg rolls.

Mrs. William D. Roddy, Jr.
(Joanne McDonald)

SPICED PEAR JAM WITH PINEAPPLE

Five ½-pint Jars

- **3 lbs. firm cooking pears**
- **1 orange, seeded**
- **1 lemon, seeded**
- **2 cups crushed pineapple**
- **4 to 5 cups sugar**
- **3 or 5 whole cloves**
- **1 6-inch stick cinnamon**
- **1 1-inch piece ginger**
- **1 cup chopped walnuts**

Peel and core pears. Wash orange and lemon well. Put fruit through a food grinder, using a coarse blade. Save juices. Add juices to fruit pulp along with pineapple, sugar, cloves, cinnamon stick, ginger and walnuts. Stir the mixture while heating it. Boil for 45 minutes. Pour into hot sterilized jars and seal.

Mrs. David B. Smith
(Marcia Williamson)

APPLE-RHUBARB JAM

6 Jars

- **3 medium cooking apples (about 1 lb.)**
- **3 cups diced rhubard (about 1 lb.)**
- **¼ cup water**
- **4 cups sugar**

Peel, core, and dice apples. Dice rhubarb. Combine fruits with water and sugar in a heavy kettle. Heat to boiling. Simmer, stirring often until sugar dissolves and fruits are soft. Boil rapidly until jam sets, about 30 minutes. Pour into hot sterilized jars and seal.

Mrs. Thomas N. Boyden
(Susan Dalton)

TARRAGON-WINE JELLY

5 Glasses

- **1 cup fresh tarragon leaves (packed)**
- **½ bay leaf**
- **1 cup boiling water**
- **1½ cups dry white wine**
- **4 cups sugar**
- **1 bottle (6 oz.) liquid fruit pectin**
- **1 scant drop green food color**
- **2 scant drops yellow food color**
- **5 fresh tarragon sprigs**

Wash and dry tarragon leaves. Chop very fine. Put into small bowl with bay leaf. Add boiling water. Let stand, covered, 5 minutes. In a 3-quart saucepan combine tarragon mixture, wine and sugar. Heat, stirring until sugar is dissolved. Bring mixture to a rolling boil. Stir in liquid pectin and boil 1 minute, stirring constantly. Remove from heat and add food color. Pour through a strainer lined with eight thicknesses of cheesecloth. In the bottom of each hot sterilized jelly glass place a sprig of tarragon. Hold in place with a hot sterilized fork. Pour hot jelly into glasses. Let stand 10 minutes. Carefully remove forks, being careful not to dislodge tarragon sprigs. Seal jars. Serve very cold with meats.

Mrs. David B. Smith
(Marcia Williamson)

CORN RELISH

6-8 Pints

- **18 ears fresh corn, husks removed**
- **1 small head cabbage, quartered, cored and shredded**
- **4 onions, peeled and chopped**
- **3 sweet red peppers, seeded, chopped**
- **3 green peppers, seeded, chopped**
- **2½ cups sugar**
- **3 T. flour**
- **2 T. salt**
- **1½ tsp. celery seed**
- **2 tsp. mustard seed**
- **1 tsp. turmeric**
- **2 qts. white vinegar**

Cook corn in salted, boiling water for 3 minutes. Cool. Cut kernels from cobs. Put cabbage, onions and peppers through a food grinder, using a coarse blade. Combine corn and ground vegetables in a large kettle. Combine sugar, flour, salt and spices in a heavy saucepan. Stir in vinegar until smooth. Heat to boiling. Pour over vegetables in kettle. Cook, stirring frequently, about 45 minutes. Spoon into hot sterilized jars and seal.

Mrs. David B. Smith
(Marcia Williamson)

CHILI SAUCE I — 2½ Pints

12 medium tomatoes
2 large onions
3 large green peppers
1 clove garlic
1 tsp. salt
1 stick cinnamon
1 tsp. whole cloves
1 T. whole pickle spice
½ cup sugar
1 T. salt
1 cup vinegar

Scald tomatoes, dip in ice water and remove skin. Chop coarsely. Skin onions. Wash and seed green peppers. Grind all together. Mash garlic with salt. Tie spices in cheesecloth. Combine ingredients in large kettle and heat to boil. Reduce heat and simmer for 2 hours or until thick. Ladle into hot sterilized jars and seal.

Mrs. John S. Jenkins
(Mary Lou Cudlip)

CHILI SAUCE II — 8 Pints

1 peck of tomatoes, peeled
4 cups vinegar
4 cups sugar
1 tsp. celery seed
1 tsp. whole mustard seed
8 onions, diced
3 green peppers, diced
1 red pepper, diced
3 tsp. salt

Bring all ingredients to a boil and simmer for 1 hour. Pour into hot sterlized jars and seal.

Mrs. James Modrall
(Nancy Anne Johnson)

LINGLE MAYONNAISE — 3 Cups

Keeps indefinitely in the refrigerator in a closed jar

4 egg yolks
1 tsp. salt
1 tsp. sugar
4 dashes cayenne pepper
2 dashes paprika
2 T. lemon juice
2 T. cider vinegar
2 cups salad oil

Place egg yolks, salt, sugar, cayenne pepper and paprika in small mixer bowl. Beat until very light colored and very thick. (You cannot overbeat at this point and you can sure get into trouble if you do not beat enough.) Mix lemon juice and vinegar. Very slowly add oil and vinegar alternately to yolks, beating constantly. (This will be much thicker than commercial mayonnaise and much tastier. It is not salty so it may be mixed with whipped cream for a fruit dressing.

Mrs. Bowman C. Lingle II
(Jennet Burnell)

BREAD AND BUTTER PICKLES — 10-12 Pints

Old family recipe

- 50 small pickling cucumbers
- 10 small onions, chopped
- 2 green peppers, chopped
- ½ cup salt
- 5 cups cider vinegar
- 5 cups sugar
- 2 T. mustard seed
- 1½ tsp. turmeric
- ½ tsp. ground cloves
- ½ tsp. cinnamon
- ½ tsp. celery seed

Slice cucumber, add onion and green peppers. Put in large kettle, sprinkle with salt; cover with ice cubes. Put dinner plate and heavy weight on top. Let stand for 3 hours. Heat vinegar with sugar and spices; do not boil; stir only with a wooden spoon. Drain vegetable mixture thoroughly; place in hot sterlized jars. Pour hot vinegar-spice mixture over. Seal tightly. Wait 4 weeks before eating.

Mrs. Henry W. Dienst
(Judy Teasdale Simpson)

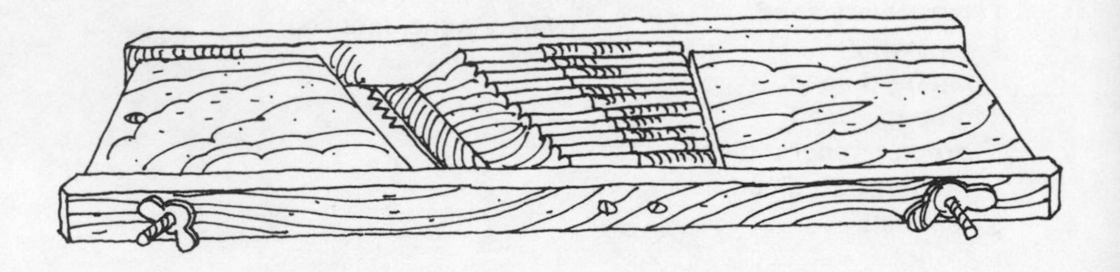

EDITH'S ZUCCHINI PICKLES — 4 to 5 Half-pints

- 2 lbs. zucchini (small to medium)
- 2 onions
- ¼ cup salt
- 2 cups white vinegar
- 2 cups sugar
- 1 tsp. celery seed
- 1 tsp. turmeric
- 2 tsp. mustard seed

Wash zucchini; cut in thin slices. Peel and quarter onion; slice thinly. Cover all with water and add salt. Let stand 2 hours. Drain thoroughly. Bring remaining ingredients to a boil and pour over vegetables. Let stand 2 hours. Put all in kettle and bring to a boil. Boil 5 minutes. Pack in hot sterilized jars and seal.

Mrs. H. Alex Vance, Jr.
(Melinda Martin)

GRANDMA'S SWEDISH DILLS

4 Quarts

Made in a crock; they can be eaten within a few hours. Will keep about 2 weeks

5 cups water
2 cups vinegar (white or cider)
½ cup salt
Small cucumbers
Dill blossoms

VARIATION:
Add 1 clove garlic to each quart

Bring water, vinegar and salt to a boil. Pack cucumbers and 2 dill blossoms in each hot sterilized quart jar. Pour brine over cucumbers. Seal. Also delicious as "fresh" pickles. Same process.

Mrs. James Modrall
(Nancy Anne Johnson)

DILLED OKRA

4 Pints

Makes a crisp hors d'oeuvre. Great for dieters

Fresh okra (3 to 4 lbs.)
4 small hot red peppers
1 qt. vinegar
1 cup water
½ cup salt
1 tsp. dill seed
4 small onions, quartered

Wash and drain fresh okra and pack into hot sterilized pint jars. Add 1 small hot red pepper and 1 onion to each jar. Mix the vinegar, water and salt and bring to a boil, then add dill seed. Pour over top of each jar and seal. Allow to stand at least two weeks before eating.

Mrs. Willaim F. Zwilling
(Diane Poppen)

FALL KITCHEN

At the Tremont House, a fashionable 19th century Chicago hotel which often played host to Abraham Lincoln, an annual Thanksgiving Day dinner was held. Only men were invited to the event, and to be included signified business and social success of the highest order.

The menu for one of these meals listed 70 offerings, most of which were seasonal specialties. Included were game broth and venison soup hunter style; baked black bass with claret; broiled leg of mountain sheep; roasts of goose, quail, duck, rabbit, partridge, elk, and pheasant; antelope steak with mushroom sauce; fillet of grouse with truffle sauce; and such "ornamental dishes" as pyramid of wide goose in liver jelly, boned quail in plumage, and red wing starling on a tree.

Anyone who survived the meal was sure to have found game and birds among the highlights of that fall repast, and the same can be said of the modern-day meals of fall. Venison and wild birds are particularly good during autumn, as are the farm-bred small birds: quail, squab, guinea hen, mallard duck, Canadian goose, and ringneck pheasant.

Pork is especially suited to the cool days of autumn, and Great Lakes mullet, yellow pike, sauger, and whitefish are also good at this time. From the oceans look for shrimp, scallops, red snapper, stripped bass, bluefish, cod and flounder.

Fall is the best season for apples. Rome Beauty and Winesap are the top choices for baking, while Baldwin, Stayman and Jersey Red should be used for pies. For eating, select Golden Delicious, Red Delicious, Jonathan, and Cortland. These are particularly good with the new walnuts, chestnuts, and pecans of fall, and with the aged

Dutch Edam and Gouda and English Cheshire cheese which are most flavorful at this time of year. Serve this apple, cheese, and nut combination as a dessert, or on an elegant fall picnic.

Other fruits of fall are cantaloupes, cranberries, grapes, kumquats, lemons, limes, oranges, pears, persimmons (try splitting a soft, ripe one in half, sprinkling it with lime juice, and eating it with a spoon), pomegranates, tangelos, and tangerines.

Salad ingredients at hand include avocados, celery, cabbage, chicory, Belgin endive, escarole, Bibb and iceberg lettuce, garlic, scallions, radishes, tomatoes, and watercress. Fall salads call for a moderately strong dressing to compliment the slightly sharp taste of the greens.

Fall's hearty cold weather vegetables also require more assertive flavorings and sauces. Vegetables that are particularly good at this time are fava beans, beets, brussels sprouts, cabbage, cauliflower, celeriac, eggplant, kale, kohlrabi, mushrooms, onions, potatoes, yams, pumpkins, winter squash, and turnips.

In fall appetites sharpen as days grow colder. Hence hearty stews, pasta dishes, roasts and braised meats are favored. A hot soup is a nice way to begin a meal. Seasonings and sauces become more important than during the warmer seasons. The cook should utilize different flavorings as a way to vary the tastes of the foods she serves.

FALL MENUS

OCTOBERFEST

LIPTAUER CHEESE SPREAD

SAUSAGE KRAUT BALLS

* *

CHEESE BEER SOUP

* *

GEORGE'S CHOUCROUTE GARNI

PUMPERNICKEL BREAD

Keg of Beer or Leibfraumilch

* *

LEMON GINGERBREAD LOG

TAILGATE PICNIC

BULLSHOTS

MUSHROOM PATE

* *

THERMOS OF CURRIED EGGPLANT SOUP

* *

SYRIAN SANDWICHES

California Grignolino Rose or Grenache Rose

* *

ASSORTED FRESH FRUIT

THANKSGIVING DINNER

HOT SPICED CIDER

CURRIED CHEESE SPREAD WITH CHUTNEY

* *

AUTUMN FRUIT WITH CRANBERRY DRESSING

* *

TURKEY WITH SAUSAGE AND CHESTNUT STUFFING

California Fruity Chenin Blanc

SWEET POTATOES IN ORANGE SHELLS

CELERY RING FILLED WITH BRUSSELS SPROUTS

* *

MOLASSES PUMPKIN PIE WITH PECAN TOPPING

Sweet Semillon or Haut Sauterne

FALL MENUS

FALL LUNCHEON

CREAMED CHICKEN WITH MELON BALLS
Vouvray

BUTTERED FRENCH STYLE GREEN BEANS
GREEN SALAD
CARAMEL CURRANT ROLLS
* *

KIRSCH TORTE
Piesporter or Wehlener Auslese

HUNTER'S DINNER

MARINATED SHRIMP PUFFS

Manzanilla Sherry

* *

PHEASANT SUPREME
Chateau Phelan Segur

BUTTERED PEAS WILD RICE CASSEROLE
* *

PUREED CHESTNUT RING

FORMAL FALL DINNER

DEFOREST'S CAVIAR PIE
French Champagne
* *

CREAM OF CHESTNUT SOUP
Fino Sherry
* *

CROWN ROAST OF PORK WITH CHAMPAGNE STUFFING
Beaune
BUTTERED GREEN PEAS
* *

LETTUCE WITH TOMATO CREAM
* *

PEAR IN CHOCOLATE SABAYON
Sauterne

FALL TABLE OF CONTENTS

SALADS AND SALAD DRESSINGS

DESSERTS AND SWEETS

BEVERAGES

HOT CIDER PUNCH

8 Servings

Great after hunting or skiing

- 3 cups sweet cider
- ½ cup brown sugar
- ¼ cup butter
- Cinnamon sticks
- 1 bottle (fifth) light rum

In a saucepan combine the cider, brown sugar and butter; heat until melted. Add the cinnamon sticks (1 or 2 to taste); simmer about 20 minutes. Add to the rum and simmer about 10 minutes, but do not boil. Serve in mugs.

Mrs. John S. Jenkins
(Mary Lou Cudlip)

HOT SPICED CIDER

- 8 pieces stick cinnamon (2-inches each)
- 1 T. whole cloves
- 1 T. whole allspice
- ½ tsp. mace
- ½ tsp. salt
- Dash of cayenne pepper
- 1 cup brown sugar
- 1 gallon cider

Tie spices loosely in a cheesecloth bag. Add spices and brown sugar to cider. Bring slowly to boiling point. Simmer 15 minutes. Remove spice bag and serve hot.

Mrs. Thomas N. Boyden
(Susan B. Dalton)

APPLE VELVET

1 Serving

- ½ cup spiced cider, chilled (see above recipe)
- 1½ oz. applejack or calvados
- 1 egg white, unbeaten
- 2 ice cubes, cracked
- Nutmeg

Combine chilled spiced cider with applejack and egg white. Add cracked ice cubes and shake. Strain drink into a glass. Grind a little fresh nutmeg on top.

Mrs. Dennis F. Muckermann
(Betty Graham)

BULL SHOTS

4 Servings

1 can (10¾ oz.) bouillon
5½ oz. vodka
2 T. lime juice
1 can (16 oz.) cocktail vegetable juice
Dash worcestershire sauce
Dash hot pepper juice
⅛ lime or 1 celery stick per glass

Combine the first six ingredients and chill thoroughly. When ready to serve, add the lime or celery sticks.

Mrs. John N. Schmidt
(Joan Slauson)

HORS D'OEUVRES AND APPETIZERS

COCKTAIL MEATBALLS — Makes 20

1 lb. ground beef
1 egg
Salt and pepper
Garlic salt
MSG
6 oz. cranberry jelly
1 cup tomato sauce
3 T. lemon juice

Thoroughly mix meat, egg and seasonings; form into small balls. Mix jelly, tomato sauce and lemon juice. Simmer for 1 hour. Bake meatballs at 350° for 7 to 10 minutes. Add sauce to meat; bake 1 hour at 350°.

Miss Gabriele Weissenberger

MUSHROOM PATE — 3-4 Small Molds

2 lbs. unsalted butter
2½ lbs. fresh mushrooms, sliced
1 lb. chicken or calves' liver
1½ T. salt
1½ T. pepper
1½ T. curry powder

In a skillet saute mushrooms in ½ lb. butter. In another skillet saute livers in ½ lb. butter. Cream remaining 1 lb. butter. Add half the salt, pepper and curry to the mushrooms while they are cooking and the other half to the liver. Mix the sauteed mushrooms and liver together; chop coarsely. Put some of the creamed butter in blender. Add some of the chopped mixture and blend until smooth but not runny. Check seasonings; add more to taste. Place in 3 or 4 small molds. Refrigerate; or freeze if you do not intend to use in a week. Unmold and leave at room temperature 30 minutes before serving. Serve with Bremmer wafers and triangles of black pumpernickel bread.

Mrs. H. Alex Vance, Jr.
(Melinda Martin)

BAGNA CAUDA

8-12 Servings

This Italian "fondue" is ideal for a light, non-filling hors d'oeuvre

- ½ cup butter
- ½ cup olive oil
- 4 cloves garlic, slivered
- 2 T. anchovy paste
- Assorted fresh vegetables

In fondue pot, melt butter with oil and garlic. Add anchovy paste. Let mixture bubble slowly about 5 minutes. Place over flame. Let guests dip fresh vegetables briefly into hot mixture. Suggested raw vegetables: carrot sticks, celery sticks, cauliflowerettes, green pepper strips, zucchini strips, whole fresh mushrooms. Bread sticks may also be used.

Mrs. Phillip J. Stover
(Annette Ashlock)

SAUSAGE KRAUT BALLS

6 Servings

- 8 oz. sausage meat, crumbled
- ⅓ cup onion, finely-chopped
- 1 can (16 oz.) sauerkraut, drained and chopped
- 2 T. dry bread crumbs
- 1 pkg. (3 oz.) cream cheese, softened
- 2 T. parsley
- 1 tsp. prepared mustard
- 1 garlic clove, pressed
- ¼ tsp. pepper
- ¼ cup flour
- 2 eggs, well-beaten
- ¼ cup milk
- 1 cup bread crumbs

Saute sausage and onion until meat is brown. Pour off fat. Add sauerkraut and 2 T. bread crumbs. Combine cream cheese, parsley, mustard, garlic and pepper; stir into sauerkraut mixture. Refrigerate. Shape mixture into small balls; coat with flour. Add the milk to the eggs and dip each ball into it. Roll balls in bread crumbs. Fry in deep fat until golden brown. Just before serving bake balls at 375° for 15 to 20 minutes.

Mrs. Gilbert P. George
(Ann Sullivan)

LIPTAUER CHEESE

6 Servings

A Hungarian cheese spread

- 1 pkg. (8 oz.) cream cheese
- ¼ cup sour cream
- ¼ cup softened butter
- 2 tsp. anchovy paste
- 2 tsp. drained capers
- 2 shallots, chopped
- ⅛ tsp. salt
- 1 T. paprika
- ½ tsp. dry mustard
- 1 oz. ale or beer

Mix all ingredients well in blender. Pour in bowl and refrigerate several hours. Serve with crackers.

Mrs. William F. Zwilling
(Diane Poppen)

DeFOREST'S CAVIAR PIE

6 Servings

- 3 hard-cooked eggs, finely-chopped
- 1 T. Bermuda onion, finely-chopped
- 5 T. butter, melted
- 1 jar caviar
- 1 cup sour cream

Combine eggs and onions with melted butter. Line a small (soup plate) shallow dish with plastic wrap and press mixture into it. Refrigerate until hard. Turn mixture out of mold and cover with caviar. Top with a thin layer of sour cream. Serve with melba toast and lemon wedges.

Mrs. Bruce G. Southworth
(Mary Monek)

CURRIED CHEESE SPREAD WITH CHUTNEY

10 Servings

- 6 oz. cream cheese
- 8 oz. sharp cheddar cheese spread
- 3 T. sherry
- ½ tsp. curry
- ¼ tsp. salt
- MSG
- 10 oz. chutney
- ¼ cup minced scallions

Mix all ingredients except chutney and onions with an electric beater. Spread in a shallow dish and chill until firm. Before serving spread chopped chutney over cheese mixture and cover with green onions. Serve with wheat or rye crackers.

Mrs. John W. Bradbury
(Mary Nolen)

COCKTAIL BRUSSELS SPROUTS

1 box fresh brussels sprouts
Water
½ tsp. salt
Juice from dill pickles

Cover sprouts with water; add salt. Cook until just barely tender. Cool and place in reserved liquid from pickle recipe below. Cover and refrigerate 12 hours. Serve with toothpicks as an appetizer.

Mrs. Edward C. McNally
(Margaret McGann)

REFRIGERATOR DILL PICKLES

1 qt. non-garlic dill pickles
2 cups sugar
1 cup cider vinegar
2½ oz. horseradish
1 sliced onion
2 tsp. dry mustard

Drain pickles, reserving liquid. Cut in small spears or circles; place pickles in a glass container. Cover with remaining ingredients. Place in refrigerator for 7 days, stirring occasionally.

Mrs. Gilbert P. George
(Ann Sullivan)

BEEF JERKY

Delicious and healthy snack for your family

Flank steak
Soy sauce
Lemon pepper
Garlic salt

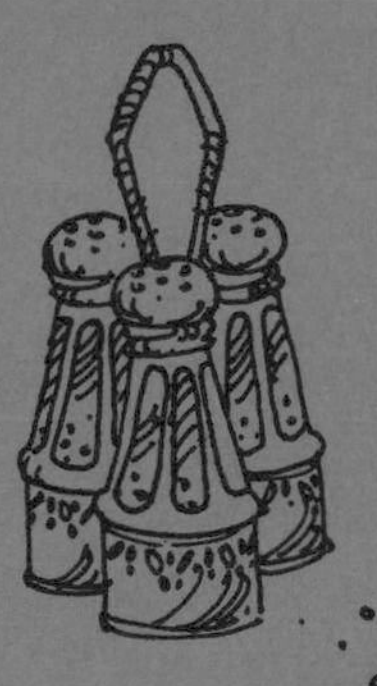

Trim steak of all fat and cut in ¼-inch thick lengthwise strips. Marinate in soy sauce 1 hour. Place strips of meat on a rack over a cookie sheet; sprinkle with lemon pepper and garlic salt. Turn and sprinkle other side. Bake at 150° for 12 hours or overnight. Strips should be chewy and not brittle. If brittle, the oven was too hot. Store in a tin.

Mrs. H. Alex Vance, Jr.
(Melinda Martin)

BACON DATE ROLL-UP 8 Servings (3-4 each)

1 lb. bacon
1 pkg. (8 oz.) dates, pitted

Wrap a half of a piece of bacon around a date and broil low in the oven until crisp. Insert a toothpick in each; serve hot.

Mrs. Peter F. Theis
(Jill Pendexter)

MARINATED SHRIMP PUFFS 3-4 Dozen

4 doz. small shrimp
1 bottle 1890's French dressing
Salt
1 or 2 large garlic cloves, pressed
2 pkgs. (8 oz. each) cream cheese, softened
2 egg yolks
½ tsp. baking powder
4 doz. bread rounds, toasted on one side
1 T. grated onion

Marinate shrimp in dressing overnight. Dissolve a dash of salt in garlic. Mix cream cheese, onion, garlic, yolks and baking powder. Place a dab of this mixture on untoasted side of bread rounds. Place a shrimp on top of each. Place another dab of mixture on top piped through a large star pastry tube. Place under broiler until puffy and lightly browned on top.

Mrs. Patrick Callahan
(Patricia Henebry)

MEXICAN QUICHE 6 Servings

A delicious, unusual appetizer

1 can (10 oz.) roasted, peeled green chilies (do not use jalapeno chilies), seeds removed
1 lb. mild cheddar cheese, grated
3 T. milk or cream
1 T. chili juice
1 egg

Line a 9-inch pie pan with the green chilies. Top with cheese. Mix the milk, chili juice and egg; pour over cheese. Bake at 350° for 40 to 45 minutes or until golden and bubbly. Slice in wedges; serve hot.

Mrs. William J. Morgan
(Keithley Piatt)

MUSHROOM TARTS

48 Tarts; 12 Servings

PASTRY:

- **⅔ cup butter**
- **2½ cups sifted flour**
- **½ tsp. salt**
- **⅓ cup sour cream**
- **1 egg, slightly beaten**

FILLING:

- **½ lb. fresh mushrooms, finely-chopped**
- **2 T. minced green onions**
- **¼ cup butter**
- **¼ cup flour**
- **½ tsp. salt**
- **1 cup whipping cream**

Cut butter into flour and salt mixture. Thoroughly blend in sour cream and egg. Press into ball. Using about 1 tsp. dough, press into bottom and sides of midget muffin pans (1¼-inches across). Bake at 400° about 12 minutes or until golden. Cool. To remove from shells, hit lightly on counter to loosen. May be frozen.

For filling, saute mushrooms and onions in butter. Stir in flour and salt. Add cream; cook, stirring constantly, until thick and smooth. Fill pastry shells ¾ full with mixture. Bake at 400° about 12-15 minutes. These may be made a day or two ahead. The filled pastry may be frozen, but defrost 1 hour before reheating.

Mrs. John N. Schmidt
(Joan Slauson)

SNAILS IN MUSHROOM CAPS

6 Servings, 4 Each

- **3 T. minced parsley**
- **3 T. minced scallions**
- **3 garlic cloves, pressed**
- **6 T. butter**
- **Salt and pepper**
- **Nutmeg**
- **2 doz. medium fresh mushrooms**
- **2 doz. snails, rinsed (7 oz. can)**

Mix parsley, scallions, garlic and butter well. Add salt and pepper to taste and a pinch of nutmeg. Remove stems from mushrooms and fill with the butter mixture. Place a snail in each mushroom cap and top with more of the butter mixture. Place in an escargot pan or on a cookie sheet; bake at 400° for about 10 minutes. Serve as a first course or pass as an appetizer.

Mrs. Denis R. Chaudruc
(Jeannene Nixon)

SOUPS

PUMPKIN SOUP

8 Servings

This may be served hot or cold

4 green onions and tops, sliced
1 onion, sliced
2 carrots, sliced
4 T. butter, melted
1 can (29 oz.) pumpkin
5 cups chicken stock
Salt to taste
½ tsp. garlic powder
2 T. flour
1 cup whipping cream
½ cup tiny home-made croutons
½ cup heavy cream, whipped

Saute all the onions and carrots in 3 T. butter until soft. Add the pumpkin and stock; blend well. Add salt to taste and garlic powder; simmer about 25 minutes. Mix the flour and 1 T. softened butter; stir into soup. Bring to a boil; remove from heat and puree in a blender. Add the cream. Return soup to heat and bring to a boil. If served cold, refrigerate until thoroughly chilled. Garnish each serving with whipped cream and croutons.

Mrs. Thomas O. Hodgkins
(Mary Ann BonDurant)

CHEESE BEER SOUP

8 Servings

¼ cup butter, melted
½ cup flour
1½ qts. chicken stock
½ cup finely-chopped onion
½ cup finely-chopped celery
½ cup finely-chopped carrots
½ lb. cheddar cheese, cubed
1½ cups milk
1 can (12 oz.) beer
½ cup chopped parsley
½ tsp. salt
Dash white pepper

Add flour to butter and brown. Slowly add stock, stirring constantly with a wisk. Cook until slightly thickened. Add vegetables; simmer 20 minutes. Stir cheese until melted. Add milk and beer; reduce heat immediately. Add parsley and cook at reduced heat another 5 minutes. Season to taste with salt and dash of white pepper. Serve hot.

Mrs. Bruce G. Southworth
(Mary Monek)

CRANBERRY BORSCH

6 Servings

- ½ cup chopped shallots
- 1 T. butter
- 1 can (1 lb.) whole beets
- 3 cups chicken broth
- 1 lb. fresh cranberries
- ¼ cup Madeira
- 1 T. lemon juice
- Salt and pepper
- Sour cream or whipped cream

Saute the shallots in butter. Chop beets and puree them in blender with the liquid and shallots. Set aside. Simmer the cranberries in stock about 5 to 7 minutes. Puree the cranberries and stock in a blender and pass them through a sieve. Combine both purees with Madeira and lemon juice. Salt and pepper to taste. Serve hot or chilled garnished with sour cream or whipped cream.

Mrs. Benson T. Caswell
(Margaret Graham)

CREAM OF CHESTNUT SOUP

8 Servings

A very rich soup

- 3 carrots, chopped
- 2 leeks, chopped
- 3 celery stalks, chopped
- 1 onion, finely-sliced
- 2 T. butter, melted
- 1½ to 2 lbs. fresh chestnuts, cooked, shelled, peeled
- 6 cups chicken stock
- Small bunch parsley
- 3 whole cloves
- ½ to 1 cup light cream
- 2 T. calvados apple brandy
- Salt, pepper and MSG to taste

Brown the carrots, leeks, celery and onion in butter. Add the chestnuts, stock, parsley and cloves. Simmer the soup 1 hour. Reserve 8 whole chestnuts for garnish. Puree the soup in the blender. Return to heat. Add ½ cup cream—more if a thinner consistency is desired. Add the calvados. Adjust seasonings and heat to boiling point. Serve warm with whole chestnuts on top.

Mrs. Gilbert P. George
(Ann Sullivan)

CURRIED EGGPLANT SOUP

8 Servings

4 T. butter
2 cups cubed, unpeeled eggplant
Salt and pepper
½ cup chopped onion
1 tsp. mashed garlic
1 T. curry powder
½ tsp. crushed rosemary
½ tsp. crushed chervil
Bouquet garni
5 cups chicken or beef stock
1 cup whipping cream
2 egg yolks
¾ cup macadamia nuts
Chopped parsley

Melt 2 T. butter in a saucepan. Add eggplant with a little salt and pepper; cook until golden. In another pan saute onion and garlic with salt and pepper in 2 T. butter until onion is limp. Add seasonings, stock and eggplant. Cover and simmer for 20 minutes. Remove bouquet. Blend thoroughly in blender. Add the cream which has been mixed with the yolks. Add ½ cup pulverized macadamia nuts and blend. Check flavor for salt, pepper and curry. Serve hot garnished with parsley and a few chopped macadamia nuts.

Mrs. H. Alex Vance, Jr.
(Melinda Martin)

JOHN'S LENTIL SOUP

8 Servings

1 cup chopped onions
4 tsp. bacon drippings
1 cup dried lentils
1 clove garlic, pressed
2 tsp. salt
1 tsp. freshly- ground pepper
2 smoked pork shanks or 1 ham bone
1 bay leaf
2 whole cloves
1½ cups sliced carrots
2 qts. cold water
2 cups cubed red potatoes
Frankfurters
Yogurt

Saute onions in bacon drippings until glossy. Add lentils, garlic, salt and pepper; stir until onion turns yellow and lentils begin to make a noise. Add pork shanks, bay leaf, cloves tied in cheesecloth, and the carrots. Add the water and bring to a gentle boil. Cover; simmer about 30 minutes. Add potatoes and cook 1½ hours. Before serving, remove cheesecloth and pass soup through food mill, reserving the whole beans if desired. Thin with water if necessary; season to taste. Garnish with sliced frankfurters and yogurt.

Mrs. John L. Tuohy
(Ann Lea)

PERSIMMON CURRANT BREAD

2 Loaves

- **2 cups fresh persimmon pulp (about 4 very ripe persimmons)**
- **1 T. lemon juice**
- **2 tsp. soda**
- **2 cups currants**
- **2 cups chopped almonds**
- **2 cups sugar**
- **2 T. salad oil**
- **3 cups flour**
- **¼ tsp. ground cloves**
- **2 tsp. cinnamon**
- **2 tsp. salt**
- **1 cup milk**

Mix persimmon pulp with lemon juice and soda. Mix currants, almonds and sugar together. Stir in oil. Add the persimmon pulp. Sift remaining dry ingredients and mix into fruit, alternating with milk. Divide batter into 2 greased 8½ x 4½-inch loaf pans. Bake at 325° for about 1 hour and 30 minutes. Cool in pan 10 minutes. Turn out on rack and cool. Serve with butter or use for a cream cheese sandwich.

Mrs. Dennis F. Muckermann
(Elizabeth Graham)

APPLESAUCE NUT LOAF

1 Loaf

- **½ cup butter**
- **¾ cup sugar**
- **2 eggs**
- **2 cups flour**
- **2½ tsp. baking powder**
- **1 tsp. salt**
- **½ tsp. baking soda**
- **1 tsp. cinnamon**
- **½ tsp. allspice**
- **1¼ cups applesauce**
- **½ cup pitted dates, cut up**
- **½ cup nuts, chopped**

TOPPING: (Optional)

- **¼ cup brown sugar**
- **½ tsp. cinnamon**
- **¾ cup nuts, chopped**

Cream butter and sugar. Beat in eggs one at a time. Combine flour, baking powder, salt, soda, and spices. Add flour mixture to creamed mixture, alternating with applesauce, reserving a little dry mixture to coat dates and nuts. Coat dates and nuts in flour; stir into batter. Pour into an 8½ x 4½ x 2⅝ inch loaf pan. Combine topping ingredients and sprinkle evenly over batter. Bake at 350° for 60 to 70 minutes. Cool in pan on a rack for 10 minutes, turn out of pan to cool.

Mrs. Philip G. Sosinski
(Nan Van Arsdale)

CRANBERRY BREAD

1 Loaf

- **2 cups sifted flour**
- **½ tsp. salt**
- **1½ tsp. baking powder**
- **½ tsp. baking soda**
- **1 cup sugar**
- **¼ cup melted butter**
- **½ cup orange juice**
- **1 egg, well beaten**
- **1 T. grated orange rind**
- **1 to 2 cups fresh cranberries, halved**
- **¾ cup chopped walnuts or pecans**

Sift flour with salt, baking powder, baking soda and sugar. Mix butter with orange juice, egg and orange rind. Add to dry ingredients, stirring quickly to moisten. Stir in berries and nuts. Pour into well greased loaf pan (8½x4½x2⅝). Bake at 350° for one hour or until top is golden and toothpick inserted in center comes out clean.

Mrs. Edward W. Hobler
(Barbara Talley)

HONEY BREAD

1 Loaf

This is wonderful with curry dishes

- **1 pkg. active dry yeast**
- **¼ cup lukewarm water (110-115°)**
- **1 egg**
- **½ cup honey**
- **1½ T. ground coriander**
- **1 tsp. ground cinnamon**
- **¼ tsp. ground cloves**
- **1½ tsp. salt**
- **1 cup lukewarm milk (110-115°)**
- **6 T. melted unsalted butter**
- **5 cups flour**

Sprinkle yeast over warm water and let stand for 2 to 3 minutes, stirring to dissolve yeast completely. Set bowl in warm draft-free place for about 5 minutes. Combine egg, honey, coriander, cinnamon, cloves and salt in a deep bowl; mix together with a wire whisk. Add yeast mixture, milk and 4 T. melted butter; beat until well blended. Stir in flour ½ cup at a time. When stiff, blend in additional flour with your fingers and knead dough until smooth and elastic. Shape into a ball; place in a large buttered bowl. Drape a kitchen towel over. Set in a warm draft-free spot for about 1 hour or until dough doubles in bulk. With a pastry brush, spread remaining butter over bottom and sides of a 3-qt. baking dish (3-inches deep). Punch dough down and knead again for 2 minutes. Shape dough into a round bulk and place in baking dish, pressing down so it covers the bottom of the dish completely. Let stand in warm draft-free place for about 1 hour or until double in bulk. Bake at 300° for 50 to 60 minutes, or until crusty and golden. Turn onto a cake rack to cool.

Mrs. Thomas C. O'Neil
(Jane Stephens)

PUMPKIN BREAD

2 Loaves

3 cups sugar
1 cup oil
4 eggs
Rind of 1 lemon, grated
2½ cups pumpkin
3½ cups flour
½ tsp. salt
2 tsp. soda
1 tsp. nutmeg
1 tsp. cinnamon
1 tsp. pumpkin pie spice
1 tsp. cloves
1½ cups walnuts, chopped

Mix the sugar and oil well. Beat in eggs one at a time. Add lemon rind and pumpkin. Sift the dry ingredients together; stir in nuts so they are well coated. Gradually add the dry ingredients to pumpkin mixture, blending thoroughly. Pour the batter into 2 well greased loaf pans (9 x 5 x 2¾). Bake at 350° about 1 hour 10 minutes. Toothpick inserted in center should come out clean. Place loaves on a cake rack to cool for 10 minutes before removing from pans.

Mrs. Ernest V. Hodge
(Claire Burghardt)

CARAMEL CURRANT ROLLS

3 Dozen Large Rolls

2 pkg. active dry yeast
½ cup water
2 cups milk
⅔ cup butter
2 eggs, beaten
½ cup sugar
1 tsp. salt
Grated rind 1 lemon
½ cup currants
5¾ to 6 cups flour
2 T. melted butter

FILLING MIXTURE:
2 cups brown sugar
2 T. cinnamon
1 cup ground pecans

TOPPING MIXTURE:
1½ cups brown sugar
¾ cup light corn syrup
6 T. butter
¾ cup chopped pecans

Dissolve yeast in lukewarm water. Scald milk; cool to lukewarm. Add butter to milk; stir in eggs, sugar, salt, lemon rind and currants. Add to yeast mixture. Add enough flour to make a soft dough. Let dough rise to double its bulk. Divide into thirds and work with only ⅓ at a time. Roll dough on floured board into a rectangular shape ¼-inch thick. Brush 2 T. melted butter over the surface. Sprinkle ⅓ filling mixture on top. Starting with the long side, roll dough jelly-roll fashion. Cut into 1-inch slices.

Combine topping ingredients; spread about 1 T. of mixture in each greased muffin tin. Place the slices on top of mixture and let rise until double in bulk. Bake at 350° for 20 to 25 minutes. Immediately remove rolls from tins. Cool.

Mrs. H. Alex Vance, Jr.
(Melinda Martin)

CHOCOLATE PRETZELS

2 Dozen

½ cup butter
¼ cup sugar
¼ cup unsweetened cocoa
3 T. hot water
2 cups flour
1 egg
1 tsp. vanilla

GLAZE:

½ cup milk
½ cup light corn syrup
⅔ cup sugar
2 oz. sweet chocolate
2 oz. unsweetened chocolate
1 tsp. butter

Cream butter and sugar. Dissolve cocoa in hot water and let cool. Beat cooled cocoa into butter. Gradually beat in the flour. Add the egg and vanilla. Shape dough into a 7 x 2-inch cylinder. Wrap in waxed paper and refrigerate 30 minutes. Slice dough into ½-inch rounds and roll each slice between hands to make rope-like length 14 x ¼-inch. Shape into a pretzel and arrange on ungreased baking sheet. Bake at 350° for 10 minutes. Cool on cake rack and dip into glaze. Dry for 15 minutes on waxed paper.

Glaze: Combine all ingredients in top of double boiler and cook until sugar is dissolved and chocolate melted, stirring constantly. Add 1 tsp. butter; remove from heat. Cool to lukewarm.

Mrs. Robert W. Buckley, Jr.
(Ann Middleton)

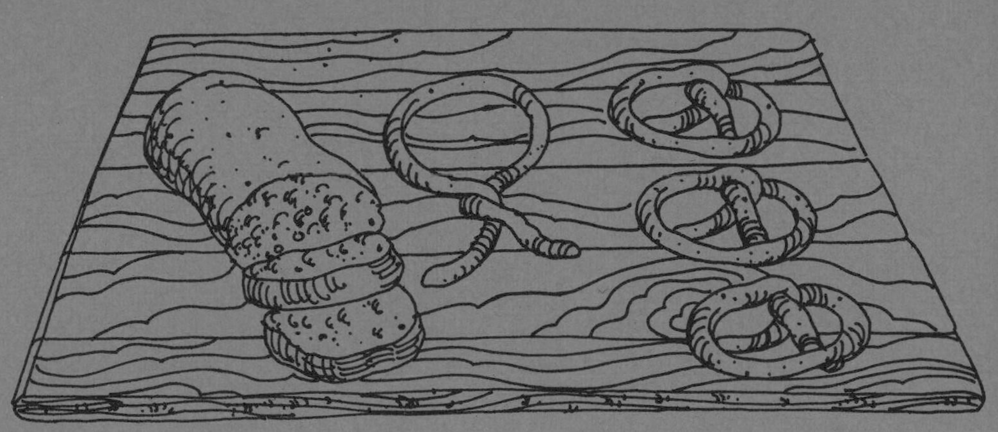

CHOCOLATE DONUTS — 3 Dozen

Have them for breakfast or with Irish coffee in late morning

2 eggs
1¼ cups sugar
3 oz. unsweetened chocolate
2 T. butter
1 cup buttermilk
1½ tsp. vanilla
4 cups flour
1 tsp. soda
1 tsp. cinnamon
½ tsp. nutmeg
¼ tsp. salt

Beat eggs and sugar until thick and lemon colored. Melt chocolate and butter over hot water; add to egg mixture. Stir in buttermilk and vanilla. Sift dry ingredients together; stir into liquid mixture. Refrigerate at least 1 hour or overnight. Divide dough in thirds. Roll out on floured board; cut all donuts before starting to fry. Heat fat to 360°. Cook in deep fat about 6 minutes, turning at least twice on each side. Remove to brown paper to drain. Shake donuts in a bag of granulated sugar to coat. Donuts are best when warmed in loosely wrapped foil before serving. Donuts may be frozen in air-tight container and heated in a 250° oven for about 15 minutes before serving.

Mrs. H. Alex Vance, Jr.
(Melinda Martin)

APRICOT NUT SQUARES — 2-3 Dozen

These are excellent for a coffee or tea

1 cup butter
2 cups flour
½ tsp. baking powder
1 pkg. (8 oz.) cream cheese
1 jar (8 oz.) apricot jam
1 cup ground pecans

VARIATION: substitute poppy seed filling for jam and pecans.

Mix first four ingredients together, roll into a ball. Chill several hours. Make filling by mixing jam and nuts together. Using ¼ of the dough at a time, roll out, cut it into 2-inch squares, fill with 1 tsp. filling and top with another pastry square. Seal around edges with a fork. Bake at 375° for 15 to 20 minutes. Sprinkle with powdered sugar. These can be frozen before baking.

Mrs. Charles H. Lueck, Jr.
(Annabelle Perry)

PUMPKIN PANCAKES

5 Servings

- **2 cups all-purpose flour**
- **2 T. sugar**
- **4 tsp. baking powder**
- **1 tsp. salt**
- **1 tsp. cinnamon**
- **1½ cups milk**
- **1 cup canned pumpkin**
- **4 eggs, separated**
- **¼ cup melted butter**

Sift together all dry ingredients. Combine milk, pumpkin, egg yolks, and butter; stir into the dry ingredients until just blended. Beat the egg whites until stiff; fold into the batter. Pour about a ⅓ of a cup at a time onto a hot, lightly-greased griddle. Cook until top is bubbly; turn. Cook the other side until browned. Serve with butter and pure maple syrup.

Mrs. H. Alex Vance, Jr.
(Melinda Martin)

SKILLET APPLE PANCAKE

3-4 Servings

- **3 eggs**
- **½ cup milk**
- **⅓ cup flour**
- **¼ tsp. salt**
- **2 green apples**
- **2 T. lemon juice**
- **¼ cup butter**
- **¼ cup sugar**
- **¼ tsp. cinnamon**
- **Calvados or lemon juice**

In a blender mix eggs, milk, flour, and salt; blend until smooth. Let the batter stand at room temperature 1 hour. Core, peel and thinly slice the apples; sprinkle with 2 T. lemon juice. In a heavy 12-inch skillet, melt 2 T. butter; pour in the batter. Cover with apple slices and bake at 375° for 10 to 15 minutes. Slide the pancake onto a serving dish and spread with 2 T. softened butter. Combine sugar and cinnamon; sprinkle over apples. Drizzle pancake with Calvados or lemon juice to taste.

Mrs. John C. Munson
(Virginia Aldrich)

TURKEY MORNAY

6 Servings

2 pkgs. (10 oz. each) frozen broccoli spears, cooked until tender-crisp
¼ lb. thinly-sliced prosciutto
1 lb. sliced cooked breast of turkey
¼ cup butter
¼ cup flour
1 cup rich chicken broth
1 cup light cream
2 T. grated parmesan cheese
2 T. grated swiss cheese
2 T. sherry
Salt to taste
Dash cayenne
¼ cup grated parmesan cheese

Drain broccoli and arrange it in a baking dish. Cover with the prosciutto, then with the turkey. Melt butter and blend in flour. Stir in the chicken stock and cream; cook, stirring constantly, until smooth and thick. Stir in cheeses, sherry, salt, and cayenne. Heat just until cheese is melted. Pour sauce over turkey; sprinkle with ¼ cup grated parmesan. Bake at 350° F. until the sauce is hot and the cheese brown and bubbly, about 30 minutes.

Mrs. David B. Smith
(Marcia Williamson)

CHICKEN RAISIN CASSEROLE

4-6 Servings

This may also be made with pheasant

1 chicken, (2½ lbs.), cut up
¼ cup butter
2 T. olive oil
1 onion, chopped
1 clove garlic, pressed
1 green pepper, chopped
2 T. flour
½ cup white wine
½ cup chicken broth
2 tomatoes, coarsely chopped
1 cup golden raisins
½ tsp. salt
Freshly-ground pepper
½ tsp. basil
Parsley for garnish
Wild rice

Brown chicken in butter and oil. Transfer to a large greased casserole. Saute onion, green pepper and garlic in remaining oil for about 3 minutes. Stir in flour. Add wine, chicken broth, tomatoes and raisins; simmer several minutes. Pour over chicken in casserole. Salt and pepper to taste. Bake in casserole at 300° for 1 hour, covered. About 10 minutes before done sprinkle basil on top. Serve on bed of wild rice.

Miss Monica Postell

CREAMED CHICKEN WITH MELON — 4 Servings

This makes a lovely fall luncheon

- 2 whole chicken breasts, boned
- 2 T. butter
- 1 small onion, chopped
- 4 oz. mushrooms,
- ½ cup apple cider or white wine
- ¼ tsp. ginger
- ¼ tsp. cinnamon
- ½ tsp. salt
- ⅛ tsp. pepper
- ½ tsp. grated lime peel
- 1 T. lime juice
- 2 T. flour
- 1 cup half and half
- Chow mein noodles
- 2 cups melon balls (cantaloupe, honeydew or Persian)

Lightly brown chicken in butter. Add onions and mushrooms and cook until lightly browned. Stir in juice or wine, ginger, cinnamon, salt, pepper, lime peel and juice. Cover and simmer until chicken is just tender, about 15 minutes. Blend the flour to a paste with the cream; gradually stir into mixture in pan. Cook and stir until thickened. Simmer 3 minutes. To serve, arrange chicken over the noodles and top with sauce. Garnish with melon balls.

Mrs. John N. Schmidt
(Joan Slauson)

CHEESE ENTREE FOR BRUNCH — 8 Servings

- 8 slices day-old bread, crusts removed
- 1½ lbs. sharp cheddar cheese, grated
- 6 eggs, lightly beaten
- 2½ cups cream (or more)
- 1 tsp. brown sugar
- ¼ tsp. paprika
- 1 green onion, minced
- ½ tsp. dry mustard
- ½ tsp. salt
- ½ tsp. worcestershire sauce
- ⅛ tsp. cayenne
- ⅛ tsp. pepper

VARIATION:
A layer of cooked sausage may be added before each layer of cheese.

Butter bread generously and cut into ¼-inch squares. Butter a 2-qt. casserole and arrange bread on bottom. Cover with half the cheese. Add another layer of bread and remaining cheese. Mix all remaining ingredients and pour over cheese. Add more cream if liquid doesn't reach top of bread. Cover well and keep refrigerated 24 hours. Two hours before serving, let stand at room temperature for ½ hour. Place in shallow pan with water 1-inch deep. Bake at 300° for 1 hour. Leave in oven an extra 20 minutes with oven off or until ready to serve.

Mrs. R. Barksdale Collins
(Lynn Snyder)

SCALLOPS WITH SAFFRON — 12-16 Servings

3 lbs. scallops
2 cups dry white wine
Rind of ½ lemon
¼ tsp. Tabasco sauce
1 tsp. worcestershire sauce
1 clove garlic, pressed
Salt and pepper to taste
1 leek, minced
¼ lb. butter
½ cup flour
1 tsp. dry mustard
1 tsp. saffron
1 cup cream
2 cans (7½ oz. each) crabmeat
Grated swiss cheese
Paprika

Cover scallops with wine, lemon, Tabasco, worcestershire, garlic, salt and pepper. Simmer about 10 minutes. In a separate saucepan saute the leek in butter until transparent. Remove from heat; stir in flour, mustard and saffron. Add wine sauce from the scallops and cream. Cook, stirring constantly, until thick. Put the scallops in sea shells; sprinkle with parsley and crabmeat. Pour a little sauce over each; top with cheese and paprika. Bake at 350° for 20 minutes.

Mrs. Robert E. King
(Emily Hauser)

CRAB LASAGNE — 8 Servings

½ lb. lasagne noodles
1 T. oil
2 cans (10½ oz. each) cream of shrimp soup
1 lb. crabmeat
2 cups small curd cottage cheese
1 pkg. (8 oz.) cream cheese
1 egg, slightly beaten
1 medium onion, chopped
2 tsp. basil
½ tsp. lemon juice
Salt and pepper
2 tomatoes, thinly sliced
Shredded cheddar cheese

Cook noodles in salted water with 1 T. oil added for 15 minutes. Drain and rinse in cold water. Combine soup and crab. In separate bowl mix cottage and cream cheeses, egg, onion, basil, lemon juice, and salt and pepper to taste. In large shallow buttered casserole place one layer of noodles, half cheese mixture and all the crab mixture. Cover with another layer of noodles and remaining cheese. Top with layer of tomatoes. Bake 15 minutes at 350°. Add layer of cheddar cheese and return to oven for 30 minutes or until brown and bubbly. Let stand several minutes before cutting in squares. Can be prepared a day ahead and refrigerated before baking.

Mrs. Kennedy W. Gilchrist
(Lynn Olson)

CAMEMBERT TART — 4 Servings

A nice quiche variation

- 4 slices ham
- 3 T. butter
- 8 small scallions, chopped
- 1 cup soft camembert cheese
- ½ cup parmesan cheese
- 4 eggs, beaten
- 2 cups whipping cream
- Dash of nutmeg
- Dash of white pepper
- 1 baked 9-inch pastry shell

Cut ham into thin strips and saute in butter. Remove ham and saute the onions until just wilted. Drain onions and combine with ham. Spread this mixture evenly over the bottom of the pastry shell. Spread camembert cheese over ham mixture; sprinkle with parmesan cheese. Beat eggs and cream, add nutmeg and pepper, and pour over the cheese. Bake at 325° for 30 minutes or until the custard is set.

Mrs. Patrick W. O'Brien
(Deborah Bissell)

ZWIEBELKUCHEN — 6-8 Servings

This German onion pie may also be served as an appetizer

PASTRY:

- ¼ lb. butter
- ¾ cup flour
- ½ cup small curd creamed cottage cheese
- Salt to taste

FILLING:

- 2 lbs. onions, diced
- ¼ lb. butter
- 3 eggs plus 1 yolk
- 2 to 3 tsp. caraway seeds
- Salt and freshly-ground pepper
- 3 slices bacon, fried crisp, crumbled

Mix all pastry ingredients well. Form into a ball; wrap in foil and place in refrigerator to chill well. Roll to ¼-inch thickness and line a 9-inch pie plate with dough. Flute edge.

Saute onions in butter until golden and clear. Cool. Mix eggs with onions, add seasonings and pour into pie shell. Top with bacon. Bake at 350° for 1 hour.

Mrs. Halbert S. Gillette
(Karla Spiel)

SYRIAN SANDWICHES

6 Servings

Perfect for a tailgate picnic

- **1 lb. hamburger**
- **3 T. tomato sauce**
- **½ pkg. chili sauce mix**

FILLINGS:

- **¼ head lettuce, shredded**
- **1 cup shredded cheddar cheese**
- **2 tomatoes, chopped**
- **1 jar pepperoncini peppers**
- **1 Bermuda onion, sliced-thinly**
- **6 loaves Syrian (pita) bread (comes frozen in boxes)**

Fry meat until brown. Add tomato sauce and chili mix. Put fillings in separate bowls; keep meat hot. Toast Syrian bread 3 to 5 min. at 400° or until crisp and hot. (Middle should pop up a bit.) Cut in half so that pocket forms. Each guest fills his bread half with mixture of ingredients. You can substitute mixed salami and pepperoni for hamburger if used for a picnic. Syrian bread will stay soft if wrapped in foil after heating.

Mrs. Walter Alexander
(Karen Bisgard)

TOMATO TART

6 Servings

- **3 ripe tomatoes**
- **1 unbaked 9-inch pastry shell**
- **1 small onion, finely-chopped**
- **2 T. butter**
- **3 eggs**
- **1½ cups whipping cream**
- **Salt and pepper**
- **¾ cup grated Swiss cheese**

Peel tomatoes, slice in half horizontally and gently squeeze out juice and seeds. Place, cut side down or in overlapping slices, in pastry shell. Saute onion in butter until soft; scatter over tomatoes. Beat eggs and cream together; season with salt and pepper. Pour over tomatoes. Sprinkle with cheese; bake at 325° for about 1 hour or until knife comes out clean.

Mrs. James F. Peil
(Nancy Rodgers)

RED BEANS AND RICE

6 Servings

This is a typical New Orleans entree
"It brings good luck all week to eat red beans and rice on Monday."

- **1 lb. red beans**
- **1 T. bacon drippings**
- **1 ham hock**
- **2 large onions, chopped**
- **2 cloves garlic, pressed**
- **1 tsp. salt**
- **½ tsp. pepper**
- **¼ tsp. red pepper**
- **4 cups water**
- **Cooked white rice**

VARIATION:

Serve with pork chops if meat is desired.

Wash beans and soak in water to cover overnight. Drain. Heat drippings in saucepan; add ham hock. Saute 10 minutes. Remove hock. Stir in onions and garlic; saute 5 minutes. Add beans, seasonings, water and ham hock. Bring to a boil, cover and cook over low heat about 6 hours. Stir and mash frequently during last 2 hours of cooking. Serve with cooked white rice.

Mrs. Victor W. Ulrich
(Ernestine Christ)

ARGENTINE AUTUMN STEW

12 Servings

A most colorful sweet stew

- **4 lbs. rump or chuck, cut in cubes**
- **2 T. butter**
- **4 medium onions, chopped**
- **3 cloves garlic, pressed**
- **2 large green peppers, chopped**
- **2 large tomatoes, peeled and chopped**
- **2 tsp. salt**
- **½ tsp. pepper**
- **2 tsp. sugar**
- **2 cans (10½ oz. each) beef broth or consomme**
- **2 doz. dried prunes**
- **2 lb. dried apricots**
- **6 yams, skinned and cubed**
- **4 pkgs. (10 oz. each) kernal corn**
- **¾ cup Madeira wine**
- **5 T. cornstarch**
- **1 pumpkin (about 8 qt. size)**

WINE SUGGESTION:
Beaujolais

Saute meat in a little butter until brown and put in an 8 qt. kettle. Saute onions, garlic, green peppers and combine with meat. Mix in all other ingredients except pumpkin; cover and simmer for 1 hour. Mix cornstarch with a little pan liquid and blend into sauce. Cut the top off the pumpkin, remove seeds and membrane and fill pumpkin with stew. Bake at 325° for 1 hour. Place pumpkin on large platter and serve from it.

Miss Heather Ramsey

BEEF TARRAGON

6 Servings

1 cup flour
2 tsp. tarragon
3 lbs. boneless beef stew meat or sirloin tip
3 T. olive oil
1 clove garlic, pressed
½ cup tarragon, red wine vinegar
1 cup beef broth
1 T. sugar
5 oz. mushrooms, sliced and sauteed in 3 T. butter
1 bunch green onions, chopped

WINE SUGGESTION:
Vintage Zinfandel

Mix flour and tarragon; coat meat. Heat oil, add garlic and brown meat. Add vinegar, beef broth and sugar; cover and simmer for 2½ hours. Check several times to see if more beef broth is needed. Add mushrooms and onions; simmer another 10 minutes. If too thin, thicken with a little flour mixed with cold water. Serve with noodles or wild rice.

Mrs. Gordon B. MacDonald
(Virginia Fagan)

BEEF NICOISE

4-5 Servings

2 large onions, chopped
6 cloves garlic, pressed
½ cup olive oil
2 large tomatoes, peeled and cut into sections
⅔ cup pitted black olives
3 T. capers
½ cup tomato puree
½ cup beef gravy
2 tsp. MSG
1 tsp. basil
¼ tsp. oregano
1 tsp. sugar
Salt and pepper
1 cup chopped parsley
2 lbs. fillet of beef, cubed

WINE SUGGESTION:
Rully

Saute onions and garlic in ¼ cup olive oil until tender. Add tomatoes, olives and capers. When mixture begins to bubble stir in tomato puree, gravy, seasonings and half of parsley. Cook mixture until slightly thick. Set aside. Heat remaining oil; saute beef cubes quickly over high heat. They should be rare. Combine beef and olive-tomato mixture. Taste for seasonings. Sprinkle with chopped parsley.

Mrs. H. Alex Vance, Jr.
(Melinda Martin)

NEW ENGLAND ROAST

8 Servings

- 1 boned and rolled bottom round beef roast (4 lbs.), or beef arm or blade
- 3 T. flour
- 2 tsp. salt
- ¼ tsp. pepper
- 3 T. bacon drippings or oil
- 1 cup whole cranberry sauce
- 1 stick cinnamon, broken in half
- 4 whole cloves
- 1 cup beef broth
- ½ cup horseradish
- 16 small onions
- 1 bunch carrots, cut in 3-inch lengths

WINE SUGGESTION:
Julienas

Dredge meat in mixture of flour, salt and pepper; brown in oil. Combine cranberry sauce, cinnamon, cloves, broth, and horseradish; add to meat. Bring beef to a boil; cover tightly and simmer 2 hours or until meat is barely tender. In separate skillet, brown onions and carrots; add to meat and cook another 25 minutes or until meat and vegetables are tender. Serve with noodles or potatoes.

Miss Sue Drymalski

SWEDISH MEATBALLS

6 Servings

- 2 eggs, slightly beaten
- 1 cup milk
- ½ cup bread crumbs
- 3 T. butter
- ½ cup chopped onion
- 1 lb. ground chuck
- ½ lb. ground pork
- 2 tsp. salt
- ¾ tsp. dill weed
- ¼ tsp. allspice
- ⅛ tsp. cardamon
- 3 T. flour
- ¼ tsp. pepper
- 1 can (10½ oz.) beef broth
- ½ cup cream

WINE SUGGESTION:
California Gamay Beaujolais

Combine the eggs, milk and dry bread crumbs in a large bowl. Saute onion in 1 T. butter until soft. Add onions to bread crumb mixture along with meat, 1½ tsp. salt, ¼ tsp. dill weed, allspice, and cardamon. Mix well. Refrigerate until mixture can be shaped into 1-inch meatballs. In 2 T. butter saute meatballs until well browned. Remove meatballs to a 2-qt. casserole. Reserve 2 T. butter or drippings in skillet. Add flour, ½ tsp. salt, and pepper; cook until smooth. Gradually add beef broth, stirring constantly. Bring to boiling point; stir in cream and ½ tsp. dill weed. Pour over meat balls; bake at 325° for 30 minutes. Serve with green noodles.

Mrs. John C. Munson
(Virginia Aldrich)

INDIVIDUAL BEEF WELLINGTON

10 Servings

May be prepared in stages over a 4 or 5 day period

MEAT AND MARINADE:

- 1 whole fillet of beef
- Suet to cover fillet
- 1 tsp. salt
- ½ cup olive oil
- ½ cup sliced onions
- ½ cup sliced carrots
- ½ cup sliced celery
- ¼ tsp. thyme
- ¼ tsp. sage
- 1 bay leaf
- 10 peppercorns
- 2 cups dry vermouth
- ½ cup cognac

PASTRY:

- 6 cups flour
- 1 T. salt
- 1 cup butter
- 1½ cups shortening
- 2 eggs, well beaten
- 2 T. vinegar
- ⅔ cup cold water

MUSHROOM FILLING:

- 3 lbs. mushrooms, finely-chopped
- 3 T. butter
- ⅔ cup finely-minced shallots
- ¾ cup Madeira
- Salt and pepper
- 8 oz. foie gras

MADEIRA SAUCE:

- Marinade
- Mushroom juices
- 2 cups beef bouillon
- 1 T. tomato paste
- 2 T. cornstarch
- ½ cup Madeira

WINE SUGGESTION:
Chambertin

Sprinkle beef with salt; place in tight-fitting casserole. Cook vegetables and herbs in oil until tender. Cover with oil-vegetable mixture, vermouth, and cognac. Cover and refrigerate 24 to 72 hours, turning occasionally.

Pastry: Mix flour and salt. Cut in butter and shortening. Combine egg, vinegar, and water. Mix with flour until all can be formed into a ball. Divide pastry into 10 equal balls. Refrigerate until 1 hour before using. (If you want decorations, make an extra half recipe of pastry.)

Filling: Twist mushrooms a handful at a time in the corner of a strong linen towel to extract as much juice as possible. Save juice. Saute mushrooms with shallots in butter 10 minutes. Add madeira; boil until liquid has evaporated. Salt and pepper to taste. Beat in the foie gras; refrigerate.

Preliminary Baking: Remove meat from marinade; scrape off vegetables. Reserve marinade together with mushroom juice for the sauce. Place suet on top of fillet; roast 15 min. in a preheated 425° oven. Let cool or refrigerate until ready to use.

Assembling and Baking: Slice meat into 10 equal pieces about 1¼-inches thick. On a sheet of waxed paper, roll out a ball of pastry into a 10-inch circle. Spread some mushroom mixture in center of dough. Place fillet on top and pat more mushroom mixture around sides and top. Wrap dough around fillet. Seal bottom, removing any excess pastry. Place, seam side down, on a cookie sheet; pat with hands to reshape. Make a small hole top center for steam to escape; decorate around it with pastry cut-outs.

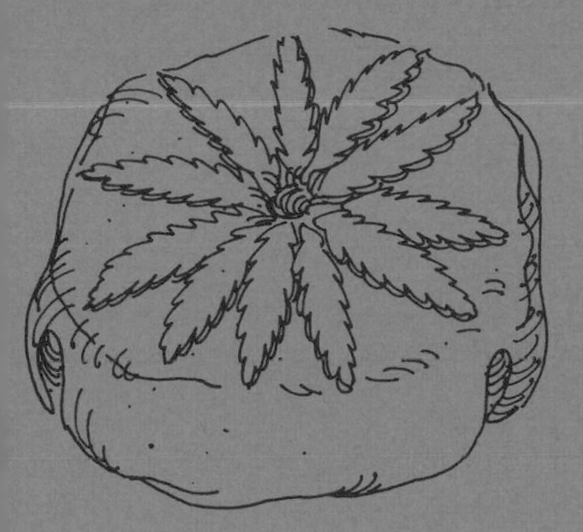

Refrigerate overnight or freeze. If frozen, wrap individually very tightly in freezer wrap. Defrost in refrigerator 6 hours before baking. When ready to bake, brush each pastry with egg glaze (2 eggs beaten with 2 tsp. water). Bake for 25 to 35 minutes at 425° or to 140° on a meat thermometer inserted in center hole in pastry. Let rest 20 minutes in a warm place before serving.

Simmer marinade, mushroom juice, bouillon and tomato paste for 1 hour, or until reduced to 2 cups. Strain, season, and thicken with cornstarch blended with madeira. Pass sauce separately.

Mrs. H. Alex Vance, Jr.
(Melinda Martin)

CUMBERLAND SAUCE

This is excellent with duck or beef wellington

1 jar (12 oz.) currant jelly
¼ to ½ cup red wine
Grated rind of 1 orange
½ tsp. ground ginger
½ tsp. prepared Dijon mustard
1 T. lemon juice
Arrowroot
¼ cup dried currants

VARIATION FOR BEEF:

Beef drippings (or bacon grease)
2 to 3 T. flour
1 can (13¾ oz.) beef consomme

Melt jelly; add wine, orange rind, ginger, mustard and lemon juice. Thicken with arrowroot mixed with a little wine. Add currants.

For Beef Wellington: Make gravy from drippings from first cooking of beef, flour, and consomme; stir in cumberland sauce.

Mrs. Halbert S. Gillette
(Karla Spiel)

CALVES' LIVER NORMANDY

4-6 Servings

8 slices calves' liver
Flour
3 onions, finely-sliced
2 T. bacon drippings
7 T. butter
4 tart apples, peeled, sliced
Salt and pepper
1 lb. bacon, cooked, crumbled
1 T. oil
2 T. chopped fresh parsley

WINE SUGGESTION:
Volnay

Flour liver well and shake off excess. Saute onions in bacon drippings and 2 T. butter until they are yellow. Add apples and salt and pepper to taste. Cover and cook 5 minutes. Add bacon and cook another 5 minutes. Meanwhile, in another pan, melt 3 T. butter and 1 T. oil. When very hot, quickly saute liver for 2 to 3 minutes on each side. Remove liver to serving plate. Melt 2 T. butter; add parsley. Pour over liver. Place apple mixture on top of liver.

Mrs. John C. Munson
(Virginia Aldrich)

BUTTERMILK SAUERBRATEN

6-8 Servings

This is an unusual German recipe

1 beef pot roast (3 to 4 lbs.)
1 qt. buttermilk
Salt and pepper
Oil or bacon drippings
1 onion, thinly-sliced
1 carrot, thinly-sliced
1 stalk celery, thinly-sliced
1 bay leaf
5 peppercorns
2 whole cloves
12 caraway seeds
½ cup sour cream
¼ cup flour
1 tsp. sugar

WINE SUGGESTION:
German Rhine Wine

Marinate meat for two days in buttermilk, in refrigerator, turning occasionally. Wipe meat dry with paper towels. Sprinkle with salt and pepper; brown well on both sides in oil or drippings. Remove meat from pan. Cook onion, carrots and celery in a little butter until wilted. Add meat. Pour in 1 cup marinade and enough water to cover meat (pan should be close-fitting); add bay leaf, peppercorns, cloves and caraway seeds. Cover and simmer, turning occasionally, until done, about 2 to 2½ hours, adding more water if necessary. Remove meat to hot platter. Stir flour into sour cream along with a little water to make a smooth paste. Stir into gravy. Simmer over a very low heat until thick. Adjust seasonings and add sugar. Return meat to saucepan and let simmer a few minutes before serving. Arrange sliced meat on a platter, pour over some of the gravy and serve the rest separately. Delicious with red cabbage cooked with apples, raisins and a touch of nutmeg.

Mrs. James F. Peil
(Nancy Rodgers)

FRENCH VEAL ROLLS

6 Servings

6 large veal cutlets
½ cup bread crumbs
¼ cup milk
¼ lb. bulk pork sausage, cooked
¼ cup chopped onion
½ clove garlic, minced
2 slices bacon, cooked and diced
1 T. minced parsley
1 egg yolk
2 T. fat
2 cups consomme
1 T. flour
Parsley
6 slices lemon

WINE SUGGESTION:
Mercurey

Pound veal until it is ¼-inch thick. Combine crumbs with milk; mix with sausage, onion, garlic, bacon, parsley and egg yolk. Put 1 T. filling across the center of each piece of veal; roll up, securing with a wooden pick. Heat fat in a skillet; saute veal rolls until browned. Add consomme and simmer until done, 45 to 60 minutes. Thicken liquid with flour. Place veal rolls on platter, cover with sauce and garnish with parsley and lemon slices.

Mrs. David B. Smith
(Marcia Williamson)

OSSO BUCO

8 Servings

A hearty and unusual Italian speciality from Giovanni's Restaurant in New York

8 veal shanks, 2-inches tall
¼ cup flour
¼ tsp. pepper
¼ tsp. salt
½ cup olive oil
2 onions, minced
2 carrots, minced
2 celery stalks, minced
1 cup marsala wine
1 cup beef broth
1 can (1 lb. 12 oz.) tomatoes, drained
2 cloves garlic
½ tsp. rosemary
½ tsp. basil

WINE SUGGESTION:
Valpolicella

Preheat oven to 350°. Flour and season shanks. Brown in ¼ cup hot oil until dark and crusty. In separate pan, saute onions, carrots and celery in ¼ cup oil; put in a large casserole. Place veal on top of vegetables with bones up to retain bone marrow. To drippings in meat skillet, add wine, broth, tomatoes and herbs; cook and stir to boiling. Pour over veal. Bake, covered, 1½ to 2 hours or until meat falls off bone. To serve, remove meat to warm platter and either strain or mash vegetables in sauce; pour over meat. Serve with herbed rice.

Mrs. John R. Gardner
(Catherine Corrigall)

PISTACHIO-STUFFED VEAL CHOPS

8 Servings

- **8 veal or pork rib chops, 1-inch thick**
- **½ lb. twice ground pork**
- **3 T. finely-chopped shallots**
- **½ cup finely-chopped onion**
- **1 clove garlic, pressed**
- **¼ lb. raw chicken livers, chopped**
- **¾ cup finely-chopped ham**
- **½ cup fresh bread crumbs**
- **¼ cup shelled pistachios**
- **2 T. chopped parsley**
- **1 beaten egg**
- **1 T. cognac**
- **Salt, pepper**
- **2 T. butter**
- **2 cups tomato sauce (see below)**
- **½ cup dry white wine**
- **1 tsp. tarragon**

TOMATO SAUCE:

- **½ lb. fresh mushrooms, sliced**
- **3 T. olive oil**
- **1 cup finely-chopped onion**
- **1 garlic clove, minced**
- **2 T. butter**
- **1 can (17 oz.) Italian plum tomatoes**
- **Salt and pepper**
- **¼ tsp. sugar**
- **½ tsp. thyme**
- **½ tsp. basil**
- **1 bay leaf**
- **2 T. tomato paste**
- **½ cup water**

WINE SUGGESTION:
Cotes du Rhone

Butterfly the chops and pound each side to flatten slightly. Brown ground pork in a skillet; add shallots, onion and garlic. Cook until meat looses pink color. Stir in chicken livers; cook briefly. Take off heat; mix in ham, crumbs, pistachios, crumbs, parsley, egg, cognac, and salt and pepper to taste. Cool. Spoon equal portions of mixture inside each split chop. Sew with string. Heat butter in skillet and brown chops on both sides. Cover and place in a 350° oven for 30 minutes. Pour off fat; add tomato sauce combined with white wine and tarragon. Cover and bake 10 to 15 minutes longer. Remove strings and serve chops on a mound of hot buttered noodles; pour tomato sauce over each chop.

Sauce: Saute mushrooms in oil. Saute onion and garlic in separate pan in butter. Add mushrooms and remaining ingredients. Simmer 45 minutes. Remove bay leaf.

Mrs. James F. Peil
(Nancy Rodgers)

VEAL CHASSEUR

6 Servings

2 lbs. veal cutlet, thinly sliced
¼ cup butter
2 minced shallots
1 lb. fresh mushrooms, sliced
½ cup dry white wine
2 T. chopped parsley
1 tsp. salt
Ground black pepper

BROWN SAUCE:

1 onion, chopped
¼ cup diced celery
1 large carrot, chopped
1 clove garlic, pressed
½ cup butter
3 T. cornstarch
3 cups beef broth
2 T. Madeira wine
½ tsp. thyme
½ tsp. salt
1 large bay leaf
6 peppercorns

WINE SUGGESTION:
Hermitage

Brown veal in butter on both sides; remove from pan. Add vegetables; saute about 5 minutes. Add wine and cook about 10 minutes at low heat until liquid is reduced to half. Stir in brown sauce, salt, pepper, parsley and meat. Cook about 5 minutes. Serve with wild rice.

Brown Sauce: Saute vegetables in butter. Stir cornstarch into cold broth; stir into vegetable mixture. Add all other ingredients. Cook and stir until mixture comes to a boil. Cover and simmer about 30 minutes. Strain.

Mrs. Donald J. Ross
(Cynthia Stiles)

PORK CHOPS AND APRICOTS IN CURRY SAUCE

8 Servings

8 thick pork chops
Salt, pepper, Italian herbs
1 can (16 ozs.) halved apricots
8 ozs. fresh mushrooms, sliced
2 medium onions, sliced
2 T. butter
2 cans (10½ ozs. each) condensed cream of mushroom soup
½ cup dry white wine
1 T. curry powder

WINE SUGGESTION:
Hermitage Blanc

Place chops in large shallow baking dish. Sprinkle lightly with salt, pepper, and herbs. Drain apricots, reserving ½ cup juice. Place 2 apricot halves on each chop, skin side up. Saute mushrooms and onions in butter until onion is soft. Stir in soup, wine apricot juice, and curry powder; pour over chops. Bake, uncovered, at 350°, for 1 hour.

Mrs. Charles G. Stemwedel
(Nancy McDonough)

CRANBERRY-STUFFED PORK CHOPS — 8 Servings

1 small onion, minced
½ cup chopped celery
1 T. butter
1 cup fresh cranberries, chopped
1 cup fresh bread crumbs
3 T. sugar
1 tsp. salt
1 tsp. grated orange rind
¼ tsp. sage
1 T. chopped parsley
Salt and pepper
8 loin pork chops with pocket

WINE SUGGESTION:
Ruby Cabernet

Saute onion and celery in butter. Combine with remaining ingredients except pork; mix well. Stuff pork chops with mixture, close openings with skewers or toothpicks. Add salt and pepper to taste; brown chops on both sides. Place in a baking dish. Bake, covered, about 40 minutes at 350°

Mrs. Benson T. Caswell
(Margaret Graham)

CINNAMON ORANGE SAUCE FOR PORK — 2 Cups

1¼ cups sugar
2 T. cornstarch
1 tsp. salt
1 tsp. cinnamon
1 T. whole cloves
2½ T. grated orange rind
1 cup orange juice

In a saucepan combine all ingredients. Cook over medium heat, stirring constantly, until thickened and clear. Serve sauce with pork chops or pork roasts.

Mrs. Thomas C. O'Neil
(Jane Stephens)

CHERRY SAUCE FOR PORK ROAST — 2 Cups

1 jar (12 oz.) cherry preserves
¼ cup light corn syrup
¼ cup red wine vinegar
¼ tsp. salt
¼ tsp. ground cloves
¼ tsp. ground nutmeg
¼ tsp. cinnamon
¼ to ½ cup toasted slivered almonds

Combine all ingredients except almonds and simmer 5 minutes. Add almonds; serve warm.

Mrs. Thomas D. Hodgkins
(Mary Ann BonDurant)

JEWELLED CROWN PORK ROAST WITH CHAMPAGNE STUFFING

8 Servings (2 Ribs Each)

1 crown roast of pork (16 ribs)
3 T. lime juice
1 T. flour
1 tsp. ginger
1 tsp. salt
½ tsp. freshly-ground pepper
2 cups champagne or dry white wine
3 chicken bouillon cubes
2 T. flour
Parsley
Clusters of green grapes
Small red crabapples
8 preserved kumquats

STUFFING:

1 cup finely-chopped onion
½ cup crushed pineapple, drained
4 strips bacon, cooked, crumbled
½ cup ripe olives, chopped
1 cup chopped fresh mushrooms
2 eggs, beaten
2 T. minced parsley
1 cup finely-chopped celery, lightly sauteed
2 cups cooked wild rice (cook in champagne or white wine)
1 tsp. marjoram
½ tsp. thyme

WINE SUGGESTION:
Chateauneuf du Pape

Place roast on rack in baking pan; pour lime juice over it. Mix flour, ginger, salt, and pepper; sprinkle over meat. Roast at 350° for 35 minutes per lb. After first hour of roasting, remove meat from oven. Drain fat from pan; remove rack and fill center with stuffing. Return roast to pan; cover stuffing. Continue baking until done. Place remaining stuffing in a tightly-covered casserole; bake about 1 hour. Drain off all fat but 3 T. Heat 1½ cups wine with bouillon until dissolved. Mix flour and remaining ½ cup cold wine; over low heat stir into drippings. Then add hot wine. Cook, stirring, until thick. To serve, place pork on a platter; surround with a wreath of parsley. Place bunches of green grapes on top of parsley. Place red crabapples between the clumps of grapes. Spear kumquats on every other rib.

Mrs. David Marchant
(Brenda Suit)

GEORGE'S CHOUCROUTE GARNI — 12 Servings

A specialty from the Alsation region of France

- 2 onions, stuck with 12 whole cloves
- 2 carrots, sliced in half
- 3 qts. sauerkraut (or more), drained and rinsed
- Coarsely-ground pepper
- 2 racks baby back ribs
- 6 pork chops
- 2 lbs. ham
- 6 bratwurst
- 6 knockwurst

SAUCE:

For each 2 cups drained sauerkraut mix:

- ¾ cup chicken broth
- ¾ cup beef broth
- ⅓ cup white wine
- 1 jigger gin

WINE SUGGESTION:
Alsatian Gewurztraminer

Rub bottom of large oven proof casserole with fat. Place vegetables on bottom. Add 1-inch layer of sauerkraut; press tightly. Add ground pepper. Place a layer of the mixed meats on top of sauerkraut (except knockwurst). Add another layer of sauerkraut. Continue layering until meat is used, finishing with a layer of sauerkraut and leaving several inches at top. Pour sauce over top. Cover and bake at 300° for 3 to 4 hours. Do not stir or open oven for 2 hours. Then lay the knockwurst on top. Most of the liquid should have evaporated at the end of 4 hours. Serve on a large platter arranging sauerkraut in a mound and piling meat around it. Serve with a baked potato, mustard and beer. No salad is necessary. If prepared in advance, reheat at 325° for 1 hour.

Mrs. Bruce G. Southworth
(Mary Monek)

STUFFED CHICKEN BREASTS WITH HAZELNUTS

8 Servings

1 lb. bulk sausage
4 cans (10½ oz. each) consomme
1 can water
½ lb. fresh mushrooms, sliced and lightly sauteed
2 cups dry wild rice
8 whole chicken breasts, skinned and boned
¼ cup butter
1 cup coarsely-chopped hazelnuts
8 slices bacon
1 cup sherry

WINE SUGGESTION:
California Vintage Pinot Chardonnay

Partially cook bulk sausage; pour off half the fat. In large casserole add consomme, water, mushrooms, rice and sausage. Cover and bake 1¼ hours at 325°. Brown chicken in butter until golden. Add hazelnuts to rice mixture. Stuff cavity of chicken breasts with rice mixture; wrap slice of bacon around each breast. Spread remaining rice mixture in large flat baking dish; place chicken on top. Pour sherry over all. Cover tightly with foil; bake at 350° for about 1½ hours or until chicken is tender.

Mrs. Phillip G. Prange
(Catherine Connor)

CHICKEN WITH PLUM SAUCE

8 Servings

2 frying chickens, quartered
½ tsp. onion salt
½ tsp. garlic salt
1 medium onion, chopped
2 T. butter
1 can (6 oz.) frozen lemonade concentrate
⅔ cup chili sauce
1 jar (12 oz.) plum preserves
1 T. soy sauce
2 tsp. prepared mustard
1 tsp. ginger

WINE SUGGESTION:
Dole (Swiss Red)

Season chicken with onion and garlic salt; brown under broiler 5 to 10 minutes. In a small saucepan saute onion in butter until tender. Add remaining ingredients; simmer 15 minutes. Place chicken in single layer in baking pan; pour sauce over. Bake at 350°, basting occasionally, 45 minutes or until tender.

Mrs. William D. Roddy
(Joanne McDonald)

SPANISH PAELLA

8-10 Servings

- 2 cloves garlic, pressed
- ½ tsp. thyme
- ½ tsp. coriander
- Salt
- 1 T. wine vinegar
- ½ cup olive oil
- 1 chicken (2½ lbs.), cup up
- ¼ lb. salt pork, diced
- 1 lb. raw medium shrimp, shelled and deveined
- 2 chorizos (Spanish sausages) or hot Italian sausages
- ¾ cup chopped onion
- 1 tsp. saffron
- 2 T. capers
- ⅓ cup fresh tomatoes, peeled and chopped
- ½ cup dry white wine
- 2½ cups uncooked rice
- 3½ cups chicken stock
- Freshly-ground pepper
- 20 mussels, scrub and remove the beards
- 20 small clams, scrubbed
- 1 lobster (2 lbs.) boiled until tender
- 1 pkg. (10 oz.) frozen artichoke hearts, partly thawed
- ⅔ cup freshly cooked or frozen peas
- 1 can (4 oz.) pimientos
- 1 tsp. anise liqueur, Pernod or Ricard
- Lemon wedges

WINE SUGGESTION:
French Chablis

In a large bowl, combine the garlic, thyme, coriander, 1 tsp. salt,, vinegar, and oil. Coat the chicken pieces with the mixture and allow to stand at least 40 minutes before cooking. In a 6-qt. flameproof casserole or paella pan, saute pork until fat is rendered and pork is brown. Remove and reserve. Saute shrimp in pork fat until bright pink; remove and reserve. In the same pan, fry chorizos until cooked, about 20 minutes. Slice and reserve. Brown coated chicken pieces in fat remaining in pan. Sprinkle with the onion, saffron, capers, and tomatoes. Return pork pieces to the pan. Add wine, rice, and chicken broth. Season with salt and pepper to taste. Cover and simmer gently about 15 minutes. Steam the mussels and clams in ¼ cup water until they open, about 5 minutes. Discard any that do not open. Remove meat from body of lobster; slice. Reserve whole claws. Add the lobster, shrimp, artichoke hearts, and peas to the chicken and rice. Cook, uncovered, 5 to 10 minutes. (If needed, add liquid from mussels and clams or more chicken broth. The rice should be moist but there should be no excess moisture.) Add pimientos, liqueur, and the chorizos. Garnish with mussels, lobster claws, and clams. Cover and place in 350° oven to reheat. Reduce to 200° to keep warm before serving. Garnish with lemon wedges.

Mrs. Denis R. Chaudruc
(Jeannene Nixon)

TUNISIAN COUSCOUS

10-12 Servings

Taught to me by a Tunisian friend's mother while visiting in their Tunis home

2 boxes (1 lb. each) couscous
Water
Salt
Olive oil
4 whole chicken breasts, split
4 chicken legs and thighs, not split
¾ cup butter
16 small white onions
1 can (15 oz.) tomato sauce
1 T. coriander
2 tsp. black pepper
2 tsp. cumin
6 large carrots, cut in 2-inch pieces
6 turnips, peeled and quartered
4 potatoes, peeled and quartered
2 cans (20 oz. each) chick peas (garbanzos)

WINE SUGGESTION:
Cotes de Provence Blanc

Place couscous in a large bowl; add 2 cups cold water, 2 ½ tsp. salt, 2 T. olive oil. Rub couscous between palms of hands until water is absorbed and each grain soft. In bottom of couscoussier place 3 inches water; bring to a boil. Line streamer (top) of couscoussier with cheese cloth; add couscous. Place steamer over bottom; cover and cook 45 minutes. Check to be sure couscous is steaming properly. In a large skillet brown chicken in ½ cup butter. Remove chicken and brown onions. Reserve both. Remove steamer; add 2 T. butter and salt to taste to couscous. Mix until all grains are well coated. Discard water from bottom section. Heat ½ cup olive oil in bottom; add onions and chicken. Mix tomato sauce, coriander, pepper, cumin, and 1 tsp. salt. Pour tomato mixture over chicken; cook 20 minutes. Add carrots, turnips, and potatoes to chicken; add just enough water to cover all ingredients. Place top of steamer over vegetables; continue steaming 20 minutes. Add 2 T. butter to couscous; steam another 20 minutes. Add chick peas to vegetables during last 10 minutes. Remove steamer; moisten couscous with 1 ½ cups liquid from bottom. To serve, heap couscous in center of a large platter. Place vegetables around edges and arrange chicken on sides and top.

NOTE: A special couscous cooker called a "couscoussier" is ideal for this dish, but a large colander snugly fitted above a deep 8 qt. kettle and lid may be improvised.

Mrs. H. Alex Vance, Jr.
(Melinda Martin)

SAGE STUFFING WITH CURRANTS

For 6-8 lb. Bird

This is excellent for a goose, duck or turkey

- 1 large onion, chopped
- ½ cup chopped celery
- ¼ cup butter, melted
- 6 cups stale cubed bread
- ⅔ cup currants
- 1 tsp. dried sage
- 2 T. chopped parsley
- Grated rind of 1 large lemon
- 1 tsp. salt
- ½ tsp. freshly-ground pepper
- 1 T. lemon juice
- Dry white wine or vermouth
- 2 tart apples, peeled and chopped

Saute onion and celery in butter until transparent; toss with bread. Add remaining ingredients, including enough wine just to moisten. Season the cavity of bird with salt and pepper. Stuff very lightly, using any left over stuffing under the neck skin.

Mrs. James F. Peil
(Nancy Rodgers)

OYSTER STUFFING

For 6-8 lb. Bird

For goose, duck or turkey

- 1 onion, chopped
- ½ cup celery, chopped
- ¼ cup butter, melted
- 1 goose, turkey or duck liver, chopped
- 6 cups stale ¼-inch bread cubes
- 1 pint oysters
- 1 egg, lightly beaten
- 2 T. chopped parsley
- 1 tsp. salt
- ½ tsp. freshly-ground pepper
- ½ tsp. thyme
- ¼ tsp. marjoram

Saute onion and celery in butter until transparent. Add liver; cook quickly 2 or 3 minutes. Toss with bread. Strain oyster liquor through cheesecloth or a fine sieve if it is gritty, and bring to a boil. Add cleaned oysters. Simmer 3 minutes or until edges just curl. Skim out the oysters and cut in quarters (or halves if small). Add to the bread. Mix in remaining ingredients and enough oyster liquor (about ⅓ cup) to moisten dressing. Season the cavity with salt and pepper; stuff very lightly, using any leftover stuffing under the neck skin.

Mrs. James F. Peil
(Nancy Rodgers)

TURKEY DRESSING WITH SAUSAGE AND CHESTNUTS

For 10-lb. Bird

1 loaf (1 lb.) day-old bread, cubed
1 T. salt
1 tsp. thyme
1 tsp. pepper
1 tsp. oregano
1 ½ cups minced onion
Chopped liver from turkey
½ cup butter
1 lb. country-style sausage
½ lb. cooked ham, ground
½ cup minced celery
⅓ cup minced parsley
3 eggs
½ cup cream
1 ½ lbs. braised chestnuts, shelled and peeled

WINE SUGGESTION:
California Johannisberg Riesling

Brown bread in 275° oven. Put bread in large bowl; add seasonings. Saute onions and liver in butter for 10 minutes. Add sausage; simmer for 5 minutes. Add ham, celery, and parsley; remove from heat. Add to bread and mix. Lightly beat eggs and cream; add to mixture. Chop chestnuts; add to bread mixture. Let cool completely. Season cavity with salt and pepper; stuff bird.

Miss Mary Whaley

SPICY ORANGE TURKEY SAUCE

About 2 cups

Also excellent with barbecued turkey

1 cup fresh orange juice
¼ cup butter
¼ cup honey
¼ cup chopped parsley
¼ cup soy sauce
Juice of 1 large lemon
1 T. dry mustard
2 garlic cloves, pressed

Mix all ingredients in saucepan; heat until blended. Use as a basting sauce for turkey, basting frequently. Turkey will brown quickly because of soy sauce, so you should cover bird with foil. Serve remaining sauce with turkey. Variation: Pour this sauce over several cut up chickens and bake at 350° for 1 hour, basting occasionally.

Mrs. Harrison I. Steans
(Lois Mae Morrison)

PHEASANT JUBILEE

8 Servings

4 pheasants, quartered
Flour
½ cup butter
1 onion, chopped
¾ cup seedless raisins
1 cup chili sauce
½ cup water
½ cup brown sugar
2 T. worcestershire sauce
¼ tsp. garlic powder
1 cup sherry
1 can (1 lb.) pitted dark sweet cherries, drained

WINE SUGGESTION:
Cabernet Sauvignon

Shake pheasants in flour; remove excess. Brown in butter. Place birds in a deep casserole. In the same skillet, combine onion, raisins, chili sauce, water, brown sugar, worcestershire and garlic. Bring to a boil. Pour over pheasants; cover and bake at 325° for 1 hour. Add sherry and cherries; bake another 20 minutes, uncovered, or until pheasants are tender.

Mrs. Dennis F. Muckermann
(Elizabeth Graham)

PHEASANT SUPREME

4 Servings

2 pheasants
Salt and pepper
2 apples, peeled and quartered
1 cup dry vermouth mixed with 1 cup water
2 T. butter
2 T. flour
¼ cup currant jelly
1 tsp. garlic powder
Pinch of curry powder
1 cup whipping cream
½ cup dry vermouth
¾ cup drippings

WINE SUGGESTION:
Pauillac

Sprinkle birds with salt and pepper; stuff apples. Roast on rack at 450° for 45 minutes. Baste every 15 minutes. with drippings and watered vermouth. (This prevents bird from drying.)

For sauce, melt butter; stir in flour. Add jelly, garlic powder, curry, cream and vermouth. Cook and stir until thickened. Stir in drippings. Add salt and pepper to taste. Cut pheasants into serving pieces and pass the sauce.

Mrs. Allan Bulley, Jr.
(Sallie Jo Bell)

PHEASANT IN SOUR CREAM — 8 Servings

6 pheasant halves or breasts
Salt and pepper
½ cup butter
2 T. grated onion
1 lb. sliced mushrooms
1 cup chicken broth
¼ cup brandy
2 T. dry sherry
1 cup sour cream
1 T. caraway seeds (optional)

WINE SUGGESTION:
Margaux

Season pheasants with salt and pepper; saute in butter until golden brown. Remove from skillet; saute onions and mushrooms in same butter until brown. Return birds to pan; add broth and simmer, covered, for 45 minutes or until tender. Remove pheasants; keep warm. Add brandy and sherry to pan; simmer 5 minutes. Stir in sour cream and caraway seeds. Simmer very gently for 2 minutes, stirring constantly. Do not boil. Pour sauce over pheasants and serve.

Mrs. J.A. Kreston
(Jeannette Boston)

ROAST QUAIL WITH PORT SAUCE — 6 Servings (2 Each)

12 ready to cook quail
½ T. salt
¼ cup chopped scallions
1 tsp. dried tarragon
12 strips bacon, simmered in water for 10 minutes
Butter
2 T. cooking oil

PORT SAUCE:

1 T. minced scallions
1 T. drippings
1 T. butter
1½ cups beef bouillon
¼ cup port

WINE SUGGESTION:
Nuits St. George

Season the cavities with salt, scallions and tarragon. Truss birds; rub with butter. Tie bacon strips around the breast of each bird. Place birds on rack. Bake at 400° for 30 to 40 minutes, basting every 10 minutes with mixture of ¼ cup melted butter and the cooking oil. For sauce, saute scallions in butter and fat from roasting pan. Add bouillon and port; boil rapidly for several minutes. Check seasonings. Spoon sauce over whole birds and serve.

Mrs. H. Dorn Stewart, Jr.
(Judith Collins)

WILD DUCKS IN HONEY

4-8 Servings

2 Mallard ducks

GAME MARINADE:

2 onions, sliced
2 carrots, sliced
2 cloves
4 crushed peppercorns
1 bay leaf
2 cloves garlic, crushed
4 sprigs parsley
2 juniper berries
3 cups red wine
1 cup olive oil
1 cup vinegar

STUFFING AND BASTING SAUCE:

4 T. salt
2 T. ground ginger
2 T. basil
1 T. freshly-ground pepper
2 cups honey
½ cup butter
¼ cup orange juice
3 T. lemon juice
2 T. grated orange rind
¼ T. dry mustard
2 oranges, sliced into 6 wedges
2 T. potato flour
¼ cup cognac

WINE SUGGESTION:
St. Emilion

Season ducks with salt and pepper and place in ceramic casseroles. Scatter vegetables and spices over them. Combine the wine, oil and vinegar; pour over ducks. Cover; place in refrigerator for 5 days, turning occasionally. Remove ducks from marinade; pat dry inside and out. Combine salt, ginger, basil and pepper. Rub half of this mixture inside ducks. Combine honey, butter, orange juice, lemon juice, orange peel, mustard and salt to taste in top of double boiler; heat thoroughly. Rub 3 T. honey mixture inside each duck. Stuff ducks with as many orange wedges as possible. Spoon 4 T. more of the honey mixture into each duck. Truss. Rub remaining basil mixture outside ducks. Place each duck on a large sheet of aluminum foil. Pour honey mixture over each; wrap securely. Bake 2 hours at 325°. Unwrap ducks and continue baking ½ hour longer, basting frequently. Pour drippings into a saucepan. Combine potato flour with a little water; stir into drippings. Bring to a boil, stirring. Pour cognac over ducks and ignite. Serve with sauce.

Mrs. James F. Peil
(Nancy Rodgers)

WILD GOOSE WITH MUSHROOM SAUCE

1 wild goose
Salt and pepper
Seasoned salt
Flour
2 T. butter

SAUCE:

1 lb. small fresh mushrooms
1 T. whipping cream
1 T. chicken stock
3 T. butter
1 tsp. flour

WINE SUGGESTION:
Margaux

Disjoint goose, including the breast. Season well with salt, pepper and seasoned salt. Sprinkle with flour and brown well in butter in a heavy skillet. Put on a rack in a covered roaster. Add small amount of water to pan drippings in skillet; pour over goose. Cover and bake for 2½ to 3 hours at 325°; add a little water if it gets too dry. (Young goose only takes 1½ to 2 hours). Prepare sauce one hour before serving; put mushrooms in a double boiler with cream and stock. Heat butter separately with salt and pepper; pour over mushrooms. Cook for one hour, tightly closed. Just before serving, add flour moistened with a bit of the sauce to make a smooth paste. Season to taste. Serve the goose with wild rice and sauce.

Mrs. John E. Rickmeier
(Mary Woehr)

VENISON WITH LINGONBERRY SAUCE

14 Servings

1 leg of venison (about 7 lbs.)
1 tsp. salt
½ tsp. ground ginger
¼ tsp. pepper
1 cup beef stock
½ cup melted butter

SAUCE:

1 cup fresh lingonberries (jarred if fresh not available)
2 T. water
6 T. sugar
1 T. cornstarch

WINE SUGGESTION:
Zinfandel

Rub venison with a mixture of salt, ginger and pepper. Place on a rack in a roasting pan; cover with foil. Bake at 325° for 2½ to 3 hours or until tender. Baste occasionally with stock mixed with butter. Let venison rest while you make sauce. Reserve drippings.

Combine lingonberries and water; simmer, covered, 15 minutes. Stir in sugar. Remove excess fat from drippings, blend in cornstarch mixed with a little water. Cook, stirring constantly, until thickened. Add water, if needed. Stir in the lingonberries and check seasonings. Spoon some sauce over venison, pass the rest.

Mrs. Dennis F. Muckermann
(Elizabeth Graham)

VENISON RAGOUT

6 Servings

3 lbs. boned venison
1 cup vinegar
1½ cups water
MSG
Salt and pepper
2 cups chopped celery
2 cups chopped onion
Pinch of rosemary
¼ cup flour
¼ cup melted butter
¼ cup red burgundy wine
½ cup sour cream

WINE SUGGESTION:
Graves Rouge

Marinate venison overnight in vinegar, ½ cup water, MSG, salt and pepper. Drain. Place in casserole with celery, onion, rosemary and 1 cup water. Cover; bake at 350° for 2 hours. Remove venison. Slice and keep warm. Strain juice. Combine flour and butter; add to juices. Cook, stirring constantly, until thickened. Stir in wine and sour cream. Heat through. Pour over venison.

Mrs. James T. W. Wheary
(Victoria Fazen)

VENISON MEATBALLS

6 Servings

1½ lbs. ground venison (may use half pork)
1 cup bread crumbs
¼ cup chopped onion
2 eggs
3 oz. dry red wine
3 T. parmesan cheese
2 T. chopped parsley
1 clove garlic, pressed
¼ tsp. dry mustard
1 tsp. pepper
1 tsp. worcestershire sauce
10 to 12 dry mushrooms (soaked in 1 cup water)

SAUCE:
2 T. flour mixed with ½ cup water
Salt and pepper
Juice from mushrooms
1 cup milk
½ cup cream of mushroom soup
1 chicken bouillon cube

WINE SUGGESTION:
Cotes du Rhone

Mix all ingredients except mushrooms very well; form into small balls. Roll each in flour and saute in equal amounts of butter and oil. Remove meatballs from pan. Mix sauce ingredients; stir into the drippings. Put meatballs and mushrooms in an ovenproof pan; cover with sauce and bake at 350° for 1 hour. Serve with noodles.

Mrs. Bruce G. Southworth
(Mary Monek)

APPLE YORKSHIRE PUDDING

8 Servings

- 6 T. butter
- ½ cup light brown sugar
- 1½ tsp. cinnamon
- 2½ cups peeled, cored and sliced apples
- 1½ cups sifted flour
- ¾ tsp. salt
- 3 eggs
- 1½ cups milk

Melt butter in 9x13-inch shallow pan. Sprinkle brown sugar and cinnamon evenly over butter. Arrange apples over sugar. Sift flour and salt together. Beat eggs until light. Add flour and ½ cup milk to eggs, beat until well blended. Gradually add last cup of milk; beat until smooth. Gently pour over apples; bake at 450° for 25 to 30 minutes. Serve at once cut in squares.

Mrs. William G. Dubinsky
(Sherrilyn Tatham)

BAKED APPLE SAUCE

- 2 lemons
- ½ cup apple cider
- 5 lbs. baking apples
- 1 whole cinnamon stick, broken in half
- ¼ cup butter
- ¼ cup brown sugar

Place grated rind of lemons in a bowl with the apple cider. Peel the apples in large wide strips; reserve peels. Core and slice apples. Place cinnamon in a pot that has a tight fitting lid. Add apple slices; pour in cider and lemon rind. Carefully cover with apple peels sealing completely. Set the pot, uncovered, on the stove; heat just until cider boils. Cover and bake at 350° for 30 minutes. Remove peels and cinnamon; discard. Pass apples through a food mill. Beat in butter and sugar. Serve hot or cold.

Mrs. Gilbert P. George
(Ann Sullivan)

BARLEY CASSEROLE

12 Servings

- ½ cup butter, melted
- 2 onions, chopped
- 1 lb. fresh mushrooms, sliced
- 1 box (1 lb.) pearl barley
- ½ cup sliced pimiento
- 3½ cups chicken stock
- Salt and pepper

Saute onions and mushrooms in butter until tender. Add barley; cook until lightly browned. Remove from heat; add pimiento, 3 cups chicken stock, and salt and pepper to taste. Place mixture in a casserole; cover and bake at 350° for 1½ hours or until liquid is absorbed. If barley seems dry, add remaining stock.

Mrs. Benson T. Caswell
(Margaret Graham)

BEETS IN SOUR CREAM

4 Servings

- 1 can (1 lb.) julienne beets or 12 small beets, sliced
- 2 T. white vinegar
- 2 T. sugar
- 2 T. flour
- 2 T. butter
- ½ cup sour cream

Drain beets, if canned; cook, if fresh. Combine remaining ingredients. Cook slowly, stirring constantly, until thick. Add the beets and cook until thoroughly heated.

Mrs. H. Alex Vance, Jr.
(Melinda Martin)

CHEESE CARROTS

8 Servings

- 20 medium carrots, sliced
- 1 small onion, grated
- ¼ cup butter
- ¼ cup flour
- 1 tsp. salt
- ¼ tsp. dry mustard
- ¼ tsp. celery salt
- ⅛ tsp. pepper
- 2 cups milk
- ½ lb. processed American cheese, sliced
- 1 cup bread crumbs

Cook carrots. Saute onion in butter; stir in flour, salt, mustard, celery salt, and pepper. Gradually add milk. Cook, stirring constantly, until thick. Arrange layers of carrots and cheese in a 2-qt. casserole, ending with carrots. Pour sauce over layers; sprinkle with bread crumbs. Bake at 350° for 25 minutes.

Mrs. John C. Munson
(Virginia Aldrich)

CELERY AMANDINE

6-8 Servings

1 bunch celery, cut in 1-inch pieces
¼ cup butter
¼ cup flour
1 cup chicken broth
¾ cup milk
¼ cup light cream
½ tsp. salt
⅛ tsp. pepper
4 green onions, thinly sliced tops and bottoms
2 oz. chopped pimiento
1 cup grated swiss cheese
1 cup toasted slivered almonds

Cook celery in salted water, covered, 5 minutes. Melt butter. Stir in flour. Slowly add chicken broth, milk, and cream. Add seasonings, onions, and pimiento. Cook, stirring constantly, until thickened. Add ½ of cheese; stir until melted. Add ½ of almonds and celery. Pour into a large baking dish or individual ramekins; top with remaining cheese and almonds. Bake at 325° for 20 minutes or until bubbly.

Mrs. Sumner W. Mead
(Nancy Price)

CELERY SOUFFLE RING

8 Servings

1½ cups chopped celery
½ cup chopped green pepper
1 large bunch parsley, chopped
1 medium onion, chopped
1 cup dried bread crumbs
¾ cup chopped pecans
1 cup milk
4 eggs, separated
2 T. butter
Salt and pepper

Grind first four ingredients. Add all other ingredients except egg whites; mix well. Beat egg whites until stiff; fold into mixture. Pour into a greased ring mold. Place mold in a pan of water. Bake at 350° for 1½ hours. This is pretty with the center filled with carrots or chicken a la king.

Mrs. John Wheelan
(Betsy Califf)

CAULIFLOWER TIMBALS WITH HOLLANDAISE SAUCE — 10 Servings

- 1½ cups warm cream
- 4 eggs
- ¾ tsp. salt
- ½ tsp. paprika
- ⅛ tsp. nutmeg
- 1 T. chopped parsley
- 1½ cups cooked, drained cauliflower pieces
- 2 cups hollandaise sauce

Beat cream, eggs and seasonings well. Toss in cauliflower pieces. Pour into 10 individual greased timbals or ovenproof dishes, leaving ½-inch space at top. Place in pan with 1 inch of water. Bake at 350° for 40 minutes or until firm. Unmold on platter; serve with hollandaise sauce.

Mrs. Bruce G. Southworth
(Mary Monek)

CORN PUDDING — 6 Servings

- 1 can (12 oz.) kernel corn or 1 pkg. (10 oz.) frozen corn, cooked
- 2 T. flour
- 2 T. sugar
- 2 T. butter
- 1 tsp. salt
- 2 eggs
- 1 small can pimiento, chopped
- 1 green pepper, chopped
- ¼ lb. grated cheddar cheese
- ½ cup milk

Mix all ingredients together, pour into a buttered baking dish. Bake at 350° about 30 minutes until brown and thickened.

Mrs. W. Gene Corley
(Lynd Wertheim)

CURRIED FRUIT CASSEROLE — 10 Servings

- 1 can (29 oz.) peach halves
- 1 can (29 oz.) pears
- 2 cans (13½ oz. each) pineapple tidbits
- 1 small bottle maraschino cherries (optional)
- ⅓ cup melted butter
- ⅔ cup brown sugar
- 2½ tsp. curry powder
- 3 T. cornstarch

Drain fruit; place hollow side up in a shallow baking dish. Mix all other ingredients; pour over top. Bake at 325° for 1 hour. This is best made a day or two in advance and reheated at 350° for ½ hour. Any fruit may be substituted.

Mrs. Benson T. Caswell
(Margaret Graham)

EGGPLANT CASSEROLE — 6 Servings

3 medium eggplants, peeled
Salt
2 T. butter, melted
1 T. flour
¾ cup beef stock
1½ lbs. tomatoes, peeled, seeded and quartered
3 onions, finely-chopped
1 tsp. sugar
Bouquet garni (bay leaf, thyme, parsley)
Salt and pepper to taste
Flour
Olive oil
Bread crumbs
1¼ cups grated gruyere cheese
2 T. butter

Cut eggplant into ½-inch slices. Sprinkle with salt; let stand ½ hour. Make a roux of butter and flour. Add stock gradually. Add tomatoes, onions, sugar, bouquet garni, salt and pepper. Cook, covered, over low heat 30 minutes. Remove bouquet garni; puree sauce in a blender. Check seasonings. Wash excess salt off eggplant under running water. Dry on paper towel. Coat eggplant with flour; deep fry in oil until browned on both sides. Drain on paper towel. Layer slices in a buttered baking dish, pouring sauce and sprinkling cheese over each layer. Sprinkle top with bread crumbs and cheese; dot with butter Bake at 350° for 25 to 30 minutes, or until bubbly. Place under broiler until top is golden brown.

Mrs. Patrick Callahan
(Patricia Henebry)

EGGPLANT DUMPLINGS — 6 Servings

They make an elegant first course

1 large eggplant
Salt
2 T. butter
2 T. flour
1 cup milk, scalded
½ cup feta cheese
1 T. freshly-grated parmesan cheese
1 T. minced parsley
⅛ tsp. nutmeg
White pepper
1 egg yolk
½ cup oil
1 egg, beaten
Dry bread crumbs

Peel eggplant; cut into ¼-inch slices. Put in colander, sprinkle with salt, let drain for 1 hour. Melt butter; stir in flour; cook over low heat stirring for 3 minutes. Slowly pour in milk; cook, stirring constantly, until smooth. Stir in cheeses, nutmeg, and salt and pepper to taste. Cool; stir in egg yolk. Pat eggplant dry; saute in ½ cup hot oil, adding more oil if necessary. Drain on paper towels. Put 1 to 2 tsp. cheese mixture in center of each eggplant slice and carefully roll up the slices, pressing ends together. Dip in egg; roll in dry bread crumbs, dip in the egg again. Fry dumplings in hot deep oil at 360° for 3 minutes or until golden. Drain on paper towel.

Mrs. Patrick W. O'Brien
(Deborah Bissell)

HOT SPICY LENTILS

8 Servings

Serve as side dish with all curries

1 lb. dried lentils
Salt, water
¼ cup butter
2 onions, finely-chopped
3 tomatoes, peeled, seeded and chopped
¼ tsp. turmeric
¼ tsp. cumin
¼ tsp. cayenne pepper
½ tsp. coriander

Place lentils in a pan with salt; cover with water. Cook until almost done. Heat butter; saute the onions and tomatoes. Add the spices and mix thoroughly. Stir into well-drained lentils; heat through.

Mrs. Benson T. Caswell
(Margaret Graham)

NOODLES DIVINE

8 Servings

1 pkg. (8 oz.) noodles
1 cup cottage cheese
1 cup sour cream
½ cup milk
2 tsp. worcestershire sauce
1 small onion, grated
1 clove garlic, pressed
1 tsp. salt
⅛ tsp. pepper
Dash cayenne
1 cup coarse bread crumbs
3 T. butter, melted
3 tomatoes, quartered

Cook and drain noodles. Add cheese, sour cream, milk and worcestershire; mix well. Blend in onion, garlic, and seasonings. Turn into shallow baking dish; top with buttered bread crumbs. Bake at 350° for 20 minutes, covered. Top with tomato wedges. Bake, uncovered, until heated through.

Mrs. William F. Zwilling
(Diane Poppen)

SCALLOPED OYSTERS

8-10 Servings

Serve this as a side dish during the holidays

1 qt. oysters
Minced parsley
½ cup diced celery
¼ tsp. salt
⅛ tsp. pepper
1½ cups soda cracker crumbs
2 eggs, slightly beaten
3 cups milk
Butter

Butter a 1½-qt. casserole. Layer oysters in bottom. Sprinkle with celery, salt, pepper and cracker crumbs. Continue to layer, ending with cracker crumbs. Beat eggs and milk together, pour over top. Dot with butter. Bake at 325° for ½ hour.

Mrs. Elbert O. Hand
(Elizabeth Howard)

POMMES ANNIE

6 Servings

2½ cups whipping cream
1 T. butter
2 cloves garlic, pressed
5 large red potatoes
¼ cup freshly-grated parmesan cheese
Salt and pepper

Simmer the cream, butter and garlic in a small pan for 15 minutes or until the cream has been reduced to half. Peel and slice the potatoes very thin; dry on paper towel. Layer in a small buttered casserole. On each layer sprinkle a little cheese, salt and pepper. Cover potatoes with reduced cream mixture, adding additional cream if necessary to cover the potatoes completely. Cover casserole; bake at 350° for 1½ hours.

Mrs. Gilbert P. George
(Ann Sullivan)

PUMPKIN RING

8-10 Servings

Perfect use for post-Halloween Jack-o-Lanterns

4 lbs. pumpkin meat, cubed
2 cups red wine
1 tsp. salt
Water
½ lb. butter
1 cup bread crumbs or herb stuffing
2 onions, finely-chopped
6 large eggs, beaten
2 tsp. allspice
1 tsp. ground ginger
1 tsp. ground cloves
Salt and pepper
MSG
3 T. orange liqueur
1 cup milk

Place pumpkin in saucepan; add wine and salt. Add just enough water to cover. Simmer until soft (about 25 minutes). Melt 4 T. butter; saute the bread crumbs, adding more butter if needed. In another pan, melt remaining butter and hold. Drain pumpkin; put through a food mill. Blend in the melted butter, half the bread crumbs, onions, eggs and spices. Work in the liqueur. Add milk and crumbs until puree holds its shape. Adjust seasoning. Butter a 2-qt. ring mold and fill with puree. Set mold in shallow pan of hot water; bake at 350° for 45 minutes. Unmold; fill center with a vegetable of contrasting color.

Mrs. Thomas D. Hodgkins
(Mary Ann BonDurant)

SPAGHETTI CARBONARA — 8 Servings

1 lb. spaghetti
Olive oil
6 eggs
1 cup grated parmesan cheese
Salt and pepper
½ pint cream
1 lb. bacon, fried and diced

Boil spaghetti with a little olive oil in water until done. Mix eggs, cheese, salt and pepper, beat until frothy. Add cream. Place egg mixture in heavy pan; add spaghetti, bacon and a little olive oil. Stir over low heat until sauce adheres to the spaghetti. Serve immediately.

Mrs. James Modrall
(Nancy Johnson)

BAKED SQUASH WITH BLUEBERRIES — 8 Servings

4 acorn squash
1 container (12 oz.) frozen blueberries; or fresh
1 apple, finely diced
6 T. brown sugar
8 tsp. butter

Cut squash in half lengthwise; remove seeds. Place in a pan that can be covered. Spoon blueberries into each squash half. Add a few pieces of diced apple. Sprinkle brown sugar over berries and squash. Place 1 tsp. butter in center of each squash. Pour ½ cup water into pan. Cover; bake at 375° for 45 minutes. Remove cover; bake 15 minutes longer.

Mrs. David B. Smith
(Marcia Williamson)

HARVEST BAKED SQUASH — 6 Servings

3 large acorn squash
1 cup water
1 can (13½ oz.) crushed pineapple, drained
1½ cups diced apple, unpeeled
1 cup chopped celery
½ cup chopped walnuts
½ cup butter
½ cup brown sugar
½ tsp. cinnamon
¼ tsp. salt

Cut squash in half so edges are scalloped. Clean out seeds. Bake in water, cut side down, at 350° for 45 minutes or until tender. Combine rest of ingredients; spoon into squash centers. Remove water from pan. Bake, cut side up, another 15 minutes.

Mrs. Edward L. Flom
(Beryl Light)

SWEET POTATOES IN ORANGE SHELLS

8 Servings

Attractive as a garnish around Thanksgiving turkey

- 3 lbs. sweet potatoes, cooked and mashed (about 6 cups)
- 2 eggs
- ¾ cup brown sugar
- ½ cup melted butter
- ½ tsp. cinnamon
- 1 tsp. salt
- 1 cup pecans, finely-ground
- Fresh orange juice (up to 1 cup)
- 8 large orange shells
- Miniature marshmallows (optional)

Place sweet potatoes in a mixing bowl. Beat in eggs, melted butter, brown sugar, cinnamon, salt, and pecans. Add the orange juice only if the sweet potatoes seem dry. Fill orange shells with sweet potatoes; refrigerate until ready to use. Bake at 375° for 20 minutes, or until heated through. Place marshmallows on top; place under the broiler until nicely browned. (To make orange shells, slice off tops of oranges; remove pulp.)

Mrs. Gilbert P. George
(Ann Sullivan)

PLANTATION SWEET POTATO PONE

8 Servings

- 4 large sweet potatoes, peeled
- 2 eggs, beaten
- ½ cup brown sugar
- Grated rind of 1 lemon
- Grated rind of ½ orange
- ½ T. cinnamon
- ½ T. nutmeg
- ½ T. ground cloves
- ½ cup butter, melted
- ½ cup molasses
- ⅔ cup milk
- ⅓ cup bourbon

Grate raw sweet potatoes. Beat eggs and sugar; stir together with the grated potatoes and grated orange and lemon rind. Add spices, melted butter, molasses, milk and bourbon; mix thoroughly. Place in buttered casserole and bake at 325° for 1 hour.

Mrs. James F. Peil
(Nancy Rodgers)

BAKED TOMATOES WITH HORSERADISH MAYONNAISE

8 Servings

8 firm medium tomatoes
1 cup grated onion
½ cup brown sugar
1 cup mayonnaise
1 to 2 T. horseradish
2 T. white sugar
Paprika

Slice the tops off the tomatoes. Scrape out seeds and watery material. Place 1 heaping tablespoon grated onion on top and in cavity of each tomato; let sit 30 minutes. Place 1 T. brown sugar on top of each. Combine mayonnaise, horseradish, and white sugar. Add more horseradish to taste. Place the mayonnaise on top of each tomato; dust with paprika. Bake 10 minutes at 450°.

Miss Virginia C. Franche

TURNIP PUFF

8 Servings

4 cups cooked mashed turnips
2 cups bread crumbs
½ cup melted butter
2 T. sugar
2 tsp. salt
¼ tsp. pepper
4 eggs, slightly beaten

Mix all ingredients together with an electric mixer. Spoon into a buttered 1½-qt. casserole. Brush top with additional butter. Bake at 375° for 1 hour.

Mrs. Patrick Callahan
(Patricia Henebry)

WILD RICE CASSEROLE

12 Servings

1 cup wild rice, washed
1 cup grated cheddar cheese
1 cup sliced ripe olives
1 cup canned tomatoes and juice
1 cup fresh sliced mushrooms
½ cup chopped onions
½ cup vegetable oil
Salt and pepper to taste
½ cup hot water

Soak rice in water overnight; drain. Mix all ingredients except the hot water and a little cheese. Place in a buttered casserole. (Prepare in advance to here). Before cooking stir in the hot water. Cover and bake at 350° for 1½ hours, checking several times to make sure it doesn't dry out. Add more water if necessary. Rice should be tender. Before serving sprinkle with extra cheese.

Mrs. C. Gary Gerst
(Virginia Caspari)

VEGETABLE CHARLOTTE

8 Servings

12 slices day-old bread, crusts removed
1¼ sticks butter, melted
2 cups pureed cooked carrots
2 cups pureed cooked turnips
2 cups pureed cooked brussels sprouts
Salt and pepper

TOMATO SAUCE:

2 lbs. tomatoes, peeled and sliced
Salt and pepper
6 shallots, finely-chopped
1 T. brown sugar
1 bay leaf
2 T. butter
2 T. flour
1 cup beef stock

Cut each piece of bread in half; dip in butter. Line a 2-qt. charlotte mold with bread. Reserve a few pieces for top. Puree all vegetables together in blender; season vegetables with salt and pepper. Place puree in mold; cover with remaining bread. Bake at 425° for 20 minutes. Unmold onto an ovenproof dish; place in oven again until bread is lightly browned. Serve with tomato sauce poured over charlotte; garnish with sprigs of parsley.

Sauce: Place tomatoes, salt and pepper, shallots, sugar and bay leaf in saucepan; bring to a boil. Simmer until tomatoes are well cooked. Remove bay leaf; put sauce in blender. Melt butter; stir in flour. Cook and stir until lightly browned. Add stock. Cook, stirring constantly, until thickened. Add to tomato mixture.

Mrs. H. Alex Vance, Jr.
(Melinda Martin)

AUTUMN FRUIT WITH CRANBERRY DRESSING

6-8 Servings

⅓ cup mayonnaise
½ cup jellied cranberry sauce
Juice of ½ lemon
Juice of ½ small orange
½ tsp. grated orange rind
¼ tsp. dry mustard
2 tsp. sugar
1 fresh pineapple, peeled, sliced into rings
3 bananas
3 ripe persimmons, sliced
Pomegranate seeds
Lettuce cups

Blend together the mayonnaise, cranberry sauce, lemon juice, orange juice and rind, mustard and sugar. Put pineapple rings in individual lettuce cups. Place banana slices in centers of the pineapple rings and arrange sliced persimmon in spoke-fashion on top. Put a generous tablespoon of dressing on each salad and sprinkle with pomegranate seeds.

Mrs. Thomas N. Boyden
(Susan B. Dalton)

AVOCADO PERSIMMON SALAD MOLD

8 Servings

1 T. plain gelatin
½ cup cold water
⅓ cup lemon juice
1 tsp. salt
1 tsp. pepper
1 T. grated onion
3 drops green coloring
2 cups mashed avocado
½ cup whipping cream, whipped
2 T. mayonnaise
1 can (16 oz.) grapefruit sections
1 can (11 oz.) mandarin oranges
2 persimmons

Soften gelatin in water and dissolve in double boiler. Add lemon juice, seasonings and coloring. Blend in mashed avocado. Chill until slightly thickened. Fold in whipped cream and mayonnaise. Pour into a 4-cup ring mold. Refrigerate several hours until set. Unmold on lettuce; fill center with dressing — a mixture of mayonnaise, sour cream and lemon juice. Surround with grapefruit, mandarin oranges, and persimmons.

Mrs. Stephen Laing
(Suzanne Reyburn)

COLD VEGETABLE SALAD

4 Servings

4 medium size tomatoes
1 pkg. (10 oz.) frozen peas, slightly cooked
½ cup mayonnaise
½ cup sour cream
3 minced shallots
1½ tsp. fresh lemon juice
1 tsp. chopped fresh parsley
¼ tsp. salt
¼ tsp. dry mustard
⅛ tsp. pepper

Peel tomatoes; remove all seeds from inside. Drain well. Mix cold, unbuttered peas with all other ingredients. Stuff tomatoes. Serve on lettuce leaf.

Mrs. Bruce G. Southworth
(Mary Monek)

LETTUCE WITH TOMATO CREAM

6 Servings

A truly beautiful salad

3 large tomatoes
1 pkg. (8 oz.) cream cheese
1 cup ricotta cheese
2 cloves pressed garlic
Salt and pepper
1 large head lettuce
French dressing

Peel tomatoes; chop fine. Combine with next four ingredients. Wash lettuce; dry well. Put tomato mixture between each leaf starting at center, being careful to keep lettuce intact. Pat lettuce into shape, wrap with plastic wrap. Chill. Cut into slices. Serve with French dressing.

Mrs. Karl V. Rohlen, Jr.
(Carolyn Walker)

FRENCH DRESSING

6-8 Servings

⅓ cup tarragon vinegar
1 T. paprika
1 tsp. salt
Dash of cayenne
1 small clove garlic pressed
¼ cup sugar
1 egg
1 cup salad oil

In blender, mix all ingredients except oil. With motor on, slowly dribble in oil until thick. Chill. Keeps in refrigerator about 5 days.

Mrs. Bruce G. Southworth
(Mary Monek)

APPLESAUCE CRANBERRY MOLD

6-8 Servings

- 2 env. plain gelatin
- ½ cup orange or cranberry juice
- ½ cup boiling water
- 2 cups chopped cooked cranberries (if you cook, cook with sugar.)
- 1½ cups applesauce
- 1 cup diced celery
- ½ cup chopped walnuts
- 1 orange, peeled and diced
- 2 T. grated orange rind

Soften gelatin in juice. Add boiling water; cool. Mix all other ingredients; add to gelatin mixture. Pour into a greased mold (2 qt.) and refrigerate several hours.

Mrs. Robert T. DePree
(Susan Barker)

STUFFED CINNAMON APPLES

6 Servings

- 6 apples
- ⅔ cup red cinnamon candies
- 2 cups water
- 1 pkg. (3 oz.) cream cheese
- 2 T. milk
- 1 tsp. lemon juice
- ⅓ cup pitted dates, chopped
- 1 can (9 oz.) pineapple bits, drained
- 2 T. chopped walnuts
- Lettuce

Pare and core apples. Mix candies and water; cook until dissolved. Add apples; simmer, uncovered, until tender; about 15 minutes. Chill in syrup several hours. Blend cream cheese, milk, lemon juice, dates, pineapple and nuts. Drain apples; place atop salad greens. Stuff centers with cream cheese mixture.

Mrs. Thomas O. Hodgkins
(Mary Ann BonDurant)

CURRIED RICE SALAD

4 Servings

Excellent with leg of lamb or fried chicken

- 2 T. salad oil
- 2 tsp. wine vinegar
- 1 tsp. curry powder
- 3 T. chopped chutney
- 2 tomatoes, seeded, chopped
- 2 T. raisins
- 1 green pepper, cut into julienne strips
- 1 stalk celery, chopped
- 2 T. parsley, chopped
- 2 cups cold cooked rice
- Salt and pepper
- Lettuce

Mix oil, vinegar, curry powder and chutney. Combine with tomato, raisins, green pepper, celery, and parsley; toss with the rice. Salt and pepper to taste. Chill several hours before serving. Serve in lettuce-lined bowl. Or rice can be pressed into individual molds and unmolded onto lettuce cups.

Mrs. Gilbert P. George
(Ann Sullivan)

DESSERTS AND SWEETS

PEARS IN CHOCOLATE SABAYON — 6 Servings

This light chocolate sauce does not overpower pear flavor

6 bartlett or comice pears (pears must be flavorful)
3 cups water
1 cup sugar
1 piece lemon rind
1 stick cinnamon (2-inch)
4 oz. semi-sweet chocolate
¾ cup coffee
9 egg yolks
5 T. sugar
¼ cup pear brandy or cognac
1 cup whipping cream
2 T. confectioners' sugar

Peel whole pears leaving stem intact. In saucepan which will hold pears, combine water, 1 cup sugar, rind, and cinnamon. Heat to boiling; add pears. Cover and poach until tender. Let pears cool in the syrup; refrigerate overnight. Melt chocolate in ¼ cup coffee. In a double boiler, mix yolks and 5 T. sugar. Add the melted chocolate and remaining coffee. Stir mixture over simmering water until creamy and thickened. Add 2 T. brandy. Whip cream; add sugar and 2 T. brandy. Place pears upright in a crystal dish. Pour sauce over and garnish with whipped cream.

Mrs. Thomas D. Hodgkins
(Mary Ann BonDurant)

SAINT-EMILION au CHOCOLAT — 8 Servings

A fantastically wickedly rich dessert

½ cup butter, softened
½ cup sugar
1 cup milk
2 egg yolks
8 oz. unsweetened chocolate
⅓ cup honey
1 tsp. vanilla
¾ lb. almond macaroons (26 to 32) or "amaretti" available at Italian food stores
½ cup dark rum
1 cup whipping cream, whipped

Cream butter and sugar until well blended. Scald milk; cool. Mix milk with yolks; beat well. Melt chocolate over low flame with honey. Gradually blend yolk mixture into chocolate. Add creamed butter in 8 additions. Over low heat stir carefully until absolutely smooth. Remove from heat; add vanilla. Dribble 1 tsp. rum on each macaroon. Cover the bottom of a glass souffle dish (1 ½ qt.) or crystal bowl with a layer of macaroons. Over and around these pour a layer of chocolate; add another layer of macaroons, and so on until the dish is filled, finishing with the macaroons. Cover; refrigerate overnight. Bring to room temperature before serving. Pass a bowl of sweetened whipped cream.

Miss Virginia C. Franche

PUREED CHESTNUT RING

10 Servings

1 qt. milk
2 cups sugar
½ piece vanilla bean
2 lbs. fresh chestnuts, peeled
¼ cup water
¼ cup boiling water
3 T. butter
2 T. cointreau
1½ cups whipping cream
¼ cup confectioners' sugar
1 tsp. vanilla
Grated sweet chocolate

VARIATION:

For individual servings, place 10 meringues on dessert plates. Pipe the puree on top, then the whipped cream and grated chocolate.

Combine milk, 1½ cups sugar, vanilla bean and chestnuts. Cover and cook 40 minutes or until tender but not mushy. Combine remaining sugar and ¼ cup water. Cook until sugar turns brown. Add boiling water and cook 3 to 4 minutes. Drain chestnuts; pass through food mill. Add sugar syrup, butter and cointreau. Cool. Put the puree into a pastry bag fitted with a "star" tube; pipe onto a round serving platter in a free form ring leaving a 4-inch well in the center. Chill completely. When ready to serve, whip the cream adding sugar and vanilla. Put in a pastry bag; fill center of the ring. Grate chocolate over top.

Mrs. H. Alex Vance, Jr.
(Melinda Martin)

PERSIMMON PUDDING

8 Servings

- **2 to 2½ cups persimmon pulp, sieved**
- **1½ cups sugar**
- **1 tsp. baking powder**
- **1 tsp. baking soda**
- **1 tsp. ginger**
- **2 tsp. cinnamon**
- **½ tsp. nutmeg**
- **½ tsp. salt**
- **1 egg, slightly beaten**
- **2 cups flour**
- **1 qt. milk**

Mix persimmon pulp, sugar, baking powder, soda, spices and salt. Beat in egg. Alternately add flour and milk, stirring well. Pour into a greased 9x9-inch pan. Bake at 325° for 60 minutes, stirring every 15 minutes. Do not cook all the syrup out. Serve cold with cream or hard sauce. This freezes well. (If desired, add 1 cup raisins or chopped nuts to batter.)

Mrs. Philip G. Sosinski
(Nan Van Arsdale)

NEW ENGLAND INDIAN PUDDING

6 Servings

- **1 qt. milk**
- **5 T. yellow cornmeal**
- **2 T. butter**
- **½ cup brown sugar**
- **½ cup dark molasses**
- **1 tsp. salt**
- **½ tsp. ginger**
- **½ tsp. cinnamon**
- **½ tsp. nutmeg**
- **½ tsp. mace**
- **2 eggs, well beaten**
- **1 tsp. grated orange rind**
- **1 cup light cream**

Place milk in double boiler; bring to a boil. Slowly add cornmeal, stirring constantly. Put over boiling water and cook for 20 minutes stirring occasionally. Add butter, sugar, molasses. Remove from heat. Add spices, eggs, and grated orange rind. Pour into a buttered 2-qt. dish; and bake, uncovered, at 300° for 2 to 2½ hours. Stir occasionally the first hour, then pour the cream over the top very carefully, and finish baking without stirring. Serve hot or warm with whipped cream or ice cream. The longer it is cooked, the darker and better the pudding.

Mrs. Edwin H. Holzer
(Josephine Earnest)

HAZELNUT SOUFFLE

6 Servings

- **5 egg yolks**
- **¼ cup sugar**
- **¼ cup flour**
- **Pinch salt**
- **1 cup hot scalded milk**
- **1 cup ground hazelnuts**
- **3 T. butter, melted**
- **1 T. rum**
- **6 egg whites, stiffly beaten**

SAUCE:

- **1 cup coffee ice cream, softened**
- **1 T. rum**
- **½ cup whipping cream, whipped**
- **Sugar to taste**
- **Confectioners' sugar**

Beat yolks with sugar until they are light. Stir in flour and salt. Gradually beat in hot milk; cook in double boiler, stirring constantly, until it thickens and coats a spoon. Cool. Saute hazelnuts in butter and rum; add to cooled milk mixture. Gently fold in egg whites. Pour into an ungreased 1½-qt. souffle dish set in a pan of hot water. Bake at 350° for 45 minutes. For sauce, beat ice cream with rum. Fold in whipped cream; add sugar to taste. Serve the sauce separately.

Mrs. Thomas B. McNeill
(Ingrid Sieder)

APPLE SOUFFLE

6 Servings

- **1 cup milk**
- **¼ tsp. salt**
- **4½ T. tapioca, instant**
- **¾ cup sugar**
- **2 red apples, peeled and grated**
- **1 T. water**
- **1 T. apricot preserves**
- **Pinch of cinnamon**
- **3 egg yolks**
- **1 T. rum**
- **3 egg whites**
- **Whipped cream**
- **Chopped pecans (optional)**

In top of double boiler, combine milk, salt and tapioca; cook over hot water until thick and smooth. Add the sugar; cook until dissolved. Cool. In separate pan combine apples, water, preserves and cinnamon; cook until soft and well done. Add yolks to milk mixture, one at a time, stirring well after each. Add rum. Combine apple mixture into milk mixture. Beat whites until stiff; fold into apple mixture. Pour into a 1-qt. souffle dish, place in pan of water 1 inch deep and bake at 350° for about 1 hour. Serve immediately topped with whipped cream and nuts.

Mrs. Edward L. Flom
(Beryl Light)

COLD PUMPKIN SOUFFLE — 4 Servings

1 env. plain gelatin
¼ cup rum
4 eggs
⅔ cup sugar
1 cup cooked or canned pumpkin
½ tsp. cinnamon
½ tsp. ginger
¼ tsp. mace
¼ tsp. ground cloves
1 cup whipping cream

Sprinkle gelatin over rum to soften. Set over simmering water until gelatin is completely dissolved. Beat eggs thoroughly, gradually adding sugar. Beat until smooth and thick. Stir in pumpkin, seasonings, rum and gelatin. Whip cream; fold into pumpkin mixture. Fill 1-qt. souffle dish or individual souffle dishes with mixture; chill until set. Serve garnished with sweetened whipped cream and salted toasted pecans.

Mrs. Donald J. Ross
(Cynthia Stiles)

BAKLAVA HEROPOULOS

A very traditional Greek dessert

1 lb. filo (cover with waxed paper and wet cloth)
1 lb. butter, melted
1½ lbs. walnuts and pecans, chopped
1 T. cinnamon
1½ tsp. ground cloves
¾ tsp. baking powder
Water

SYRUP:

7 cups sugar
2½ cups water
Juice of 1 lemon
1 stick cinnamon

Bring above to boil and cook until syrup-like, about 20-30 minutes.

Butter a large 17 x 17 x 2-inch baking pan. Lay 6 to 7 sheets of filo on pan, buttering each layer with pastry brush. Mix nuts, cinnamon, cloves and baking powder. Sprinkle some of this mixture lightly on top of buttered filo in pan. Add one sheet of filo, butter it, sprinkle with nuts. Do this layer after layer until you have 7 sheets left. Cut edges off with scissors; put them in pan. Use remaining nuts and butter and top with 7 sheets of filo. Fold the edges under; and cut in lengthwise pieces so syrup will drip through. Sprinkle a little water on top. Bake at 350° for 45 to 60 minutes or until nicely brown. Remove from oven and let sit 10 minutes. Slowly pour syrup over baklava being careful to let syrup drip down into cuts made before baking. Let it stand 4 to 5 hours. After it cools, cut into triangles. If freezing, do not bake first. Store in refrigerator. To serve: Heat oven to 400° for 10 minutes, turn oven off, put baklava in oven for 10 minutes.

Mrs. Bruce G. Southworth
(Mary Monek)

FROZEN PUMPKIN PIE

6-8 Servings

A delightful change from the traditional pumpkin pie

- 1 cup canned pumpkin
- ½ cup packed brown sugar
- ½ tsp. salt
- ½ tsp. ginger
- ½ tsp. cinnamon
- ¼ tsp. nutmeg
- 1 quart French vanilla ice cream

CRUST:

- 1 cup ground pecans
- ½ cup ground ginger snaps
- ¼ cup sugar
- ¼ cup soft butter

VARIATION:
The filling may also be served as ice cream atop mincemeat pie.

Beat pumpkin, brown sguar, salt and spices with beater several minutes. Stir in softened ice cream. Pour into crust; freeze overnight. Remove from freezer about 15 minutes before serving. Top with whipped cream if desired.

Crust: Combine pecans, cookie crumbs, sugar and butter, press into the bottom of 9-inch pie pan. Bake at 450° for 5 to 7 minutes.

Mrs. Arthur S. Bowes
(Patricia Kelly)

MOLASSES PUMPKIN PIE WITH PECAN TOPPING

8 Servings

- ¾ cup sugar or 1 cup brown sugar
- 1 T. flour
- ½ tsp. salt
- 1 tsp. ground ginger
- ½ to 1 tsp. cinnamon
- ¼ tsp. ground cloves
- ⅓ cup molasses (unsulphured)
- 2 cups cooking pumpkin, cooked and mashed; or 1 can (16 oz.) pumpkin
- 3 large eggs
- 1 cup evaporated milk
- 1 unbaked 9-inch pie shell

TOPPING:

- ½ cup dark corn syrup
- ¾ cup pecans, coarsely chopped

Mix dry ingredients together. Add molasses and pumpkin. Add the eggs, one at a time, beating well. Stir in the milk; pour mixture into pie shell. Bake at 400° for 40 minutes. Cool. Serve with sweetened whipped cream or pecan topping. For the topping, combine the corn syrup and pecans. Pour over the pie, spreading evenly. Broil about 4 inches from the heat until bubbly. Cool a few minutes before serving.

Mrs. Dennis F. Muckermann
(Betty Graham)

APPLE PIE WITH SOUR CREAM — 6 Servings

A delicious variation on America's favorite pie

- 2 T. flour
- ¾ cup sugar
- ¾ tsp. cinnamon
- ⅛ tsp. salt
- 1 egg
- ½ tsp. vanilla
- 1 cup sour cream
- 6 medium apples, peeled and sliced
- 1 unbaked chilled 9-inch shell

TOPPING:

- ⅓ cup flour
- ⅓ cup sugar
- ½ tsp. cinnamon
- ¼ cup butter

Sift together flour, sugar, cinnamon and salt. Stir in egg, vanilla and sour cream. Fold in apples; spoon into pie shell. Bake 15 minutes at 400°. Reduce oven to 350°; bake another 30 minutes. Mix topping ingredients together with a pastry blender until mixture is crumbly. Sprinkle over pie; bake another 10 minutes at 400°

Mrs. James F. Peil
(Nancy Rodgers)

FRENCH APPLE PIE — 6 Servings

- 1 lb. cooking apples, peeled and thinly sliced
- 2 T. lemon juice
- ¼ tsp. nutmeg
- ¼ tsp. cinnamon
- ½ cup sugar
- 2 T. seedless golden raisins
- 1 cup brown sugar
- 2 T. flour
- ½ cup chopped pecans
- 2 T. butter
- ¼ cup water
- 1 unbaked 9-inch pie shell and top

HARD SAUCE:

- ½ cup butter
- 1 T. water
- 1½ cups confectioners' sugar
- 1 T. brandy or rum

Arrange sliced apples in unbaked pie shell. Sprinkle with lemon juice, nutmeg and cinnamon. Spread sugar and raisins over apples. Combine brown sugar and flour; spread mixture over all. Sprinkle pecans over top, dot with butter; and sprinkle with water. Place top crust over top; brush lightly with a little milk. Bake at 350° for 45 to 60 minutes. Serve warm with hard sauce.

Hard Sauce: In saucepan over low heat melt butter with water. Remove from heat; beat in sugar and brandy or rum until smooth. If too thick, add few drops of water.

Mrs. James F. Peil
(Nancy Rodgers)

FROZEN CRANBERRY VELVET PIE

10-12 Servings

1¼ cups crushed vanilla wafers
6 T. butter, melted
1 cup whipping cream
¼ cup sugar
½ tsp. vanilla
1 pkg. (8 oz.) cream cheese
1 can (1 lb.) whole cranberry sauce (or cranberry orange relish)

Combine crumbs and melted butter; press firmly onto bottom and sides of 9-inch pie plate. Chill until firm. Beat cream cheese until fluffy. Combine whipping cream, sugar, and vanilla; whip until thickened but not stiff. Gradually add to cream cheese, beating until smooth and creamy. Fold in cranberry sauce reserving a few whole cranberries for garnish. Spoon into crust; freeze until firm. Remove from freezer 10 minutes before serving. Top with additional whipped cream and reserved cranberries.

Mrs. Roger P. Eklund
(Sally Strothman)

"NUTTY" POPCORN BALLS

Makes 18

2 cups sugar
⅔ cup apple cider
⅔ cup maple syrup
½ cup butter
1½ tsp. salt
½ tsp. vanilla
4 cups warm popped corn
1 cup salted peanuts
1½ cups chopped dates

VARIATION:

For Halloween it is fun to substitute the dates for black and orange gumdrops or corn candy and wrap in orange cellophane tied with black yarn.

Combine sugar, apple cider, syrup, butter and salt in a heavy saucepan. Bring to a boil, stirring occasionally. Remove sugar from sides of pan with wet brush. Cook without stirring until mixture reaches soft ball stage or 270° on a candy thermometer. Add vanilla. Pour mixture over popcorn, peanuts and dates. Mix well; shape into 3-inch balls with buttered hands.

Mrs. Thomas D. Hodgkins
(Mary Ann BonDurant)

CHOCOLATE MOUSSE TORTE 10 Servings

- 8 oz. semisweet chocolate
- 1 T. instant coffee
- 1/4 cup boiling water
- 2/3 cup sugar
- 8 eggs, separated
- 2 1/2 tsp. vanilla
- 1/8 tsp. salt
- Fine bread crumbs
- 1 1/2 cups whipping cream
- 1/4 cup sifted confectioners' sugar

Preheat oven to 350°. Put chocolate in top of double boiler; add coffee dissolved in boiling water. Cover; let stand over very low heat, stirring occasionally, until chocolate is melted and smooth. In a separate bowl beat egg yolks until thick. Gradually beat in sugar, beat until mixture is lemon colored. Slowly beat the chocolate into the egg mixture. Add 1 tsp. vanilla. In separate bowl, beat egg whites and salt until stiff but not dry. Fold whites into chocolate mixture slowly until blended. Butter and dust a 9-inch pie plate with bread crumbs. Fill with mousse until just level with edge; refrigerate remainder. Bake at 350° for 25 minutes. Turn oven off; leave in 5 minutes longer. Cool 2 hours on wire rack so that mousse sinks in middle to form pie shell. Fill with chilled uncooked mousse. Chill 2 hours. Beat cream with remaining vanilla and confectioners' sugar. Spread over pie or use piping bag to make a lattice pattern.

Mrs. Christopher Stack
(Adelia Morris)

LINZERTORTE

A blue ribbon winner in a Jr. League contest!

- 1 1/2 cups butter
- 1 cup confectioners' sugar
- 2 3/4 cups sifted flour
- 1 1/2 cups ground hazelnuts
- Pinch of salt
- 1/2 tsp. cinnamon
- 2 cups raspberry jam
- 2 tsp. lemon juice
- 1 egg

Cream butter and sugar until light and fluffy. Beat in egg. Stir flour into creamed mixture alternately with a mixture of hazelnuts, salt and cinnamon. Chill dough. Line a 9-inch spring-form pan, making a rim 1-inch up sides. Reserve a little dough for lattice strips. Spread dough with a mixture of 1 1/2 cups raspberry jam and lemon juice. Cut strips of dough; form a lattice over the jam. Bake at 375° for 40 minutes. When cool fill squares formed by lattice with extra jam; sprinkle with more confectioners' sugar.

Mrs. Thomas B. McNeill
(Ingrid Sieder)

KIRSCH TORTE

10 Servings

This is certainly worth the extra trouble

SPONGE CAKE:

4 eggs, beaten
¾ cup sugar
¾ cup sifted cake flour
½ tsp. baking powder
¼ tsp. salt

MERINGUE:

3 egg whites
⅛ tsp. cream of tartar
1 cup sugar
1 cup ground almonds

KIRSCH SYRUP:

6 T. water
3 T. sugar
6 T. Kirsch

BUTTERCREAM FROSTING:

¾ cup unsalted butter
2 egg yolks
¾ cup confectioners' sugar
1 T. Kirsch

GARNISH:

½ cup slivered almonds, toasted
Confectioners' sugar

For cake, beat eggs and sugar until thick and lemon-colored. Sift together dry ingredients; fold into eggs. Pour into a greased and floured 9-inch spring-form pan. Bake at 325° for 40 to 50 minutes or until springy to touch. Turn upside down and cool on a rack.

Meringue: Beat egg whites with cream of tartar until foamy; slowly beat in sugar, continuing beating until stiff peaks form. Fold in nuts. Pour into greased and floured 9-inch round cake pans (lined with greased waxed paper). Bake at 275° for 1 hour. Turn oven off and leave layers in with door closed another hour. Cool.

Syrup: Bring water and sugar to boiling; cool. Stir in Kirsch.

Frosting: Beat butter and egg yolks about 10 minutes. Add sugar; beat until fluffy. Add Kirsch.

To Assemble: Place one layer of meringue on a cake plate; cover it with ¼ of the buttercream. Place sponge cake on top; pour the Kirsch solution over cake very slowly. Spread another layer of buttercream on cake. Top with meringue. Spread remaining buttercream around the sides of cake; press almonds around the sides. Lightly sift confectioners' sugar on top.

Mrs. James F. Peil
(Nancy Rodgers)

SACHER TORTE — 10 Servings

10 egg whites
1/8 tsp. salt
3/4 cup sugar
3/4 cup butter
7 sq. semi-sweet chocolate
1 tsp. vanilla
8 egg yolks
1 cup flour
3 oz. unsweetened chocolate
1 cup whipping cream
1 T. corn syrup
1 cup sugar
1 egg, lightly beaten
1 tsp. vanilla
1 cup apricot preserves
Whipped cream
Crystalized violets

Beat egg whites and salt until soft peaks form. Add 3/4 cup sugar very gradually, beating constantly until stiff peaks form. Melt butter and semi-sweet chocolate in a double boiler. Cool slightly. Add chocolate mixture with 1 tsp. vanilla to egg yolks. (This will be thick.) Fold 1/4 of meringue mixture into chocolate mixture. Pour over remaining meringue and sprinkle flour on top. Fold all together very gently, leaving no lumps of white. Pour into three 9-inch buttered, waxed-paper-lined cake pans. Bake at 350° for 25 or 30 minutes. Turn out onto a rack; remove wax paper. Cool. Combine unsweetened chocolate, cream, corn syrup, and 1 cup sugar in pan. Heat until mixture reaches 225° on a candy thermometer. Beat hot mixture slowly into egg. Cool to room temperature. Add 1 tsp. vanilla. Spread apricot preserves between 2 layers. Place the third layer on top and pour cooled frosting over cake. Refrigerate 3 hours or overnight. Bring to room termperature before serving. Serve with slightly sweetened whipped cream and crystalized violets.

Mrs. H. Alex Vance, Jr.
(Melinda Martin)

RASPBERRY CHESTNUT CREAM — 6 Servings

Delicious, unusual and so simple

1 can (16 oz.) sweetened chestnut puree
1 cup whipping cream
1 T. light rum
1/4 cup confectioners' sugar
1 sq. semi-sweet chocolate, grated
1 pt. fresh raspberries

Beat chestnut puree until it is very smooth; divide among 6 stemmed dessert glasses, chill. Whip cream with rum and sugar until it holds a soft shape; spoon over puree. Sprinkle grated chocolate on cream. Spoon the raspberries on top.

Miss Virginia C. Franche

GRANDMA'S DEVIL'S FOOD CAKE 10 Servings

½ cup butter
2 cups light brown sugar
2 eggs, beaten
½ cup buttermilk
2¼ cups flour
Pinch of salt
½ cup boiling water
1 tsp. soda
½ cup grated bitter chocolate or ½ cup cocoa plus 1 T. butter
1 tsp. vanilla

FROSTING AND FILLING:

2 cups light brown sugar
½ cup butter
½ cup milk or cream

Cream butter and sugar until smooth. Add eggs, one at a time; and beat well. Mix flour and salt; and add to creamed mixture alternately with milk. Dissolve soda and chocolate in water; when cool add to other mixture. Add vanilla. Place in 3 greased 8-inch layer cake pans. Bake at 350° for 20 to 25 minutes. Frost while still slightly warm.

Frosting: Cook all ingredients slowly until it spins a thread. Let cool to 160°; beat until creamy. If too thick, add more cream.

Mrs. Patrick W. O'Brien
(Deborah Bissell)

DATE ORANGE LAYER CAKE 10 Servings

A very moist rich cake

2½ cups sifted flour
½ tsp. salt
1 tsp. soda
1 tsp. baking powder
1 cup softened butter
2 cups sugar
2 eggs
1 cup chopped nuts
1 cup cut-up dates
Grated rind of 2 oranges
1 cup buttermilk
1 tsp. vinegar
Juice of 2 oranges

ICING:

1 cup sweet butter
Juice of 2 oranges
Grated rind of 1 orange
4 cups confections' sugar

Sift dry ingredients together. Cream butter and 1 cup sugar. Add eggs; beat well. Sprinkle a little flour over nuts and dates, reserve. Add rind to butter. Stir in dry ingredients, buttermilk and vinegar alternately. Mix well; add nuts and dates. Turn into 2 greased and waxed-paper-lined 9-inch cake pans. Bake at 350° about 25 minutes or until done. Remove cake from oven; leave in pans. Combine orange juice and 1 cup sugar and pour over cake. Leave in pan until cool. For icing, beat butter until fluffy. Add orange rind. Add confectioners' sugar gradually; thin with enough orange juice until frosting is of spreading consistency.

Mrs. Gordon B. MacDonald
(Virginia Fagan)

LEMON GINGERBREAD LOG

10 Servings

¾ cup sifted flour
½ tsp. salt
½ tsp. baking soda
½ tsp. baking powder
½ tsp. ginger
½ tsp. cinnamon
¼ tsp. cloves
¼ tsp. allspice
4 eggs
½ cup sugar
⅓ cup light molasses
Confectioners' sugar
1 qt. lemon sherbet

Combine flour, salt, soda, baking powder and spices. In large bowl beat eggs at top speed until very thick and lemon colored. Continue beating, gradually adding sugar until mixture is very very thick, about 8 minutes. Reduce speed; add dry ingredients. With spoon fold in molasses. Pour into greased and waxed-paper-lined 12 x 18 x 1-inch pan; bake about 12 minutes at 375° until done. Invert onto waxed paper which has been sprinkled with confectioners' sugar. Remove old waxed paper. Sift another layer of sugar onto gingerbread; cover with a towel and gently roll with the towel. Cool in rolled position, seamside down, on wire rack. Gently unroll; quickly spread with softened sherbet. Reroll, wrap and freeze. Remove from freezer several minutes before serving.

Mrs. Bruce G. Southworth
(Mary Monek)

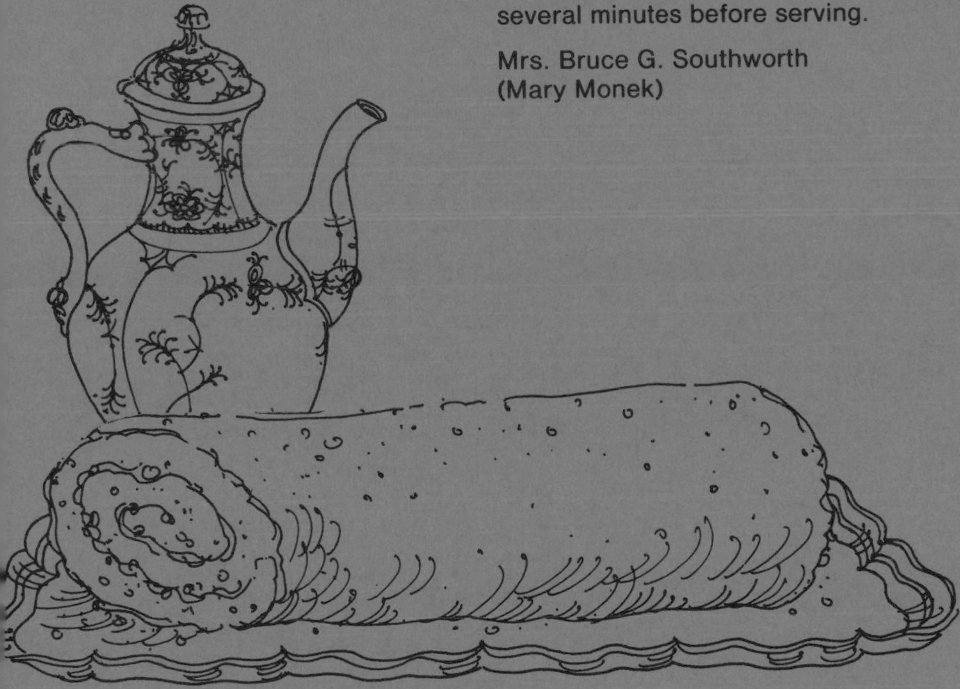

Flour

WINTER KITCHEN

Father Jacques Marquette, the first of the French explorers to enter Illinois, became ill during the expedition and was forced to spend the winter in a rude hut on the south branch of the Chicago River, about five miles from its mouth. That December, 1674, he described the food of the winter season available to himself and his two French companions in his journal: "Pierre and Jacques killed three buffaloes and four deer . . . They contented themselves with killing three or four turkeys out of the many which came around our cabin, and Jacques brought a partridge which he had killed." This bounty, along with the grain, dried pumpkin and corn provided by friendly Indians, comprised the winter fare for the good priest and his friends during that early Chicago sojourn.

Although wild buffalo and partridge no longer abound in Illinois, birds and wild game still provide a major eating pleasure during winter—a time of year which offers little variety in the way of fruits and vegetables. Today's produce selection may be better than dried corn and pumpkin, but it is still sufficiently limited to call for great creativity on the part of the cook, who must prepare the few fresh foods at hand in a variety of ways if they are not to become boring.

Winter's cold weather brings hearty appetities, as well as more time to work in the kitchen. Foods served from December through February are heavier than those of other seasons, and are often accented with sauces and dressings which provide the variety of tastes that nature has neglected.

Winter is also a time of holidays and entertaining, with Christmas and the celebration of the New Year providing the occasions for many gastronomic delights. Homemade foods are welcome gifts, and the efforts of the cook in preparing breads, cakes, puddings, cookies, tureens and pates for friends and relatives are always appreciated.

Specific foods which are best in winter are:

In meat and game prepare dishes of venison, rabbit, goose, quail and turkey.

In fruits, look for apples, cranberries, grapefruit, kumquats, oranges, pears, tangelos, tangerines and ugli fruit.

In salads, use avocados, chinese or celery cabbage, white celery, chicory, cucumbers, scallions, green peppers, spinach and watercress along with bibb, Boston, iceberg, or romaine lettuce. Since winter greens are the least delicate of all varieties, select the strongest flavored dressings to accompany them.

Winter vegetables, too, call for pungent sauces and strongly spiced butters to compliment their coarser taste and textures. Experiment with different ways to serve artichokes, green beans, beets, broccoli, brussels sprouts, cabbage, carrots, cauliflower, celeriac, Jerusalem artichokes, mushrooms, onions, leeks, parsnips, potatoes, spinach, turnips or rutabagas, and winter squash.

Ice holes in the Great Lakes yield pickerel, lake smelt, herring and sauger, while clams, crabs, shrimp, and tiny bay scallops, flown in fresh, are a true delight.

The recipes that follow illustrate interesting and delicious ways to prepare some of these foods of winter.

WINTER MENUS

CAROLING PARTY

WASSAIL

* *

CANNELLONI

Italian Barbera

SPINACH SALAD   FRENCH BREAD

* *

ASSORTED HOLIDAY COOKIES AND CONFECTIONS

CHRISTMAS DINNER

CAVIAR MOUSSE

Brut Blanc de Blancs Champagne

* *

CONSOMME

Fino Sherry

* *

ROAST GOOSE WITH RASPBERRY SAUCE

Clos de Vougeot

BRUSSELS SPROUTS ROYALE   WILD RICE

* *

MIXED GREEN SALAD WITH BLUE CHEESE DRESSING

* *

MOCHA FRENCH YULE LOG

Chateau d'Yquem

FIVE COURSE SIT DOWN DINNER WITHOUT HELP

KIR

* *

CLEAR SOUP

* *

MUSHROOMS SUPREME

Chablis

* *

CROWN ROAST OF PORK WITH SPICED APRICOT STUFFING

Santenay

BRUSSELS SPROUTS

* *

MIXED GREEN SALAD

* *

BRANDY ALEXANDER PIE

WINTER MENUS

12th NIGHT FORMAL DINNER

BRANDIED CHICKEN LIVER PATE
Pouilly Fuisse
* *

JELLIED CONSOMME
* *

VEAL NICHOLAS
St. Emilion Chateau

BUTTERED PEAS   BROILED TOMATO
* *

MIXED GREEN SALAD
* *

GRAND MARNIER SOUFFLE

MEXICAN FIESTA

GUACAMOLE
* *

TACOS   SOUR CREAM ENCHILADAS
Beer or Rioja Blanco

REFRIED BEANS
* *

MEXICAN CREAM TORTE

ST. PATRICK'S DAY

MUSHROOM ROLL-UPS
* *

SPICED CORNED BEEF
Fruity Chenin Blanc

LIMA BEAN CASSEROLE   BOILED BUTTERED POTATOES
IRISH SODA BREAD
* *

PEARS AND SHERBET IN RUM SAUCE
* *

IRISH COFFEE

WINTER TABLE OF CONTENTS

ENTREES: POULTRY

ENTREES: SEAFOOD

VEGETABLES AND ACCOMPANIMENTS

SALADS AND SALAD DRESSINGS

DESSERTS AND SWEETS

BEVERAGES

HOT BUTTERED RUM

50 Servings

1 lb. brown sugar
1 lb. powdered sugar
1 lb. butter
1 qt. vanilla ice cream
1 tsp. allspice
1 tsp. cinnamon
1 tsp. nutmeg
Rum
Brandy

Mix all ingredients except rum and brandy; heat slowly over low heat until like cake batter. Put in freezer. To serve: Place 1 heaping teaspoon of batter into each mug; add 1 jigger rum and 1 jigger brandy. Fill with hot water and mix. Sprinkle nutmeg on top; add piece of cinnamon stick, if desired.

Mrs. John H. McDermott
(Ann Pickard)

TOM AND JERRY

48 Servings

12 egg whites, stiffly beaten
12 egg yolks, beaten until light
3 lbs. powdered sugar
2 tsp. cinnamon
2 tsp. allspice
1 tsp. vanilla
½ tsp. clove
Rum, brandy or bourbon

Fold whites into yolks. Stir in sugar and flavorings. To serve: Place 2½ tablespoons of mixture in mug. Add 1 to 2 oz. rum, brandy or bourbon. Slowly fill mug with boiling water; stir. Top with dash of nutmeg.

Mrs. Timothy E. Thompson
(Susan Falk)

SWEDISH GLÖG

About 1 Gallon

2 fifths claret wine
2 fifths port wine
20 cardamom seeds
20 cloves
2 oz. cinnamon seeds
¾ cup raisins
¼ cup blanched almonds
1 orange, cut up
2 cups sugar
1 pt. brandy

Pour port and claret in large kettle. Tie spices in cheese cloth. Add to wine along with raisins, almonds and orange. Simmer 30 minutes. Remove spice bag; strain, if desired. Remove from heat; add sugar and brandy. Cover and simmer slowly for 15 minutes. Serve warm.

Miss Frances Ann Rohlen

Mrs. Karl V. Rohlen, Jr.
(Carolyn Walker)

HOT RED WINE — 5 Quarts

- 4 to 6 very ripe red apples
- 2 T. cardamon seeds
- 4 sticks cinnamon
- 2 T. whole allspice
- 1 gallon port wine
- 1 fifth bourbon
- ½ cup sugar
- 1 small can frozen orange juice, thawed
- 1 tsp. ground nutmeg
- 1 tsp. ground cinnamon

Pierce underside of apples several times with fork. Tie whole spices in cheesecloth bag. Then place all ingredients in large pan; heat slowly. Do not boil. Serve in punch cups.

Mrs. John Mangel II
(Hilda Brumbaugh)

PERCOLATOR MULLED WINE — 8-10 Servings

- 2 to 2½ qts. red wine
- 3 cinnamon sticks, broken
- 3 T. whole allspice
- 2 T. whole cloves
- 1 cup brown sugar

Place spice and sugar in strainer of pot with wine below. Heat. Let wine percolate slowly through sugar and spices until it is of desired strength as determined by color and flavor. Avoid boiling of beverage in pot.

Miss Jeanne W. Smith

HOT SPICED TEA — 8 Servings

Outstanding for cold winter days

- 1 cup sugar
- 1 T. whole cloves
- 2 cinnamon sticks
- 4 cups water
- 2½ tsp. tea leaves
- 4 cups boiling water
- Juice of 4 oranges
- Juice of 1 lemon

Combine the first 4 ingredients in saucepan; bring to a boil. Boil 10 minutes. Steep tea leaves in 4 cups boiling water for 10 minutes. Combine all ingredients; bring to a simmer. Serve very hot. Can be made and refrigerated for later use. Just reheat.

Mrs. H. Alex Vance, Jr.
(Melinda Martin)

SPICED CRANBERRY PUNCH — 12 Servings

½ cup sugar
1 cup water
½ tsp. whole cloves
3 cinnamon sticks
2 cups cranberry juice
½ cup lemon juice
1 cup orange juice
3 cups ginger ale
1 fifth rum

Mix first four ingredients; boil 5 minutes. Strain; cool. Mix with fruit juices. Just before serving, pour into a punch bowl over a decorative ice ring mold (use holly leaves and red cranberries). Add ginger ale and rum.

Mrs. Patrick Callahan
(Patricia Henebry)

MILK PUNCH — 35 Servings

4 qts. milk
1 fifth of whiskey
1 cup brandy
2½ cups rum
1 qt. vanilla ice cream
Nutmeg

Combine milk, whiskey, brandy, and rum. Stir well. Pour into punch bowl. Use vanilla ice cream to float in punch bowl, keeping punch cool and enriching it. Garnish with nutmeg.

Mrs. John S. Jenkins
(Mary Lou Cudlip)

WASSAIL

6 Servings

6 small tart apples
3 pts. ale, at room temperature
1 cup brown sugar
1 tsp. ginger
1 tsp. cinnamon
1 tsp. nutmeg
2 to 3 whole cloves
Thin strips of rind from one lemon
1 pt. Malaga wine or sherry

Core apples; dry-roast them without sugar in a 350° oven until they almost burst and are white and frothy. Combine 1 pint ale with brown sugar, spices and lemon peel; simmer for 15 minutes. Add the rest of the ale and wine; heat thoroughly, but do not boil. To serve: Put an apple in each mug; ladle hot beverage over it.

Mrs. Robert T. DePree
(Susan Barker)

UNBEATABLE EGG NOG

8 Servings

6 eggs, separated
½ cup sugar
1 pt. whipping cream
2 cups milk
¼ cup superfine sugar
1 pt. good blended whiskey
1 oz. Jamaican rum

Beat egg yolks until light. Add sugar, cream and milk. Beat egg whites until stiff. Gradually add sugar, continuing to beat until stiff peaks form. Add whiskey and rum to egg yolk mixture. Fold in ½ of the egg white mixture until well blended. Top with remaining egg whites, spread evenly over top of mixture. Let stand in refrigerator for at least 24 hours.

Mrs. Jerome E. Hickey
(Denise Coakley)

HOT CRABMEAT DIP

8-10 Servings

1 pkg. (8 oz.) cream cheese
3 T. mayonnaise
2 T. white wine
1 tsp. Dijon mustard
½ tsp. sugar
¼ tsp. salt
1 can (7½ oz.) crabmeat

In double boiler, combine all ingredients except crabmeat; cook until blended and heated through. Stir in crabmeat; serve in chafing dish with crackers.

Mrs. Bruce G. Southworth
(Mary Monek)

GREEK SPINACH-FILLED PASTRY

Makes 40

1 medium onion, finely-chopped
¼ cup mixture butter and olive oil
1 pkg. (10 oz.) frozen spinach, defrosted and drained
½ lb. feta cheese (crumbled)
¾ cup bechamel sauce
3 eggs, well-beaten
1 tsp. dill (optional)
½ lb. phyllo pastry
½ cup melted butter

Saute onion in butter and olive oil until transparent. Add spinach; simmer until most of moisture has evaporated. Combine feta cheese with bechamel sauce. Add eggs and dill; mix well. Blend into spinach-onion mixture.

Defrost phyllo pastry. Cut each sheet lengthwise into 4 strips. Brush with some of the melted butter. (Work quickly or it will dry out. Keep sections you are not working with covered with a damp towel). Place 1 tablespoon filling on bottom end of each strip; fold the pastry over it to form a triangle. Continue folding the pastry in triangles down the full length of the strip to make one multilayered triangle. Prepare remaining strips in the same way. Brush with more melted butter; bake at 400° for 20 minutes or until lightly browned. (May be frozen and reheated).

Mrs. William G. Dubinsky
(Sherrilyn Tatham)

SHRIMP SAGANAKI

Makes about 3 Dozen

This may also be served with rice for an entree
Saganaki is Greek for "hot pan"

1 pkg. (8 oz.) frozen artichoke hearts
¼ cup olive oil
1 lb. raw medium shelled shrimp
¼ lb. small whole mushrooms
2 cloves garlic, pressed
½ tsp. salt
Freshly-grouna pepper
½ tsp. oregano
2 T. lemon juice
2 T. minced fresh parsley

Blanche artichokes in boiling salted water for 2 minutes. Drain. Heat olive oil in a skillet; add shrimp and mushrooms. Cook until shrimp turn pink. Add artichoke hearts, garlic, salt, pepper, and oregano. Heat until hot. Sprinkle with lemon juice; stir lightly. Sprinkle with parsley. Serve in a chafing dish with toothpicks or keep warm in a mongolian fire pot.

Mrs. Suzanne Robison
(Suzanne Dohse)

CHUTNEY CHEESE BALL

6-8 Servings

¼ lb. blue cheese
½ lb. cream cheese
¼ cup chopped chutney
½ cup toasted almonds, chopped

Mix the blue cheese, cream cheese, and chutney; form into a ball. Roll the cheese ball in the chopped almonds. Chill. Serve with crackers. (May be frozen).

Mrs. Bruce G. Southworth
(Mary Monek)

MUSHROOM ROLL-UPS

16-18 Servings

- 1 loaf thin-sliced bread, trimmed
- ½ lb. fresh mushrooms, chopped
- ½ cup butter
- 3 T. flour
- 1 cup light cream
- ¾ tsp. salt
- ¼ tsp. MSG
- 2 tsp. chives
- 1 tsp. lemon juice
- Butter, softened

Roll bread slices thin and flat. Saute mushrooms in butter for 5 minutes. Stir in flour until well blended. Stir in cream; cook, stirring constantly, until thickened. Stir in salt, MSG, chives, and lemon juice. Remove from heat. Place 1 to 2 teaspoons of the mixture on each slice of bread. Roll; butter the top side of each. Freeze. When ready to serve, cut in half; place on baking sheet. Bake at 400° for about 10 minutes or until light brown.

Mrs. Raymond Olson, Jr.
(Carol Johnson)

BRANDIED CHICKEN LIVER PATE

8-10 Servings

- 2 lbs. chicken livers, chopped
- ½ cup butter
- 2 medium onions, chopped
- 1 tsp. paprika
- 1 tsp. curry powder
- ¼ tsp. salt
- ¼ tsp. pepper
- 1 cup softened butter
- ¼ cup brandy

Combine in a saucepan the first 7 ingredients. Cover and cook over low heat for 10 minutes. Puree in a blender or force through a sieve. Stir in the softened butter and brandy. Put the pate in a covered dish; chill until firm. Serve with crackers or melba toast.

Mrs. Thomas C. O'Neil
(Jane Stephens)

SMOKED SALMON SPREAD

- 1 lb. smoked salmon, cut in thin short strips
- ½ cup sour cream
- ½ cup mayonnaise
- 1 onion, coarsely grated
- 1 T. capers
- 2 tsp. fresh dill, chopped; or 1 tsp. dill weed
- Pepper
- Parsley, minced

Combine all ingredients; mix until well blended. Serve with toast triangles with the crusts removed.

Mrs. John C. Munson
(Virginia Aldrich)

NOVA SCOTIA MOLD

12 Servings

1 envelope unflavored gelatin
¼ cup cold water
½ cup hot cream
1 pkg. (8 oz.) cream cheese, softened
1 cup sour cream
1 tsp. worcestershire sauce
Dash Tabasco sauce
2 T. chopped chives
1 tsp. lemon juice
1 T. chopped parsley
1 T. horseradish
½ lb. Nova Scotia or smoked salmon, coarsely chopped
4 oz. red caviar

Soak gelatin in cold water for 5 minutes. Stir gelatin mixture into hot cream; stir until dissolved. Cool. Cream the cheese until smooth; blend in sour cream, worcestershire sauce, Tabasco, and chives. Stir into gelatin-cream mixture. Add lemon juice, parsley, horseradish, and salmon. Gently fold in caviar. Pour into a well-greased 3-cup mold. Refrigerate until firm. Unmold onto a lettuce-lined serving plate. Garnish with watercress and cherry tomatoes. Circle mold with party rye slices or black bread.

Mrs. George H. Cross III
(Gwendolyn Rendall)

CAVIAR MOUSSE

10 Servings

1 env. unflavored gelatin
1 tsp. worcestershire sauce
Juice of 1 lemon
2 T. mayonnaise
1 pt. sour cream
4½ oz. black caviar
1 T. onion juice
1 to 2 dashes dry mustard

Soak gelatin until soft in 2 tablespoons cold water; add ½ cup boiling water; stir until dissolved. Add lemon juice and worcestershire sauce. In another bowl, combine mayonnaise and sour cream. Pour in gelatin mixture and remaining ingredients (be sure caviar has been rinsed well and drained). Mix gently. Pour into lightly-greased 1 qt. mold; chill for 6 hours. Unmold and serve with crackers.

Mrs. Robert W. Buckley, Jr.
(Ann Middleton)

GUACAMOLE

8 Servings

- **2 large cloves garlic**
- **2 large ripe avocados**
- **2 T. fresh lime juice**
- **¼ cup butter**
- **2 to 4 tsp. canned chili pepper, drained, very finely minced**
- **2 tsp. juice from chili pepper**
- **2 tsp. grated onion**
- **2 tomatoes, seeded, chopped**
- **2 T. cream**
- **Salt and freshly-ground pepper**

Mash garlic by putting it through a press. Mash avocado well with a fork. Stir lime juice into mixture. Melt butter; heat until it turns nutty brown. Add to avocados. Add remaining ingredients; mix well. Salt and pepper to taste. Serve with corn tortilla chips.

Mrs. Peter Werner
(Kathy Collins)

SHRIMP TREE WITH SHERRIED SHRIMP DIP

- **1 cup mayonnaise**
- **1 T. tarragon vinegar**
- **1 T. red wine vinegar**
- **2 tsp. anchovy paste**
- **1 tsp. dry mustard**
- **2 T. sherry**
- **¼ cup parsley, minced**
- **1 T. grated onion**
- **¼ cup capers**
- **¼ tsp. garlic powder**
- **Medium shrimp**

Combine all ingredients except shrimp; refrigerate, covered, 24 hours.

Shrimp Tree: Cover a large styrofoam cone with fresh parsley. Force a dowel up center of cone. Secure other end of dowel in a decorative container. Cover top of container with parsley. Secure shrimp to tree with red toothpicks; place extra shrimp around base. Serve with chilled sauce.

Mrs. Gordon B. MacDonald
(Virginia Fagan)

AVOCADOS WITH HOT DRESSING

4 Servings

- 2 T. sugar
- 2 T. water
- 2 T. vinegar
- 2 T. catsup
- 2 T. butter
- Salt
- Pepper
- 2 ripe avocados, halved, pits removed
- 6 slices cooked bacon, crumbled

In saucepan, heat sugar and water until sugar is dissolved. Stir in vinegar, catsup, butter, salt and pepper. Cook over low heat 15 to 20 minutes. Pour dressing into cavities of avocados; sprinkle bacon over the top. Dressing can be made in advance and reheated.

Mrs. William G. McMillan
(Florence Dalrymple)

SHRIMP ROCKEFELLER

8 Servings

- 2 pkgs. (8 to 10 oz. each) frozen cooked, cleaned shrimp
- 2 pkgs. (10 oz. each) frozen chopped spinach
- ¼ cup water
- ½ cup minced onion
- ¾ tsp. salt
- 3 slices white bread, crusts removed, cubed
- ½ cup butter
- 1½ tsp. worcestershire sauce
- ¼ tsp. hot pepper sauce
- 1 tsp. celery salt
- ½ tsp. garlic powder
- ½ cup dry bread crumbs
- 2 T. melted butter
- ¼ cup grated parmesan cheese

Thaw shrimp. Cook spinach with water, onion and salt just until spinach separates. To undrained spinach, add bread, butter, worcestershire sauce, hot pepper sauce, celery salt and garlic powder. Simmer 10 minutes. Reserve 8 shrimp for garnish. Divide remaining shrimp among 8 scallop shells; cover with spinach mixture. Moisten bread crumbs with butter; sprinkle over spinach. Top with parmesan cheese and 8 shrimp. Bake at 400° for 15 minutes or until lightly browned.

Mrs. John N. Schmidt
(Joan M. Slauson)

MUSHROOMS SUPREME

8 Servings

To serve in place of a fish course at a formal dinner

1 lb. fresh mushrooms, sliced
¾ cup butter
¼ cup flour
1 tsp. salt
¼ tsp. white pepper
1½ cups milk
½ cup half and half
1 cup grated swiss or gruyere cheese
2 T. brandy
8 slices toast, crusts removed

Saute mushrooms in ½ cup butter; set aside. Melt remaining butter in heavy saucepan; blend in flour and seasonings. Stir in milk and half and half. Cook, stirring constantly, until thickened. Stir in cheese; cook slowly until melted. Add mushrooms and brandy; heat thru. Serve over toast points.

Mrs. Phillip J. Stover
(Annette Ashlock)

HOT BRANDIED GRAPEFRUIT

2 Servings

1 grapefruit, halved, sections loosened
2 T. brown sugar
1 tsp. butter
1 T. brandy

Combine brown sugar, butter and brandy. Spread on top of grapefruit halves. Broil slowly until heated and bubbling. Serve hot for appetizer.

Mrs. Charles H. Lueck
(Annabelle Perry)

BEEF-NOODLE SOUP WITH CARAWAY DUMPLINGS

6 Servings

Robust cold-day main dish

1 to 1½ lbs. meaty beef soup bones
8 cups water
1 onion, sliced
1 bunch celery tops and leaves, unchopped
1 rib celery, sliced
2 tsp. salt
2 cloves garlic, minced
2 bay leaves
½ tsp. savory
¼ tsp. pepper
1 cup uncooked noodles
½ cup (or more) frozen peas

CARAWAY DUMPLINGS
1 cup flour
1 T. parsley flakes
1½ tsp. baking powder
1 tsp. caraway seeds
¼ tsp. salt
1½ T. margarine
½ cup milk

In kettle, combine bones, water, onion, celery tops and leaves, sliced celery and seasonings. Cover, simmer for 3 hours or until meat is very tender. Remove bones, bay leaves and most celery tops. Add noodles and peas. For dumplings, mix flour, parsley, baking powder, caraway seeds, and salt; cut in margarine until crumbly. Add milk; stir just until moistened. Drop 6 spoonfuls of dumpling batter on top of bubbling soup. Cover, steam for 15 minutes; do not peek.

Mrs. Phillip J. Stover
(Annette Ashlock)

BLACK BEAN SOUP

8 Servings

2 cups black turtle beans
Water
1 bay leaf
1 ham bone
1 grapefruit, peeled, coarsely chopped
1 beef bouillon cube
1 small green pepper, minced
1 garlic clove, crushed
¼ cup dry sherry
1 cup fluffy buttered rice
½ cup finely-chopped onion

Wash beans; cover with cold water. Soak overnight; drain. Add 3 quarts water, bay leaf and ham bone. Boil gently until the beans are completely soft and the liquid fairly thick, adding more water if necessary. Do not puree or sieve. Add the pulp from the grapefruit, the bouillion cube, green pepper, garlic and sherry. Simmer ½ hour longer. Let each dinner guest garnish their soup with rice and chopped onion.

Mrs. William A. Patterson, Jr
(Marcia Motley)

CORN-OYSTER CHOWDER

8 Servings

- **¼ cup butter**
- **1 large onion, chopped**
- **2 stalks celery, chopped**
- **3 cups water**
- **2 carrots, sliced**
- **4 potatoes, peeled and diced**
- **¼ cup chopped fresh parsley**
- **1 tsp. salt**
- **¼ tsp. black pepper**
- **¼ tsp. sugar**
- **1 can (16 oz.) cream style corn**
- **2 cups milk**
- **1 can (4 oz.) chopped pimientos, drained**
- **1 pt. fresh oysters with liquid**

Melt butter in large soup kettle. Add onion and celery; saute until limp. Add water, carrots, potatoes, parsley, salt, pepper and sugar. Cook about 20 minutes or until vegetables are almost tender. Add corn, milk, pimiento and oysters. Heat just to boiling; turn down heat; simmer until the oyster edges curl. Serve hot.

Mrs. Robert T. DePree
(Susan Barker)

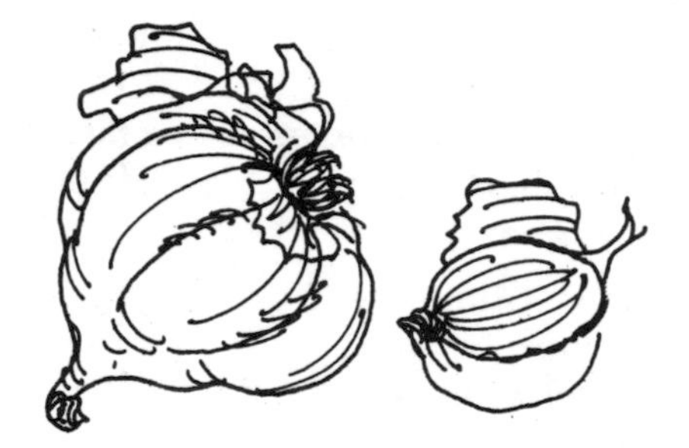

GARLIC SOUP

8 Servings

To combat an aromatic house, make the day before!

- **12 large cloves garlic, peeled and slightly crushed**
- **2½ qts. chicken stock**
- **2 to 2½ T. tapioca**
- **2 egg yolks**
- **¼ cup heavy cream**
- **Chopped fresh basil (or 1 tsp. dried)**
- **2 T. chopped fresh parsley**

Simmer garlic and half the chicken stock, uncovered, for 25 to 30 minutes or until garlic is tender. Remove garlic and puree it. Add remaining stock, reduce over high heat to 7 cups. Reduce heat; add garlic puree and tapioca; cook, stirring constantly, until thickened and smooth. Add more tapioca if not thick enough. Beat egg yolks with cream. Add basil to soup. Add a little hot soup to cream mixture; then pour back into soup, stirring constantly. Do not boil. Serve in soup cups garnished with parsley.

Mrs. Thomas C. O'Neil
(Jane Stephens)

MULLIGATAWNY SOUP — 8-10 Servings

A variation of an old dish from India; the name means pepperwater

1 broiler-fryer chicken (3 to 4 lbs.) cut up
1 qt. water
1 T. salt
1 tsp. curry powder
⅛ tsp. mace
⅛ tsp. cloves
1 small bunch parsley
1 medium onion, sliced
1 medium carrot, sliced
1 stalk celery, sliced
1 green pepper, diced
1 medium apple, pared and sliced
¼ cup butter
1/3 cup flour
1 can (8 oz.) stewed tomatoes

VARIATION:
Excellent recipe to use with turkey carcass. Double or triple ingredients, depending on size of carcass.

In large saucepan, combine chicken, water and next 5 seasonings; cover and simmer 45 minutes or until chicken is tender. Remove chicken from broth. Measure broth; if necessary, add water to make 1 quart. Remove bones and skin from chicken and cut meat into pieces. In large saucepan, cook onion, carrot, celery, green pepper and apple in butter until tender. Remove from heat; stir in flour. Gradually stir in broth and tomatoes. Add chicken. Heat to boiling, stirring constantly. Boil 1 minute. Cover and simmer 1 hour. To serve Indian style, bring to the table in shallow soup plates and top each with a spoonful of hot rice.

Mrs. Sumner W. Mead
(Nancy Price)

MUSHROOM BARLEY SOUP — 10-12 Servings

1 onion, chopped
¼ cup bacon drippings
4 cups beef broth
1 cup barley
1 lb. mushrooms, sliced, sauteed
1 T. lemon juice
1 cup cream or milk
3 egg yolks
Salt and pepper

Saute onion in drippings until transparent. Stir in beef broth; add barley. Cook until tender (about 45 minutes). Add mushrooms and lemon juice; cook 15 minutes longer. Combine milk and egg yolks; slowly stir into soup. Season with salt and pepper. Heat thoroughly but do not boil. Serve hot.

Mrs. Karl V. Rohlen, Jr.
(Carolyn Walker)

MUSHROOM-CHEESE SOUP

4 Servings

Hearty and delicious

1 T. butter
1 T. olive oil
1 onion, grated
1 clove garlic, pressed
1 lb. mushroom caps, sliced
3 T. tomato paste
3 cups chicken broth
2 T. sweet vermouth
½ tsp. salt
⅛ tsp. pepper
4 egg yolks
2 T. minced parsley
2½ T. parmesan cheese, grated

Melt butter and oil in saucepan. Saute onion until brown. Add garlic and mushrooms; saute for 5 minutes. Add the tomato paste; and stir until smooth. Slowly pour in chicken stock; add vermouth, salt and pepper. Simmer for 10 minutes. Beat the egg yolks, parsley and cheese; stir a small amount of stock mixture into the eggs. Slowly stir into the remaining chicken stock, stirring constantly. Serve hot.

Mrs. Charles H. Lueck
(Annabellc Perry)

FRENCH ONION SOUP

4-6 Servings

12 to 16 red onions, peeled and thinly sliced on the bias
¼ cup olive oil
¼ cup butter
Salt
Freshly-ground pepper
2 T. sugar
6 cups beef broth
¼ cup brandy
French bread
Grated parmesan cheese

Saute onions in olive oil and butter until limp; add salt, pepper, sugar and beef broth. Simmer for 20 minutes; add brandy. Lightly brown French bread under broiler and place in soup bowls. Pour soup over; sprinkle parmesan cheese on top.

Mrs. John S. Jenkins
(Mary Lou Cudlip)

SAUSAGE AND PEA SOUP

8 Servings

1 bag (1 lb.) split peas
Water
1 beef soup bone
1 to 2 lbs. ham
1 bay leaf
¼ tsp. cayenne
¼ tsp. thyme
½ lb. seasoned sausage (veal sausage or other in casing)
¼ lb. salt pork
1 onion, minced

Cover peas with water and soak overnight; drain. In a kettle combine 6 cups water, drained peas, beef bone, ham, bay leaf, cayenne and thyme. Bring to boil; cover and simmer for 2 hours. Add sausage, salt pork and onion. Simmer another hour. Discard beef bone. Cut up sausage, ham and salt pork; return them to soup. Refrigerate overnight; skim off fat. Reheat and serve hot.

Mrs. Karl V. Rohlen, Jr.
(Carolyn Walker)

OXTAIL SOUP

6 Servings

- **2 lbs. oxtail, cut into 2-inch pieces**
- **½ cup sliced onions**
- **2 T. butter**
- **8 cups water**
- **1½ tsp. salt**
- **3 peppercorns**
- **½ cup diced carrots**
- **½ cup diced celery**
- **1 bay leaf**
- **¼ cup barley**
- **½ cup tomato pulp**
- **1 tsp. dried thyme**
- **1 T. flour**
- **2 T. butter**
- **½ cup burgundy**

Brown oxtail pieces in butter. Add water, salt, and peppercorns; simmer about 4½ hrs. Add vegetables and seasonings; simmer for ½ hr. or until they are tender. Strain soup. If desired meat can be diced and added to the soup. Brown flour and butter; add stock slowly. Stir in burgundy; adjust seasonings.

Mrs. William W. Lane
(Pamela Coles)

DRESDEN CHRISTMAS STOLLEN

2 Large Loaves

This is richer, more moist and longer-keeping than most stollen

- **1¼ cups diced mixed candied fruit**
- **½ cup sultana raisins**
- **½ cup currants**
- **½ cup glaceed cherries, cut in half**
- **¼ cup dark Jamaican rum**
- **2 oz. fresh yeast (cake)**
- **½ cup sugar**
- **1 tsp. salt**
- **½ cup cold milk**
- **1 cup sour cream**
- **2 tsp. lemon juice**
- **2 tsp. vanilla**
- **3 egg yolks**
- **1½ cups butter, softened**
- **5 to 6 cups flour**
- **1 cup blanched slivered almonds**
- **½ cup melted butter**
- **Confectioners' sugar**

Combine fruits, raisins, currants and cherries; toss with rum. Marinate 1 hour. Drain. Cream yeast with sugar and salt to make a syrup. Add milk, sour cream, lemon juice and vanilla; stir in egg yolks and softened butter. Add enough flour to make a medium-firm dough. Knead at least 10 minutes, adding more flour if necessary. Dough should be smooth and elastic. Cover bowl and refrigerate for at least 4 hours. It will raise in refrigerator and should be punched down each time. It may be kept 3 days in refrigerator.

Knead fruit and almonds into dough. Work only until fruit is evenly distributed. Cut in half. On a floured surface, roll out each half to a rectangle 13x8 inches. Fold each loaf over on itself lengthwise, not quite in half (as for a Parker House roll); press edges together with a rolling pin. Place on 2 greased baking sheets; allow to rise until almost doubled. Brush with melted butter. Bake at 375° for 45 minutes. Brush with melted butter while warm. Brush again when cool; sift sugar over them. Wrap until needed. Sift sugar over them again, just before serving. Cut into thin slices.

Mrs. H. Alex Vance, Jr.
(Melinda Martin)

FRUIT CAKE

3 Loaves (or 1 Tube Pan)

1 lb. golden raisins
1 lb. mixed candied fruit
½ lb. candied red cherries
1 cup ruby port
1 lb. butter, softened
¾ lb. powdered sugar
7 eggs, separated
4 cups flour (scant)
1 tsp. baking powder
½ tsp. salt
½ tsp. cinnamon
1 lb. whole pecans

DECORATIONS:
Green and red candied cherries, whole pecans, candied pineapple.

Place raisins in large bowl. On top put mixed fruit and cherries. Add the port. Cover bowl; let sit 2 days. Cream butter; add sugar and egg yolks. Whip until light. Sift flour, salt and cinnamon; gradually add to mixture. Stir in nuts and fruit mixture. Beat egg whites until stiff; fold into batter. Ready three 9x5-inch loaf pans; grease and line with waxed paper. Divide batter among pans. Bake at 250° for 25 minutes. At this point, remove cakes and add decorations. Continue baking 1 hour or until done; top should be lightly browned. Cool on wire racks. Remove from pans; trim off paper to cake top level. Wrap in plastic, then foil. Store in refrigerator.

Mrs. Halbert S. Gillette
(Karla Spiel)

CHRISTMAS JAM

6-8 Half-pint Jars

1 pkg. (12 oz.) dried apricots, chopped
1 can (1 lb. 14 oz.) crushed pineapple
3½ cups water
1 jar (8 oz.) maraschino cherries, quartered
6 cups sugar

In large saucepan, combine apricots, pineapple and juice, water and cherry liquid; let stand 1 hour. Cook slowly until apricots are tender. Add sugar; cook slowly, stirring often until thick and clear. Add cherries; cook a few minutes longer and pour into hot sterilized jars; seal.

Mrs. David B. Smith
(Marcia Williamson)

CATHERINE BYRNE'S PLUM PUDDING

3 Molds; 8 Servings each

3 lb. raisins
1 lb. citron
½ lb. glaceed cherries
½ lb. currants
1 lb. beef suet, ground
½ cup brandy
1 lb. fresh bread crumbs
1 T. flour
1 tsp. baking powder
1 whole nutmeg, grated
1 tsp. cinnamon
1 tsp. allspice
1 tsp. cloves
1½ tsp. salt
12 egg yolks
1 lb. brown sugar
1 pt. whipping cream
1 tsp. baking soda
¼ cup maple syrup
7 egg whites, stiffly beaten

Combine raisins, citron, cherries, currants and suet. Add brandy; toss until well mixed. Combine the bread crumbs, flour, baking powder and seasonings; stir into fruit. Beat egg yolks until thick and lemon colored. Gradually beat in sugar. Slowly beat in cream. Add baking soda dissolved in maple syrup. Pour over the fruit mixture. Stir vigorously until all ingredients are blended. Carefully fold in egg whites.

Separate mixture into 3 equal parts; place each in a greased 1½-qt. pudding basin or plain mold. Fill ¾ full. Cover tightly; steam 3 hours. Cool. Refrigerate pudding at least 3 weeks before serving. When ready to serve, steam mold 1½ hours. Turn out on a serving platter; decorate with a sprig of holly. Accompany with hard sauce.

VARIATION:
To serve pudding aflame, heat ½ cup brandy over low flame; ignite, and pour flaming over pudding.

Mrs. Robert H. BonDurant
(Irene McCausland)

HONEY PECAN LOAF — 1 Loaf

- ¾ cup milk
- ¼ cup orange juice
- 1 tsp. grated orange rind
- 1 cup honey
- ½ cup sugar
- ¼ cup butter
- 2 eggs
- 2¼ cups flour
- 1 tsp. baking soda
- ½ tsp. salt
- ½ tsp. cinnamon
- ¼ tsp. nutmeg
- ⅛ tsp. cloves
- 1 cup chopped pecans
- ¼ cup brown sugar
- ½ tsp. cinnamon
- ¼ cup chopped pecans

Combine milk, orange juice, rind, honey, sugar and butter; heat, stirring until well blended. Cool. Stir into eggs. Sift flour with baking soda, salt, cinnamon, nutmeg and cloves; add to honey mixture, stirring just until blended. Stir in nuts. Pour into a greased 9 x 5-inch loaf pan. Combine the brown sugar, cinnamon and remaining pecans. Sprinkle evenly over batter. Bake at 350° 1 hour, 10 minutes or until done. Cool in pan for 10 minutes. Turn out onto cake rack.

Mrs. Edward L. Flom
(Beryl Light)

GRAND MARNIER CAKE — 12 Servings

- 1 cup butter
- 1 cup sugar
- 3 eggs, separated
- 1½ tsp. Grand Marnier
- 2 cups flour, sifted
- 1 tsp. baking powder
- 1 tsp. baking soda
- 1¼ cups sour cream
- 1½ T. fresh grated orange rind
- 1 cup chopped walnuts

TOPPING:

- ½ cup sugar
- 1 cup orange juice
- ½ cup Grand Marnier

Whipping cream

Beat butter and sugar together until light. Add egg yolks, one at a time, beating well after each addition. Add Grand Marnier. Sift dry ingredients together; add to creamed mixture alternating with the sour cream. Stir in the orange rind and walnuts. Beat egg whites until stiff; fold into batter. Pour into a 9 or 10-inch greased tube pan. Bake at 350° for 50 to 60 minutes. For topping, combine sugar and orange juice in saucepan; heat until dissolved. Add Grand Marnier. Pour topping over hot cake while it is still in the pan. When all liquid has been absorbed and cake is cool, remove from pan. Serve with whipped cream.

Mrs. William G. Dubinsky
(Sherrilyn Tatham)

SPICED CRANBERRIES

6-8 Half-pint Jars

2 quarts cranberries
1⅓ cups cider vinegar
⅔ cup water
6 cups sugar
2 T. ground cinnamon
1 T. ground cloves
1 T. ground allspice

Wash and inspect cranberries. Place in large kettle and add remaining ingredients. Cook slowly over low heat for 45 minutes. Pour into hot sterilized glasses and seal.

Mrs. David B. Smith
(Marcia Williamson)

MUSTARD

Tangy, sweet-sour

1 jar (4 oz.) mustard, (A & P brand preferred)
1 cup vinegar
3 eggs
1 cup sugar

Combine vinegar and mustard and let stand overnight. Next day, beat eggs and sugar together. Stir into mustard-vinegar and cook in double boiler over boiling water, stirring constantly until thickened. Fill jars and let cool. Store in the refrigerator.

Mrs. G. Dodge Ferreira
(Noni Harrington)

CRANBERRY-TANGERINE CHUTNEY

Nice to serve with meats or poultry

4 tangerines
2 cups fresh cranberries
1 medium apple peeled, diced
½ cup golden raisins
½ cup orange marmalade
½ cup vinegar
1½ cups water
1¼ cups sugar
1 T. curry powder
¾ tsp. cinnamon
½ tsp. ginger
¼ tsp. ground cloves
Dash of allspice

Peel tangerines; remove all membranes and seeds. Cut sections in half. Combine all ingredients in a saucepan; bring to a boil over medium heat. Reduce heat, cover and simmer for 30 minutes, stirring occasionally to prevent sticking. Pour into hot sterilized jars; seal. Or store in refrigerator in covered containers.

Mrs. Dennis F. Muckermann
(Elizabeth Graham)

MINCEMEAT

2 lbs. lean beef
2 lbs. beef tongue
1 lb. beef suet
4 cups seedless raisins
4 cups seeded raisins
2 cups currants
1 cup diced citron
1 cup diced orange peel
½ cup diced lemon peel
1 cup chopped figs
2½ cups sugar
2 tsp. salt
2 tsp. nutmeg
2 tsp. cinnamon
2 tsp allspice
1½ tsp. cloves
5½ cups cognac
4½ cups sherry
1 cup chopped tart apples

Cook beef and tongue in water until tender; coarsely grind it, passing the suet through the meat grinder, too. Combine meat mixture and all remaining ingredients except cognac and sherry. Add enough brandy and sherry to just cover. Place all in a crock; let stand in a cool place or refrigerator 1 month. Check once a week; as liquid is absorbed, add enough to moisten it again. It will keep indefinitely. Add 1 cup chopped apples to each 1½ cups drained mincemeat before using or packaging for gifts.

Mrs. Gordon B. MacDonald
(Virginia Fagan)

PEAR CHUTNEY

8 Half-pint Jars

½ tsp. whole allspice
½ tsp. whole cloves
10 cups sliced (about ¼-inch thick) cored and pared pears (4 to 5 lbs.-15 pears)
1½ cups seedless raisins
½ cup finely-chopped green pepper
4 cups sugar
½ cup crystallized ginger
3 cups cider vinegar
½ tsp. salt
2 2-inch sticks cinnamon

Tie allspice and cloves in double thickness of cheesecloth. Combine all ingredients in large saucepan; leave uncovered. Bring to a boil; reduce heat. Simmer slowly 1 hour or until thick. Discard spices. Spoon into hot sterilized jars; seal.

Mrs. J. Stephen Laing
(Suzanne Reyburn)

GINGERBREAD HOUSE

Make this recipe in 3 batches:

1 T. butter, softened
6¼ cups flour
6 T. baking powder
1½ tsp. cinnamon
1 tsp. ground cloves
¼ tsp. nutmeg
¼ tsp. cardamon
⅛ tsp. salt
¾ cup honey
1¾ cups sugar
¼ cup butter
1/3 cup fresh lemon juice
1 T. grated lemon rind
1 egg
1 egg yolk

ICING:

2 egg whites
2½ cups powdered sugar (a second batch of icing may be needed)

DECORATION:

Mixed colorful candies and cookies
1 to 2 cups granulated sugar

Make cardboard patterns for the house and base as shown in illustration. Lightly grease and flour 3 11-inch x 17-inch jelly-roll pans. Set patterns and pans aside.

Sift flour, baking powder, cinnamon, cloves, nutmeg, cardamon and salt together. In a 5 qt. saucepan bring honey, sugar and butter to a boil; cook until sugar is dissolved. Stir in lemon juice and rind. Cool. Beat in 2 cups of flour-spice mixture; add egg and egg yolk; add 4 more cups flour-spice mixture. Knead dough until smooth and still slightly sticky; if still too sticky, beat in more flour by the tablespoon. Evenly press dough into prepared pans, forcing it into corners. Bake at 325° for 35 minutes. Let cake cool in pans 5 minutes. Place patterns on top of gingerbread and cut out shapes. Set pieces aside on wax paper until completely cooled.

Beat egg whites until frothy. Alternate beating whites and sifting sugar over them. Beat until stiff icing is formed. Fill a pastry bag with a small decorative tip. Pipe windows, door, etc. on pieces of gingerbread while still flat. When icing is completely dry, assemble house using icing as cement to hold pieces together. As you assemble each piece, hold it until frosting is set. Finally, lay roof pieces on top; they should meet, but not overlap. Fill space between them with icing. Use your imagination to decorate house with candies and cookies; cement them in place with icing. When house is done to your taste, sprinkle the roof and base with snowdrifts of sugar.

Mrs. Robert W. Buckley, Jr.
(Ann Middleton)

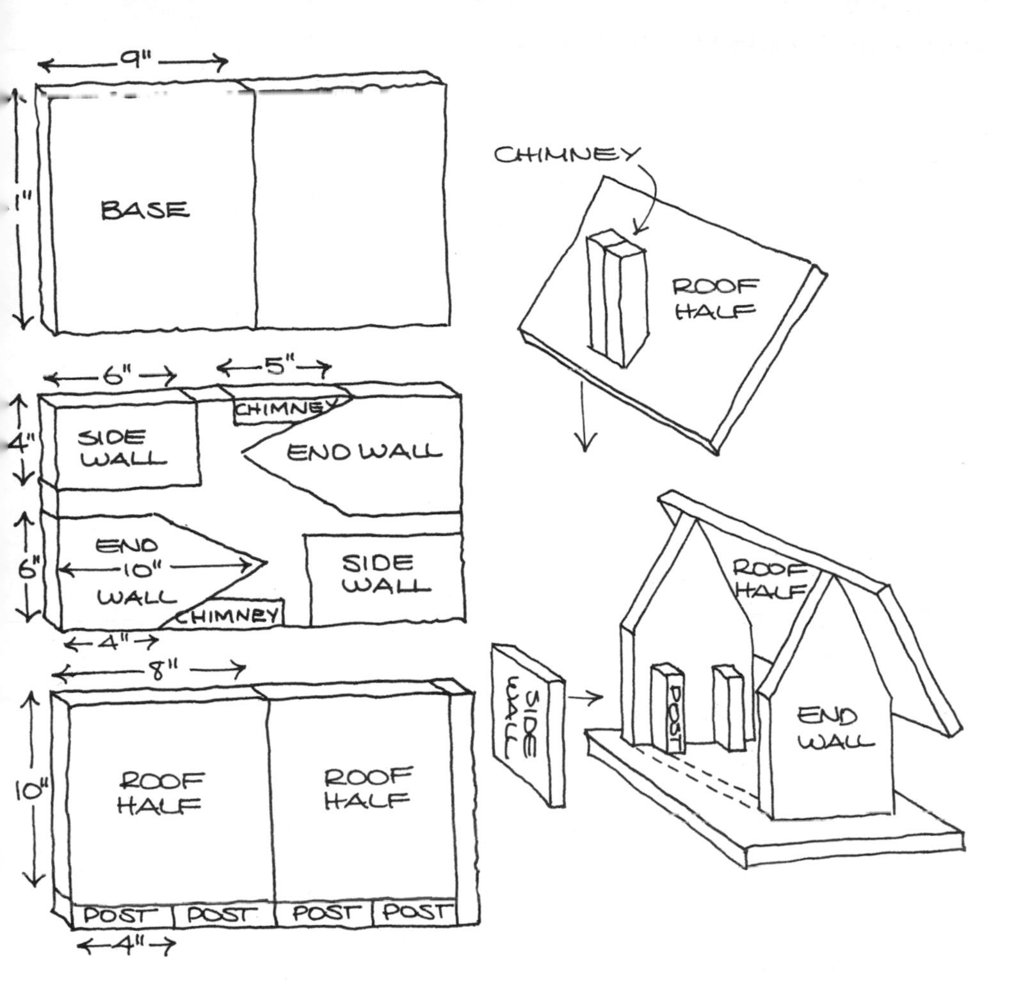

SWEDISH NUTS

1 lb. pecans
3 egg whites
Dash salt
1 cup sugar
1 cup butter

Toast pecans in 325° oven until light brown. Beat egg whites with salt until foamy. Gradually add sugar, continuing to beat until stiff peaks form. Fold in cooled nuts. Melt butter in 15x10x1-inch jelly roll pan. Spread nut mixture over butter. Bake at 325° about 30 minutes, stirring carefully about every 10 minutes, or until light brown. Cool; break into pieces.

Mrs. Peter A. Bergsten
(Sally Jo Spicher)

BYZANTINE SUGAR PLUMS

- 3 lbs. combined pitted dates, peeled figs, seeded raisins, currants, apricots, prunes
- ½ lb. blanched walnuts or almonds
- ½ lb. unsalted, shelled pistachio nuts
- ½ lb. crystallized ginger
- Grated rind of 2 oranges
- 3 T. lemon juice or brandy, or as needed
- Confectioners' or granulated sugar

Put fruits, nuts, ginger and rind through the coarsest blade of the meat grinder. Add just enough lemon juice or brandy to enable mixture to stick together. Shape into balls, 1 to 1½ inches in diameter. Roll in sugar before wrapping. Vary assortment of fruits and nuts to suit your own taste, using any one or all of those suggested.

Mrs. Thomas N. Boyden
(Susan Dalton)

CHOCOLATE PEANUT BUTTER CONFECTIONS

48 Confections

- 1 cup peanut butter
- 2 cups confectioners' sugar
- ½ cup butter
- Dash salt
- 1 pkg. (6 oz.) semisweet chocolate bits
- ½ stick paraffin

Mix peanut butter, sugar, butter and salt. Form into small balls; place a toothpick in each. Chill about 2 hours. In top of double boiler over hot water, melt chocolate and paraffin. Dip peanut butter balls into chocolate; drop onto waxed paper. Chill. Store in refrigerator.

Mrs. John W. Bradbury
(Mary Nolen)

RUSSIAN TEA CAKES

4 Dozen Cookies

- 1 cup soft butter
- ½ cup sifted confectioners' sugar
- 1 tsp. vanilla
- 2¼ cups flour
- ¼ tsp. salt
- ¾ cup finely-ground pecans

Cream butter, sugar and vanilla. Combine flour with salt; add to butter mixture. Mix in nuts. Chill. Roll into 1-inch balls and place on ungreased cookie sheet. Bake at 400° for 10 to 12 minutes until set but not brown. While warm, roll in more sifted confectioners' sugar. Cool. Roll again.

Mrs. Halbert S. Gillette
(Karla Spiel)

BERLINER KRÄNSE — 6 Dozen 2-inch Cookies

- ¾ cup butter
- ¾ cup margarine
- 1 cup sugar
- 2 tsp. grated orange rind
- 2 eggs
- 4 cups sifted flour
- Red candied cherries, chopped
- Green candied cherries, chopped
- 1 egg white
- 2 T. sugar

Cream butter, margarine and sugar. Add orange rind and eggs; mix well. Stir in flour. Chill dough. Break off small pieces; roll to pencil-size thickness, 4-inches long. Form into wreaths. Into them press bits of red and green candied cherries for holly berries and greens. Beat egg white until stiff; gradually beat in sugar. Brush wreaths with meringue. Bake at 400° for 10 to 12 minutes, until set but not brown.

Mrs. Halbert S. Gillette
(Karla Spiel)

DANISH COOKIES

- ½ lb. butter
- ⅔ cup sugar
- 4 egg yolks
- 2½ cups flour
- ½ tsp. vanilla
- Whole pecans
- Currant jelly

Cream butter and sugar. Add egg yolks, flour and vanilla; mix thoroughly forming a firm dough. Chill dough for 30 minutes. Make small balls (about ¾-inch) with hands; place on greased cookie sheet. Press a pecan into half the balls. Make a small indentation in remaining balls with your thumb; fill with currant jelly. Bake at 350° for 12 minutes.

Mrs. Calvin Adams
(Ann Thomas)

CHRISTMAS CASSEROLE COOKIES

36 Cookies

- 2 eggs
- 1 cup sugar
- 1 cup pitted dates, cut up
- 1 cup coconut
- 1 cup chopped nuts
- 1 T. rum

Beat eggs; add sugar, continuing to beat until light. Blend in remaining ingredients. Turn into an ungreased 2-quart casserole. Bake at 350° for 30 minutes. While still hot, beat well with a wooden spoon. Cool. Form into balls; roll in granulated sugar.

Mrs. David B. Smith
(Marcia Williamson)

FLORENTINES

16 Confections

½ cup sugar
⅓ cup heavy cream
⅓ cup honey
2 T. butter
¼ cup candied orange peel, very finely-chopped
1½ cups blanched slivered almonds
3 T. flour
8 oz. semisweet chocolate
1 T. vegetable shortening

Combine sugar, cream, honey and butter in a saucepan; stir over low heat until sugar is dissolved. Raise heat and boil until candy therometer is 238°; cool slightly. Stir in orange peel, nuts and flour. Drop small rounds of batter on greased baking sheets, leaving 2 inches between cookies; flatten with greased fork. Bake at 400° 8 to 10 minutes or until golden. Pull each cookie back into shape with a 3-inch round cookie cutter. When firm, remove to a rack. Melt chocolate; stir in shortening. Thinly coat underside of each cookie with chocolate. Refrigerate until chocolate is set.

Mrs. Thomas D. Hodgkins
(Mary Ann BonDurant)

GINGERBREAD MEN

36-48 Cookies

2 cups sugar
½ cup shortening
½ cup butter
2 eggs
½ cup dark molasses
4 cups flour
2 tsp. cinnamon
1 tsp. ginger
1 tsp. cloves
1 tsp. nutmeg
1 tsp. soda
¼ tsp. salt
Confectioners' icing
Decorations: colored sugars, raisins, citron, chocolate chips

Cream sugar, shortening and butter until light. Stir in eggs, one at a time, blending well. Stir in molasses. Sift together dry ingredients; stir into the sugar-egg mixture, mixing until thoroughly blended. Roll into a ball; wrap in waxed paper. Chill 3 hours. Roll out on floured board to about ¼ inch thickness. Cut out with cutters; placed on greased cookie sheets. Bake at 325° for 10 to 12 minutes. Holes can be made in tops of cookies before baking so they can be hung on the Christmas tree. Spread with icing; decorate as desired.

Mrs. R. Thomas Howell
(Karen W. Corbett)

PFEFFERNUSSE

30 Cookies

Delicious German spice cookies

4 cups flour
1 tsp. baking powder
1 tsp. ground cloves
½ tsp. ground allspice
½ tsp. ground cinnamon
¾ cup honey
1 cup dark corn syrup
¾ cup sugar
2 T. butter
1 T. shortening

ALMOND GLAZE:

1 cup confectioners' sugar
½ tsp. almond extract
1 tsp. fresh lemon juice or rum
2 T. cold water

Combine flour, baking powder and spices. In a large saucepan bring honey, corn syrup and sugar to a boil over medium heat. Stir until sugar dissolves. Reduce heat to low and simmer for 5 minutes. Remove from heat; add butter and shortening; stir until dissolved. Beat in flour mixture, 1 cup at a time, until smooth. Drop by teaspoon onto buttered baking sheets, leaving 1-inch between cookies. Bake at 400° for 15 minutes. Sprinkle with powdered sugar or coat with almond glaze. For glaze, stir sugar, almond extract and juice or rum together. Add cold water, 1 teaspoon at a time, until of spreading consistency. Can be stored for 6-8 weeks in tightly sealed tins or jars. These cookies are very hard.

Mrs. Robert W. Buckley, Jr.
(Ann Middleton)

SWEDISH COOKIES

2 Dozen Cookies

3 egg whites
1 cup sugar
½ cup ground almonds
6 slices melba toast, whirled in a blender

ICING No.1:

¾ cup sweet butter, softened
½ cup powdered sugar
1 T. cocoa, unsweetened
1 tsp. vanilla

ICING No. 2:

⅔ cup powdered sugar
2 to 3 T. water
¼ cup cocoa, unsweetened

Beat egg whites until foamy. Gradually add sugar, one tablespoon at a time, beating until stiff peaks form. Fold in ground nuts and toast crumbs. Drop in even rounds on a greased and floured cookie sheet. Bake at 300° until lightly browned, about 20 minutes. Cool 10 minutes, then remove carefully from cookie sheet. Beat ingredients for icing No. 1 until fluffy; smear on underside of cookies. Chill (icing side up). Beat ingredients for icing No. 2; smear on top of icing No. 1, leaving a rim of icing No. 1 showing. Top with a toasted almond. Chill; store in tightly closed tin in refrigerator.

Mrs. James F. Peil
(Nancy Rodgers)

THREE-TIERED OMELET WITH WINE SAUCE

6 Servings

12 eggs, separated
1 tsp. salt
1 tsp. seasoned salt
Freshly-ground pepper
3 T. parsley, minced
3 shallots, finely-chopped
6 T. flour
4½ T. white wine or dry vermouth

SAUCE:
¼ cup butter, melted
¼ cup flour
1 cup whipping cream
2 chicken bouillon cubes
2 tsp. chopped chives
1 tsp. worcestershire sauce
½ cup dry white wine
1 tsp. fresh lemon juice
1 T. fresh dill or
1 tsp. dill weed
Dash salt

VARIATIONS:
Use other sauces. Sprinkle grated cheese or sauteed mushrooms between layers.

Beat egg yolks until light. Add both salts, pepper, parsley, shallots and flour. Beat until thoroughly blended. Beat egg whites together with wine until stiff but not dry. Carefully fold whites into yolk mixture. Grease three 8-inch pie plates. Divide egg mixture between them. Bake at 350° for 15 minutes or until set.

For sauce, melt butter; stir in flour. Gradually add cream. Add bouillon cubes, chives and worcestershire. Cook, stirring constantly, until thickened. Stir in remaining ingredients. Simmer 10 minutes. Stir occasionally. Stack each omelet layer with sauce between; pour sauce over top. Cut in wedges.

Mrs. Thomas C. O'Neil
(Jane Stephens)

CHICKEN MOUSSE WITH SAUCE AURORE — 8 Servings

A delicate winter luncheon dish

1½ lbs. skinned, boneless chicken breasts, cubed (about 3 cups)
Salt and pepper to taste
¼ tsp. nutmeg
⅛ to ¼ tsp. cayenne pepper
2 cups whipping cream
1 egg white, lightly beaten

SAUCE AURORE:
4 T. butter
3 T. finely-chopped onion
3 T. finely-chopped shallots
2 cups tomatoes, seeded, chopped, put through food mill
Salt and pepper
½ bay leaf
½ tsp. tarragon
1½ T. flour
1 cup chicken broth
½ cup whipping cream
1 T. chopped parsley
½ tsp. thyme

Place a few chicken cubes in blender; blend until smooth; scrape into a bowl, repeat until all the chicken has been blended. If necessary, a small amount of cream can be added. Add salt, pepper, nutmeg and cayenne. Chill well. Set the bowl in a bowl of ice cubes; gradually beat in remaining cream. Beat in egg white; chill. Place in buttered 1½-qt. mold; smooth top. Cover with a buttered ring of paper. Place in a baking dish; add about 1-inch of boiling water. Bake at 400° 25 to 35 minutes.

Sauce: Melt 1 T. butter; add onion and shallots. Saute until wilted. Add tomatoes, salt, pepper, bay leaf, tarragon and thyme. Cook, stirring frequently, about 30 minutes. Meanwhile, melt another 1 T. butter; stir in flour. Add chicken broth; simmer, stirring occasionally, about 10 minutes. Add tomato sauce; cook 15 minutes longer. Strain; stir in cream. Adjust seasonings. Heat through. Swirl in remaining butter. Unmold mousse; spoon some sauce over. Sprinkle with parsley. Pass remaining sauce.

Mrs. James F. Peil
(Nancy Rodgers)

CRABMEAT CASSEROLE — 6 Servings

2 cans (7½ oz. each) crabmeat
4 hard boiled eggs, chopped
2 cups bread cubes, crusts removed
2 T. chopped parsley
1 T. grated onion
2 cups mayonnaise
2 cups half and half
1 T. sherry
½ tsp. Durkee sauce
Buttered breadcrumbs

Combine crabmeat, eggs, bread cubes, parsley and onion in an ungreased casserole. Combine mayonnaise, half and half, sherry and Durkees; stir into crabmeat mixture; blend well. Cover with breadcrumbs. Bake, uncovered, at 350° for 45 minutes or until done.

Mrs. Reed M. Badgley
(Mary H. Montgelas)

SPINACH QUICHE

8 Servings

16 slices bacon, fried, crumbled
1 unbaked 10-inch pastry shell
2 large onions, thinly sliced
12 oz. swiss cheese, grated (imported preferred)
1¼ cups cooked chopped spinach, well drained
6 eggs, slightly beaten
3 cups half and half
Salt and pepper
Grated parmesan cheese

Sprinkle bacon on bottom of pie crust. Saute onions in bacon drippings; place onions over bacon. Sprinkle cheese over onion layer; add layer of spinach. Beat together eggs and half and half. Season with salt and pepper; pour over pie. Sprinkle with parmesan cheese. Bake 10 minutes at 450°, then reduce heat to 300° and bake an additional 45 to 50 minutes or until custard is set.

Mrs. William G. Dubinsky
(Sherrilyn Tatham)

SOUR CREAM ENCHILADAS

6 Servings

12 corn tortillas
Corn oil
1 can (10 oz.) enchilada sauce
1 pt. sour cream
1 cup green onions and tops, thinly sliced
½ tsp. ground cumin
1 lb. (about 4 cups) shredded longhorn cheddar cheese

Fry tortillas one at a time in corn oil over high heat about 15 seconds or less. Drain briefly on paper towel and immediately dip each tortilla on all sides in enchilada sauce; set aside. Blend together sour cream, sliced green onion, cumin and 1½ cups shredded cheese. Place 2 overlapping tortillas at one end of a 9 x 13-inch baking dish, allowing part of tortillas to extend over edge of dish. Spread 1/6 of the sour cream mixture down center of tortillas and fold extending section over it. Repeat this process until all six enchiladas are formed side by side covering bottom of dish. Sprinkle remaining cheese over top. Cover and refrigerate overnight or until ready to bake at 375° for 20 minutes.

Mrs. Robert T. DePree
(Susan Barker)

SEAFOOD RICE CASSEROLE

8 Servings

- **2 cups cooked rice**
- **½ cup chopped green pepper**
- **1 cup chopped celery**
- **½ cup chopped onion**
- **1 can (5 oz.), water chestnuts, drained, sliced**
- **1 bag (8 oz.) frozen cooked shrimp**
- **1 can (7½ oz.) crab meat (or frozen)**
- **1 cup mayonnaise (Hellman's preferred)**
- **1 cup tomato juice**
- **¼ tsp. salt**
- **⅛ tsp. pepper**
- **⅛ tsp. paprika**
- **1 small box fresh mushrooms, sliced, sauteed**
- **½ cup sliced almonds**
- **½ cup grated cheddar cheese**

Combine rice, green pepper, celery, onion, water chestnuts, seafood, mayonnaise, tomato juice, spices and mushrooms. Mix well. Pour into a buttered 2½-qt. casserole. Saute almonds in 2 T. butter; sprinkle over casserole. Sprinkle with cheddar cheese. Bake at 350° for 35 minutes, or until bubbly and golden on top. This can be prepared ahead and frozen. Thaw before baking.

Mrs. Bruce G. Southworth
(Mary Monek)

SCALLOPS BRUNI

4-6 Servings

- **¼ cup butter**
- **½ cup chopped onion**
- **½ cup chopped leeks (white part only)**
- **1 lb. raw scallops, cubed**
- **2 T. flour**
- **1 unbaked 9-inch pastry shell**
- **4 eggs, slightly beaten**
- **2 cups whipping cream, scalded**
- **½ tsp. salt**
- **¼ tsp. black pepper**
- **⅛ tsp. nutmeg**

Melt butter; add the onions and leeks. Saute for 5 minutes. Sprinkle the scallops with flour; add to onion and leek mixture. Cook over high heat for about 5 minutes, stirring constantly. Place mixture in pastry shell. Blend eggs, cream, salt, pepper and nutmeg. Pour over scallops. Bake at 375° until light brown and custard is set.

Mrs. Earl F. Ronneberg
(Christiane Wills)

SHRIMP MOUSSE WITH SOLE

8 Servings

8 sole fillets (2¼ lbs.), thawed
2 T. lemon juice
1 tsp. salt
⅛ tsp. white pepper
Butter

MOUSSE:
10 to 12 oz. shelled shrimp, halved
2 egg whites
1 cup whipping cream
1 tsp. salt
1 T. catsup
1 T. chopped parsley
2 T. sherry

SAUCE:
¼ cup butter
¼ cup flour
½ tsp. salt
1 cup light cream
1 T. catsup
2 egg yolks, beaten
½ cup dry sherry
½ lb. fresh mushrooms, thinly-sliced, sauteed
Watercress

Rinse sole under cold water; dry on paper towels. Brush both sides with lemon juice. Sprinkle with salt and pepper. Lightly butter a 5-cup ring mold. Line with fillets, dark side up, narrow end to center, overhanging outside and inside rims. To prepare mousse, place in electric blender shrimp, egg whites, cream, salt, catsup, parsley, sherry. Blend until smooth. Fill mold. Fold ends of fillets, overlapping, over top of filling. Spread top with 1 T. soft butter. Cover loosely with waxed paper. Place mold in 14 x 10-inch baking dish; pour 1-inch of boiling water around mold. Bake at 350° for 30 minutes or just until firm. Do not overbake. (Fish should flake with fork.) In double boiler top over direct heat, melt ¼ cup butter; stir in flour and salt. Slowly add cream and catsup; cook, stirring constantly until thickened. Stir a little hot sauce into egg yolks; add to sauce. Add sherry. Stir over low heat until hot. Keep warm over hot water. With spatula, loosen edge of ring. Pour off any liquid into sauce. Invert over heated platter; lift off mold. Spoon sauce over ring. Pass rest of sauce. Garnish with mushrooms and with watercress.

Mrs. J. Stephen Laing
(Suzanne Reyburn)

SWEET AND SOUR CHICKEN

8 Servings

In spite of unusual ingredients, it's delicious

4 whole chicken breasts, split
4 chicken leg-thighs, not split
1 jar (18 oz.) apricot preserves
1 bottle (8 oz.) Russian dressing
1 envelope onion soup mix

Place the chicken in a large shallow baking dish. Combine remaining ingredients; pour sauce over the chicken, trying to coat all pieces. Bake at 350° for 1 hour 15 minutes. Serve with brown rice and spoon some of the sauce over it.

Mrs. Gilbert P. George
(Ann Sullivan)

CURRIED SALMON SOUFFLE WITH GOLDEN SAUCE

4 Servings

1 T. minced onion
1 tsp. curry powder
3 T. butter
3 T. flour
1 can (7¾ oz.) salmon
Milk
2 tsp. cornstarch
1 T. water
½ tsp. salt
Dash cayenne pepper
4 large eggs, separated

GOLDEN SAUCE:

2 T. butter
3 T. flour
1 tsp. curry powder
½ tsp. salt
Dash cayenne pepper
1 cup milk
2 egg yolks
¼ cup half and half
2 T. sherry

Saute onion with curry in butter until transparent. Stir in flour. Drain salmon, reserving liquid; add enough milk to liquid to make 1 cup. Gradually stir liquid into flour mixture. Cook, stirring constantly, until thickened. Combine cornstarch and water; stir into sauce. Cook 1 minute longer, stirring. Add salt and cayenne. Remove from heat. Slowly add egg yolks. Cook over very low heat, stirring constantly, until it begins to bubble around edge. Stir in salmon. Beat egg whites until stiff but not dry. Thoroughly fold half the whites into salmon mixture. Add remaining egg whites and fold in lightly. Turn into a 1½-quart souffle dish greased on bottom and sides with butter. Bake at 375° for 35 minutes.
NOTE: To hold souffle for up to 1 hour before baking, cover with a large empty bowl or kettle to protect from drafts.
Golden Sauce: Melt butter; stir in flour, curry powder, salt and cayenne. Cook slowly, stirring, for 3 minutes. Gradually add milk. Cook, stirring, until thickened. Cook over low heat for 2 minutes; stir occasionally. Combine yolks, half and half, and sherry. Stir into sauce. Cook 1 minute, stirring constantly; do not boil. Keep warm over hot but not simmering water. Serve over souffle.

Mrs. Henry W. Banister
(Rodney M. Davis)

MUSHROOM CASSEROLE

10-12 Servings

This is also an excellent vegetable accompaniment to roasts

8 to 10 slices bread, buttered, cut into 1-inch squares
2½ lbs. fresh mushrooms, sliced, sauteed
1 cup chopped celery
1 cup chopped onion
1 cup chopped green pepper
2 cups mayonnaise
2 cups milk
4 eggs
Salt and pepper
½ tsp. dry mustard
2 cans (10½ oz. each) cream of mushroom soup
½ cup buttered bread crumbs or grated parmesan cheese

Butter a 9x13-inch casserole. Place half the bread squares on bottom. Place half the sauteed mushrooms on bread. Combine chopped vegetables with mayonnaise; spread half this mixture over mushrooms. Repeat layers. Mix milk, eggs and seasonings; pour over top. Cover and refrigerate overnight. Before baking spread mushroom soup on top; sprinkle with bread crumbs or parmesan cheese. Cover and bake at 325° for 50 minutes. Uncover; bake 10 to 15 minutes, until brown.

Mrs. Thomas D. Hodgkins
(Mary Ann BonDurant)

ENTREES: MEATS

CARBONNADES FLAMANDES

6 Servings

A Flemish stew that men especially love. It's flavored with beer!

- 2 lbs. boneless beef chuck or round steak, cut in 1-inch cubes
- Flour
- 3 T. cooking oil
- 2 T. minced parsley
- 1½ tsp. salt
- ½ tsp. marjoram
- ½ tsp. thyme
- ½ tsp. pepper
- 4 medium onions, sliced
- 2 cloves garlic, minced
- ⅓ cup butter
- 2 T. cornstarch
- 1 T. brown sugar
- 1 beef bouillon cube dissolved in ½ cup boiling water
- 1 can (12 oz.) beer
- 1 bay leaf
- 4 to 6 cups cooked noodles

Dredge meat in flour. Brown in oil. Mix with seasonings. In separate skillet, lightly saute onions and garlic in butter. Layer meat and onions in a casserole dish. Combine cornstarch and brown sugar; stir in bouillon and about half of beer. Cook, stirring constantly, until thickened. Add remaining beer; pour over meat and onions. Add bay leaf. Cover and bake at 300° for 2 to 2½ hours, or until tender. (If liquid appers thin, add 1 to 2 T. cornstarch dissolved in a little water about 15 minutes before end of baking. Stir every 5 minutes.) Serve over noodles.

Mrs. Phillip J. Stover
(Annette Ashlock)

DANISH PATE

8 Servings

Serve as an entree, then cold on crackers as an hors d'oeuvere

- 1 lb. calves' liver (uncooked)
- ¾ lb. pork fat
- ½ small onion
- 2 eggs, beaten
- 1 T. salt
- ¼ tsp. pepper
- 2½ cups milk
- ½ cup bread crumbs
- 3 T. flour

WINE SUGGESTION:
Chenin Blanc

Grind liver, fat and onion through a meat grinder. Stir in eggs, salt and pepper. Stir in milk. Mix in bread crumbs and flour. Place in an 8½ x 4½-inch meat loaf pan; bake at 350° for 1 hour 15 minutes to 1½ hours. It is done when browned and holds together to the touch. Serve hot as a main course with bread, salad and pickles. Keeps 10 days, refrigerated, to use for hors d'oeuvres or sandwiches.

Mrs. Barbara T. Whitney
(Barbara Thiele)

ESTOUFFADE DE NOEL

10 Servings

Pork rind or split pig's foot
7 or 8 shallots, cut in pieces
3 or 4 onions, cut in wedges
1 carrot, cut in long strips
1 tsp. thyme
1 garlic clove
1 boneless Boston pot roast, rolled, tied (about 6 lbs.)
Nutmeg
Salt
1 cup Armagnac
2½ cups burgundy or other red wine

NOTE: Pork rind is impossible to find at the butchers. Whenever you have a Virginia ham, save the rind in the freezer for the day you want this pot roast.

WINE SUGGESTION:
Pinot Noir

Line a casserole with a piece of pork rind or put a split pig's foot on the bottom. Make a bed on top with shallots, onions and carrot. Add thyme, garlic, and a sprinkling of nutmeg. Make indentation in center of vegetables; in it lay pot roast, salted. Add Armagnac and burgundy. Cover with aluminum foil and the casserole lid. Bake at 350° for 35 minutes. Reduce heat to 300°; cook for 1 hour. Reduce heat to 250°; cook for 2 to 3 hours longer. Remove from oven about an hour before serving to let the fat settle on top. Skim off fat, correct seasoning, and reheat if necessary. (If made a day ahead, the flavors blend better).

Mrs. Otto F. G. Schilling
(Dorothy Stanton)

STUFFED CABBAGE

6 Servings

1 large cabbage (Savoy is best)
1½ lbs. sausage meat
3 onions, chopped
½ cup milk
½ cup bread crumbs (can substitute rice)
1 egg
Salt and pepper
Chives (lots to taste)
¼ lb. bacon
1 can (10½ oz.) beef bouillon
Carrot, onion, celery
1 can (10½ oz.) water

Blanch cabbage in not water tor 7 to 10 minutes. Drain on a towel. Open cabbage carefully by laying back each leaf until you almost reach the center. To make stuffing, combine sausage, onions, milk, bread crumbs, egg, and seasonings. Spread some stuffing over each leaf reforming the cabbage as you go. Tie the cabbage back into a head. Place the bacon in the bottom of a dutch oven, covering the whole surface. Add the cabbage, the beef bouillon, and cut up vegetables, and 1 can water. Cover and simmer slowly for 3 hours. Serve with boiled potatoes and beer.

Mrs. H. Alex Vance, Jr.
(Melinda Martin)

CANNELLONI

8 Servings

CREPES:
1 cup flour
Dash salt
3 eggs
1½ cups milk
½ cup oil for frying crepes

FILLING:
¼ cup finely-chopped onions
1 tsp. minced garlic
2 T. olive oil
1 pkg. (10 oz.) frozen chopped spinach, defrosted, squeezed dry and chopped again
2 T. butter
1 lb. twice-ground round steak
2 chicken livers
5 T. parmesan cheese
2 T. cream
2 eggs, lightly beaten
½ tsp. oregano
Salt, freshly-ground pepper

BESCIAMELLA:
6 T. butter
6 T. flour
1 cup milk
1 cup whipping cream
1 tsp. salt
⅛ tsp. white pepper

TOMATO SAUCE:
¼ cup olive oil
½ cup finely-chopped onions
4 cups Italian plum tomatoes, coarsely-chopped, undrained
3 T. tomato paste
1 tsp. dried basil
1 tsp. sugar
Freshly-ground pepper

WINE SUGGESTION:
Barbera

Crepes: Prepare batter 1 or 2 hours before frying crepes so they will be more tender. Put flour, salt, eggs and milk into blender. Blend until smooth. Refrigerate. Then make crepes in the usual manner.

Filling: Cook onions and garlic in olive oil until soft. Stir in spinach; cook 3 to 4 minutes. Transfer to a large bowl. Melt 1 T. butter in a skillet and brown meat. Add to spinach-onion mixture. Melt remaining butter; cook livers 3 to 4 minutes, turning frequently. Chop; add to mixture in bowl along with remaining ingredients.

Besciamella: Melt butter; stir in flour. Gradually add milk and cream, whisking constantly. Cook over high heat stirring constantly. When sauce comes to a boil, reduce heat and simmer 2 to 3 minutes. Season with salt and pepper. (Sauce will be heavy).

Tomato Sauce: Cook onion in olive oil until tender. Add remaining ingredients; simmer, partially covered, for 40 minutes. Press through a food mill.

To Assemble: Place a spoonful of filling on each crepe; roll up. Pour a thin film of tomato sauce into two 13 x 9-inch shallow baking dishes. Add cannelloni in one layer. Pour besciamella over; spoon rest of tomato sauce over all. Sprinkle with parmesan chesse; dot with butter. Bake for 20 minutes at 375°. Broil for 30 seconds to brown top. (Crepes can be filled and combined with sauces a day in advance; cover lightly with plastic wrap. Remove plastic, then bake until hot).

Mrs. James F. Peil
(Nancy Rodgers)

MARINATED SHORT RIBS OF BEEF — 4 Servings

3 lbs. short ribs of beef
1 T. powdered mustard
2 T. water
1 small onion, chopped
¼ cup olive oil
2 T. wine vinegar
1 T. fresh lemon juice
1 T. salt
1½ tsp. chili powder
1 tsp. ground black pepper
¼ tsp. cayenne pepper
¼ tsp. garlic powder

WINE SUGGESTION:
Cote de Nuits

Trim excess fat from ribs. Mix mustard with water; let stand 10 minutes for flavor to develop. Add remaining ingredients; pour over meat. Cover and marinate in the refrigerator overnight or about 12 hours, turning occasionally. Place meat in a casserole or roasting pan, saving marinade. Bake, uncovered, at 450°' for 20 minutes. Pour off any fat; then pour marinade over ribs. Cover and bake at 325° for 1½ to 2 hours, or until meat is tender, basting occasionally with marinade. Thicken gravy with 2 T. flour mixed until smooth with 3 T of water. Stir and cook 1 to 2 minutes, or until thickened. Serve with hot buttered noodles.

Mrs. Robert T. DePree
(Susan Barker)

SPICED CORNED BEEF — 18 Servings

9 lbs. corned beef brisket (may need two pieces)
Water
Whole cloves
1 cup brown sugar
½ cup fine dry bread crumbs
1 tsp. dry mustard
Grated peel and juice of 2 medium oranges
Grated peel and juice of 2 lemons
2 cups cider or apple juice

WINE SUGGESTION:
Graves

Cover meat with cold water; bring to a boil and remove scum. Cover and simmer slowly 3 hours, or until just tender. Cool in cooking liquid. Place drained corned beef in baking pan; score fat and stud with cloves. Combine brown sugar, crumbs, mustard, and grated peels. Pat meat with crumb mixture. Place in 350° oven to brown slightly. Baste frequently with a mixture of the orange and lemon juices and cider. Continue baking 30 minutes or until heated through. Slice to serve.

Mrs. Thomas N. Boyden
(Susan Dalton)

MOUSSAKA

6 Servings

A Greek specialty for a casual company supper

1 lb. ground beef
1 medium onion, chopped
1 large clove garlic, minced
½ cup white wine
¼ cup water
2 T. tomato paste
2 T. parsley flakes
½ tsp. salt
¼ tsp. each: pepper, cinnamon, ground cloves
1 eggplant (1 lb.)
3 med. potatoes (1 lb.)
Olive oil
½ cup dry bread crumbs

SAUCE
3 T. butter
3 T. flour
½ tsp. salt
¼ tsp. nutmeg
Dash pepper
2 cups milk
2 large eggs, beaten

WINE SUGGESTION:
Roditis

Brown beef, onion, and garlic; pour off drippings. Add wine, water, tomato paste and seasonings; cover and simmer about 30 minutes. Slice eggplant; sprinkle with salt. Let stand about 30 minutes. Slice potatoes; brown lightly in olive oil. Pat eggplant with paper towel; brown in olive oil. Sprinkle 2 T. bread crumbs in bottom of 2-qt. casserole; mix ¼ cup crumbs with meat.

For Sauce: Melt butter; add flour, salt, nutmeg and pepper. Gradually stir in milk. Cook, stirring constantly, until slightly thickened. Stir a little hot mixture into eggs. Return all to pan. Layer ⅓ of meat, ⅓ of potatoes, and ⅓ of eggplant in casserole; add a little sauce. Repeat layers. Pour remaining sauce over top; sprinkle with 1 T. crumbs. Bake at 350° for 40 minutes.

Mrs. Phillip J. Stover
(Annette Ashlock)

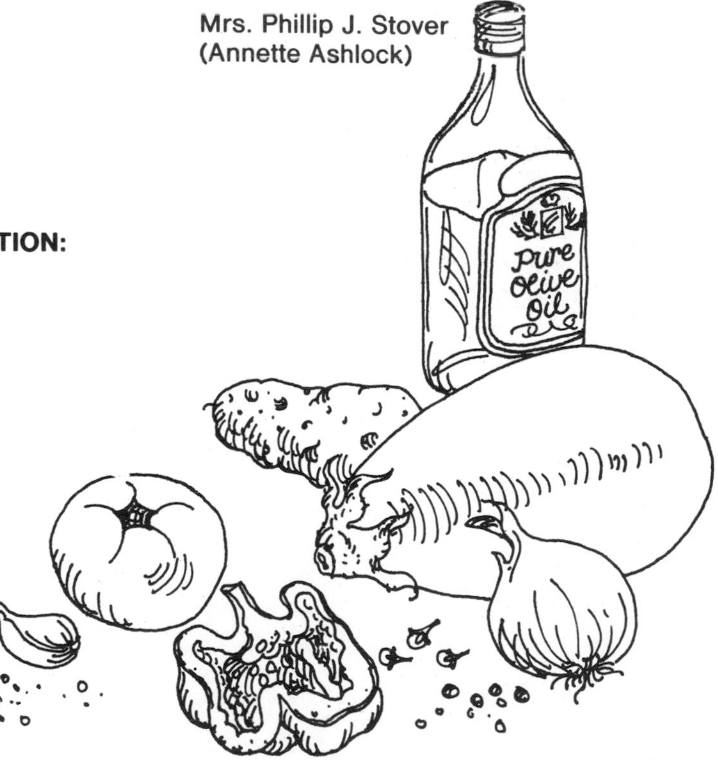

GERMAN SAUERBRATEN

6-8 Servings

1 rump roast (4 lbs)
1 clove garlic
2 cups mild vinegar
2 cups water
½ cup sugar
3 bay leaves
1 T. peppercorns
2 onions, sliced
Flour for dusting meat
4 strips bacon
1 large onion, chopped
6 to 8 beef bouillon cubes
4 T. flour
¾ cup water
½ cup whipping cream

WINE SUGGESTION:
German Rhine Wine

Rub meat well with garlic. Heat vinegar, water, sugar, bay leaves, peppercorns and onions; do not boil. Place meat in a deep bowl; pour hot mixture over it; cover tightly, refrigerate at least 4 to 5 days, turning once daily. When ready to cook meat, drain and reserve marinade., Flour meat. Render bacon; brown meat slowly in bacon fat. Add chopped onion and brown. Add marinade; cook slowly in Dutch oven on top of stove at least 2 hours or until well done. Remove meat. Let the sauce cool slightly; pass through food mill; skim off fat. If sauce is too sour add more sugar. Add beef bouillon cubes. Just before serving thicken sauce with flour-water mixture; add whipping cream. Serve with buttered parsley noodles and red cabbage.

Mrs. Freeman J. Wood, Jr.
(Roswitha Stephan)

MUSKY AND WALLEYE STEW

6-8 Servings

This is not a fish stew but rather a hearty beef stew for a cold winter's night!

3 lbs. stewing beef cut in 1½-inch cubes
2 cans (10¾ oz. each) cream of mushroom soup
2 cans (3 to 4 oz. each) mushrooms, drained
¾ cup sherry
1 pkg. dry onion soup mix
½ tsp. Crazy Mixed Up Salt
Freshly ground pepper

WINE SUGGESTION:
Pinot Noir

Combine all ingredients in a large casserole. Cover and bake at 325° for 3 hours. Serve on top of noodles and with tossed salad.

Mrs. Edward Hines
(Marcia D. McMillan)

BEEF STANDING RIB WITH HERBS

6-8 Servings

- 1 beef standing rib roast (4 to 5 lbs.)
- 1 clove garlic
- 3 T. lemon juice
- 1 tsp. dried mustard
- 1 tsp. ground ginger
- 1 tsp. onion powder
- 1 tsp. salt
- ½ tsp. cayenne pepper

MIXED HERBS:

- 1 T. savory
- 1 T. sweet basil
- 1 T. celery flakes
- 1 T. dried parsley
- 1 T. marjoram
- 1 T. rosemary
- 1 T. tarragon

WINE SUGGESTION:
Clos de Vougeot

Sliver garlic clove; insert it into beef, pricking the meat with a sharp knife. Pour lemon juice over it. Sprinkle with the spices. Combine the mixed herbs and sprinkle beef with 1 T. of mixture. Reserve rest for future use. Place roast on foil-lined broiling pan and broil for 12 minutes each side. Wrap roast tightly in foil. Bake at 400° (rare: 18 minutes per lb.). Slice very thin.

Mrs. Frank W. Gordon II
(Judith Bracken)

VEAL STEW WITH SAUSAGE

6 Servings

- 1½ lbs. veal stew meat, cut into 1-inch cubes
- 3 T. flour
- 3 T. salad oil
- 1 link of Italian hot sausage, cut into ½-inch thick slices
- 1 large onion, chopped
- ½ lb. fresh mushrooms, sliced
- 1 tsp. salt
- 1 envelope (1½ oz.) spaghetti-sauce mix with mushrooms
- 1 can (8 oz.) tomato sauce
- 6 medium sized carrots
- 3 medium sized zucchini, sliced ¼-inch thick

WINE SUGGESTION:
Barbera

Coat veal with flour and brown quickly in hot oil in a 4 quart dutch oven; remove as browned. Add sausage, onion and mushrooms to pan drippings; saute until golden brown. Return the browned veal to the dutch oven. Stir in salt, spaghetti sauce mix, 2 cups water and the tomato sauce until well blended; bring to boiling. Reduce heat and simmer, covered, 1 hour. Pare carrots; cut in 3-inch pieces. Add to veal mixture. Simmer 30 minutes. Add zucchini and simmer 30 minutes or until meat and vegetables are tender.

Mrs. David B. Smith
(Marcia Williamson)

ITALIAN VEAL WITH MADEIRA MUSHROOM SAUCE

6 Servings

2 eggs, lightly beaten
⅔ cup dry vermouth or ½ cup dry white wine plus ¼ cup dry vermouth
⅓ cup lemon juice
1 tsp. dried tarragon
¾ tsp. salt
¼ tsp. freshly-ground pepper
1½ lbs.veal scaloppine, pounded very thin and cut into serving pieces
1 cup fine dry bread crumbs
¼ cup butter
¼ cup oil
¼ lb. prosciutto, thinly sliced
¼ lb. swiss or gruyere cheese, thinly sliced
1 cup whipping cream

SAUCE:
2 shallots, finely-chopped
1 T. butter
1 can (10½ oz.) condensed chicken broth
½ cup madeira
2 T. lemon juice
1 T. chopped parsley
⅛ tsp. dried tarragon
Pinch of ground cloves
1 T. cornstarch
2 T. water
2 T. cognac
¼ lb. mushrooms, sliced, sauteed in 2 T. butter
Salt, freshly-ground pepper

WINE SUGGESTION:
Barolo

Place eggs, vermouth, lemon juice, tarragon, salt and pepper in a bowl and beat together lightly. Add the veal and set aside at room temperature for ½ hour. Preheat oven to 400°. Remove veal from mixture and dredge in bread crumbs. Heat butter and oil in skillet and brown veal slices on one side. Place, browned side down, in a single layer in a large shallow baking dish. Cover tops of veal with thin slices of prosciutto and cheese. Stir cream into the remaining egg mixture and pour around the veal. Cover with foil, greased lightly on underside, and bake 15 minutes. Remove foil and place casserole under broiler until cheese bubbles and is very lightly browned. While veal is cooking, make sauce by sauteing shallots in butter until tender. Add chicken broth, madeira, lemon juice, parsley, tarragon and cloves. Bring to boil and cook until reduced by ⅓. Mix cornstarch with water and add to sauce. Stir until mixture thickens. Add cognac, sauteed mushrooms and salt and pepper to taste. Reheat and serve. Sauce can be made ahead.

Mrs. Kennedy W. Gilchrist
(Lynn Olson)

VEAL NICHOLAS

8 Servings

An elegant party dish that can be prepared ahead of time

1 boned veal roast (3 lbs.), tied at 2-inch intervals
11 T. butter
1 chopped carrot
1 chopped onion
2 sprigs parsley
1 bay leaf
⅓ cup white wine
2 T. minced shallots
½ lb. fresh mushrooms, minced
Salt, pepper
¼ cup white wine
3 T. flour
2 cups milk, heated to boiling
Nutmeg
2 egg yolks
½ cup grated gruyere cheese
8 thin slices ham
8 thin slices gruyere cheese
1 T. grated gruyere cheese

WINE SUGGESTION:
Petite Sirah

Place veal in 4 T. melted butter in roasting pan large enough to hold veal. Bake at 375° for 15 minutes, turning veal on all sides. Remove. Make a bed of carrots, onions, parsley and bay leaf; place veal on top. Bake 15 minutes. Add ⅓ cup wine; bake for 20 minutes or until juices run clear. Remove from oven and let veal rest 20 minutes. Prepare duxelles by melting 4 T. butter in skillet. Add shallots and cook for 2 minutes. Add mushrooms and salt and pepper to taste. Cook until moisture evaporates. Add ¼ cup wine; cook until liquid has reduced completely. Prepare sauce by melting 3 T. butter in pan. Add flour; stir together for 2 minutes. Remove from heat; add milk. Whisk together. Add salt, white pepper and nutmeg to taste. Cook, stirring constantly, until thickened; boil 1 minute. Remove from heat; beat in 2 egg yolks. Stir in ½ cup cheese; cook until cheese melts. Slice veal into 8 pieces. On an ovenproof platter place pieces of veal; on each piece place a bit of the mushroom mixture, 1 slice of ham and 1 slice of cheese. Cover with sauce and sprinkle 1 T. cheese on top. This dish can be prepared ahead up to this point. When ready to serve, bake at 375° for 30 minutes until veal is hot. Put under broiler for 3 minutes for color.

Mrs. J.D. MacDonald
(Charie Roberson)

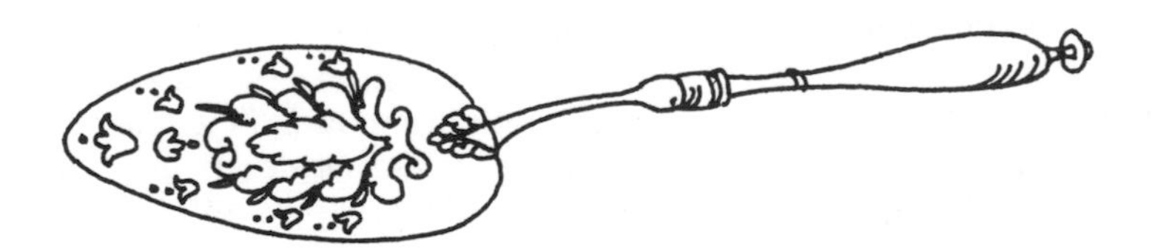

EGGPLANT-STUFFED CROWN ROAST OF LAMB

8 Servings (2 ribs each)

- 1 small eggplant, peeled, cubed (about 1 qt.)
- 3 T. olive oil
- ¼ cup diced celery
- 4 oz. elbow macaroni, cooked, drained
- ¼ lb. ground lamb
- ½ tsp. oregano
- Pinch cinnamon
- Salt and pepper
- 2 cups tomato sauce (preferably homemade)
- ¼ cup bread crumbs
- 1 crown roast of lamb (16 ribs)
- 2 T. lemon juice
- 3 T. grated parmesan cheese
- 4 oz. mozzarella cheese, thickly-sliced

WINE SUGGESTION:
Bordeaux Superior

Saute eggplant in olive oil until lightly browned. Combine with the celery and macaroni in a large bowl. Saute ground lamb; add oregano and cinnamon. Add to macaroni mixture. Stir in tomato sauce and bread crumbs; season to taste with salt and pepper. Rub the crown roast all over with lemon juice; season with salt and pepper. Stuff with the eggplant mixture, piling it up and placing any extra in a small baking dish. Sprinkle with parmesan cheese. Place roast on a rack in a shallow pan. Roast at 350° for 1 hour and 20 minutes or until done. Arrange mozzarella slices on top of stuffing and on extra dish of mixture; sprinkle with more parmesan cheese. Bake for an additional 20 minutes or until done. Extra dish should be placed in oven for last 20 minutes only. (Stuffing makes a delicious casserole for a luncheon).

Mrs. James F. Peil
(Nancy Rodgers)

LAMBS SHANKS WITH ORANGE LIQUEUR

6 Servings

- 1 bottle kumquats
- 2 oz. Triple Sec
- 6 lamb shanks
- ¼ cup olive oil
- 2 garlic cloves, pressed
- 3 cups beef broth
- 3 T. tomato paste
- 1 tsp. rosemary
- 1 bay leaf, crumbled
- 1 tsp. salt
- ½ tsp. pepper
- 1 to 2 T. flour

WINE SUGGESTION:
Grignolino

Soak kumquats in Triple Sec for several hours. In a heavy kettle, brown shanks on all sides in olive oil and garlic. Pour in broth, tomato paste and spices. Add liquid from kumquats, reserving kumquats for garnish. Cover and simmer for about 1½ hours or until tender. Remove shanks to platter and thicken sauce with flour. Pour sauce into blender and blend at high speed until smooth. Serve shanks on a large platter with kumquats as a garnish and sauce in a separate dish. This is delicious accompanied with noodles.

Mrs. Bruce G. Southworth
(Mary Monek)

SOUTH AFRICAN LAMB CURRY

6 Servings

A delicious and typical African dish

1 cup dried apples
½ cup dried, pitted prunes
½ cup seedless raisins
1½ cups water
1½ lbs. boneless lamb shoulder (or beef chuck), cubed
1 tsp. salt
2 T. vegetable oil
1 cup finely-chopped onion
2 T. curry powder
2 T. red wine vinegar
1 T. lemon juice
¼ cup chopped salted peanuts
2 medium bananas, sliced ⅛-inch thick

WINE SUGGESTION:
Tavel

Combine apples, prunes, raisins and water; soak at least 1 hour, turning frequently. Salt meat and brown in oil. Transfer to a plate. Pour off all fat but 2 T. and cook onions until soft. Reduce heat and add curry powder; cook another 2 minutes. Return meat to skillet along with fruits and their liquid, vinegar and lemon juice. Bring to a boil and reduce heat. Simmer, covered, for 1 hour or until meat is tender. (Simmer beef 2½ to 3 hours.) Stir occasionally and add up to ¼ cup water if necessary. To serve, mound meat on a platter and sprinkle with chopped peanuts. Arrange slices of banana around the meat. Serve with rice.

Mrs. James F. Peil
(Nancy Rodgers)

PORK CHOPS IN ORANGE WINE SAUCE

4 Servings

This sauce is also delicious served with a pork roast

8 pork chops
Cooking oil
2 T. butter, melted
2 T. flour
1½ cups orange juice
½ cup white wine
¼ cup brown sugar
1 T. salt

WINE SUGGESTION:
Morey St. Denis

Brown pork chops in oil; drain. In a saucepan, add flour to butter, stirring until thick. Slowly stir in orange juice and wine. Cook and stir until thick; add brown sugar and salt. Place chops in shallow casserole and pour sauce over them. Cover and bake at 350° for 45 to 60 minutes.

Mrs. Peter F. Theis
(Jill Pendexter)

FRUIT-STUFFED PORK CROWN ROAST

14 - 16 Servings (one rib each)

Impressive main course for winter formal dinner

- **1 pork crown roast (14 to 16 ribs)**
- **1 can (16 oz.) halved appricots**
- **6 cups cubed day-old bread**
- **2 cups diced peeled apples**
- **1½ cups chopped cooked prunes**
- **2 onions, chopped**
- **½ cup butter, melted**
- **1 tsp. salt**
- **1 tsp. cinnamon**
- **½ tsp. ground cloves**
- **½ tsp. savory or thyme**
- **Honey**
- **1 cup water (about)**
- **½ cup sherry**

WINE SUGGESTION:
St. Emilion

Place roast on rack in roasting pan. Drain apricots, reserving liquid; chop. Combine cubed bread, fruits, onions, butter and seasonings. Add enough apricot liquid to moisten. Bake pork roast at 350° for 25 to 30 minutes per pound, or until meat thermometer registers 170°. One hour before end of baking time, place stuffing in center of roast. Place extra stuffing in casserole dish to bake while meat finishes baking. Baste meat with honey during last 20 minutes. Remove meat to heated platter. Skim fat from baking pan. Add water to drippings. Cook, stirring up brown particles. Add sherry; simmer a few minutes. Decorate tips of ribs with paper frills. Spoon sauce over slices.

Mrs. Phillip J. Stover
(Annette Ashlock)

HUNGARIAN GOULASH

8 Servings

6 slices bacon, diced
3 large onions, sliced
2½ lbs. pork tenderloin, cut into 1-inch cubes
1 large garlic clove, pressed
1 tsp. dill seed
1 tsp. caraway seed (optional)
1 tsp. paprika
1 tsp. salt
1 tsp. pepper
1 (1 lb. 13 oz.) can sauerkraut, drained
2 T. brown sugar
1 lb. veal steak, cubed
2 cups sour cream

WINE SUGGESTION:
Egri Bikaver

Fry chopped bacon until crisp. Remove to a casserole dish. Saute onions in bacon grease until golden and add to casserole along with cubed pork, garlic and seasonings. Cover these ingredients with sauerkraut. Sprinkle with brown sugar. Cover tightly and bake at 350° for 1 hour. Remove cover, add veal and mix thoroughly. Cover and bake another 45 minutes. Refrigerate covered overnight. When ready to serve, reheat at 350° for 20 to 30 minutes or until heated through. Top with sour cream the last 15 minutes.

Mrs. Allan E. Bulley, Jr.
(Sallie Jo Bell)

PORK TENDERLOIN IN MUSTARD SAUCE

6-8 Servings

2 pork tenderloins
Salt and pepper to taste
3 T. butter
⅓ cup vinegar
Freshly-ground pepper
2 cups cream
⅓ cup Dijon style mustard
2 T. cold butter
Salt to taste

WINE SUGGESTION:
Savigny les Beaune

Cut pork in ¾ -inch slices and flatten between waxed paper until ½ -inch thick. Sprinkle with salt and pepper. Saute in butter about 5 minutes on each side or until done. Put on platter and keep warm. Add vinegar and freshly-ground pepper to pan. Boil mixture, scraping bottom of pan. Cook mixture until it is reduced in volume by one half. Stir in cream; simmer 5 minutes. Remove from heat; stir in mustard, remaining butter and salt to taste. If a smoother sauce is desired, pour in blender and blend one minute. Serve sauce hot over pork tenderloins with wild rice.

Mrs. Bruce G. Southworth
(Mary Monek)

CASSOULET

20 Servings

There are as many versions of this country French dish as there are good cooks. Anything goes!

BEANS:
3 lbs. Great Northern beans
Water
½ lb. fresh pork rind
10 sprigs parsley
8 garlic cloves
4 whole cloves
½ tsp. thyme
2 bay leaves
1 lb. lean salt pork
2 cups sliced onions

Add beans to 5 qts. boiling water; boil 2 minutes. Remove from heat; let beans soak 1 hour. Put pork rind in cold water; boil 1 minute. Throw out water; repeat process twice. Cut rind into small triangular pieces; boil in 1 qt. water 30 minutes. Tie parsley, garlic, cloves, thyme and bay leaves in a cheesecloth bag. Add along with salt pork and onions to beans. Simmer about 1½ hours. Add water, if necessary. Let beans cool in liquid.

PORK:
1 boned pork loin roast (4 lbs.)
1 tsp. salt
½ tsp. pepper
¼ tsp. thyme
1 tsp. allspice
2 cloves garlic, halved
1 onion, sliced
1 carrot, sliced
2 garlic cloves, peeled
½ cup stock or wine

Pork: Rub pork with seasonings; insert the garlic. Refrigerate overnight. Brown roast; place in casserole. Brown onion, carrot and garlic. Add to casserole. Cover and roast at 325° for 2 hours. Reduce juices left in pan with ½ cup stock. Mash vegetables and reserve in the pan juice.

DUCK:
1 or 2 ducks (5 lbs. each)

Duck: Roast at 325° for 2½ to 3 hours. Cut into pieces, discarding bones.

LAMB:
2½ lbs. boneless lamb shoulder
3 T. pork grease and olive oil (mixed)
1½ lbs. cracked lamb bones
2 cups chopped onions
6 tomatoes
4 cloves garlic, pressed
½ tsp. thyme
2 bay leaves
3 cups dry white wine
3 cups beef broth
Salt and pepper

Lamb: Cube lamb in 2-inch pieces. Brown in very hot fat. Remove meat; brown bones. Remove bones; brown onions. Drain. Return meat and bones to pan. Peel, chop and seed tomatoes. Add with remaining ingredients to meat. Cover and simmer 1½ hours. Discard bones and bay leaves. Adjust seasonings.

SAUSAGE CAKES (12):
2½ lbs. lean ground pork
⅔ lb. ground pork fat
½ tsp. pepper
1 tsp. salt
¼ tsp. allspice
¼ tsp. ground bay leaf
3 garlic cloves, mashed
½ cup cognac
1 T. sage
Pinch of ginger and mace
½ onion, grated

TOPPING:
2 cups bread crumbs
1 cup minced parsley

WINE SUGGESTION:
Moulin a Vent

Sausage: Mix all ingredients together very well. Form into about 12 sausage cakes. Brown quickly on both sides and drain on paper towel.

To assemble: Drain beans, reserving liquid. Cut salt pork into ¼-inch slices. Cut pork loin into 1-inch slices. Drain lamb and reserve liquid. Arrange a layer of beans in bottom of an 8 to 10 qt. casserole. Cover with layers of salt pork, pork loin, duck, lamb and sausage. Repeat, ending with beans and sausage. Mix reserved juices and liquids; pour over casserole until beans are barely covered. Mix crumbs and parsley and sprinkle on top. Bake, uncovered, at 350° for 1 hour. Every 20 minutes, break crust that has formed. Leave final crust intact. Refrigerate overnight. Bring to room temperature before final reheating. Add reserved juices if liquid in casserole becomes too thick.

Mrs. H. Alex Vance, Jr.
(Melinda Martin)

CORNISH HENS WITH TANGERINES

8 Servings

- **4 tangerines, peeled and sectioned**
- **8 cornish hens (12 to 14 oz. each)**
- **6 T. butter**
- **2 T. vegetable oil**
- **¼ cup brandy**
- **¼ cup shallots**
- **½ lb. sliced mushrooms**
- **1 T. lemon juice**
- **1 tsp. salt**
- **¼ tsp. pepper**
- **1 cup dry marsala**
- **1 tsp. potato starch (or cornstarch)**
- **1 T. cold water**
- **2 T. gin (or 20 crushed juniper berries)**
- **1 bunch watercress for garnish**

WINE SUGGESTION:
Gewurztraminer

Stuff tangerines into hens and truss. Heat 4 T. of the butter and all of the oil in a heavy skillet and, over high heat, brown the hens all over. Place them in a large heavy casserole. Pour off fat from skillet and degrease with brandy; pour over hens. Heat remaining 2 T. butter in skillet; add shallots, and cook for a minute or two. Add mushrooms, lemon juice, salt and pepper. Stir over high heat for 3 minutes. Add marsala; heat to boiling. Remove from heat; stir in potato starch which has been dissolved in cold water. Return to heat and cook over high heat until sauce thickens. Pour mushroom sauce over hens in casserole. Sprinkle crushed juniper berries (or gin) over all. Cover casserole; bake at 400° for about 30 minutes or until juices run clear when the thick part of the leg is pricked with a fork. Remove trussing strings, arrange hens on a serving platter, spoon sauce with mushrooms over each and garnish with watercress.

Mrs. Thomas N. Boyden
(Susan Dalton)

CHICKEN PAPRIKA

6 Servings

1 large onion
2 T. butter, melted
1 T. paprika
4 whole chicken breasts
Salt
Pepper
½ cup water
1 pint sour cream
2 T. flour
1 box (1 lb.) spaghetti broken into 2-inch pieces
½ cup butter
½ cup fine bread crumbs

WINE SUGGESTION:
Chenin Blanc.

Saute onion in butter until glossy; stir in paprika. Wash chicken, dry, and season with salt and pepper. Place chicken in pan and cover with onions and paprika. Add water, cover and simmer slowly until chicken is tender. Scrape off onion and paprika and remove chicken. Remove bones and skin. Stir flour into sour cream. Stir through strainer into pan liquids. Heat, stirring constantly, until mixture thickens. Do not boil. Stir in chicken. Cook the spaghetti as directed on package. Rinse with cool water. In skillet melt butter. Stir in spaghetti until well coated. Mix in bread crumbs and simmer until light brown. Serve chicken over spaghetti.

Mrs. Nelson Shaw
(Judith Ann Kocns)

CHICKEN A L'ORANGE

6 Servings

6 whole chicken breasts, boned
Salt
Pepper
Flour
½ cup butter, melted
2 cups chicken stock
1 cup port
¾ cup orange juice
1 T. currant jelly
1 orange, peeled, sectioned
Grated rind of 1 orange
Grated rind of 1 lemon
Pinch of ginger
2 T. sherry
2 T. cornstarch
1 orange rind, shredded and blanched

WINE SUGGESTION:
Johannisberger Riesling

Season chicken breasts with salt and pepper and dredge in flour. In a flame-proof casserole, saute breasts in butter until golden. Add chicken stock; bake, covered, at 350° for about 20 minutes or until they are tender. Remove chicken breasts from casserole; keep warm. To stock in casserole add port, orange juice, jelly, orange sections, rinds and ginger. Cook for 15 minutes; season to taste. Add enough corn-starch, mixed to a paste with cold sherry, to slightly thicken the sauce; strain. Add shredded and blanched orange rind. Return chicken to casserole and simmer for a few minutes before serving. Serve with wild rice.

Mrs. John N. Schmidt
(Joan M. Slauson)

CHICKEN ENCHILADAS AND BEANS 8 Servings

BEANS:

1 lb. pinto beans
Water
Salt
½ cup bacon fat (approx.)
8 tortillas, quartered, fried until crisp

SAUCE:

½ ancho (dried pepper). If not available, substitute ¼ T. or less cayenne
½ cup water
1 slice toast
1 can (8 oz.) tomatoes or tomato sauce
½ tsp. black pepper
½ tsp. oregano
1 small onion, chopped
Dash cloves
Salt
½ T. oil

TORTILLAS:

2 doz. frozen tortillas
Melted bacon fat or oil
4 whole chicken breasts, cooked, skinned and shredded
1¼ cups freshly-grated parmesan cheese
½ small head lettuce, shredded

WINE SUGGESTION:

Rioja Burgundy

Soak beans overnight in water to cover. Then simmer slowly until very tender, approx. 3 hours. Add salt to taste, drain and mash. Melt bacon fat; add beans. Mix well. Cook, stirring frequently, until thick and all fat is absorbed. Spoon beans into casserole or individual dishes; stand several tortilla pieces upright in beans.

Boil ancho in water until soft. Soak toast in ancho water. Put ancho, toast, tomatoes, pepper, oregano, onion, cloves, salt and ½ cup of water the ancho was cooked in, in blender and mix well. In a saucepan, warm oil. Strain sauce and add to oil. Simmer 10 minutes; keep warm.

Dip each tortilla into 1-inch bacon fat or oil. Fry just a few seconds until limp; do not fry until crisp. Remove with tongs; dip into heated sauce. Lay dipped tortilla out flat; fill with warm shredded chicken and ½ T. grated parmesan cheese. Roll and place 3 on each plate. Top with additional sauce, cheese and lettuce. (You may make 8 hours ahead of time and warm in sauce in oven; but better made and served immediately).

Mrs. John H. McDermott
(Ann Pickard)

BREAST OF CHICKEN MEXICAN STYLE

8 Servings

4 whole chicken breasts, each split in half
3 cups water
Salt and pepper
1 rib celery with leaves
1 T. butter
1 medium onion, finely chopped
1 clove garlic, finely minced
2 green peppers, cored, seeded, finely chopped
1 cup thinly-sliced mushrooms
1 can (16 oz.) Italian plum tomatoes
¼ cup chopped parsley
1 tsp. oregano
1 tsp. chili powder
1 T. cornstarch

WINE SUGGESTION:
Bourgogne Blanc

Place chicken breasts in saucepan; add water, salt, pepper, and celery. Cover, bring to boil, reduce heat and simmer until tender, 30 to 45 minutes. Remove from heat and let chicken cool in broth. When cool, remove chicken from broth. Remove bones and skin, keeping meat intact. Return bones and skin to broth. Return to boil; reduce heat and simmer, uncovered, until liquid is reduced to 2 cups. Strain. Meanwhile, melt butter in skillet and cook onion, garlic, green peppers and mushrooms, stirring occasionally until onions are translucent. Add tomatoes, parsley, sugar, oregano, chili powder, and chicken broth. Cook, uncovered, for 15 minutes. Taste for seasoning. May add more salt, pepper or chili powder, if desired. Combine cornstarch with a little cold water and stir it into sauce. Cook, stirring, 1 minute. Place chicken in ovenproof dish and pour sauce over it; cover. When ready to serve, reheat at 400° until bubbly. Serve with rice.

Mrs. Earl F. Ronneberg
(Christiane Wills)

ROAST GOOSE WITH RASPBERRY SAUCE

6 Servings

- 1 young goose (8 to 10 lbs.)
- ½ lemon
- Salt and freshly-ground pepper
- 2 apples, cored and chopped
- 1 large onion, sliced

RASPBERRY SAUCE:

- 1 T. butter
- ½ cup black raspberry jelly
- Juice of ½ lemon
- ½ cup water
- 1 tsp. salt
- ¼ cup port
- 1 cinnamon stick

WINE SUGGESTION:
Nuits St. George

Wash goose in cold water, pat dry and rub bird inside and out with cut side of lemon. Salt and pepper cavity and stuff with apples and onion. Close opening and truss the bird securely. Roast on a rack for 3½ hours. Basting is not necessary. When the juice runs clear the bird is done. Allow to set covered for 15 minutes before carving. Discard stuffing.

Sauce: Combine all ingredients and simmer for 5 minutes. Serve hot with goose.

Mrs. H. Dorn Stewart, Jr.
(Judith Collins)

BRUNSWICK STEW

10-12 Servings

- 1 large stewing hen (or 2 fryers)
- 1 lb. lean pork (optional)
- 1 or 2 squirrels (optional)
- 4 potatoes, peeled and diced
- 4 onions, diced
- 2 cans (28 oz. each) tomatoes (3, if pork or game are used)
- 1 pkg. (10 oz.) frozen lima beans
- 1 T. salt
- ¼ tsp. pepper
- Few dashes Tabasco sauce (to taste)
- ⅛ tsp. garlic powder
- Few dashes worcestershire sauce
- 1 can (1 lb. 1 oz.) creamed corn

WINE SUGGESTION:
German Rheinhessen

Day before serving: Cook meats in enough water to cover until tender. Bone and cut up when cool. Cook all vegetables but corn in broth while boning meat. Add meat and seasonings. Simmer, uncovered, 4 to 5 hours. Add corn during last 30 to 45 minutes. Then stir frequently to prevent sticking. Only occasional stirring needed before this. Cool. Cover. Refrigerate. Warm slowly before serving. Good with crackers or corn sticks. (Cracker crumbs may be added before serving if too thin.)

Mrs. Walter L. Jones, Jr.
(Jane Frederick)

STUFFED FILLET OF SOLE FLORENTINE

6 Servings

2 pkg. (10 oz. each) chopped spinach, cooked and drained
Salt and pepper
1 cup dry bread stuffing
Basil or savory
½ cup chopped raw oysters
6 fillets of sole

WINE SAUCE:

1 cup medium white sauce
1 chicken bouillon cube
½ cup sauterne
½ cup freshly-grated parmesan cheese
1 tsp. lemon juice
½ tsp. worcestershire sauce
Salt and pepper

WINE SUGGESTION:
Pinot Chardonnay

Season spinach with salt and pepper; put into bottom of a shallow casserole. Combine bread stuffing, pinch basil or savory and oysters. Spread each piece of sole with stuffing; roll up and secure with toothpick. Place on top of spinach. Heat white sauce; add all remaining ingredients and heat to blend. Pour the sauce over sole. Bake at 350° for 30 minutes or until fish is done.

Mrs. John R. Lee
(Lydia Kerr)

FISH AU GRATIN WITH MUSHROOM SHERRY SAUCE

6-8 Servings

2 pkgs. (16 oz. each) flounder fillets, thawed
Salt and white pepper
½ cup chopped parsley
2 T. butter
2 T. fresh lemon juice
1 lb. fresh mushrooms, sliced
1 T. flour
1½ cups whipping cream
2 to 3 T. sherry
2 T. grated parmesan cheese
2 to 3 T. fine bread crumbs
Paprika

WINE SUGGESTION:
Sancerre

Sprinkle separated fillets with salt and pepper. Arrange in shallow baking dish; sprinkle with parsley. Melt butter with lemon juice. Add mushrooms and saute over low heat 10 to 12 minutes, stirring occasionally. Blend in flour. Gradually add cream; simmer until thickened, stirring. Simmer 10 minutes longer, stirring occasionally. Add sherry and a pinch of salt and pepper. Pour sauce over fish and sprinkle with cheese, bread crumbs and a little paprika. Bake at 450° for 20 to 25 minutes or until fish is white and flakes easily and top is well browned.

Mrs. J. Stephen Laing
(Suzanne Reyburn)

FINNAN HADDIE DUGLERE

2 Servings

1 lb. smoked haddock
1 white onion, chopped
1 T. butter
1 T. flour
⅓ cup white wine
½ cup whipping cream
1 can (1 lb.) Italian plum tomatoes, thoroughly drained and cut into strips
Freshly-chopped parsley

WINE SUGGESTION:
Hermitage Blanc

Divide haddock into two pieces; heat in cold water over moderate flame until heated through; drain. Melt butter in skillet and cook onion until soft. Add flour and stir until blended. Gradually add the white wine and when thickened, stir in the cream. Let cook briefly, then stir in the tomatoes. Place fish in a small deep casserole, pour sauce over and bake at 350° for about 20 minutes. Serve in casserole sprinkled with chopped parsley.

Mrs. Roderick W. Lamm
(Barbara Deringer)

VEGETABLES AND ACCOMPANIMENTS

ARTICHOKE PUREE

6 Servings

3 cups canned diced artichokes (hearts and/or bottoms)
1 cup whipping cream
Salt and pepper to taste
½ cup finely-chopped pistachio nuts

Place diced artichokes in blender and mix in the cream. Puree this mixture. Heat the puree in double boiler. Season to taste. Keep warm until ready to serve. Sprinkle chopped pistachios over the top.

Mrs. Thomas C. O'Neil
(Jane Stephens)

BEETS A LA ORANGE

4 Servings

½ cup orange juice
2 T. lemon juice
1 T. vinegar
½ tsp. salt
Dash pepper
1 T. sugar
1 T. cornstarch
1 T. water
1 (16 oz.) can small whole beets, drained
2 T. butter

Combine in double boiler orange juice, lemon juice, vinegar, salt, pepper and sugar. Mix cornstarch and water to a smooth paste; stir into juice. Cook until clear, stirring constantly. Add beets and heat thoroughly. Add butter and blend well. Serve hot.

Mrs. Robert T. DePree
(Susan Barker)

BRUSSELS SPROUTS ROYALE

10 Servings

Here's how to keep the sprouts bright green

2 pounds fresh brussels sprouts
2 qts. water
1 T. salt
1 T. sugar
1 can (5 oz.) water chestnuts, sliced
⅓ cup butter, melted

Remove tough end and little leaves from base of each sprout. With narrow-bladed sharp knife, cut cross in each stem end. (This helps the center cook faster.) Place water, salt, and sugar in large saucepan; heat to boiling. Add sprouts. Boil, uncovered, for 6 to 7 minutes. Immediately plunge sprouts into cold water; hold in refrigerator until just minutes before serving. Heat water chestnuts in butter; keep warm. Heat a large pan of water to boiling. Add sprouts; boil about 3 minutes. Drain; toss with water chestnuts and butter.

Mrs. Phillip J. Stover
(Annette Ashlock)

BROCCOLI WITH LEMON CREAM

6-8 Servings

- 2 lbs. fresh broccoli
- Boiling salted water
- 2 pkgs. (3 oz. each) cream cheese, room temperature
- 6 T. milk
- 1 tsp. grated lemon peel
- 1 T. lemon juice
- ½ tsp. ground ginger
- ½ tsp. cardamom
- ½ cup sliced or slivered almonds
- 1 T. butter

Trim and peel stem ends of fresh broccoli spears; cook in boiling water just until tender-crisp, about 7 minutes. Drain and arrange neatly, with spears all pointing in same direction, in a heatproof serving dish. Combine the cream cheese with milk, lemon peel and juice, ginger and cardamom; beat until smoothly blended. Spoon the cheese mixture over broccoli stems, leaving some of the green heads showing. (This much can be done ahead; then cover and refrigerate.) To serve, cover with the casserole lid or with foil and bake at 350° for about 15 minutes (25 if refrigerated), or until heated through. Saute almonds in the butter in a small pan until toasted. Sprinkle over top of vegetables before serving.

Mrs. John N. Schmidt
(Joan M. Slauson)

BUTTERNUT BAKE

6-8 Servings

- 1 large butternut squash (2 to 3 lbs.)
- ¼ cup butter
- 1 T. brown sugar
- ¼ tsp. salt
- Dash of pepper
- ¼ cup sugar
- 1½ quarts peeled and sliced Jonathan apples (about 2 lbs.) or any tart apple

TOPPING:

- 3 cups corn flakes, crushed coarsley
- ½ cup chopped pecans
- 2 T. melted butter
- ½ cup brown sugar

Cut squash in half lengthwise; clean out seeds. Bake, face down, in shallow pan of water until tender, about 30 minutes. Scrape out pulp and mash in mixer until smooth. Stir in butter, brown sugar, salt and pepper; set aside. Heat butter in skillet, add apples and sprinkle with sugar. Cover and simmer over low heat until just barely tender. Spread apples in a large flat buttered casserole. Spoon squash mixture evenly over apples. For topping, combine cornflakes, pecans, melted butter and brown sugar, mixing well. Spread over squash. Bake at 350° for 15 to 20 minutes or until lightly browned.

Mrs. James Modrall
(Nancy Anne Johnson)

RED CABBAGE STUFFED APPLES — 12 Servings

Delicious with roast goose

- 2 lbs. red cabbage, finely-shredded
- 2 cups boiling water
- ⅔ cup white vinegar
- 2 apples, peeled, cored and thinly-sliced
- 2 cups red wine
- ¼ cup lingonberry preserves
- 2 T. lemon juice
- ½ tsp. sugar
- ¼ tsp. cinnamon
- Salt and pepper
- 2 onions, chopped
- 3 T. butter, melted
- 1 tsp. sugar
- 1 cup beef broth
- 12 large baking apples

Place cabbage in boiling water and vinegar for 3 minutes. Remove from heat and drain well. Mix cabbage with apples, wine, lingonberry preserves, lemon juice, ½ tsp. sugar, cinnamon, salt and pepper to taste. Cover mixture and refrigerate overnight. Saute onions in butter until golden. Add cabbage mixture, 1 tsp. sugar and broth. Simmer covered 1 hour or until cabbage is tender. Drain the mixture, check seasonings and serve as is or stuffed into baked apples. Peel top quarter of apples and hollow out center as for stuffed tomatoes. Place them on a rack above a pan of water and steam in a 350° oven 15 to 20 minutes or until barely tender. Fill them with hot cabbage.

Mrs. Gordon B. MacDonald
(Virginia Fagan)

CAULIFLOWER MOUSSE IN AVOCADO — 6 Servings

- 1 head of cauliflower (or 2 boxes frozen)
- ½ cup bechamel sauce
- ¼ cup hollandaise sauce
- ½ tsp. salt
- ¼ tsp. pepper
- 3 large ripe avocados
- 1 T. melted butter
- 4 strips pimiento

Cook cauliflower buds in boiling water for 15 minutes, slightly undercooked; drain. Blend in blender for a short time; do not puree. Stir in bechamel sauce, hollandaise sauce, salt and pepper. Keep warm. Cut avocados into halves and brush the insides with melted butter. Put in a shallow pan and bake at 400° for 8 minutes or until heated through. Fill with mousse and return to the oven for 10 minutes Garnish with pimiento.

Mrs. Denis R. Chaudruc
(Jeannene Nixon)

CURRIED STUFFED ONIONS

8 Servings

8 onions, peeled
2 cups chopped broccoli
1 pkg. (8 oz.) cream cheese, softened
Herbed bread crumbs mixed with parmesan cheese

SAUCE:
¼ cup butter
¼ cup flour
2½ cups onion liquid
1 tsp. thyme
2 tsp. curry powder
Salt and pepper to taste
Chopped onion centers

Cook onions in salted water until barely tender. Drain and reserve onion liquid. Cut out centers. Add broccoli to cream cheese; stuff onions. Top with bread crumbs and parmesan cheese; place in a shallow buttered baking dish. Heat at 325° for 30 minutes. Stir flour into melted butter. Gradually add onion liquid; cook, stirring constantly, until thickened. Add seasonings and chopped onion centers. Pass in sauce dish to be served over onions.

Mrs. Thomas D. Hodgkins
(Mary Ann BonDurant)

CARROT SOUFFLE

6-8 Servings

4 or 5 carrots
1 T. grated orange peel
¼ cup butter
¼ cup flour
¾ cup milk
¼ cup orange juice
5 beaten egg yolks
1 tsp. salt
¼ tsp. white pepper
2 T. chopped parsley
7 egg whites
½ tsp. cream of tartar

Use a 6-cup souffle dish with a paper collar. Peel and slice carrots crosswise into 1-inch pieces; boil in water to cover over high heat until tender. Puree in a blender (makes about 1 cup). Stir in grated orange peel; set aside. Melt the butter in a saucepan and stir in flour. Cook, stirring over high heat for 2 minutes; do not let brown. Stir in milk and orange juice, continuing to stir until sauce thickens. Remove from heat. Stir several tablespoons of the hot sauce quickly into the beaten egg yolks. Quickly stir the egg yolk mixture into the hot sauce. Add salt, pepper, carrot puree and chopped parsley; blend thoroughly. Beat egg whites until foamy; add cream of tartar and beat until stiff but not dry. Fold egg whites gently into souffle base and pour into souffle dish. Bake in a preheated 425° oven for 25 minutes.

Mrs. Thomas C. O'Neil
(Jane Stephens)

LIMA BEAN CASSEROLE — 8 Servings

1 can (11 oz.) condensed cheese soup
½ cup milk
½ cup mayonnaise
2 pkgs. (10 oz.) frozen lima beans, cooked and drained
¾ cup chopped celery
¼ cup chopped parsley
2 T. chopped pimiento
2 cans fried onion rings

Blend cheese soup with milk and mayonnaise; add beans, celery, parsley, pimiento and ½ can of the onion rings. Pour into casserole. Bake at 350° for 35 minutes covered. Then, uncover and bake for 10 more minutes with the remaining onion rings on top.

Mrs. Thomas C. O'Neil
(Jane Stephens)

HONEY PARSNIPS — 6 Servings

Especially good with ham or pork

6 medium parsnips (1½ lbs.), peeled
1 tsp. salt
¼ cup butter
¼ cup honey
Cinnamon

Cut parsnips lengthwise in thin slices, then cut slices into pieces about 1½ inches long. Cover parsnips with boiling water; add salt and cook until tender, about 20 minutes. Do not overcook. Drain. Melt butter and add honey, stirring until bubbly. Add parsnips, cover and heat about 5 minutes. Sprinkle with cinnamon and serve.

Mrs. Patrick Callahan
(Patricia Henebry)

STRING BEAN FRITTAIA — 6-8 Servings

½ lb. string beans, cooked, drained and finely-chopped
1 onion, finely-chopped
Salt and pepper
5 T. butter
1 T. flour
1⅔ cups milk
Mace
2 T. freshly-grated parmesan
4 eggs, separated

VARIATION:
Substitute brussels sprouts, broccoli or spinach for beans.

Saute beans with onion, salt and pepper in 3 T. butter until onions are golden. In the meantime, make a sauce with 2 T. butter and 1 T. flour, adding milk and mace gradually. Mix in cheese, yolks and beans. Put all this mixture in the blender and puree. Now fold the stiffly beaten egg whites into the bean mixture. Heavily butter a 5-cup ring mold or a flan pan and place a buttered piece of waxed paper on the bottom. Place the mixture in the mold and set it in a pan of warm water. Bake at 350° for 35 to 40 minutes or until texture on top is rather hard. Demold and serve with a tomato sauce or bechamel sauce.

Mrs. Gilbert P. George
(Ann Sullivan)

DEVILED PEAS

12-16 Servings

1 can (1 lb.) plus 1 can (8 oz.) tiny peas, drained
½ lb. fresh mushrooms, sliced and sauteed
1 small jar pimiento, chopped
1 bell pepper, chopped
1 cup chopped celery
1 can tomato soup
1 cup grated cheese
½ cup chili sauce
1 T. worcestershire sauce
2 cups thick cream sauce
6 hard-cooked eggs, chopped
Bread crumbs
Butter

Mix vegetables, soup, cheese, chili sauce, and worcestershire sauce. Into a buttered casserole put a layer of mixture and a layer of sauce mixed with eggs. Continue until dish is full. Top with bread crumbs dotted with butter. Bake at 350° for 20 to 30 minutes.

Mrs. Harrison I. Steans
(Lois Mae Morrison)

POTATOES ROMANOFF

8 Servings

6 large baked potatoes
1 bunch green onions, chopped
1½ cups grated sharp cheddar cheese
4 cups sour cream
1½ tsp. salt
¼ tsp. pepper
Paprika

Peel baked potatoes and cut into cubes. Combine all ingredients except paprika in greased casserole dish. Cover and refrigerate overnight or 3 hours. When ready to use, sprinkle with paprika and bake at 350° for 30 minutes.

Mrs. Frank Jacobsen
(Julie Hasselbalch)

CRAB POTATOES

12 Servings

8 potatoes
½ cup butter
¾ cup milk
1 to 1½ cups sour cream
6 T. grated onion
Salt and pepper to taste
2 cans (6½ oz. each) crabmeat, drained

Bake potatoes. Halve them. Scoop out and mash potatoes while still hot, adding first the butter then other ingredients and mix well. Refill potato skins (or put into sea shells) and bake for 20 minutes at 400°. Can be made in advance.

Mrs. Elwood R. Mons
(Jane Allen)

ARTICHOKE-SPINACH-CHEESE BAKE

8 Servings

- **2 jars (6 oz. each) marinated artichoke hearts, drained**
- **2 pkgs. (10 oz. each) frozen chopped spinach, thawed, squeezed dry**
- **1 pkg. (8 oz.) cream cheese, softened**
- **2 T. butter, softened**
- **6 T. milk**
- **Freshly ground pepper**
- **½ cup grated Parmesan cheese**

Put artichoke hearts in 1½ to 2-qt. casserole. Arrange spinach evenly over artichoke hearts. Beat cream cheese and butter until smooth; gradually add milk. Spread cream cheese mixture over spinach; give it a good grinding of pepper. Sprinkle with Parmesan cheese. May be made ahead and refrigerated overnight. Bake covered at 350° for 30 minutes. Uncover and bake an additional 5 minutes.

CUCUMBER MOUSSE

6-8 Servings

Good with cold roast beef

- **5 medium cucumbers, peeled**
- **2¼ cups water**
- **2 T. lemon juice**
- **4 green onions with tops**
- **½ cup parsley, no stems**
- **1 cup mayonnaise**
- **4 tsp. Worcestershire sauce**
- **1½ tsp. salt**
- **¼ tsp. pepper**
- **Dash MSG**
- **Dash hot pepper sauce**
- **3 envelopes unflavored gelatin**
- **1 cup whipping cream**

Slice cucumbers in ½ lengthwise. Scrape spoon down middle to remove seeds. Cook cucumbers in 2 cups of water and lemon juice in covered saucepan until tender, about 20 minutes. Drain well. Puree in blender with onions and parsley. (Do not over-puree.) Add mayonnaise and seasonings. Blend. Soften gelatin in ¼ cup water; heat until dissolved. Stir into cucumber mixture. Chill until mixture mounds in spoon. Whip cream; fold into mixture. Adjust seasonings. Pour into oiled 6-cup ring mold. Chill overnight.

EASY NOODLES

6-8 Servings

- **1 pkg. (8 oz.) narrow egg noodles**
- **1 envelope dry onion soup mix**
- **1 lb. small curd cottage cheese**
- **1 pt. sour cream**

Cook noodles following package directions. Mix ingredients together. Place in casserole. Bake at 350° for 30 minutes until hot.

LEMON RICE WITH ALMONDS

4-6 Servings

- 1 large lemon
- 1 cup uncooked rice
- 1 ½ cups chicken broth
- 1 T. butter
- ½ tsp. salt
- ½ tsp. cinnamon
- ¼ tsp. nutmeg
- 1 cup dry white wine
- ⅔ cup coarsely ground almonds
- ½ cup currants
- 1 cup cooked peas, fresh or frozen
- ¼ cup honey

Grate rind of lemon and reserve. Squeeze juice and pulp from lemon; reserve. Place rice, broth, butter, salt, cinnamon, and nutmeg in top of double boiler. Cover and set over simmering water and steam about 30 minutes. Combine wine, almonds, and currants in a small pan. Simmer 10 minutes. Add to rice. Stir in peas. Transfer to serving dish. Drizzle honey over top.

TANGY COOKED DRESSING

3 Cups

Creamy and sweet

- 3 T. cornstarch
- 2 tsp. paprika
- 1 tsp. salt
- 1 tsp. dry mustard
- 4 eggs or 8 egg yolks
- 1 cup vinegar
- 1 cup water
- 1 cup sugar
- 2 tsp. butter, melted

In top of double boiler, mix cornstarch, paprika, salt and dry mustard. Add eggs; beat. Stir in vinegar, water, sugar and melted butter. Cook over boiling water, stirring constantly, until thickened.

CHEESE AND ONION BAKE

8 Servings

Good side dish with roasts

- 2 T. butter
- 2 large onions, sliced
- 1 can (10½ oz.) cream of chicken soup
- 1 soup can milk
- ½ to ¾ cup grated Swiss cheese
- 6 slices French bread, buttered (preferably sourdough)

Slowly cook onions in butter until limp and golden, about 20 minutes. Place in a 2-qt. casserole. Combine soup, milk, cheese, salt, and pepper. Heat. Pour ½ the mixture over the onions. Place 6 slices of bread on top (if bread is too fresh, toast slightly). Pour remaining soup mixture over bread. May be made day ahead. Bake at 350° for 1½ hours.

RUTABAGA AND CARROT PUREE

8 Servings

- 2 lbs. rutabagas, peeled and cut in 1½-inch pieces
- 6 carrots, peeled and cut into 2-inch pieces
- 1 onion, sliced
- 6 T. butter
- 2 T. brown sugar
- Salt, pepper, nutmeg

Just barely cover vegetables with salted water and bring to a boil. Boil vegetables 30 minutes. Drain vegetables and pass them through a food mill. Heat puree until moisture has evaporated. Beat in butter, sugar and seasonings to taste.

Mrs. Patrick Callahan
(Patricia Henebry)

CARIBBEAN SWEET POTATOES

6 Servings

- 4 sweet potatoes
- 3 bananas
- ½ cup butter
- ½ cup milk
- 1 egg, beaten
- ⅓ tsp. salt
- ¼ tsp. nutmeg

Boil sweet potatoes. Peel and mash with bananas, butter, milk and egg; season with salt and nutmeg. Add more liquid if needed. Place in a 2 quart casserole. Bake at 350° until thoroughly heated.

Mrs. Arthur S. Bowes
(Patricia F. Kelly)

SPINACH FLORENTINE

6-8 Servings

- 1 lb. fresh mushrooms, sliced
- ¼ cup chopped onion
- ¼ cup butter
- ¼ tsp. garlic salt
- 1 tsp. salt
- 2 pkgs. (10 oz. each) frozen spinach, thawed and all water squeezed out
- 1 cup finely grated cheddar cheese

Saute mushrooms and onion in butter until transparent. Stir in garlic salt and salt. Place one package of spinach in bottom of casserole. Pour half of mushroom mixture on top of spinach; sprinkle half of cheese over top. Repeat layer one more time. Bake uncovered at 350° for 20 minutes.

Mrs. Suzanne Robison
(Suzanne Dohse)

LIME SALAD SUPREME

9 Servings

- **2 pkgs. (3 oz. each) lime gelatin (or lemon)**
- **2 cups boiling water**
- **1½ cups cold water**
- **1 can (13½ oz.) crushed pineapple, drained**
- **2 bananas, diced**
- **1 cup small marshmallows**
- **2 T. butter**
- **1 T. flour**
- **1 egg, beaten**
- **½ cup sugar**
- **1 cup pineapple juice**
- **1 cup whipping cream, whipped**
- **½ cup grated swiss cheese**

Dissolve gelatin in boiling water. Stir in cold water and let stand about ½ hour or until slightly set. Add pineapple, bananas and marshmallows. Pour into a 9-inch square pan; refrigerate until firm. Melt butter; add flour and egg. Stir until smooth. Add sugar and pineapple juice; cook and stir until thick. Cool. Fold in the whipped cream; pour over top of gelatin. Sprinkle with grated cheese; refrigerate. Cut in squares.

Mrs. Bruce G. Southworth
(Mary Monek)

GREEK SALATA

8-10 Servings

Nice to serve with moussaka

- **1 cup greek olives**
- **1 cup hot peppers**
- **½ cup olive oil**
- **½ cup red wine vinegar**
- **3 to 4 heads of lettuce**
- **4 large tomatoes, cut in wedges**
- **2 large cucumbers, cut in long spears**
- **1 lb. feta cheese, cut into small pieces**
- **1 small can anchovy fillets**
- **Oregano**

The day before, marinate olives, peppers, olive oil and vinegar together. Just before serving, drain olives and peppers reserving marinade. Place olives and peppers in large mixing bowl; add lettuce, tomatoes and cucumbers; toss lightly. Arrange on salad plates; add pieces of feta cheese and anchovy fillets. Sprinkle with oregano. Use remaining marinade sparingly on salad as salad dressing.

Mrs. John Mangel II
(Hilda Brumbaugh)

CHERRY MOLD

8 Servings

- 2 pkgs. (3 oz. each) cherry gelatin
- 2 cups boiling water
- 1 can (20 oz.) cherry pie filling
- ⅓ cup claret wine
- 2 T. lemon juice
- 1 pkg. (3 oz.) cream cheese
- 1 cup evaporated milk

Dissolve gelatin in water; cool. Add pie filling, wine and lemon juice. Beat cheese with electric mixer until fluffy; beat milk in gradually. Add to first mixture; chill until partly set. Stir mixture until cherries are evenly distributed. Turn into an 11x7x2-inch pan, or individual molds. Chill until firm.

Mrs. David B. Smith
(Marcia Williamson)

GREEN BEAN SALAD

8 Servings

Delicious with beef and ham

- 2 cans (1 lb. each) of petite (size 1) whole green beans
- 1 onion, sliced
- Salt and pepper
- 2 T. salad oil
- 2 T. vinegar
- ½ cup mayonnaise
- ½ cup sour cream
- 1 tsp. prepared horseradish
- 1 T. lemon juice
- ½ tsp. dry mustard

Marinate beans and onions, salted and peppered, in oil and vinegar for several hours (all day is best), in refrigerator. Drain. Combine remainder of ingredients; stir into salad.

Mrs. Barbara T. Whitney
(Barbara Thiele)

VEGETABLE MEDLEY SALAD

4-6 Servings

- 1 pkg. (10 oz.) frozen mixed vegetables
- 2 cups mixed salad greens torn into bite-size pieces
- ⅓ cup chopped celery
- ⅓ cup mayonnaise
- 1 T. minced onion
- 1 tsp. worcestershire sauce

Cook vegetables in boiling, salted water until tender; drain. Add celery and greens. Blend remaining ingredients and add to vegetables; toss lightly. Chill.

Mrs. David B. Smith
(Marcia Williamson)

TANGERINE WALNUT TOSS

6-8 Servings

- 7 cups torn lettuce
- 2 cups tangerine sections, membrane removed
- ½ cup olive oil
- ⅓ cup vinegar
- 2 T. water
- 1 medium onion, sliced
- 1 T. sugar
- 1 clove, garlic, minced
- 1 tsp. celery seeds
- ½ tsp. salt
- Dash pepper
- ½ cup walnut pieces
- 1 T. butter
- ¼ tsp. salt

Place lettuce and tangerine sections in salad bowl; chill. Place olive oil, vinegar, water, onion, sugar, garlic, celery seeds, salt and pepper in a saucepan. Bring to a boil; remove from heat and chill. Just before serving pour dressing over lettuce and tangerine sections; toss well. Saute walnuts in butter and salt. Stir until walnuts are crisp and butter browned. Sprinkle over salad.

Mrs. David B. Smith
(Marcia Williamson)

MIXED GREEN SALAD WITH BLUE CHEESE DRESSING

12-16 Servings

- 1 cup sour cream
- 2 oz. blue cheese, crumbled
- ¼ cup thinly-sliced green onions with tops
- 1 T. lemon juice
- 1 tsp. sugar
- ½ tsp. salt
- ½ tsp. celery seeds (optional)
- ¼ tsp. pepper
- 1 lb. fresh spinach
- 2 small heads Boston lettuce or 1 head iceberg lettuce

For dressing, combine sour cream, cheese, onion, lemon juice, sugar, salt, celery seeds and pepper in blender container. Blend until almost smooth. Chill. Wash greens; pat dry. Tear into pieces. Toss with dressing in salad bowl.

Mrs. Phillip J. Stover
(Annette Ashlock)

WINTER SALAD

6-8 Servings

1 cup diced carrots, cooked
1 cup chopped beets, cooked
1 can (8 oz.) white beans, drained
1 cup green peas, cooked
½ cup diced potato, boiled
4 hard-cooked eggs, chopped
1 sour pickle, chopped
1 cup sour cream
2 T. mayonnaise
Salt and pepper to taste

Combine the vegetables, eggs and pickles; chill. Just before serving combine sour cream, mayonnaise, salt and pepper; toss with vegetables.

Mrs. J.L. Harper
(Sally S. Kelley)

MOLDED BEET SALAD

8 Servings

½ envelope plain gelatin
¼ cup cold water
1 pkg. (3 oz.) lemon gelatin
1 cup boiling water
¾ cup canned pickled beet juice
3 T. vinegar
½ tsp. salt
4 tsp. minced onion
2 T. prepared horse-radish
½ cup finely-chopped cucumbers
½ cup finely-chopped celery
1 cup finely-diced pickled beets

Sprinkle gelatin in cold water. Let stand 5 minutes. Add lemon gelatin and boiling water; stir until dissolved. Add beet juice. Chill until of egg white consistency. Stir in remaining ingredients. Pour into a greased ring mold. Chill until firm.

Mrs. William P. Sutter
(Helen Yvonne Stebbins)

BRANDY ALEXANDER PIE

6-8 Servings

1 env. plain gelatin
½ cup cold water
⅔ cup sugar
⅛ tsp. salt
3 eggs, separated
¼ cup cognac
¼ cup creme de cocoa
2 cups whipping cream, whipped
1 graham cracker crust (9 or 10-inch)

Sprinkle gelatin over water in a heavy saucepan. Add ⅓ cup sugar, salt and egg yolks. Stir to blend. Cook over low heat, stirring until the gelatin dissolves and mixture thickens. Do not boil. Stir in cognac and creme de cocoa. Chill until mixture starts to mound slightly. Beat egg whites until foamy. Gradually beat in remaining ⅓ cup sugar, continuing to beat until stiff peaks form. Fold into thickened mixture. Fold in half the whipped cream. Turn into crust. Chill several hours or overnight. Decorate with remaining whipped cream and chocolate curls.

Mrs. James F. Peil
(Nancy Rodgers)

EGG NOG PIE

6-8 Servings

2 cups light cream or milk
3 eggs, separated
½ cup sugar
Dash salt
⅛ tsp. nutmeg
1 envelope plain gelatin
2 T. cold water
1 to 2 T. rum
1 tsp. vanilla extract
½ cup whipping cream, whipped
1 prepared 8-inch crumb crust

Scald cream in a double boiler. Beat egg yolks with half the sugar until pale. Add salt and nutmeg. Add yolk mixture to cream. Cook, stirring constantly, over simmering water until it coats a spoon. Soften gelatin in the water; add to custard. Stir until dissolved. Strain. Add the rum and vanilla extract. Chill until it begins to set. Beat egg whites until foamy. Gradually add remaining sugar and beat until stiff. Fold into custard. Fold in whipped cream. Pour into crust; chill until firm. Garnish with more whipped cream and nutmeg.

Miss Linda R. Smith

PARTRIDGE-IN-A-PEAR TREE PIE

6-8 Servings

2 T. cornstarch
1¼ cups sugar
¼ tsp. salt
1¼ cups water
1 cup seedless raisins
2 cups cranberries
1 T. butter
Pastry for 2-crust pie
1 T. melted butter
1 can (8 oz.) pear halves drained, sliced
Sugar

Blend 1¼ cups sugar, cornstarch and salt. Add water slowly. Cook until mixture thickens, stirring constantly. Add raisins, cranberries and butter; cook 5 minutes. Line a 9-inch pie plate with half of pastry; brush with melted butter. Add cranberry-raisin filling. Gently press pear slices into filling in a spoke-like design. Roll out remaining pastry; make partridge and tree designs to top pie. Sprinkle cut-outs with sugar. Bake at 450° for 20 minutes.

Mrs. Robert T. DePree
(Susan Barker)

PEARS AND SHERBET IN RUM SAUCE

4 Servings

A light dessert to end a dinner party

4 pear halves (canned or very-ripe fresh, peeled)
4 scoops pineapple sherbet
½ cup berry syrup
2 T. rum

Place pear halves in sherbet dishes. Top with sherbet. Mix syrup and rum; pour over desserts. (For syrup, use blackberry, elderberry, blueberry, or red raspberry.)

Mrs. Phillip J. Stover
(Annette Ashlock)

CASSATA ALLA SICILIANA

16 Servings

- 1 bakery pound cake (about 9-inches long)
- ⅔ cup orange juice
- ¼ cup rum
- 1 lb. creamed cottage cheese
- ¼ cup sugar
- ½ cup semi-sweet chocolate pieces, chopped
- ¼ cup chopped candied cherries or maraschino cherries, drained on paper towels
- ¼ cup chopped golden raisins

CHOCOLATE FROSTING:

- 2 squares unsweetened chocolate, melted
- 2½ cups confectioners' sugar
- 3 T. butter or margarine
- 2 T. hot coffee
- 1 egg yolk

Split cake into 5 layers. Combine orange juice and rum; reserve 3 tablespoons. Sprinkle remainder over cake layers. Process cheese, sugar and 3 tablespoons rum mixture in blender until smooth (best to do in several batches). Stir in chocolate, cherries and raisins. Place bottom cake layer on long platter; spread filling between layers, while stacking them. Chill. Combine ingredients for frosting, adding hot water or confectioners' sugar as necessary to give spreading consistency. Spread ¾ on top and sides of cake; press remainder through pastry tube to make decorative swirls. Refrigerate at least 1 day. Garnish base with decorative candies, flowers or leaves.

NOTE: This is a very rich dessert, great for dessert parties. It would probably be too rich to follow most meals. The cake is served in Sicily for weddings, Christmas and Easter. It signifies the beginning of a new way of life.

Mrs. Phillip J. Stover
(Annette Ashlock)

APPLE CRISP

8 Servings

6 to 8 apples, cored peeled and sliced
½ cup sugar
½ tsp. cinnamon
Juice of ½ a lemon
1 cup flour
1 cup brown sugar
½ cup butter, softened

VARIATION:
Add ⅓ cup chopped pecans to topping.

Mix apples with sugar, cinnamon and lemon juice. Lay apples in buttered 8-inch pan to a depth of 1½ inches. Mix flour, brown sugar, and butter; spread on top. Bake at 350° for 30 minutes. Serve with hard sauce.

Mrs. Marquis Bowman, Jr.
(Joan Osborne)

PLANTATION CAKE

6-8 Servings

This is a delicious old southern recipe

½ cup butter
½ cup firmly-packed brown sugar
2 cups sifted flour
¼ tsp. salt
⅔ cup water
⅔ cup molasses
¾ tsp. soda

CREAM CHEESE FLUFF:
1 pkg. (3 oz.) cream cheese
1 T. powdered sugar
1 T. cream

LEMON SAUCE:
1 T. cornstarch
1 cup sugar
⅛ tsp. salt
1½ cups water
2 egg yolks, slightly beaten
2 T. butter
1½ T. lemon juice
Grated rind of 1 lemon

Cream butter and sugar together; stir in flour and salt. Divide into 3 parts. Set aside. Mix water, molasses and soda. In a buttered 9-inch layer cake pan place ⅓ of crumbs. Carefully pour ⅓ of molasses mixture over crumbs, taking care not to disturb crumbs. Repeat 2 more layers. Bake at 350° for 30 minutes. Serve warm topped with a large spoonful of cream cheese fluff and hot lemon sauce.

For Fluff: Beat all ingredients until fluffy.

For Sauce: Mix cornstarch, sugar and salt; stir in cold water. Bring to a boil. Cook, stirring, until thickened. Add a little hot mixture to egg yolks; return all to pan for 1 minute, stirring constantly. Remove from heat; add butter, lemon juice and lemon rind.

Mrs. James F. Peil
(Nancy Rodgers)

CARROT CAKE

10 Servings

1½ cups salad oil
2 cups sugar
4 eggs
2 cups sifted flour
2 tsp. baking soda
2 tsp. baking powder
2 tsp. cinnamon
½ tsp. salt
¼ tsp. nutmeg
1 cup chopped pecans
3 cups grated carrots
1 cup golden raisins
1 tsp. vanilla

FROSTING:

¼ lb. browned butter
1 lb. confectioners' sugar
1 tsp. vanilla
3 to 4 T. cream

Blend oil and sugar. Add eggs one at a time. Sift together dry ingredients; add to mixture and blend well. Add remaining ingredients. Pour into three 9-inch greased and floured cake pans; bake at 350° about 25 minutes or until done.

Combine frosting ingredients. Frost cake while warm.

Mrs. Frank L. Phillips
(Jane Bennett)

BUCHE DE NOEL AU CHOCOLAT 10-12 Servings

CHOCOLATE SPONGE CAKE:

6 eggs, separated
Pinch of salt
¾ cup sugar
6 oz. semisweet chocolate, melted
2 T. strong coffee
1 tsp. vanilla
½ cup dark unsweetened cocoa

CHOCOLATE BUTTER CREAM:

3 egg whites
Pinch of salt
¼ tsp. cream of tartar
1⅓ cups sugar
⅓ cup water
2 cups (12 oz.) semisweet chocolate bits, melted with
3 T. strong coffee or rum
1 T. vanilla
½ lb. sweet butter, softened

Cake: Beat egg whites with salt until they hold soft peaks. Add sugar gradually, continuing to beat until stiff peaks form. Lightly beat egg yolks. Stir in chocolate, coffee and vanilla. Fold ¼ of egg whites into chocolate mixture. Pour back over remaining egg whites; fold together. Pour into greased, waxed-paper-lined 15 x 10-inch jelly-roll pan. Bake at 375° 10 minutes. Reduce heat to 350°, bake 5 minutes longer or until top is firm. Cool in pan. Sift cocoa evenly over a sheet of waxed paper; turn pastry onto cocoa. Butter Cream: Beat egg whites until foamy. Add salt and cream of tartar. Beat until stiff. Meanwhile, dissolve sugar in water over high heat; boil to soft ball stage (238°). While continuing to beat egg whites, pour in the sugar syrup in a thin stream. Beat at high speed for 5 minutes. Reserve ½ cup meringue for decorative mushrooms. Beat melted chocolate, coffee and vanilla into meringue. Gradually beat in butter. Chill until of easy spreading consistency. Spread ½ the butter cream on cake; roll up, starting with a short end. Cut off the two ends on the bias and cut each into short branches. Cut holes ½-inch deep at two locations on log; insert branches. Frost with remaining butter cream, reserving 1 to 2 T. With a fork create a bark-like effect. Refrigerate until set, (or freeze). Place reserved meringue in a pastry bag. With a 3/16-inch tube, create domes for mushroom caps and short cylinders for stems. Drop onto a lightly-floured baking sheet; bake at 200° for 40 to 60 minutes. Pierce hole in bottom of each cap; fill with dab of reserved butter cream and insert stem. Remove log from refrigerator 20 minutes before serving. Press mushrooms into base and top of log; sprinkle with cocoa and a little powdered sugar for snow.

Mrs. Dennis F. Muckermann
(Betty Graham)

NUT TORTE WITH BRANDY SYRUP — 24 Servings

2 cups zwieback crumbs
2 cups chopped pecans
½ tsp. cinnamon
½ tsp. salt
2 tsp. baking powder
1 T. grated lemon rind
2 tsp. vanilla
6 eggs, separated
1 cup sugar

BRANDY SYRUP:

4 cups water
2 cups sugar
¼ cup brandy
2 T. grated orange rind

Thoroughly mix first 6 ingredients; add vanilla. Beat egg yolks until thick and lemon colored. Gradually add sugar, continuing to beat until well mixed. Add to dry ingredients; mix thoroughly. Beat egg whites until stiff; fold into mixture. Pour into a greased 13x9-inch pan. Bake at 325° for 30 minutes or until top springs back. Meanwhile prepare brandy syrup: Place water and sugar in saucepan; heat to boiling, stirring to dissolve sugar. Continue cooking over medium heat for 30 minutes. Stir in brandy and orange rind. Slowly pour syrup over hot torte until it is completely absorbed.

Mrs. Thomas N. Boyden
(Susan Dalton)

MEXICAN CREAM TORTE — 8 Servings

Light and refreshing after a heavy meal

1 pkg. (8 to 12 oz.) coconut macaroons
3 pints chocolate ice cream (softened)
1 jar (12 oz.) chocolate syrup (Smuckers Chocolate Fudge preferred)
1½ pints orange sherbet (softened)
2 cups crushed peanut brittle

Press macaroons into the bottom of a 9-inch spring-form pan. Cover bottom completely. Layer with half the chocolate ice cream, 6 oz. chocolate syrup, all the orange sherbet, 4 more ounces chocolate syrup and remaining chocolate ice cream. Sprinkle peanut brittle over top. Freeze at least 3 hours or overnight. Remove sides of pan and slide onto a serving plate. Cut into wedges.

Mrs. H. Alex Vance, Jr.
(Melinda Martin)

PEPPERMINT BROWNIES

3 Dozen Small Squares

Serve these alongside of French vanilla ice cream

2 squares unsweetened chocolate
½ cup butter
2 eggs
1 cup sugar
½ cup flour
½ tsp. baking powder
¼ tsp. peppermint flavoring

FROSTING:

1 cup confectioners' sugar
2 T. butter, softened
1 T. milk
½ tsp. peppermint flavoring
Few drops green food coloring

TOPPING:

1 square (1 oz.) semisweet chocolate
1 T. butter

For brownies, melt chocolate and butter in top of double boiler. Beat eggs and add with sugar to chocolate mixture. Stir in remaining ingredients. Turn into buttered 9-inch square baking pan. Bake at 350° for 20 to 25 minutes. Cool.

For frosting, beat ingredients together; spread on brownies. Chill about 30 minutes.

For topping, melt chocolate with butter and drizzle over frosted brownies. Refrigerate again until chocolate is firm. Cut into squares.

STRAWBERRY TORTE

6 Servings

9-inch pastry shell
1 cup whipping cream
3 T. confectioners' sugar
1 to 2 tsp. vanilla
1 to 2 pts. ripe strawberries
¼ cup red currant jelly

Line a 9-inch tart pan (with removable sides if possible) with pastry, cover with tin foil. Fill with dried beans and bake at 375° 15 to 20 minutes or until golden brown. If using a pan with removable sides, remove pastry shell from tin and cool. Otherwise allow to cool in pan. Whip cream with confectioners' sugar and vanilla. Spread over the bottom of cooled pastry shell. Trim strawberries so that they conform in size and place them attractively in the cream. Heat currant jelly with a bit of water and brush onto each strawberry to glaze.

WALNUT-RASPBERRY TORTE

9 Squares

- **3 eggs, separated**
- **1 cup sugar**
- **1 cup graham cracker crumbs**
- **½ cup chopped walnuts**
- **1 pkg. (3 oz.) cream cheese**
- **½ cup confectioners' sugar**
- **½ tsp. milk**
- **½ cup seedless raspberry jam**

Beat egg whites until stiff. Set aside. Combine the yolks, sugar, graham cracker crumbs, and walnuts. Fold into egg whites. Pour into a 9-inch x 9-inch pan. Bake at 325° for 20 to 30 minutes. Cool. Blend cream cheese, confectioners' sugar, and milk until smooth. Spread cake with jam and frost with cheese mixture. Cut into squares.

ORANGE-DATE SWIRLS

5 Dozen

- **1 lb. chopped dates**
- **½ cup sugar**
- **½ cup water**
- **2 tsp. grated orange rind**
- **1 cup sugar**
- **1 cup brown sugar**
- **1 cup butter**
- **3 eggs, beaten**
- **4 cups flour**
- **1 tsp. baking soda**
- **½ tsp. salt**
- **1 tsp. vanilla**

Boil dates and sugar in water until thick. Add 1 tsp. of orange rind and cool. Set date mixture aside. Cream sugars and butter. Add eggs. Add flour, soda, salt, and remaining orange rind. Add vanilla. Refrigerate dough. Roll out dough into a rectangle on waxed paper. Spread with date mixture. Roll up like a jelly roll, cover with waxed paper and refrigerate. Can be kept in refrigerator up to 3 weeks. Slice into ¼-inch slices. Bake on ungreased cookie sheet for 8 to 10 minutes at 400°.

CHOCOLATE-WHEAT GERM PIE

6 Servings

- **½ cup butter, softened**
- **¾ cup sugar**
- **2 eggs**
- **1½ tsp. vanilla**
- **1 pkg. (6 oz.) semisweet chocolate pieces**
- **1 cup plain wheat germ**
- **1 unbaked 9-inch pastry shell**
- **Ice cream or whipped cream**

Using electric mixer, cream butter; gradually beat in sugar. Add eggs and vanilla; beat well. Mix in wheat germ and chocolate pieces. Pour into pastry shell. Bake at 350° about 50 minutes, or until knife inserted in center comes out clean. Serve with ice cream or whipped cream.

SNOW PUDDING WITH LEMON SAUCE

5-6 Servings

Light and fluffy

PUDDING:

1 envelope (1 T.) unflavored gelatin
3 T. cold water
1 cup boiling water
½ cup sugar
Dash salt
1 T. vanilla
3 egg whites
⅓ cup graham cracker crumbs, buttered, toasted

LEMON SAUCE:

3 egg yolks
½ cup sugar
⅓ cup melted butter, cooled
Juice and rind of 1 lemon
½ cup whipping cream, whipped

For pudding, soften gelatin in cold water. Add hot water, sugar, vanilla and salt. When cool, add unbeaten egg whites and beat until stiff but not dry. Turn into large individual goblets or brandy snifters. Top with crumbs. Chill until set. For sauce, beat yolks with sugar until thick and lemon colored. Beat in butter, lemon juice, and rind. Just before serving, fold in whipped cream. Serve generous amount of sauce over each serving of snow pudding.

SWISS TORTE

10-12 Servings

12 oz. ground almonds or walnuts
1½ cups sugar
1 cup butter
2 whole eggs
2 egg yolks
2 T. flour
Raspberry jam
Confectioners' sugar
Whipped cream (optional)

Cream almonds, sugar and butter until light and fluffy. Beat egg and yolks together and add with flour to creamed mixture. Line bottoms of 3 spring-form pans with buttered waxed paper. Put ⅓ of mixture in each pan. Bake at 350° for 20 minutes. Remove from pans while still warm. Spread each layer with raspberry jam. Place layers together; sprinkle with confectioners' sugar. Whipped cream may be passed when serving, if desired.

SOUR CREAM PEACH SQUARES

12 Servings

Tastes best warm

- **2 cups sifted flour**
- **¾ cups sugar**
- **¼ tsp. baking powder**
- **1 tsp. salt**
- **¾ cup butter, softened**
- **4 cups sliced fresh peaches, sugared (or 1 can (30 oz.) sliced cling peaches, drained)**
- **1 tsp. cinnamon**
- **2 egg yolks**
- **1 cup sour cream**

Sift together flour, ¼ cup sugar, baking powder, and salt. Cut in butter until crumbly. Turn into a lightly greased 13 x 9-inch baking pan. Press crumbs firmly over bottom and up sides of pan to form an even crust. Arrange peaches over crust. Combine remaining ½ cup sugar and cinnamon; sprinkle over peaches. Bake at 400° for 15 minutes. Meanwhile, beat egg yolks and sour cream; spoon over peaches. Bake 15 minutes longer or until peaches are glazed and golden brown. Serve warm with ice cream, if desired. Other fruits may be substituted for or mixed with the peaches.

RICH BUTTER NUT CAKE

- **1 pkg. (17 oz.) pound cake mix**
- **½ cup butter, melted**
- **4 eggs**
- **1 pkg. (8 oz.) cream cheese**
- **½ tsp. vanilla**
- **2½ cups confectioners' sugar**
- **1 cup chopped nuts**

Combine cake mix, butter, and 2 eggs, stirring until well blended. Beat for 1 minute. Spread batter in greased 9 x 13-inch baking pan. Beat cream cheese with electric mixer until light and fluffy. Beat in remaining 2 eggs and vanilla. Set aside ½ cup confectioners' sugar. Beat remaining sugar into cream cheese mixture. Pour evenly over cake batter in pan. Sprinkle with nuts. Bake at 350° for 35 to 45 minutes, until cake pulls away from sides of pan. Cool 20 minutes. Sprinkle with remaining confectioners' sugar.

CHOCOLATE JAM TORTE

12-16 Servings

- **8 eggs, separated**
- **1 cup sugar**
- **¼ tsp. salt**
- **½ lb. finely-ground pecans**
- **1 large jar raspberry jam**

FROSTING:

- **¼ lb. sweet chocolate (Baker's German preferred)**
- **¼ cup water**
- **¾ cup sugar**
- **¾ cup softened, unsalted butter**
- **2 egg yolks**
- **Finely-chopped nuts or chocolate shot**

Beat egg yolks until thick and lemon colored. Gradually beat in ½ cup sugar. Beat egg whites and salt until foamy; gradually beat in ½ cup sugar, continuing to beat until stiff peaks form. Gently fold yolks into whites. Fold in nuts. Turn into 2 greased and floured 9-inch cake pans. Bake at 350° for 50 minutes. Turn out on racks; cool. Split layers in two. (Use a very sharp, thin knife and cut slowly). Place one layer on serving tray; spread with jam. Repeat with second and third layers. Place fourth layer on top.

To prepare frosting: melt chocolate. Dissolve sugar in water (heat if necessary); blend with chocolate. Cool. Cream butter until fluffy; add egg yolks. Beat thoroughly. Add chocolate-sugar mixture.

Frost top and sides of torte. Garnish sides with chocolate shot or finely-chopped nuts. Keep refrigerated. After frosting hardens, wrap in plastic wrap. (This torte is very rich, so thin slices are ample. Torte may be frozen).

Mrs. Halbert S. Gillette
(Karla Spiel)

MINTED POTS DE CREME

6 Servings

- **1 cup semi-sweet mint chocolate chips**
- **1¼ cups half and half, scalded**
- **2 egg yolks**
- **2 to 3 T. brandy or rum**
- **Whipping cream**

Place all ingredients in a blender; blend at high speed until smooth. Pour into pot-de-cremes and chill for at least 3 hours. If desired whipped cream with chocolate shavings on top can be used as a garnish.

Mrs. Frank W. Gordon, II
(Judith Bracken)

MOCHA FRENCH YULE LOG — 12 Servings

5 eggs, separated (at room temperature)
½ cup sugar
3 T. cocoa
½ cup sifted cake flour
½ tsp. salt

MOCHA BUTTER CREAM:

¾ cup sweet butter
¾ cup sifted confectioners' sugar
1 T. cocoa
2 tsp. instant coffee
2 egg yolks

FILLING:

1 cup whipping cream
¼ cup granulated sugar

Beat egg whites until they form stiff peaks; set aside. Beat egg yolks until lemon colored; gradually beat in sugar and cocoa, continuing to beat until thick. Blend in flour and salt. Gently fold yolk mixture into egg whites. Pour into a greased jelly roll pan (15 x 10 x 1-inch) lined with greased waxed paper. Bake at 375° for 15 minutes or until done; do not over bake. Turn out onto dish towel which has been sprinkled with powdered sugar. Roll up from narrow end. Cool.

For butter cream: Cream butter, sugar, cocoa and coffee until fluffy. Beat in egg yolks.

For filling: Whip cream until thick; stir in sugar.

Unroll cake; spread with thin layer of butter cream (about ⅓ cup). Spread with whipped cream filling; reroll. Frost with remaining butter cream. Refrigerate 24 hours. Allow cake to stand ½ hour at room temperature before slicing.

Mrs. Walter G. Larkin
(Kathryn Comfort)

RUM CREAM — 8-10 Servings

1½ T. plain gelatin
½ cup cold water
6 egg yolks
¼ cup strong coffee
½ cup light rum
1 cup sugar
2 cups whipping cream
Ladyfingers, split
Slivered toasted almonds

Soften gelatin in cold water; dissolve over boiling water. Beat egg yolks until thick and lemon colored. Beat in coffee and rum. Gradually beat in sugar. Beat gelatin into egg mixture. Chill until mixture begins to thicken. Whip cream; fold in egg mixture. Pour into mold lined with ladyfingers, letting ½-inch show around edge. Garnish with almonds. (This can also be served in individual dessert glasses, omitting lady fingers.)

Mrs. Edward C. McNally
(Margaret McGann)

ORANGE CHEDDAR CHEESECAKE

8 Servings

- **1 cup crushed orange cookie wafers**
- **2 T. melted butter**
- **2 packages (8 oz. each) cream cheese, softened**
- **½ cup finely-shredded cheddar cheese**
- **¾ cup sugar**
- **2 T. flour**
- **3 eggs**
- **¼ cup beer**
- **¼ cup whipping cream**
- **¼ tsp. grated orange rind**
- **¼ tsp. grated lemon rind**
- **½ tsp. vanilla**

Mix cookie crumbs with butter; pat into a buttered 8-inch spring-form pan. Bake at 350° for 8 minutes. Whip cream cheese until light and fluffy in an electric mixer; blend in cheddar cheese. Gradually beat in sugar mixed with flour. Add eggs, one at a time, beating until smooth. Mix in beer and cream. Add rinds and vanilla; mix well. Turn into crumb-lined pan; bake at 350° for 30 to 45 minutes. Test with toothpick. Cool, then chill or serve at room temperature. Garland the cake with clusters of frosted grapes nestled on leaves.

Mrs. John L. Tuohy
(Anne LaVerne Lea)

CHOCOLATE CHEESECAKE

10 Servings

- **¾ cup graham cracker crumbs**
- **5 T. melted butter**
- **2 T. sugar**
- **2 T. grated semisweet chocolate**
- **3 eggs**
- **1 cup sugar**
- **3 (8 oz. each) pkg. cream cheese**
- **12 sqs. (1 oz. each) semisweet chocolate**
- **1 cup sour cream**
- **¾ cup butter**
- **1 tsp. vanilla**
- **1 cup pecans, coarsely chopped**
- **Whipping cream (optional)**

Combine the first four ingredients; press into bottom of 8-inch spring-form pan. Beat with electric beater the eggs and sugar until pale yellow. In a separate bowl beat cheese until softened; add to egg mixture and mix well. Melt chocolate in double boiler; stir in sour cream, butter and vanilla. Stir this mixture into the cheese mixture and fold in nuts. Pour batter into pan; bake at 325° for 2 hours or until center is firm. Cool on wire rack; remove from pan. Chill and serve with whipped cream.

Mrs. John N. Schmidt
(Joan Slauson)

CRANBERRY PUDDING 8-10 Servings

- **2 tsp. soda**
- **½ cup hot water**
- **½ cup molasses**
- **2 cups raw cranberries, sliced in half**
- **1⅓ cups flour (unsifted)**
- **2 tsp. baking powder**

Dissolve soda in hot water; add molasses and berries. Mix flour and baking powder; add to other mixture. Pour into greased pudding mold with top. Cover and place on rack in kettle. Add water to come half way up side of mold. Cover kettle and steam 2 hours. Can be made ahead and reheated. Serve with egg nog sauce or brandy sauce.

Mrs. Herbert Knight
(Nancy Gordon)

STEAMED CHOCOLATE PUDDING 8 Servings

- **2 T. butter to grease mold**
- **6 oz. dark sweet chocolate**
- **3 eggs**
- **1½ cups sugar**
- **3 T. soft butter**
- **3 T. orange marmalade**
- **3 cups flour**
- **2 tsp. baking powder**
- **½ tsp. salt**
- **1½ cups whipping cream**
- **Hard sauce**

Heavily butter an 8-cup steamed pudding mold. Melt chocolate over very low heat, stirring constantly; set aside. Beat eggs; add sugar gradually, beating until light and fluffy. Beat in cooled (but not set) chocolate, soft butter and orange marmalade. Sift flour with baking powder and salt; beat into egg-sugar mixture alternately with cream. Pour batter into mold to about ¾-inch from top. Fasten lid tightly; stand mold on a rack in a large pot. Pour boiling water half way up the sides of the mold. Steam on top of stove for 2 hours. Replenish boiling water as necessary. Turn pudding out onto a platter; serve with hard sauce.

Mrs. David B. Smith
(Marcia Williamson)

BRANDY SAUCE

½ lb. butter
1 lb. brown sugar
Juice and grated peel of 1 lemon
2 eggs
½ cup brandy or rum

Mix all ingredients; heat in double boiler until thick, beating constantly so eggs do not curdle. (This sauce may be refrigerated, then reheated over hot water. Very good on plum pudding and mincemeat pie).

Mrs. Brian Baldwin
(Elizabeth Voris)

EGG NOG SAUCE

4 egg yolks
1 cup powdered sugar
2 T. brandy
1 cup whipping cream, whipped
1 tsp. vanilla
Pinch of salt

Beat yolks until light and lemon colored. Gradually add sugar and brandy, beating constantly. Fold into whipped cream. Add vanilla and salt. This is good on plum pudding.

Mrs. Edward Hines
(Marcia McMillan)

CUMBERLAND RUM BUTTER

¼ cup unsalted butter, softened
½ cup light brown sugar, sieved
¼ cup light rum
⅛ tsp. freshly-grated nutmeg

Cream butter and sugar; add rum and nutmeg. Refrigerate until firm. Very good on plum pudding.

Mrs. Arthur S. Bowes
(Patricia F. Kelly)

BRANDY CREAM SAUCE

8 Servings

Fantastic rich sauce for puddings and fruit cake

¼ cup butter
2 cups powdered sugar
2 eggs, well beaten
Pinch of salt
5 T. brandy (or other liqueur such as cointreau)
1 pt. whipping cream, whipped

Cream butter and sugar. Add eggs and beat until very smooth. Add salt and brandy. Fold in the whipped cream; refrigerate. If made ahead, sauce will separate, but, be perfect when beaten again.

Mrs. John R. Gardner
(Catherine Corrigall)

CHOCOLATE FLOAT

8 Servings

1 sq. unsweetened chocolate
2 T. butter
½ cup milk
1 tsp. vanilla
1 cup flour
¾ cup sugar
¼ tsp. salt
2 tsp. baking powder
½ cup pecans, chopped (optional)

TOPPING:

½ cup white sugar
½ cup dark brown sugar
2 T. cocoa
1 cup boiling water
1 cup whipping cream, whipped

Melt chocolate and butter in a double boiler. Add milk. Remove from heat; add vanilla. Mix remaining ingredients; add to chocolate mixture and blend. Pour into ungreased 8-inch square baking pan. For topping, combine white sugar, dark brown sugar and cocoa. Cover batter with this topping; pour boiling water over all. Bake at 325° for 45 to 55 minutes. Serve warm topped with whipped cream.

Mrs. Robert W. Buckley, Jr.
(Ann Middleton)

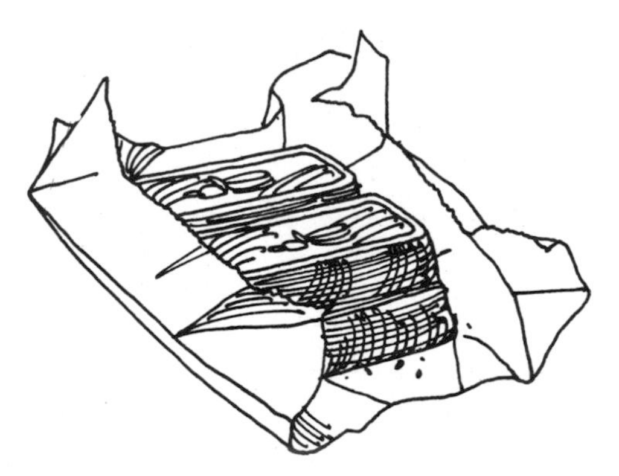

CHOCOLATE MOUSSE

8 Servings

4 oz. unsweetened chocolate
8 eggs, separated
1 cup confectioners sugar, sifted
1½ oz. bourbon
¾ cup whipping cream, whipped
1 T. sugar
1 tsp. bourbon

Melt chocolate. Beat yolks, adding confectoners' sugar gradually, until yolks are pale yellow. Slowly mix yolks into chocolate over a low heat until very smooth. Add 1½ oz. bourbon. Beat whites until almost stiff. Fold whites into chocolate mixture until no whites show. Refrigerate, covered, overnight. When ready to serve, decorate with whipped cream flavored with sugar and 1 tsp. bourbon.

Mrs. Benson T. Caswell
(Margaret Graham)

GRAND MARNIER SOUFFLE

4-6 Servings

2½ T. unsalted butter
3 T. flour
1 cup milk
5 eggs, separated
1 cup confectioners' sugar
Grated rind of 1 orange
1 tsp. vanilla
⅓ to ½ cup Grand Marnier

Melt butter; stir in flour. Add milk gradually; stir mixture over low heat until it thickens and is very smooth. Cool. Beat yolks with sugar until pale; add orange rind and vanilla. Mix yolks with sauce and Grand Marnier. (This mixture may be held over lukewarm water). When ready to bake, beat egg whites until very stiff. Gently fold in Grand Marnier mixture. Butter a 1½-qt. souffle dish; sprinkle with sugar. Tie a waxed paper collar around dish. Fill with souffle. Bake at 350° for 25 to 30 minutes. Dust top with confectioners' sugar.

Mrs. H. Alex Vance, Jr.
(Melinda Martin)

CHOCOLATE SOUFFLE WITH CREME ANGLAISE

4-6 Servings

1 T. sugar
3 T. unsalted butter
2 T. cake flour
1 cup milk, scalded and cooled
½ cup sugar
3 oz. melted unsweetened chocolate
3 T. creme de cacao
4 egg yolks, beaten
5 egg whites, stiffly beaten

CREME ANGLAISE SAUCE:

½ cup sugar
4 egg yolks
1 T. cornstarch
1¾ cups boiling milk

Butter well a 6-cup souffle dish. Sprinkle with 1 T. sugar; shake excess out. Place a paper collar on dish. In a saucepan, melt butter; stir in flour. Add milk slowly. Cook, stirring constantly, until thick. Add ½ cup sugar to melted chocolate and cacao. Combine both mixtures. Cool 15 minutes. Add yolks. Fold in beaten egg whites. Pour into a 1½-qt. souffle dish. Bake at 350° for 25 minutes or 30 minutes for a less-runny souffle.

Sauce: Gradually beat sugar into yolks, beating until very pale yellow. Beat in cornstarch. Continue beating and very gradually add boiling milk. Cook slowly, stirring constantly, until mixture coats a spoon. Strain sauce through a sieve. Add a little cacao flavoring, if desired. Serve at room temperature over souffle. Pass sauce in a bowl.

Mrs. Thomas C. O'Neil
(Jane Stephens)

COOK'S
NIGHT
OUT!

CHICAGO RESTAURANTS

he first restaurant in Chicago was the Wolf Tavern, founded in 1828 at a site on the Chicago River where the Merchandise Mart now stands. Food was a sideline at the Wolf. Whiskey and gin were its main drawing cards.

Chicago restaurants have changed greatly since the days when the Wolf prospered. Today a person wishing to dine out can select from among hundreds of eating establishments throughout the city. These offer a wide range in style, atmosphere, and price, with food, not drink, the main attraction.

Many of the city's most popular restaurants are found in ethnic residential neighborhoods, for Chicago is still largely a city so comprised. Chinese, Japanese, Germans, Greeks, Poles, Czechs, and other nationality groups maintain their distinct communities from generation to generation, and their cooking, like their other cultural traits, adds diversity and excitement to the city.

Also evident in Chicago are regional restaurants, with styles of cuisine that have been brought from other sections of the country and now thrive in the midwest. Such cooking is equally enjoyed by transplated natives of the areas where the style originated and those more recently won over to the new taste sensations.

Finally, classic gourmet cooking is well represented by Chicago restaurants, many of which are among the most popular in the city.

For SOUPÇON we have selected 15 of our favorite Chicago restaurants. This is not meant to be a definitive enumeration of the best in the city, but rather a sampling of some of those our members consistently enjoy. Each was chosen for its general level of excellence, and the total list reflects the large diversity in styles Chicagoans are fortunate to have available to them.

Each restaurant selected has provided menus and recipes for some of its best liked meals. These are included in the book, along with appropriate wine suggestions, so that the reader may either duplicate them in his or her own home, consider possible course selections before visiting one of the 15, or simply dream of delicious gastronomic delights still to be enjoyed.

THE ABACUS

Love of the Oriental gourmet

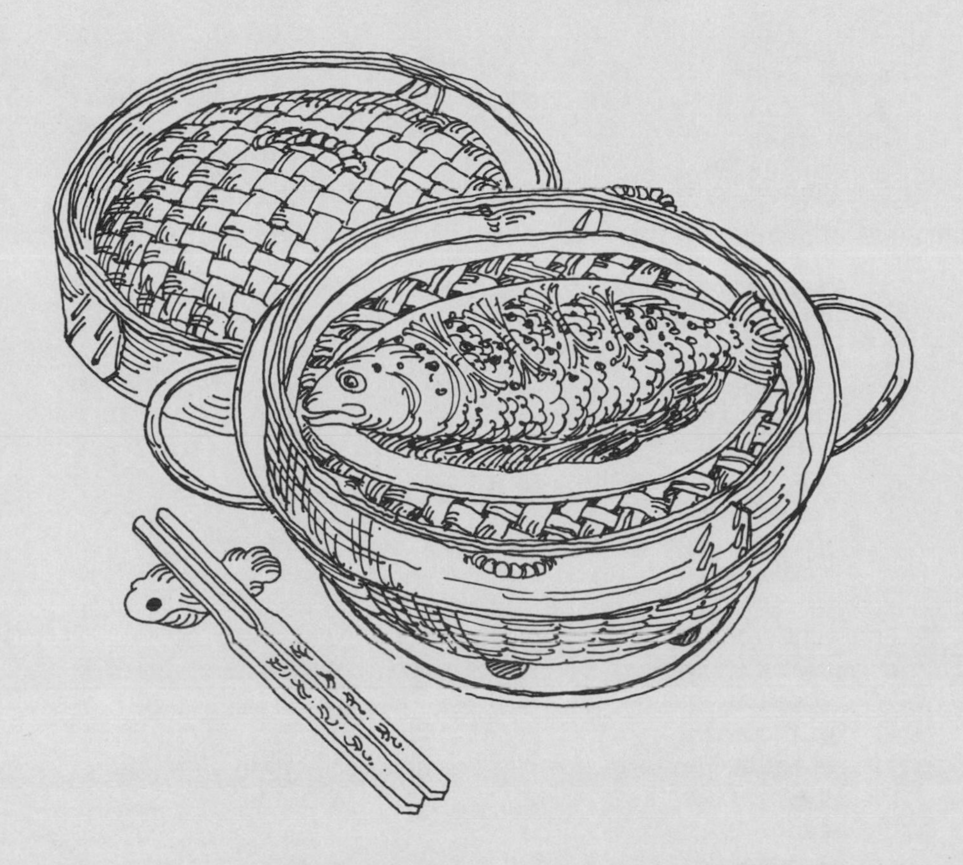

MANDARIN SIZZLING RICE SOUP
Dry Chenin Blanc
**
MONGOLIAN BEEF
**
MONK'S DELIGHT
**
STEAMED FISH WITH BLACK BEAN SAUCE
Blanc de Blancs, Cote de Provence
**
SPUN APPLES
Vintage Port

STEAMED FISH WITH BLACK BEAN SAUCE

4 Servings

1 whole fresh Walleye pike (2 lbs.)
4 oz. minced, salted black beans
2 T. shredded fresh ginger root
1 clove garlic, minced
½ tsp. salt
Pinch of pepper
½ cup soy sauce
1 T. sesame oil
½ tsp. sugar
2 green onions, shredded
½ cup vegetable oil

Slash both sides of fish 4 times about ¾-inch deep across body at slight slants. Mix next 8 ingredients; brush over entire fish, inside and out. Lay fish in fish steamer; sprinkle with green onions. Steam for 15 minutes. Shake pepper over fish. Heat vegetable oil to about 350°. Splash over fish.

SPUN APPLES

8 Servings

1 egg, lightly-beaten mixed with ½ cup and 2 T. cold water
1 cup flour
3 cups and 1 T. peanut oil
1 cup sugar
¼ cup ice water
1 T. sesame seeds
2 apples, peeled and cut into eighths

Add egg and water mixture to flour slowly, stirring constantly, until batter is smooth. In a saucepan heat 3 cups of oil until a haze forms. In a 12-inch wok or 10-inch skillet, heat 1 T. oil with sugar and water; bring to a boil, stirring until sugar dissolves. Cook mixture briskly without stirring until syrup is 300°. Add sesame seeds and lower heat. Drop apple wedges into batter. Transfer to heated oil and deep fry for 1 minute, or until light brown. Remove with slotted spoon and place in syrup. Stir wedges to coat thoroughly. Drop one at a time into a bowl of ice water, to harden syrup coating. Place finished wedges on greased serving plate. Serve immediately; candy glaze will soften if allowed to stand.

(Bananas may be substituted for apples.)

THE BAKERY

Excellent continental cuisine in a lively setting

RADISHES, BUTTER AND BLACK BREAD

**

CLEAR TOMATO SOUP

Pouilly Fume or Fume Blanc

**

SPINACH-MUSHROOM SALAD

**

POACHED SALMON IN CHAMPAGNE SAUCE

Meursault

ASPARAGUS　　PAN ROASTED POTATOES

**

LEMON CREPE SOUFFLE'

Chateau Coutet

CLEAR TOMATO SOUP

12 Servings

2 lbs. veal bones
1 coarsely-chopped carrot
1 chopped parsley root or parsnip
1 cut up celery stalk
½ onion, unpeeled
5 to 6 black peppercorns
1 T. salt
1 bay leaf
1 clove garlic
3 T. sugar
1 tsp. butter
1 can (6 oz.) tomato paste
1 can (46 oz.) tomato juice
2 T. dried tarragon
2 T. dried dill weed
6 T. cornstarch
Liquid from 2 ripe tomatoes, chopped and run through a blender
Fresh lemon juice to taste
Fresh dill weed, if available

CHEF'S SECRET:

Adding sugar to the tomato juice and tomato paste brings out a fresh tomato flavor and reduces some of the acidity.

The addition of fresh lemon juice before serving adds a tang, and using cornstarch instead of flour as a thickening agent makes a translucent and syrupy soup which is very different from other tomato soups.

In a large soup pan, place veal bones, carrot, parsley root or parsnip, celery, onion, peppercorns, salt, bay leaf and garlic. Add about 3-qts. of water. and cook slowly for at least 4 hours. The amount of stock should then be approximately 2-qts.

Strain the stock into another pot, skim the top if necessary.

Dissolve the sugar in the butter, heating until it starts to caramelize. Pour 1 qt. of stock over the butter-sugar mixture. Add this to the tomato paste and tomato juice. Bring to a boil; reduce heat and simmer.

In the meanwhile, cool 1 pt. of stock and bring another pint to a boil.

Sprinkle into the boiling stock the tarragon and dried dill weed. Let boil for 2 minutes. Strain this stock, removing the herbs, into the simmering tomato soup.

Stir the cornstarch into the cold pint of stock and slowly pour the starch-stock mixture into the simmering soup. This will make the soup syrupy-thick and clear.

Add chopped dill weed if you have fresh dill. Correct the seasoning of the soup with lemon juice, sugar and salt. Pour the liquid from the fresh tomatoes into the soup tureen and ladle the hot soup over it. Serve immediately.

POACHED SALMON IN CHAMPAGNE SAUCE

8 Servings

8 salmon steaks, 5 oz. each
4 T. butter
1 T. flour
1 T. cornstarch
1 tsp. granulated sugar
⅛ tsp. mace
Salt and white pepper to taste
1 cup half and half
1 cup dry champagne or, if not available, dry white wine
1 egg yolk
8 slices black truffle or 4 black olives (optional)

CHEF'S SECRET:

The mace enhances the champagne flavor but too much of it would spoil the sauce, so be very careful when using it.

The egg yolk will give the desirable faint yellow hue to the sauce. If for any reason you want to omit it, replace it by adding 1 tsp. more cornstarch and one drop of yellow food coloring to the sauce. Of course, the starch is added with the other dry ingredients.

If you must use an ordinary white wine instead of champagne, add a few drops of lemon juice or orange juice and 2 to 3 T. ginger ale or club soda to it before stirring the wine into the sauce.

In a shallow pan poach the salmon steaks in simmering, lightly salted water for 6 to 8 minutes, depending on their thickness. Remove them carefully with a wide spatula to a warm serving platter.

Melt the butter in a saucepan. In a bowl mix the flour, cornstarch, sugar, mace, salt, and pepper. Slowly stir in the half and half, mixing until the mixture is completely free of lumps.

Pour this mixture into the warm butter and stir until it starts to bubble. Immediately remove from the fire and stir in the champagne or wine, reserving 3 T. of the champagne.

When the champagne is completely mixed into the sauce, put the sauce back on low heat and stir until it boils again. Remove and set it in a warm place and let it stand until serving time.

Just before serving, mix the reserved champagne with the egg yolk. Spoon a little of the hot sauce into the yolk-champagne mixture; stir it and then pour slowly into the sauce. Spoon the sauce over the salmon. Decorate with truffles or halved olives; serve immediately.

THE BERGHOFF

German efficiency in both preparation and service

FLAEDLE SOUP
Schloss Vollrads
**
GREEN SALAD
**
RAGOUT A LA DEUTSCH
Chateau Cheval Blanc

STRING BEANS SWISS STYLE
**
GERMAN CHOCOLATE CAKE
Niersteiner Auslese

FLAEDLE SOUP

5 Servings

1⅓ cups flour
1¼ cups milk
Pinch of salt
4 eggs
2 T. minced chives
10 T. butter
4 to 5 cups hot consomme

Mix flour, milk and salt until smooth. Add eggs and chives; mix for 1 minute. Heat 2 T. butter in 10-inch frying pan. Add ½ cup batter. When golden brown, turn and brown other side. Repeat with remaining batter. Cool pancakes for ½ hour. Cut into julienne strips. Put pancake julienne in soup bowl. Add hot consomme.

RAGOUT A LA DEUTSCH

5 Servings

1¾ lbs. beef sirlion
Butter
1 green pepper, diced
1 onion, diced
¼ lb. mushrooms, sliced
1 cup thick brown gravy
½ cup white wine
1 jar (4 oz.) pimientos
1 tsp. salt
Dash of hot pepper sauce
Dash of worcestershire sauce

Cut beef in ½ oz. strips; saute in a small amount of butter. Saute vegetables in butter; add beef. Add gravy, wine, pimientos, salt, pepper sauce, and worcestershire sauce. Cover and simmer for about ½ hour, or until done.

THE BON TON

Pastry shop and Hungarian restaurant

HUNGARIAN GOULASH

Pinot Noir de Bourgogne

BUTTERED NOODLES

* *

GREEN SALAD WITH TOMATOES

* *

RASPBERRY SLICES

Tokay Aszu

HUNGARIAN GOULASH

6 Servings

2 lbs. lean stew beef cut into bitesize pieces
5 tsp. oil
2 onions, diced
1 green pepper, chopped
2 tsp. red paprika
1 tsp. salt
1 cup water

Brown meat in oil, adding onions, green pepper, paprika and salt. Slowly add water. Cover and simmer for 2 to 3 hours, or until tender. If desired, thicken liquid with flour.

NOTE:
Any meat, such as lamb or chicken, may be substituted for the beef.

RASPBERRY SLICES

MACAROON:
1 lb. almond paste, cut into small pieces
1 cup granulated sugar
4 egg whites
Pinch of salt

DOUGH:
2 lbs. butter
1 lb. 12 oz. confectioners' sugar
2 lbs. 8 oz. flour
4 egg yolks
1 T. grated lemon rind
Pinch of salt
1 T. vanilla flavoring
Raspberry jam

Mix almond paste with sugar in mixer at slow speed. Gradually add egg whites and pinch of salt. Store in refrigerator until ready to use.

Mix all ingredients, except the raspberry jam, together very well. Put the dough on a pan and cover with a clean dish towel. Store in a cool place for several hours. Roll out dough on dusted towel into 3 thin sheets and place them on flat pans. Spread thinly with raspberry jam one of the sheets of dough. Press macaroon mixture through decorating tube with star fixture in close, diagonal straight lines on top of jam.

Bake the two plain sheets of dough for 15 minutes (until golden brown) at 320°. Cook the sheet with the jam until the macaroon is light brown.

Cool the sheets, then spread jam on one, put the other on top of it and spread jam on it as well. Place the macaroon decorated sheet on top of the other two, with macaroon decoration facing upward. Fill corating bag with raspberry jam and thinly fill in between the macaroon lines. Refrigerate overnight and cut into slices the next day.

THE CAPE COD ROOM

Charming atmosphere of traditional New England

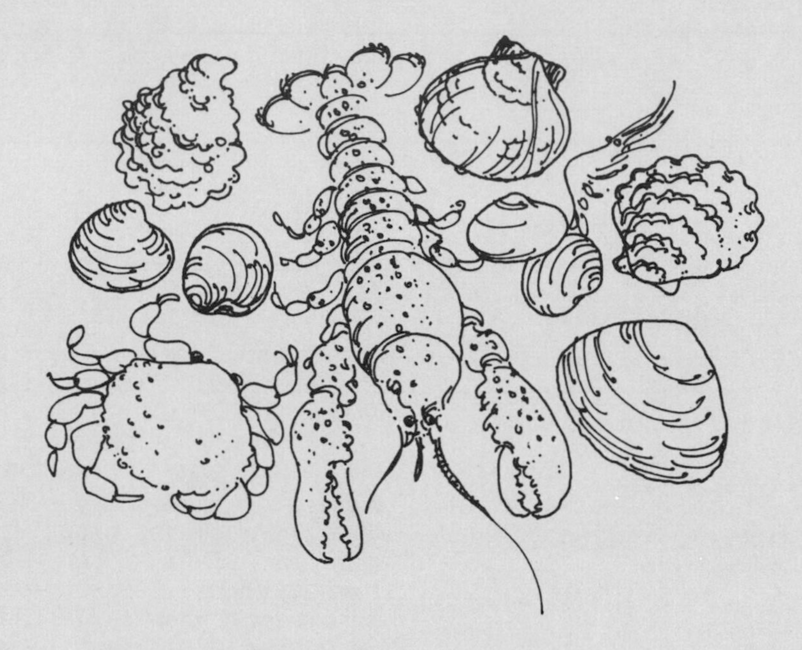

BOSTON CLAM CHOWDER
Muscadet
**
NEW ENGLAND SCROD CHASSEUR
Chablis

BOILED BERMUDA POTATOES

CAPE COD COLE SLAW
**
ICE CREAM PEARS ANDALUSIAN

BOSTON CLAM CHOWDER 10-12 Servings

12 large fresh clams
2 qts. water
1 lb. potatoes, diced
½ green pepper, diced
1 diced onion
4 cups celery, diced
1 tsp. cornstarch
1 tsp. flour
Pinch of thyme
Salt
1 T. worcestershire sauce
1 can (3 oz.) minced clams
½ pt. cream

Wash clams in shells; boil in water for 10 minutes. Remove clams from shells, clean and return to broth. Add potatoes, green pepper, onion, and celery. Cook for 1 hour. Thicken with cornstarch and flour. Add remaining ingredients except cream; cook for 15 minutes. Remove from heat; add cream. Adjust seasoning. Serve hot.

NEW ENGLAND SCROD CHASSEUR 8 Servings

8 fillets of scrod (6 oz. each)
2 fresh tomatoes, peeled and chopped
1 onion, chopped
2 T. butter, melted
¾ cup water
½ cup white wine
1 tsp. worcestershire sauce
1 tsp. cornstarch
Pinch of rosemary
Chopped parsley

Place scrod in buttered pan; top with tomatoes, onions, butter, water and wine. Bake at 350° for 30 minutes. Place scrod on warm platter. Thicken liquid with cornstarch. Add worcestershire sauce and rosemary. Pour over scrod; sprinkle with parsley.

THE CREOLE HOUSE

Authentic Creole and Cajun cooking
in a charming Victorian house

SHRIMP PATE
Entre-deux-Mers

**

CREOLE HOUSE PEANUT SOUP

**

GREEN SALAD WITH HOMEMADE GARLIC DRESSING

**

JAMBALAYA
St. Perey

HUSH PUPPIES

**

FUDGE MINT AND ICE CREAM PIE

CHICORY COFFEE

CREOLE HOUSE PEANUT SOUP

8 Servings

¼ lb. butter
1 small onion, diced
2 ribs celery, diced
8 cups chicken broth
3 T. flour
1 cup peanut butter
¼ tsp. celery salt
½ tsp. salt
1 T. lemon juice
Ground peanuts

Melt butter in heavy pot and saute celery and onion for 5 minutes, but do not brown. Add flour and mix well. Stir in chicken broth and cook 30 minutes. Remove from heat, strain and stir in peanut butter, celery salt, salt, and lemon juice. Stir until peanut butter is dissolved. Serve hot with a sprinkling of ground peanuts.

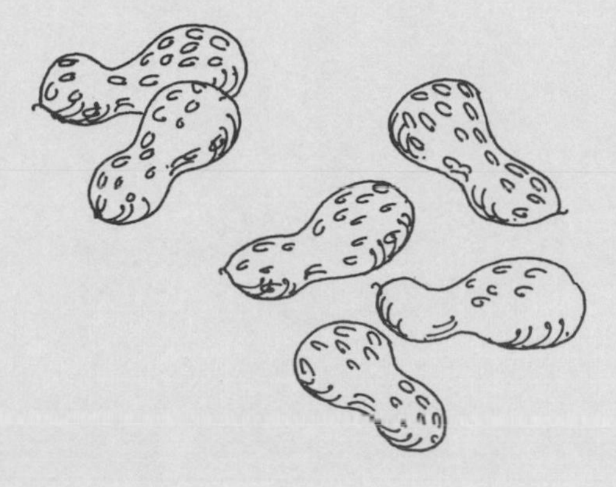

HUSH PUPPIES

3-4 Servings

½ cup white cornmeal
½ cup all purpose flour
2 tsp. baking powder
½ tsp. salt
1 small onion, chopped
1 egg
¼ cup beer

Mix together the cornmeal, flour, baking powder, salt, and onion. Break in egg and add the beer; mix vigorously. Batter should not be too stiff. Drop from a teaspoon into deep hot fat. Fry until golden brown and serve hot.

DON THE BEACHCOMBER

Cantonese cooking with exotic atmosphere and beverages

CRAB MEAT MUSHROOMS
Bourgogne Aligote
**
EGG ROLLS
**
BEEF LOTUS
Chateau Duhart Milon

LONG GRAIN STEAMED RICE
**
HAWAIIAN PINEAPPLE WITH KUMQUATS
**
KONA COFFEE GROG

EGG ROLLS

12 Egg Rolls

6½ oz. dungeness or king crab meat
1 cup cooked, diced pork
1 cup finely-chopped white mushrooms
1 cup finely-chopped bamboo shoots
3 T. oil
12 egg roll wrappers

Fry crab, pork, and vegetables in oil, mixing together well. Fill egg roll wrapper, wrapping carefully, making sure all ends are tucked in. Stick edges down with a touch of egg yolk. Deep fry at 375° or fry in pan, turning so egg rolls brown evenly.

BEEF LOTUS

Serves 6

1½ lbs. tender, lean beef, diced
¼ lb. smoked Virginia ham, diced
1 lb. Chinese lotus nuts, whole
1 lb. water chestnuts, sliced
1 cup chopped onions
2 T. oil
1 cup beef broth

Saute beef and onion (preferably in wok) with oil. Add salt to taste. Add remaining ingredients; saute lightly. Add broth; heat. If desired, thicken with cornstarch.

THE ITALIAN VILLAGE

Three regional Italian dining rooms

ANTIPASTO

**

SALTIMBOCCA ALLA ROMANA

Classico Chianti

GREEN SALAD

ITALIAN BREAD

**

ZABAIONE

Asti Spumante

**

ESPRESSO

SALTIMBOCCA ALLA ROMANA

4 Servings

8 small veal cutlets
3 T. flour
3 T. butter, melted
Grated mozzarella cheese
8 small sage leaves
8 slices prociutto
1 cup chicken broth
¼ cup white wine
Parsley flakes

Flatten cutlets to less than ¼-inch thick. Dust with flour and brown on both sides in butter; remove from pan. Top meat with cheese, sage. Attach prociutto by threading veal with toothpick. Return meat to pan; add chicken broth and wine. Cover and simmer for 5 to 6 minutes. Sprinkle lightly with chopped parsley.

ZABAIONE

6 Servings

8 egg yolks
2 egg whites
½ cup sugar
1 cup marsala

Beat in the top of double boiler egg yolks, egg whites, and sugar until very thick and creamy. Add marsala. Place pan over simmering water; heat gradually, never ceasing to beat it with a rotary or electric beater. When very thick and hot, but just before it reaches the boiling point, spoon into stemmed glasses and serve at once.

JOVAN

Intimate French dining

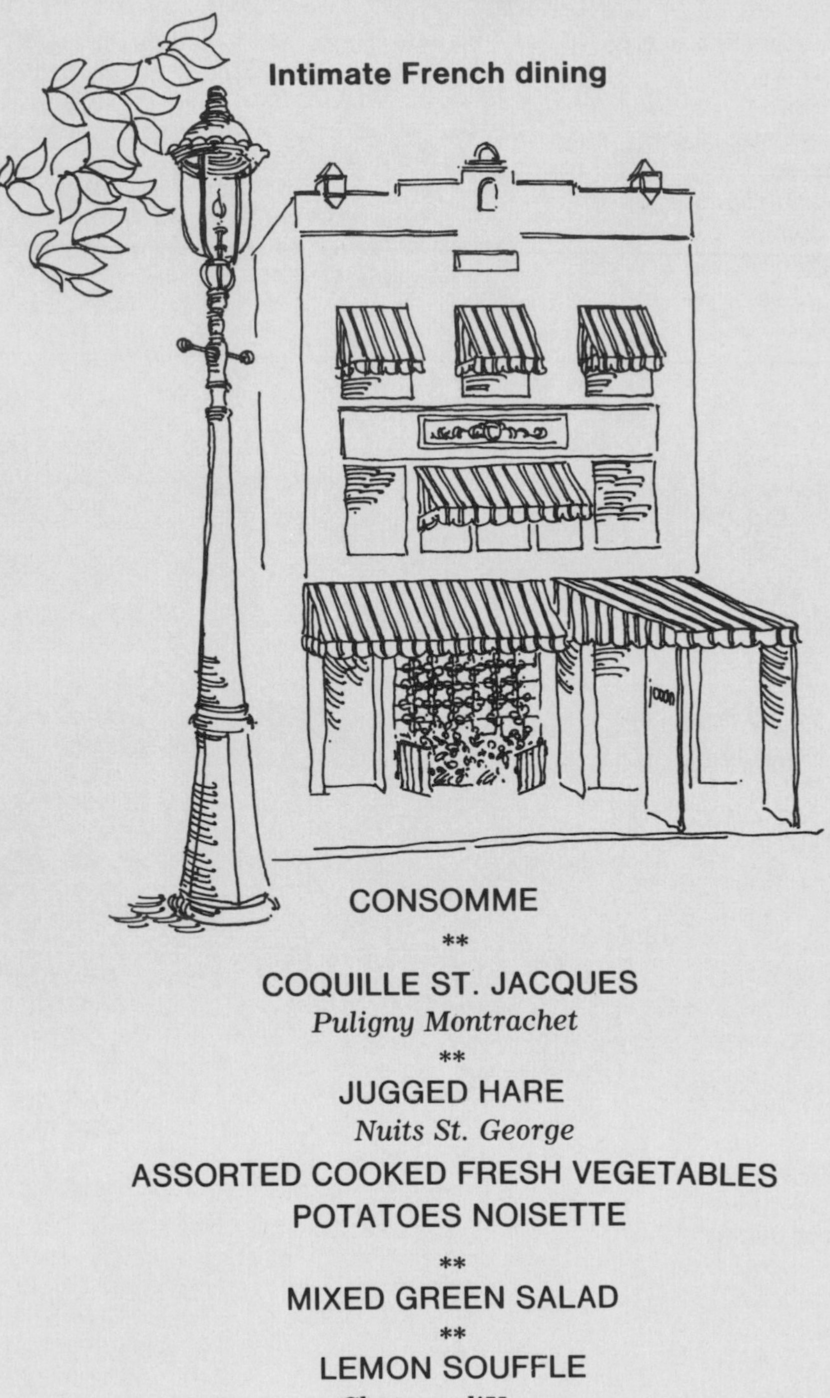

CONSOMME

**

COQUILLE ST. JACQUES

Puligny Montrachet

**

JUGGED HARE

Nuits St. George

ASSORTED COOKED FRESH VEGETABLES

POTATOES NOISETTE

**

MIXED GREEN SALAD

**

LEMON SOUFFLE

Chateau d'Yquem

COQUILLE ST. JACQUES

6 Servings

2 cups dry white wine
8 shallots, finely-chopped
8 mushrooms, sliced, sauted
2 lbs. fresh scallops
¼ lb. butter
2 T. flour
Salt
Pepper
6 egg yolks
½ cup cream
2 T. butter
Bread crumbs
Parmesean cheese

Reduce wine with shallots; add mushrooms and scallops, cover and simmer until done. Remove scallops. Melt ¼ lb. butter. Add flour; stir. Gradually add wine broth. Add salt and pepper. Cook, stirring constantly until sauce thickens. Mix in cream. Pour over scallops; mix. In double boiler, beat egg yolks with 4 T. of wine until thick. Add 2 T. butter. Stir; pour over scallops. Mix gently; pour into shells. Top with bread crumbs or parmesan cheese. Bake for 15 minutes at 350°.

JUGGED HARE

4 Servings

1 hare
2 cups red wine
2 onions, sliced
1 carrot, chopped
1 cup chopped celery
1 clove garlic, chopped
1 tsp. peppercorns
Pinch of thyme
2 bay leaves
Pinch of rosemary
½ tsp. chopped parsley
1 cup cognac
Liver, heart and blood of hare
¼ cup flour
2 T. butter
2 cups hare or veal stock
Salt
Pepper
¼ lb. butter
2 T. flour
1 truffle, chopped
½ cup chopped mushrooms, sauted

Marinate hare for two days in next 10 ingredients. Turn hare occasionally. Marinate liver, heart and blood of hare in cognac. Dust hare in ¼ cup flour; brown in 2 T. butter. Saute vegetables from marinade in heavy saucepan. Add wine from marinade; simmer for 10 minutes to reduce wine. Add hare and stock. Salt and pepper to taste. Simmer until hare is tender, about 30 minutes. Remove hare. In separate saucepan melt ¼ lb. butter. Add 2 T. flour; and mix until smooth. Strain harestock mixture and add to flour and butter. Simmer, stirring constantly. Chop liver and heart in blender; mix with sauce. Simmer for 10 minutes. Pour over hare. Garnish with truffles and mushrooms.

KAMEHACHI OF TOKYO

Japanese cuisine complete with sushi chefs working at their art

JAPANESE PICKLES

MISO SOUP

* *

BEEF KUSHI YAKI OR CHICKEN EN SAKE

Beaune les Greves

STEAMED RICE

GREEN TEA

* *

SLICED FRUIT

Malmsey Madiera

BEEF KUSHI YAKI

6 Servings

2 lbs. boneless tender beef (or chicken breasts or lamb)
1 cup soy sauce
1 cup mirin
1 T. sugar
18 small mushrooms
3 or 5 stalks green onion, cut in 2-inch pieces

Cut meat into 1-inch cubes. Combine soy sauce, mirin, sugar and soup bone or chicken bone in saucepan. Boil, uncovered, until liquid is reduced to ¼ quantity. Cool. Dip meat in sauce. Alternate meat and vegetables on bamboo skewers. Dip skewer in sauce. Place under broiler or grill over charcoal about 10 minutes. May be dipped in sauce while cooking.

CHICKEN EN SAKE

4 Servings

1 chicken
Garlic salt
1 egg, well beaten
½ cup flour
Salad oil
¼ cup sake or white wine
½ cup soy sauce
½ cup sugar
Salt
2 cups bread crumbs

Cut chicken in small pieces. Sprinkle with garlic salt. Dip in beaten egg then flour. Fry in deep fat. Combine wine, soy sauce, sugar, and salt; cook together until sugar is dissolved. Dip chicken in sauce, then in bread crumbs. Place chicken in pan. Bake at 350° for 15 minutes.

LE PERROQUET

Gracious dining complements the French haute cuisine

CHEESE TART WITH LEEKS
Sauvignon Blanc
**
CHICKEN FOR ALL SEASONS
Schloss Furstenberg
**
BOSTON LETTUCE AND WATERCRESS SALAD
**
STRAWBERRY SOUFFLE
Cream Sherry
**
TURKISH COFFEE

CHEESE TART WITH LEEKS

6 Servings

4 large leeks
3 T. butter
3 T. flour
1 cup consomme
¾ cup light cream
1 thin onion slice
1 cup grated swiss cheese
½ cup grated parmesan cheese
8-inch pastry shell, baked
½ tsp. grated nutmeg

Boil leeks in salted water for 15 minutes; drain and cut into 1-inch pieces. Melt butter; stir in flour. Add consomme and cream slowly; add onion slice. Cook, stirring constantly, until thickened. Remove onion slice. Add ½ cup swiss and parmesan cheese; stir until smooth. Pour cheese sauce into pastry shell, arrange leeks in sauce. Sprinkle with remaining swiss cheese and nutmeg. Bake 20 minutes at 350° or until set.

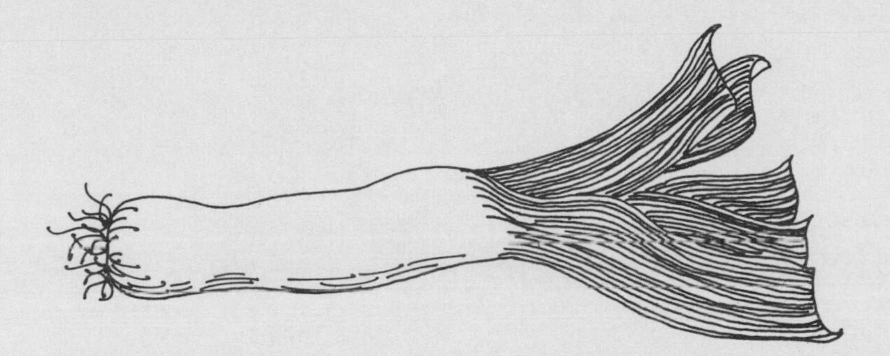

CHICKEN FOR ALL SEASONS

4 Servings

1 chicken (3 lbs.), quartered
½ cup butter
Salt
Pepper
1 cup dry white wine
1 cup chicken broth
2 egg yolks, beaten
2 oz. port
1 cup heavy cream

Saute chicken in butter, salt and pepper. Add wine and broth. Simmer for 45 minutes, or until done. Remove chicken. Add to sauce egg yolks, port and cream; stir until smooth. Pour over chicken and serve with rice.

L'EPUISSETTE

Specialties of fish in an elegant atmosphere

ESCARGOTS BOURGUIGONNE

Bourgogne Blanc

**

ROCKY MOUNTAIN BROOK TROUT L'EPUISSETTE

Heitz Pinot Chardonnay

PARSLEY BOILED POTATO

**

SLICED AVOCADO SALAD

**

LIME SHERBET

ESCARGOTS BOURGUIGNONNE

6 Servings

3 doz. canned snails
3 doz. snail shells
½ cup sherry
½ cup butter
1 clove garlic, minced
1 tsp. finely-chopped shallots
1 tsp. chopped parsley
½ cup white wine
1 T. lemon juice
3 T. bread crumbs

Insert snails in shells and pour sherry over them. Melt butter, add remaining ingredients. Mix well and pour over snails. Bake at 400° about 10 minutes.

ROCKY MOUNTAIN BROOK TROUT L'EPUISSETTE

4 Servings

4 boneless trout
4 oz. crabmeat
5 mushrooms
1 tsp. minced shallots
1 tsp. chives
⅓ cup sauterne wine
9 oz. butter
Flour
Salt
White pepper
⅓ cup cream
Lemon
Parsley

Dip boneless trout in flour and shake well. Trout to be open as a butterfly. Saute trout for 10 minutes on both sides in 3 oz. of butter. Keep trout warm.

In saucepan melt 2 oz. butter; add 2 oz. of flour, stir well. Remove pan from heat, add ⅓ cup of cream, stir well until smooth. Cook and stir at moderate heat for 10 minutes. Remove from heat. Add ⅓ cup sautern wine, 1 tsp. chopped chives, 1 tsp. chopped shallot, 5 sliced mushrooms, 4 oz. crab meat, salt and white pepper to taste.

Mix all above ingredients with sauce and heat for 5 minutes.

Butter a platter lightly; put stuffing on each open trout; close trout and heat in pre-heated oven for 5 minutes. Melt 4 oz. butter in saucepan until golden brown, squeeze one lemon into the brown butter, remove trout from oven, pour brown butter over the trout, garnish with parsley and lemon slices and serve.

MAXIM'S DE PARIS

Elegance in true Parisian tradition

CROQUETTES DE CREVETTES
Chassagne Montrachet
**
DOUBLE PROVENCALE
Musigny, Conte de Vogue

POMMES VAPEUR
**
SALAD
**
CREPES VEUVE JOYEUSE
Cristal Roderer Champagne

CROQUETTES DE CREVETTES

4 Servings

3 slices stale white bread
2 cups milk
7 oz. cooked shrimp
¼ cup chopped walnuts
3 egg yolks
¼ cup butter, softened
Pinch of curry powder
Bread crumbs
4 T. butter

Soak stale bread in milk; squeeze dry. Mash or put in blender with shrimp, walnuts, egg yolks, butter and curry. Blend two minutes. Add salt if necessary. Form the resulting puree into small patties; dredge in bread-crumbs and saute in butter until browned on all sides. Garnish with parsley.

DAUBE PROVENCALE

6 Servings

2 oz. salt pork, diced
1 T. lard
1 T. olive oil
2 oz. thick bacon, diced
2 onions
2 cloves
2 carrots, sliced
½ calf's foot
2 lbs. boneless beef, chuck or round
1 sprig thyme, crushed
1 bay leaf, crushed
1 clove garlic, minced
2 tomatoes, quartered
2 shallots, cut up
1 stalk celery and root, cut up
1 cup dry red wine
Pinch of cinnamon
Pinch of ginger
½ tsp. peppercorns
½ orange peel, grated
½ tsp. salt

Heat salt pork in stew pan with lard and oil. Add bacon; brown. Cut 1 onion into quarters and stick the other with two cloves. Add carrots, onions and calf's foot to pot. Cut beef into 2½-inch pieces. Brown them in pot. Add thyme, bay leaf and garlic. Turn meat often to brown on all sides. Add tomatoes, shallots, celery, celery root, wine, cinnamon, ginger, peppercorns, orange peel, and salt. Bring to boil. Cover and lower heat. Simmer for 4 to 6 hours, or until tender. Serve with boiled potatoes.

PARTHENON

Varietes of authentic Greek cooking in a typical festive Greek atmosphere

SPINACH AND CHEESE PIE
Mount Ambelos White
**
LAMB WITH ARTICHOKES
Roditis

FRESH ROE SALAD
**
BAKLAVA
**
GREEK COFFEE

SPINACH AND CHEESE PIE

12 Servings

2 lbs. fresh spinach
Olive oil
2 onions, finely-chopped
2 tsp. dill weed
1 cup milk
4 eggs, beaten
¾ lb. feta cheese
2 tsp. salt
¼ tsp. pepper
1 pkg. (1 lb.) phyllo leaves

Cook spinach; drain well. Saute onion in 2 T. oil. Add spinach and dill. Add milk, cooking over low heat for 10 minutes. Add eggs, cheese, salt and pepper; mix. Grease 2 pie pans with oil; line with phyllo. Leaves should hang over edge of pan so they can later be folded on top of pie. Brush leaves well with oil. Pour in spinach mixture. Fold over phyllo leaves; brush well with oil. Add 2 leaves to top; brush with oil. Cut into serving pieces before cooking. Cook at 275° for 45 minutes, or until brown. Cool slightly before serving.

LAMB WITH ARTICHOKES

6 Servings

6 lbs. lamb breast or 6 lamb shanks
2 onions, finely chopped
½ lb. butter
1 tsp. dill
2 lemons
Salt
Pepper
3 egg yolks
1 tsp. cornstarch
5 cups water
12 artichoke hearts

Saute lamb and onion in ¼ lb. buttter. Add dill, 1 sliced lemon and salt and pepper to taste. Cover and simmer in water for 1½ hours. Add artichoke hearts and ¼ lb. butter; cook another 30 minutes. Remove lamb and artichokes; keep warm. Mix egg yolks, juice of 1 lemon and cornstarch. Add 3 cups cooled broth. Cook, stirring constantly, until thickened. Pour over lamb and artichokes.

SU CASA

Delightful Mexican food and decor where MI CASA ES SU CASA

MARGARITA OR TEQUILA SUNSET

CHILI CON QUESO DIP

**

SPICY BEEF CHILI RELLENO

Marques de Riscal

RICE AND REFRIED BEANS

**

FLAN OR SHERBET

Cream Sherry

**

CAFE CHIPAS

CHILI CON QUESO DIP

6 Servings

- **1 lb. Velvetta cheese**
- **½ lb. cheddar cheese**
- **½ cup seeded and diced tomatoes**
- **½ cup finely-chopped onion**
- **2 T. parsley, finely-minced**
- **2 hot green chilies, chopped (add more if you like it hotter)**

Place cheese in a double boiler and add remaining ingredients. Heat until cheese is completely melted and onion is soft. Serve with tortilla chips.

SPICY BEEF CHILI RELLENO

6 Servings

- **6 medium bell peppers**
- **Oil and vinegar**
- **2 lbs. ground round**
- **1 cup finely-chopped onion**
- **½ cup finely-chopped green pepper**
- **Salt and pepper**
- **Ground rosemary**
- **½ cup raisins**
- **⅓ cup finely-chopped almonds**
- **⅓ cup finely-chopped pecans**
- **5 eggs, separated**
- **Flour**
- **Oil for deep frying**

Place peppers on a baking sheet and broil about 6-inches from heat on all sides. Remove from oven and immediately place them in a paper bag and close tightly. Allow them to steam in closed bag; peel outer skin. Cut off ½-inch from stem end and remove seeds. Marinate pepper overnight in equal parts oil and vinegar. Saute beef, onion and green pepper until done. Add seasonings to taste. Refrigerate meat. When ready to stuff add raisins and nuts to meat mixture and check seasonings. Drain peppers and stuff them. Beat egg whites until stiff. Fold in slightly beaten egg yolks. Roll peppers in flour and dip in egg mixture one at a time. Drop in deep frying pan with enough hot oil to cover. Brown evenly and drain.

SAUCE:

- **1 onion, finely-chopped**
- **1 garlic clove, mashed**
- **1 T. olive oil**
- **2 cups tomatoes, drained**
- **2 cups chicken stock**
- **½ cup white wine**
- **½ bay leaf**
- **3 pepper corns, crushed**
- **3 drops hot pepper sauce**
- **Salt to taste**

SAUCE:

Saute onion and garlic in oil until onion becomes transparent. Pass tomatoes through a sieve or food mill and add them to the onions and garlic. Add the stock and wine and remaining seasonings. Bring sauce to a boil and simmer 10 minutes. Check seasonings. Twenty minutes before serving place peppers in sauce and simmer until thoroughly heated. Spoon over peppers.

INDEX

C

D

E

F

G

H

I

J

K

L

M

N

O

P

Q

R

S

T

FOREIGN AND REGIONAL DISHES

VARIATIONS OF MY FAVORITE RECIPES

VARIATIONS OF MY FAVORITE RECIPES

VARIATIONS OF MY FAVORITE RECIPES

VARIATIONS OF MY FAVORITE RECIPES

VARIATIONS OF MY FAVORITE RECIPES

Soupcon I & II

The Junior League of Chicago, Inc.
1447 North Astor Street, Chicago 60610

Please send me ________ copies of Soupçon I
Please send me ________ copies of Soupçon II

Name ________________________________

Address ________________________________

City ______________ State ______________ Zip ______________

	Price Ea.	Qty.	Total Price
Soupçon I	$11.95		$
Soupçon II	$11.95		$

Sub-Total $ ________

Shipping @$1.55 ea. $ ________

Illinois delivery add $.72 sales tax $ ________

Gift Wrap $.50 $ ________

TOTAL $ ________

☐ Check or money order enclosed. Make checks payable to Soupçon, The Junior League of Chicago, Inc.

Charge: ☐ MasterCard ☐ Visa/BankAmericard

Account Number:

All digits, please.

Expiration Date ______________ Signature ________________________________
(required) (required for charge orders only)

- -

Soupcon I & II

The Junior League of Chicago, Inc.
1447 North Astor Street, Chicago 60610

Please send me ________ copies of Soupçon I
Please send me ________ copies of Soupçon II

Name ________________________________

Address ________________________________

City ______________ State ______________ Zip ______________

	Price Ea.	Qty.	Total Price
Soupçon I	$11.95		$
Soupçon II	$11.95		$

Sub-Total $ ________

Shipping @$1.55 ea. $ ________

Illinois delivery add $.72 sales tax $ ________

Gift Wrap $.50 $ ________

TOTAL $ ________

☐ Check or money order enclosed. Make checks payable to Soupçon, The Junior League of Chicago, Inc.

Charge: ☐ MasterCard ☐ Visa/BankAmericard

Account Number:

All digits, please.

Expiration Date ______________ Signature ________________________________
(required) (required for charge orders only)

All copies will be sent to same address unless otherwise specified. If you wish one or any number of books sent as gifts, furnish a list of names and addresses of recipients. If you wish to enclose your own gift card with each book, please write name of recipient on outside of the envelope, enclose with order, and we will include it with your gift.

All copies will be sent to same address unless otherwise specified. If you wish one or any number of books sent as gifts, furnish a list of names and addresses of recipients. If you wish to enclose your own gift card with each book, please write name of recipient on outside of the envelope, enclose with order, and we will include it with your gift.

Soupçon I&II

The Junior League of Chicago, Inc.
1447 North Astor Street, Chicago 60610

Please send me ________ copies of Soupçon I
Please send me ________ copies of Soupçon II

	Price Ea.	Qty.	Total Price
Soupçon I	$11.95		$
Soupçon II	$11.95		$

Sub-Total $ ________

Shipping @$1.55 ea. $ ________

Illinois delivery add $.72 sales tax $ ________

Gift Wrap $.50 $

TOTAL $ ________

Name ________________________

Address ________________________

City ________ State ________ Zip ________

☐ Check or money order enclosed. Make checks payable to Soupçon, The Junior League of Chicago, Inc.

Charge: ☐ MasterCard ☐ Visa/BankAmericard

Account Number: ☐☐☐☐ ☐☐☐ ☐☐☐ ☐☐☐ ☐☐☐

All digits, please.

Expiration Date ________ (required)

Signature ________________________ (required for charge orders only)

- - - - - - - - - - - - - - - - - - - -

Soupçon I&II

The Junior League of Chicago, Inc.
1447 North Astor Street, Chicago 60610

Please send me ________ copies of Soupçon I
Please send me ________ copies of Soupçon II

	Price Ea.	Qty.	Total Price
Soupçon I	$11.95		$
Soupçon II	$11.95		$

Sub-Total $ ________

Shipping @$1.55 ea. $ ________

Illinois delivery add $.72 sales tax $ ________

Gift Wrap $.50 $ ________

TOTAL $ ________

Name ________________________

Address ________________________

City ________ State ________ Zip ________

☐ Check or money order enclosed. Make checks payable to Soupçon, The Junior League of Chicago, Inc.

Charge: ☐ MasterCard ☐ Visa/BankAmericard

Account Number: ☐☐☐☐ ☐☐☐ ☐☐☐ ☐☐☐ ☐☐☐

All digits, please.

Expiration Date ________ (required)

Signature ________________________ (required for charge orders only)

All copies will be sent to same address unless otherwise specified. If you wish one or any number of books sent as gifts, furnish a list of names and addresses of recipients. If you wish to enclose your own gift card with each book, please write name of recipient on outside of the envelope, enclose with order, and we will include it with your gift.

All copies will be sent to same address unless otherwise specified. If you wish one or any number of books sent as gifts, furnish a list of names and addresses of recipients. If you wish to enclose your own gift card with each book, please write name of recipient on outside of the envelope, enclose with order, and we will include it with your gift.